Patterns of European Industrialization

£35,

H2c

Patterns of European Industrialization

The nineteenth century

Edited by

Richard Sylla and Gianni Toniolo

London and New York

Fondazione Adriano Olivetti

First published in 1991
by Routledge
11 New Fetter Lane, London EC4P 4EE

Simultaneously published in the USA and Canada
by Routledge
a division of Routledge, Chapman and Hall Inc.
29 West 35th Street, New York, NY 10001

© 1991 Richard Sylla and Gianni Toniolo

Typeset by Leaper & Gard Ltd, Bristol
Printed in Great Britain by
Mackays of Chatham PLC, Chatham, Kent

British Library Cataloguing in Publication Data
Patterns of European industrialization : the nineteenth
  century.
  1. Europe. Industrialization, history
  I. Sylla, Richard   II. Toniolo, Gianni
  338.094

  ISBN 0-415-06214-4

Library of Congress Cataloging in Publication Data
Patterns of European industrialization : the ninteenth century /
  edited by Richard Sylla and Gianni Toniolo.
        p.   cm.
  Includes bibliographical references and index.
  ISBN 0-415-06214-4
    1. Europe–Industries–History–19th century.   I. Sylla, Richard
  Eugene.   II. Toniolo, Gianni. 1942–
  HC240.P27   1991
  338.94′009′034–dc20   90-21798
                                                                   CIP

Contents

Figures

Tables

Contributors

N.F.R. Crafts, Professor of Economics, University of Warwick.

Olga Crisp, Reader in Economic History (emeritus), School of Slavonic and East European Studies, University of London.

Giovanni Federico, Assistant Professor of History, University of Pisa.

David F. Good, Professor of History and Director, Center for Austrian Studies, University of Minnesota – Twin Cities.

Paul R. Gregory, Professor of Economics, University of Houston.

C. Knick Harley, Professor of Economics, University of Western Ontario.

Michel Lescure, University of Paris X – Nanterre.

Maurice Lévy-Leboyer, Professor of Economic History (emeritus), University of Paris X – Nanterre.

S.J. Leybourne, University of Leeds.

Donald N. McCloskey, John F. Murray Professor of Economics and Professor of History, University of Iowa.

T.C. Mills, Midland Montague Centre for Financial Markets, City University Business School, London.

William N. Parker, Philip Golden Bartlett Professor of Economics and Economic History (emeritus), Yale University.

Richard Sylla, Henry Kaufman Professor of the History of Financial Institutions and Markets and Professor of Economics, Stern School of Business, New York University.

Richard Tilly, Professor of Economic History, Institute for Economic and Social History, University of Münster.

Gianni Toniolo, Professor of Economics, Ca' Foscari – the University of Venice.

Preface

This book is a result of our mutual interest in the economic history of modern Europe and of our association as scholars, which dates from the late 1960s when we were both members of Alexander Gerschenkron's Economic History Workshop at Harvard. At that time US economic history was receiving new intellectual stimulus from the so-called cliometric revolution of which Gerschenkron was a leading instigator through the support he gave to his many students. He also instilled in them an abiding interest in Europe through both the depth of his knowledge and his 'approach', as he liked to call it, to Europe's modern economic history.

In the years that have passed since the 1960s, the application of economic theory and quantitative analysis to economic history has made rapid strides, and Gerschenkron's approach – which brought the diverse economic histories of the various European countries into a unified story of industrialization and modern economic growth – has received many challenges. But a new synthesis of Europe's experience with industrialization has not yet emerged.

Our objective in planning this volume was to evaluate the current state of Europe's economic historiography in order to see whether the elements of a new synthesis could be detected and advanced. With that objective in mind, and because Gerschenkron's approach provided the leading, if dated, example of the desideratum we and others are seeking, his work quite naturally lent itself as a framework around which to organize our papers and deliberations. This book, however, is not intended to be a study of Gerschenkron's approach and how it has fared over the decades since he first advanced it. Rather, the aim of these essays is to stress the intellectual utility of an approach – any approach – which can bring a certain unity to diverse economic experiences and to note the considerable problems that arise in the effort to construct such an approach.

As it is often the case with projects involving a relatively large number of scholars, we could not proceed without a conference for the discussion of the first drafts of the papers. The Fondazione Adriano Olivetti sponsored a meeting which was held at Bellagio (Italy) during the week of October 3–7, 1988. We enjoyed the invaluable hospitality of the Rockefeller Foundation at Villa Serbelloni. Additional support was provided by Banca Commerciale Italiana. The

Conference was particularly successful thanks to the quality of the participants – both authors and discussants – and to the special attention devoted to us by our hosts, the late Roberto Celli and his wife, Susan Garfield, manager of the Foundation's Bellagio Center Office in New York was ever helpful as was Geraldine Ludbrook who helped both in organizing the meeting and in the first editing of some of the papers. For editorial help we are also indebted to Alison Walters of Routledge, Harriet Stewart-Jones for copy editing, and Beth Scott for indexing. We received encouragement and support from our colleague Giovanni Maggia to whom we are particularly grateful.

Richard Sylla and Gianni Toniolo

Chapter 1

Introduction: patterns of European industrialization during the nineteenth century

Richard Sylla and Gianni Toniolo

EUROPE, NOW AND THEN

While these lines are being written, Europe is changing at a breathtaking speed. In the East, the revolutions of 1989 have taken everybody by surprise, unleashing enormous hopes for freedom and economic development. At the same time, by upsetting well-established equilibria, they have produced great uncertainty regarding the future and have created the potential for new instability in the Old Continent. Meanwhile, Western Europe is not only putting the finishing touches to the single European market to meet the 1992 deadline but also embarking on fresh negotiations for political unity among the Twelve.

Experts in social and political sciences have been surprised by the speed at which reality has surpassed their most optimistic forecasts. It is therefore natural for the economic historian to reach for the tools of his or her trade in trying to make sense of the overwhelming unfolding of history that, thanks to live television broadcasting, is taking place literally under one's eyes.

Needless to say, such epochal upheavals defy any attempt at drawing 'lessons from history'. For sure, we know only that the 'long-postwar' is over. The political and economic setting in which the future generations of Europeans are likely to live will be different from that in which we grew up. It is likely that similarities will be found more with previous periods in history than with the most recent one. On the one hand, some aspects of the pre-1914 *'belle époque'* are likely to revive: free movement of goods, capital and labour in a context of fixed exchange rates. On the other hand, the collapse of a large empire and the re-emergence of nationalism within small, newly-independent states will re-create some features of Europe as it emerged from the Treaty of Versailles, which put an end to the First World War. Which of these two contrasting forces will eventually prevail? To a considerable extent, the future of Europe will depend on the answer to this question.

For most of the Eastern European countries economic development will be the crucial issue for many years to come. The survival of democracy is to a large extent linked to delivering both bread and freedom. Potential for growth is difficult to assess since recent history does not offer a fruitful insight for the understanding of the problems connected with the process of transition to a market economy. The experience of industrialization during the nineteenth century, on the other hand, may prove to be of some interest from that particular point of view. Convinced as we are that the study of economic history is interesting *per se*, we cannot escape the feeling that in this particular moment it may also be useful for the understanding of some aspects of our present and that it may help in framing interesting questions about future development patterns.

During the nineteenth century, many of the ancient walls that constrained Europe two centuries ago – feudal vestiges, poverty, ignorance, primitive technologies and organizations, limited capital and finance, destructive regional and national rivalries, among others – came tumbling down as the processes of industrialization and modern economic growth spread across the continent. The *'ancien régimes'* came slowly to an end everywhere: autocracy and mercantilism were replaced by democracy and market economy. In the sweep of human history, it was a century of hitherto unknown economic prosperity and progress in science and technology. Kuznets's 'epochal innovation' – modern economic growth – gained a momentum that proved to be irreversible. Industrialization, a synonym for modern economic growth that focuses on its essential ingredient, changed forever the ways in which people lived and worked, usually for the better but not without attendant political, social, and ideological strains.

Two strains – nationalism and class conflict – bequeathed to the twentieth century a legacy of wars, revolutions, depressions and, eventually, an iron curtain that divided Europe until recent days. Nationalism and class conflict drew energy from industrialization and possibly contributed to its buoyancy. Often in the nineteenth century they were so powerful that they obscured the uniformities of the economic process that was transforming Europe. Since industrialization came to European countries and regions at different times, it tended to accentuate the differences that were already present in languages, customs, politics, religions, cultures, and the like. In time, however, the economic transformation that spread across Europe would reduce backwardness and narrow the very economic differences that it at first accentuated between countries, regions and classes. But this longer-term perspective on the transformation was not so evident to Europeans in the nineteenth century, or even to those who witnessed the political and economic disasters of the first half of the twentieth century.

Now, as the end of the twentieth century nears, those who seek to understand the current problems and the future potential of the European economy would do well to understand its past. As we have said, there are similarities between some of the challenges Europe faces today and those it had to meet 70 or 150 years ago. In economic life – our concern in this book – there are not only different degrees of 'relative backwardness' but different obstacles on the road to further development as well. This is true both within the European Community and between the countries of Western and Eastern Europe. In the years and decades ahead, these economic differences will condition the flows of products, services and productive resources within Europe and the rest of the world, just as they did in the past. Differing levels of development will continue to create tensions between the 'haves' and the 'have nots', between the advanced and the backward countries and regions. Within nations as well as among countries moving along the road of full integration, there will be disagreement concerning economic goals and policies. These will come as no surprise to one who knows Europe's economic past.

ALEXANDER GERSCHENKRON AND HIS SYNTHESIS

The twentieth century's most influential interpretation of European industrialization in the nineteenth century and its implications for subsequent history is that of the late Alexander Gerschenkron (Gerschenkron 1962, 1968, 1970, 1977). Gerschenkron's conception of Europe as an economic entity which, despite all its national and regional differences, led the world into a new era of economic transformation, was both bold and fruitful. His interpretation and its influence are the motivations for this book; they are represented throughout the chapters that follow. The chapters are organized into two parts which reflect the main categories of Gerschenkron's thought: (1) the key factors that propelled industrialization, (2) the nation states that were the settings for industrialization.

Why has Gerschenkron's analysis of European industrialization proven so influential? More than other scholars, Gerschenkron comprehended the varieties of the European experience with industrialization while also understanding that it was a European experience and not merely a variety of experiences. Others, especially economists, viewed industrialization as a uniform process of modernization that had unfolded in some places and would eventually unfold everywhere. Still others, especially historians, felt that each country or region was unique in its history and economic path, which might or might not have led to industrialization. In this view, attempts to impose some notion of an orderly economic process on the varieties of unique historical circumstances were doomed to failure. Gerschenkron understood and appreciated both points of view and strove to reconcile them in his work. He was not entirely successful, as will become evident in the studies published here, but he was successful enough not only to have made a lasting impact as an economic historian but to have stimulated a flow of very influential research in the field.

To understand and appreciate Gerschenkron's work, it is helpful to know some facts about his life (Rosovsky 1979; Tilly 1986). His experiences in life steeped him in many cultures and traditions. He was born in 1904 at Odessa in the Russian Empire. In 1920, after the Russian revolution, he migrated with his family and settled in Austria. He studied economics and political science at the University of Vienna, receiving his doctoral degree in 1928. For the next ten years he held a variety of business, teaching and research posts in Austria. The deteriorating situation in central Europe in the 1930s led Gerschenkron, now with a family of his own, to emigrate to the United States in 1938. For the next six years he taught and carried on research at the University of California in

Berkeley. In 1944, he became a member of the staff of the Board of Governors of the Federal Reserve System. In 1948, he joined the Harvard faculty, in the Economics Department, where he specialized in economic history and Soviet studies over the course of the next three decades. Gerschenkron died in Cambridge, Massachusetts, in October 1978.

Before Gerschenkron, a fashionable view was that economic history in general and industrialization in particular could be best analysed in terms of stages of economic growth through which every society passed and in which every society could locate itself at a given point in historical time. These ideas, originated by the German historical school, were reformulated and made popular by W.W. Rostow's *The Stages of Economic Growth – A non-Communist Manifesto* (1961), which appeared in the middle of Gerschenkron's Harvard career and became quite influential in scholarly discussions. Gerschenkron, in his writings and his teaching, reacted negatively to the uniform paths of development and rigid determinism that stage analysts imposed on economic history, especially their notion – typified by Rostow in one of his stages – that prerequisites had to emerge before a society would industrialize or, in general, move from one stage to another.[1] But as an analytical economist, Gerschenkron did not want to go to the opposite extreme, espoused by traditional historians, that each case of industrialization or economic development was unique, with no lessons to be learned from studying other cases, which – in this view – were also unique. Gerschenkron rejected both the determinism of stage analysts and the emphasis on uniqueness of traditional historians. Instead, he fashioned an approach to modern European economic history that emphasized industrialization as a process exhibiting many uniformities across societies, but also one that demonstrated many deviations from the 'necessary prerequisites' of industrialization.

Gerschenkron shared an understanding and appreciation of the uniformities of the industrialization process with his friend and Harvard colleague, Simon Kuznets, who called the process 'modern economic growth' and carefully documented its characteristic uniformities from the historical statistics of fifteen nations, including ten in Europe (Kuznets 1966). Kuznets, like Gerschenkron, also knew that there was much variability and diversity in modern economic growth across countries, but, unlike Gerschenkron, he regarded them as elements of disorder in the orderly uniformities of modern economic growth. As a scientific economist, Kuznets thought that explanations of variability and diversity in the growth process 'must be ad hoc and incomplete, not so much because of insufficient data, but essentially because we are dealing with experimentally uncontrolled situations in which the variety of possible causative factors cannot be exhaustively tested' (Kuznets 1966: 1).

The work of these two great scholars and friends might be contrasted by saying that Gerschenkron, the economic historian, was fascinated by and wanted to bring order to the elements of historical variability and diversity in economic growth that Kuznets, the statistical economist, regarded as rather intractable.

The difference in attitude and interest is still evident in discussions between economists and economic historians.

Gerschenkron's principal contribution to economic historical scholarship was to organize the deviations into coherent patterns built around his concept of 'relative economic backwardness', which referred to economic conditions in a particular society at the time it began to industrialize. Thus, when it embarked on industrialization in the mid-nineteenth century, Germany was more backward than Britain had been when it experienced the first industrial revolution. And Russia, when it began to industrialize at the end of the nineteenth century, was more backward than Germany had been half a century earlier.

From his concept of economic backwardness and his detailed knowledge of the histories of European nations, Gerschenkron derived a number of hypotheses about the patterns of European industrialization. Among them are:

1   The more backward the country, the more rapid will be its industrialization, i.e. the faster will be its rate of growth of industrial production.
2   The more backward the country, the greater will be its stress on producer (capital) goods as compared with consumer goods.
3   The more backward the country, the larger will be the typical scale of plant and firm, and the greater will be the emphasis on latest, up-to-date technology.
4   The more backward the country, the greater will be the pressure on the consumption levels of the population; consumption levels will be squeezed to promote a high rate of capital formation.
5   The more backward the country, the less will be the role of the agricultural sector as a market for industrial goods and as a source of rising productivity in its own right.
6   The more backward the country, the more active will be the role of special institutional factors – great banks as in Germany, the government ministry of finance as in Russia – in supplying capital and promoting industrialization.
7   The more backward the country, the more important will be ideologies of industrialization in the shaping of policies and events.

During the years that have elapsed since Gerschenkron formulated his hypotheses about European industrialization, many scholars have questioned and even rejected important elements of his work. But no analytical insights or grand syntheses comparable to Gerschenkron's have come in the wake of the critical work his seminal ideas stimulated. Scholars and teachers of European economic history have been left with little more than discussions of amorphous long-run trends, tiny regional patterns, and individual 'causes' that inevitably are shown to be unimportant. On the whole, the subject of European industrialization seems to have become more precise but at the same time less intellectually appealing, at least for the younger generation of students from whom will come tomorrow's scholars.

A look at the timing and character of industrialization as it spread across Europe in the nineteenth-century – what we now know, or think we know – will serve to indicate how recent research has modified some of Gerschenkron's characterizations, and to introduce the reader to the chapters that follow. Gerschenkron studied Europe's industrialization, he posed questions about it, and, using the evidence available to him, he provided answers to those questions. We now know that his answers often must be modified in the light of more recent findings. It is also often the case that we have these findings because of the questions Gerschenkron posed and the captivating attractiveness of his answers. That is the essence of what makes a scholar influential.

RELATIVE BACKWARDNESS IN NINETEENTH-CENTURY EUROPE

According to Gerschenkron, relative backwardness – however measured – is a powerful explanatory variable of such characteristics of industrial development as timing, growth rates and structural change. Gerschenkron's definition of backwardness is not based on any one indicator such as per capita income. Of his two souls, it was that of the historian rather than of the economist that surfaced when he defined and discussed economic backwardness. In his university lectures, he hinted that no specific definition was needed, since any knowledge-able economic historian would be able to rank European countries in their order of relative backwardness at any chosen moment during the nineteenth century. The variables to be considered, however, should be those most relevant for the emergence of preconditions for subsequent economic development. Among such variables he therefore included savings ratios, literacy, some technology-related indicators (e.g. patents), per capita social overhead capital, and even less measurable ones such as ideology.

Gerschenkron's overall appraisal of the various degrees of backwardness of the individual European countries around the middle of the nineteenth century was simple and convincing. He seemed to argue that travelling from the northwest of Europe to the east and southeast, one would be met by increasing degrees of economic backwardness. Thus, for instance, within Germany, Prussia was more backward than the Rhineland, within the Habsburg Empire Hungary was more backward than Austria, and in the Italian Peninsula the Kingdom of the Two Sicilies lagged behind Piedmont and Lombardy. Europe was made up of a number of independent countries that had in common a number of economic, political and cultural factors but that at the same time were made different not only by language and local traditions but, much more fundamentally, by their relative degrees of economic backwardness.

Such a broad concept of backwardness cannot be fitted into standard procedures of empirical testing. Measures based on some proxies, however, confirm Gerschenkron's view of relative backwardness within nineteenth-century Europe. Barsby (1969) provided a first quantitative assessment. In more recent years various attempts have been made at estimating GNP per capita in various

European countries during the nineteenth century. Such measures can be taken only as rough indicators of overall orders or magnitude and they may be used in comparative analysis only with great caution given the complexity of the well-known index number problem implicit in such bold attempts. Moreover, and not surprisingly, different authors by using different sources and methodologies arrive at quite dissimilar results. Chapters 7 and 10 discuss the issue in more detail. What matters here is simply to note that Gerschenkron's ranking of countries in terms of relative backwardness around 1850 is basically confirmed by whatever comparisons are possible from the historical national account statistics. Moreover, those statistics convey the impression that differences in the degree of backwardness (when measured in terms of GNP per head) were by no means trivial.

Empirical economists have established a link between the level of per capita income and a number of economic variables that describe the 'structure' of an economy. The pioneer in this field was Colin Clark, followed by Kuznets and Abramowitz, and by the econometrically more sophisticated work of Chenery and his team. These scholars established that increasing levels of per capita income are associated with changes in such variables as the agricultural labour force over total labour force, the sectoral composition of industrial output and foreign trade, savings ratios and capital accumulation, and the quantity and quality of financial assets over total wealth (Goldsmith 1969). In such studies, therefore, the level of per capita income is an 'explanatory' variable for a number of qualitative features of the economy. The 'explanation', of course, is only statistical, as is the case in general with regression analysis, and *per se* it does not say anything about causality.

Gerschenkron's broad definition of backwardness was meant to supply an explanatory variable in the literal meaning of the word. A backward country not only was less endowed with such factors of production as skilled labour, up-to-date technology, infrastructure and financial capital but was likely to be burdened with a ruling class whose very interests would be at least partially jeopardized by successful industrialization. Such a country was likely to encounter many obstacles on its way to industrial progress. Moreover, the majority of its ruling class would not perceive the advantages of such progress. In these circumstances, market forces alone would be rather slow in generating the conditions for rapid economic growth. A short-cut along the road of industrialization could be taken if those among the ruling class who could see the advantages of taking that road could also get hold of a tool capable of surmounting the major obstacles to industrialization. These tools might be a financial innovation such as the 'mixed bank' or the very power of the state, according to the country's degree of backwardness. They are briefly discussed later in this introduction and in more detail in Chapters 2–5.

THE TIMING AND RATE OF INDUSTRIALIZATION

Historical statistics of industrial output available to Gerschenkron were confined to a limited number of countries. Moreover, their reliability was often questionable from the point of view of both sources and methodology. Thus, when he had to analyse the Italian case, he found the existing indices of value added by manufacturing less than satisfactory and he set out to construct one of his own. He did the same for Bulgaria.

In the period that followed Gerschenkron's seminal work on European industrialization, considerable progress has been made in the field of economic historical statistics, including time series of industrial output. Much of that progress is due to the work of economic historians – or 'historical economists', as the French call them – familiar with econometric and statistical tools as well as with economic theory. Whatever the merits of cliometrics in producing 'new' results, it is impossible to deny that it produced and stimulated a true revolution in historical quantification. If the discovery of sources for new evidence about the past and the assessment of their validity constitutes the basis of the historian's craft, then cliometricians proved to be excellent historians: they produced a wealth of carefully selected data and made them available to the entire profession. Their debates on the virtues and pitfalls of individual time-series and on the insights yielded by such time-series opened new lines of research into past economic phenomena. Gerschenkron is to be credited for helping these developments in at least two ways. First, he asked relevant questions that could not be answered without improving our quantitative knowledge of the past and, second, he recognized quite early the importance of cliometrics, which he endorsed and supported. It is not a coincidence that his students have made many important contributions to theory-informed quantitative economic history ever since the 1950s.

One of the aims of the essays collected in this volume is to account for the progress made in recent years in the understanding of the time-pattern of the process of industrialization that took place in the largest European countries during the 'long' nineteenth century. Here we briefly review the evidence emerging from the individual country studies. The reader is referred to the relevant chapters for more detailed factual and bibliographical analyses.

Great Britain – and particularly England – has stimulated the largest body of literature directly or indirectly drawing on quantitative analysis. This is due both to the inherent interest of the subject, the 'pioneer' of industrialization and modern economic growth, and to a well-established British tradition in quantitative economic history that also attracted the attention of a number of qualified economists. However, until not long ago, the most relevant studies were devoted to national accounts and investment (e.g. Dean and Cole 1962; Feinstein 1972, 1978, 1988) rather than to improvement of the old Hoffmann index of industrial production (Hoffmann 1955) on which Gerschenkron's own observations were based. Such improvements came only in the late 1970s and in the 1980s (Lewis 1978; Harley 1982; Crafts *et al.* 1990).

On the basis of new statistical evidence, Crafts shows that British industrial production exhibits a long-run increase throughout the eighteenth century, with an acceleration in trend growth around 1750 and continuing until the 1830s. Thereafter, the long-run rate of growth in industrial output declines from an average of about 3 per cent per annum to slightly more than 2 per cent per annum.

The picture of British industrialization that emerges from the new quantitative findings seems to be more in accordance with the way Gerschenkron saw it than with the view still held by most historians. There was no 'kink', no take-off in a Rostovian sense. Neither was there a 'discontinuity' around 1780, where a time-honoured tradition places the beginning of the so-called Industrial Revolution. If anything, the start of the Industrial Revolution has to be pushed three decades back, but even then, the acceleration that took place hardly allows one to speak of a sudden substantial change in the growth of industrial output.

As Crafts points out in his essay, our perception of the British growth pattern as that of a slow-growing early-comer to industrialization has been reinforced by recent research. Innovations in the textile sector were slow in producing a tangible impact on total factor productivity. Fixed investment was based on wood and water, and did not become an important fraction of aggregate demand until well into the nineteenth century. Productivity gains in agriculture played a major role in inducing industrial growth as well as in increasing per capita incomes. Financial markets were more sophisticated than elsewhere in Europe. Whatever financial innovation took place, however, did not concern large-scale investment banking for which there was no great need, at least as far as the manufacturing sector was concerned.

The above-mentioned stylized facts seem now to be rather well-established by the most recent quantitative findings. On the other hand, the debate on the performance of late Victorian Britain remains to a certain extent unresolved. Crafts finds that a slowdown of industrial growth that might indicate the presence of a climacteric took place at the middle rather than at the end of the century, and he provides a number of quantitative arguments that run counter to McCloskey's (1970, 1971) earlier optimistic view of Victorian England. But 'failure', the word most often used in the debate, has subjective connotations that might hide different assumptions. Those who argue in favour of a poor performance do so mostly in comparative terms, looking either at previous British rates of growth or at the accomplishments of foreign countries, particularly Germany, during the same period of time. Those who believe that there was not, after all, much failure do so within the economic framework of British 'potential output'. In these terms, the debate relates more to ability of market forces to promote long-term productivity growth and to possible market and policy failures (particularly in education and training) than to the quantitative appraisal of actual growth in industrial output.

French economic growth during the nineteenth century has bewildered more than a generation of economic historians. The contrast between France's military weakness in 1870 and in 1914 and the mighty years under the first Napoleon, along with the exceptionally low rate of growth of her population, have led to the assumption that something must have gone wrong with the French economy. Roehl summarizes the conventional view on the subject as follows:

> The French economy in the early modern period, until, say, the late 17th century, is relatively strong and healthy; by the 19th century it is troubled and stagnant ...; the 18th century usually appears as the period during which those roots of subsequent problems are implanted.

(Roehl 1976: 238)

The most reliable quantitative evidence now available provides a different picture. Crouzet, an authority in both French and English industrial history, maintains that during the eighteenth century the rates of growth of manufacturing in the two countries were roughly the same (Crouzet 1966: 266). And it may be the case that toward the end of the century per capita incomes in France and Britain were of the same order of magnitude. The Napoleonic wars likely had a differing impact on the two economies; there seems to be a consensus that France lagged behind. For the nineteenth century, the paper by Lévy-Leboyer and Lescure (Chapter 8) presents the results of the most recent quantitative research to which Maurice Leboyer himself made major contributions (Lévy-Leboyer 1978; Lévy-Leboyer and Bourguignon 1985). The record of industrial growth from the Restoration to the early 1860s is rather impressive. The modest performance of the economy from that decade to the end of the century is due to a slowdown in agricultural rather than in industrial output, except for the 1880s. Both sectors participated in the expansion that took place from the end of the century to the outbreak of the First World War. On the whole, the cyclical pattern from 1850 to 1914 is roughly similar to that of most other European economies, with the possible exception of Germany.

The secular trend in France's industrial output compares well with that of Britain. The two countries share the absence of a 'take-off' or a 'spurt': their rates of growth were moderate but steady; both seem to experience a mild climacteric in the second half of the century that does not seem, however, to have a long-lasting 'retardation-effect'. The real peculiarity of France was its demographic pattern. If by the nineteenth century we may take French fertility rates as exogenous, then the relatively slow growth in *total* output may have been the result of slow population growth. Nonetheless, in 1913 France's per capita income was probably the highest of the large continental countries.

Gerschenkron's appraisal of French industrial growth depended upon the quantitative evidence then available to him. He knew that France was the most advanced continental power, but he probably overestimated her backwardness relative to Britain. An upward revision in favour of France of the relative position of the two countries on the eve of modern industrialization would lead one, in a Gerschenkron framework, to expect a similar pattern of industrial growth on the two sides of the channel. And that is precisely what seems to emerge from the quantitative analysis of the French case developed over the last two or three decades.

Located at the heart of Europe, Germany is probably the main character on the stage of Gerschenkron's play. Ex post, the reasons for such a central role may be seen in the overwhelming success of German industry. From an early nineteenth-century viewpoint, Germany's ability to seize the growth opportunities implicit in its export-oriented eastern agriculture, in its flourishing handicrafts, and in its resource endowments, could set the path for the industrialization of the Continent and challenge British superiority. Friedrich List, the German economist and nationalist, did not fail to see these opportunities. In addition, a successful Germany would provide not only a paradigm but an actual stimulus as well to the more backward countries east and south of its 1871 borders.

In spite of the important progress made in the last two decades, German quantitative economic history has not as yet produced a new set of industrial statistics extending back to the early nineteenth century. Scholars are still relying on partial revisions of Hoffmann's index of 1965. The timing of industrialization that emerges from such revisions, from estimates of output in agriculture and of GNP, as well as from case studies of individual industries is the following: There were important instances of 'protoindustrialization' during the eighteenth and early nineteenth centuries. Precise quantification in this area is still scanty, but some scholars believe that their weight eventually could have been sufficient to induce investment leading to growth acceleration. There is little doubt among scholars that during the 1840s and 1850s German industry made important progress. This phase of industrial development has been seen by some as fitting Gerschenkron's definition of 'great spurt', both because of its speed and because of its emphasis on producers' goods. The achievements of the two preceding decades are less clear and the subject of an ongoing debate. It is possible that German industrial output and investment had relatively high rates of growth from the end of the Napoleonic wars onward.

The progress of German industry continued in the second half of the century. Scholars are increasingly sceptical about the existence of a twenty-year-long 'great depression' anywhere in Europe, and even more so in the case of Germany. The rate of growth of manufacturing output seems to be only slightly lower than that of the preceding twenty years, if one is to trust Hoffmann's index. Toward the end of the century an acceleration took place, in tune with the international business cycle.

If the available quantitative evidence is correct, Germany experienced almost a century of high growth of industrial output, outperforming Britain possibly by a factor close to two.

The Habsburg Empire was a complex multi-ethnic entity enclosing within its borders a variety of economic regions with varying degrees of economic backwardness and performance. Chapter 11 focuses on Austria and Hungary, the core of the Empire. The former country was more advanced than the second;

both were 'relatively backward in the nineteenth century and, despite economic growth in the nineteenth century, remained so on the eve of the First World War' (Chapter 11, p. 226). The discussion must therefore stress not only the timing but also the relative speed of industrialization to see if part of the gap existing between Austria and the most advanced countries at the end of the Napoleonic wars was narrowed a century later.

Quantitative historians tell a story that by now will sound quite familiar to the reader: they see industrial growth taking place at a non-negligible pace during the first half of the nineteenth century (Rudolph 1975; Huertas 1977). An index of industrial production constructed by Komlos (1983) provides overwhelming evidence of sustained growth for Austria, between 1830 and 1913.[2] Hungary developed later, but by the 1870s that country too was changing over to sustained growth (Chapter 11, p. 227). There were, of course, cycles and even moments of rapid increase in the rates of growth, but on the whole, today's scholars are rather reluctant to pinpoint a particularly relevant spurt, or even any spurt at all.

Debates as well as quantitative investigations are continuing. The current revival of interest in Eastern Europe – a substantial part of which was in the Habsburg Empire before 1914 – will certainly speed up research in this area. As economic historians, we are sure that a better understanding of pre-communist economic development will provide insights into today's potential for growth and comparative advantages of individual countries in Eastern Europe and help in framing meaningful policy-oriented questions. For the time being, it should be noted that quantitative historians have revised a traditional pessimistic view of the economic weakness of the Empire on the eve of the First World War. The sustained industrial growth that had taken place for over a century, even if slow to spread to the whole territory under the Habsburg Monarchy, had an important impact. And some scholars argue that the War cut short a process of economic integration that ran against the disintegrating forces of nationalistic policies.

In 1913, Italy was probably more backward than Austria and more advanced than Hungary. It was, at any rate, an area in which an industrial spurt could be anticipated within the framework of Gerschenkron's approach to European industrialization. He built his own index of industrial production covering the years from 1881 to 1913. On that basis, Gerschenkron was able to see a great spurt taking place between 1896 and 1908.

Quantitative economic history has not made as much progress in Italy during the last thirty-odd years as it did in other countries covered by this survey. To be sure, competent research has widened the quantitative records available on individual industries and regions, while three other indices of industrial output have been produced (ISTAT 1957; Fenoaltea 1983; Carreras 1982). The latter indices, however, cannot claim an unmistakable statistical superiority over that of Gerschenkron. Moreover, they describe a cyclical pattern displaying a broad similarity to his index. All the indices show that industrial growth accelerated in the early 1880s, that a serious setback took place early in the following decade, and that after 1896–8 a long period of industrial development occurred until 1913, growth rates being exceptionally high until 1907–8 and slowing down somewhat thereafter. Given this evidence, the existence of a 'spurt' is largely a matter of semantics. Gerschenkron disregarded the boom of the 1880s on grounds that it was too short and that it was followed by a major recession. Others, like Fenoaltea, prefer to shy away from such words as spurts and take-offs, opting instead for a business-cycle approach to fluctuations in industrial output. It is, however, undeniable that the upward swing that began in the late 1890s was more pronounced, longer, and had a wider impact on the economy than the relatively short-lived one of the 1880s.

The industrial development of Italy in the years before 1880 remains quantitatively under-researched. Gerschenkron's index did not extend backward beyond that year. The other available indices go back to 1861: they describe a process of slow growth during the first two decades after political unification. No aggregate statistics of industrial output are available for the first part of the century, when Italy was divided into several independent states. On the basis of existing evidence, scholars such as Cafagna and Bonelli have pointed to slow but steady industrial growth in the textile industry, particularly in silk-spinning.

In the case of Italy, as for the Habsburg Empire, regional differences were particularly pronounced. The so-called Kingdom of the Two Sicilies (southern Italy and Sicily itself) was by far less developed than the Po Valley during the first part of the century: the gap in per capita incomes, if anything, widened after the unification of the country. Most of the pre-1914 industrial growth took place in the northern regions.

Russia, the least developed part of Europe, provided Gerschenkron with the extreme case for verifying the explanatory potentials of his paradigm. His view of the timing and structural characteristics of industrialization is summarized in Chapters 4 and 12. He saw a very slow growth until the mid-1880s followed by a sudden acceleration that lasted until 1900. The so-called heavy industries led this 'spurt' with exceptionally high rates of growth in such sectors as steel-making and engineering.

Gerschenkron's work was based on statistical evidence that had been scrutinized and developed to form an index of industrial production or a series of national accounts. Goldsmith's (1961) estimates of Russian economic growth appeared after Gerschenkron conceived his approach to European industrialization and wrote his essay on 'Russia: Patterns and problems of economic development' (Gerschenkron 1962: 119–51). We reiterate this point on the availability of historical statistics because we feel that Gerschenkron can be fully appreciated as a path-breaking scholar only in the historiographic context of his time. At the same time, we would also emphasize that economic history, like any other field of scholarship, makes slow but steady progress based on new discoveries. The availability, reliability and sophistication of quantitative evidence, as well as its compilation according to standards allowing cross-country and cross-time comparisons are keys to the progress in the discipline.

In the 1970s and 1980s several quantitative studies on Russia's economic development were published by Soviet and Western scholars: Chapters 4 and 12 provide the essential bibliography. While offering somewhat different inter-pretations of Russia's pattern of industrialization, both Crisp (Chapter 12) and Gregory (Chapter 4) convey the impression that the coverage and extension over time of industrial statistics are not entirely satisfactory. We are not yet able to make a precise assessment of the rate of growth and structural transformation of Russian industry prior to the 1880s, when Gerschenkron detected the 'kink' or sudden acceleration that characterizes the 'spurt'. Existing statistics, however, leave little doubt that the 1880s and 1890s witnessed a rapid expansion in the industrial sector. We are less sure about previous developments. Gregory hints at labour mobility soon after the Emancipation Act, a possible sign that industry was not stagnant. Crisp is inclined to see a long-run build-up rather than a sudden discontinuity around 1885. But we are not yet able to measure the order of magnitude of the acceleration in the rate of industrial growth that took place during the 1880s. What we do know now is that Russian agriculture also was expanding, a fact that Gerschenkron failed to see. As for the early beginnings of industrialization during the eighteenth century stressed by Crisp, they did not escape Gerschenkron's observation. He saw in the 'Old Believers' a social group providing a number of successful entrepreneurs in early modern Russia.

AGENTS OF INDUSTRIALIZATION

Gerschenkron saw both the state, i.e. the government, and a certain type of bank as particular agents of industrialization in countries characterized by economic backwardness. These were part of a more general concept of substitutions that sometimes were made for 'prerequisites' of industrialization that were missing in backward countries that nonetheless industrialized. Moreover, he viewed ideologies favouring industrialization as another agent of industrialization that tended to be stronger in backward countries. In this section we review current thinking on these agents of industrialization from the perspective of research after Gerschenkron; more detail is provided in the chapters that follow.

The unit of observation

Since Gerschenkron used nations or countries as his units of observation, it is appropriate at the start to ask whether this is still a valid way to proceed. Since Gerschenkron wrote, some writers have argued that it is more appropriate to study economic regions than political states or nations. Within nations, after all, industrialization invariably is a regional phenomenon, usually displaying a strongly uneven pattern, sometimes described as 'dualistic growth'.

The choice of the unit of observation depends on the purpose of the research and the aim and interest of the researcher. If research questions relate to comparative advantages, resource endowments, externalities, forward and backward linkages of particular industries, and so on, then regions may well be appropriate units of observation. Moreover, when questions relate to economic imbalances between regions, the choice of regions as units is obviously necessary.

For many purposes, however, the nation or country remains of paramount importance in modern historical research. One practical reason is that data are often collected and presented at the level of the nation, although this in no way denies the usefulness of geographically disaggregated data. More importantly, nation states historically tend to have common languages, laws, customs, public institutions, monies, bureaucracies and economic and social policies, as well as élites that shape all of these characteristics. These variables have a profound influence on the industrialization process and vary much more between nations than within them. Moreover, if one believes that economic policy matters then the national approach cannot be avoided. Therefore, those who use nations as units of observation in economic history usually do so for good reasons. In the chapters that follow, the authors often disagree with Gerschenkron's findings and they suggest numerous modifications of, and qualifications to, his approach. None, however, denies the validity of the nation state as a proper unit of observation, even though most find references to regional developments to be instructive within national contexts.

Substitutions for prerequisites

Patterns of substitution for 'prerequisites' are features of Gerschenkron's approach to European industrialization. They reconcile the interests of economists in identifying the common factors and economic processes that promote successful industrializations with the interests of historians in identifying the particular and possibly unique aspects of each individual case of industrialization. Any comparative approach to European industrialization, of course, would give attention to both the common and the particular features of the cases considered. What made Gerschenkron's comparative approach so influential among economists and historians studying historical economic development was the linking together of the common and the unique aspects of individual cases by means of his concept of relative backwardness. There were, according to Gerschenkron, patterns of substitution for alleged prerequisites that could be understood as responses to varying degrees of economic backwardness among countries when they began to industrialize.

Chapter 2 shows that Gerschenkron's insights into patterns of substitution continue to inform the work of economists on the optimal choice among various institutional forms of economic organization as well as the work of economic historians on the relative successes or failures of countries not only when they first industrialized but also as their industrializations continued in later decades. These remain contentious issues, as Chapter 2 and other chapters here demonstrate. As far as Gerschenkron's approach is concerned, most of the country studies here raise questions about the emphasis to be placed on particular institutions, for example, the role of joint-stock banks in financing industrial investment in France and Italy, and the role of the state in promoting industry in Russia. Nonetheless, Harley's main point, which he derives from Gerschenkron and from more recent analysts of economic institutions such as Oliver Williamson, is that the forms institutions take at particular times and in particular countries are to a considerable extent determined endogenously by economic conditions that prevail then and there. To Gerschenkron, differences in economic conditions were essentially varying degrees of backwardness. Harley indicates, however, that economic conditions may mean more than backwardness. Such an insight is helpful, but future work in economic history will derive the most benefit from it if the results flowing from differences in economic conditions form a systematic pattern, as Gerschenkron argued with such force. If differences in conditions merely lead to differences in results and there is no pattern of substitution that organizes the differences, the discipline of economic history will not have advanced very far by attempting to make Gerschenkron's insight about backwardness more general.

The role of the state

Gerschenkron saw in the state – in the broad sense, the government of a nation – a potential agent of industrialization. The state was particularly needed in conditions of extreme backwardness or, as one might put it today, in situations where markets fail to promote industrialization. Most modern economists accept that the state can influence the economy of a nation in a variety of ways. Some of these influences are conducive to economic development, while others hinder it. Even those who believe in rational expectations and therefore doubt that the monetary and fiscal policies of the state can have real economic effects would not deny that state policies affecting relative prices, for example, tariffs, subsidies, and government purchases, can have an impact in the real economy. On a broader level, the state can promote – or fail to promote – political and social stability; such stability contributes to economic development by stabilizing expectations and reducing the risks of private economic decision making.

Compared to the state as it has developed in the twentieth century, the European state of the nineteenth century typically was much smaller in relation to its national economy. In such a setting, the monetary and fiscal policies of the state may have affected individual business cycles, but they hardly mattered in the long run, except perhaps when they stabilized expectations about exchange rates and the price level by adherence, for example, to the gold standard. Another consequence of the small relative size of the government sector is that its direct impacts on industry were also rather limited. Tariffs and subsidies may have favoured some sectors and industries but often with the result that others were harmed. Direct purchases by the state also had mixed impacts, as did state-operated enterprises. The net economic impacts of such state policies and activities likely were small, and those who would argue otherwise typically fail to consider all of the impacts or to specify what the economic results would have been had the state not done what it actually did. These considerations suggest that the more efficiently markets functioned, the less was the net impact of state intervention. If markets were absent or inefficient in situations of backwardness, as Gerschenkron suggested, the net economic impact of state intervention was likely to be greater than where markets were well-developed.

The one exception to an argument that the direct economic impact of nineteenth-century states was negligible is the railway sector. Here the capital requirement was large relative to other types of enterprise and it was necessary to secure rights of way. Both of these characteristics prompted state intervention, and the consensus of today's economic historians is that railways on the continent would have developed more slowly without state intervention. Nonetheless, the assessment of the net benefit of this intervention remains problematical. In Chapter 8, Lévy-Leboyer and Lescure indicate that French railways, largely as a result of state intervention, were overbuilt with generally negative impacts on industry and the French economy. Chapters 9–11 on Germany, Italy and Austria-Hungary are consistent in the view that railway development was an important factor in the internal integration of those economies and possibly had net positive effects on industrial development. Chapters 4 and 12 on Russia take an even more positive view of the economic impact of railways on the Russian economy and the Russian state's large role in that development. These findings regarding the one great area of direct state intervention in the economy are fairly consistent with Gerschenkron's approach even though the authors question many of his other interpretations.

If apart from the railways the nineteenth-century state had minor direct impacts on industry, what were its indirect impacts? Most likely they were in the area of creating and fostering or abolishing institutions that either helped or hindered industrialization. On the beneficial side were the creation and protection of property rights, the dismantling of outmoded institutions such as serfdom, the promotion of national economic integration in ways other than railways (for example, monetary integration), the provision of elementary education – often compulsory – which the market would have been slower to provide, and the sometimes creative response of the state to social problems resulting from industrialization itself (Tilly here refers to Germany's 'ambitious program of social insurance', which eased class tensions arising from industrialization). But state action could also impede industrialization. Gerschenkron argued, for example, that Russia's emancipation provisions of 1861 inhibited agricultural productivity in the following decades and therefore delayed Russian industrialization. Gregory responds that Gerschenkron mistook bureaucratic intent for actual results, and that market forces and incentives overcame the economic inefficiencies inherent in the legal provisions. That may indeed have been the case. But there remains the issue of what costs were involved in getting around ill-conceived laws and institutions. Often these costs were not trivial; to that extent the laws and institutions did function as drags on development.

Views on the role of the state in economic development often have tended to reflect the political stance of the investigator as much as the historical evidence investigated. Those who are troubled by the excesses of *laissez-faire* results and market failures often extol the virtues of state intervention. Those who are troubled by the excesses of state intervention and the problems of making rational collective choices extol the virtues of market solutions. The history of European industrialization rarely offers clear and consistent support for either of these stances. Progress in understanding the role of the state in industrialization requires both hard economic analysis of specific state actions and a certain amount of scholarly detachment from any tendency to draw current political implications out of past events.

The role of financial institutions

'German' banks, i.e. mixed or universal banks that combined commercial and investment banking, are another important agent of industrialization in Gerschenkron's approach. He argued that such banks actually did play the key role of financing modern industry in conditions of moderate economic backwardness such as those of Germany, and that they might therefore be expected to play the same role in other moderately backward situations such as in Austria and Italy. The contrast is with Britain, where the absence of backwardness made such banks unnecessary, and with Russia, where a more extreme degree of backwardness made such banks impossible.

In Britain, original accumulation and the profits of pioneer industrialists were sufficient to meet the long-term financing needs of modern industry. Britain had a well-developed financial system that met commercial (short-term) lending needs and the portfolio diversification needs of private wealth-holders without mixed banking of the German variety. The Bank of England and city banks provided liquidity and discount facilities. Country banks provided discount facilities and probably some amount of long-term credit. Sophisticated insurance brokers (e.g. Lloyds) and efficient securities exchanges making markets in public and private bonds and equities completed the advanced British financial system.

During the first half of the nineteenth century, financial systems on the Continent were much less developed than the British system. There the financing needs of states and of large enterprises such as railways and some metal and mining firms were met by private banking houses. These houses were 'universal' in their lending operations, but they generally did not collect deposits; their resources were derived from persons and institutions of wealth. Smaller inter-mediaries – local banks, savings banks and mortgage/land banks – developed to provide financing for small local enterprises. In this context, Gerschenkron viewed the 1852 appearance of the Pereires' Crédit Mobilier in France as a major financial innovation. It was a joint-stock institution that, in contrast with earlier continental bankers, mobilized savings – small, medium and large – and concentrated the disposition of its large financial resources on major projects such as railways, canals, utilities and foreign investment. The establishment by the Crédit Mobilier of foreign affiliated institutions led to yet another financial innovation. Some of these affiliates began to gather deposits and channel them toward the development of manufacturing enterprises. They provided all the credit facilities, short- and long-term, needed by these new enterprises, as well as entrepreneurship and industrial coordination (avoiding harmful competition) among the enterprises financed by the bank.

It was this latter innovation, an offshoot of the Crédit Mobilier, that Gerschenkron called the 'German' mixed bank, although it had precedents as well in Belgium and in German private banks. The innovation spread also to Austria, to Hungary, to Italy, and to Spain, among other nations. It did not, however, have much influence on French banking, which moved slowly closer to the English pattern. Some local and regional banks, as Lévy-Leboyer and Lescure point out in Chapter 8, did practise a form of mixed banking but only in later stages of French industrialization rather than at the outset.

Gerschenkron argued that the specific financial innovation of mixed or universal banking with an accompanying supply of industrial entrepreneurship from the bankers themselves was an important agent of industrialization in contexts of moderate economic backwardness. In these contexts the supply of savings – at least that part of savings available to industry – was limited, as was the availability of industrial entrepreneurship for large-scale ventures. The mixed bank, especially in Germany, substituted for these missing 'prerequisites' of industrial modernization. Gerschenkron's proposition, especially as concerns banker entrepreneurship, is not easily tested, as he himself recognized (Gerschenkron 1967: 450). Detailed archival research in the banking and firm records of a number of countries is needed to clarify the issues and place them in a comparative context. A start has been made on this, as noted by Toniolo and Federico in Chapter 10, but much more remains to be done by future researchers.

The present state of our knowledge (see Chapter 3, among others, for more detail) may be summarized as follows: It is difficult to accept the extreme version of Gerschenkron's hypothesis that banks were the only agents of industrialization in moderately backward countries, although he himself came close to holding to this version in the Italian case (Gerschenkron 1967: 450). On the other hand, it is difficult to reject the argument that industry-oriented financial institutions promoted industrialization in ways that made major differences in some cases, particularly those in which the cultural and financial environments associated with powerful 'landed interests' were present and industrialization was regarded with suspicion both for its socio-political effects and for its high financial risks. Such environments are aspects of moderate economic backwardness. It is also likely that mixed, universal banks helped to shape the industry mix of the countries in which they were active, especially by concentrating resources in more technologically advanced and capital-intensive sectors. Thus, the banks had an uneven impact on industry. The case of Germany most amply, and by fairly general agreement (see Chapters 3 and 9), illustrates these propositions; the case of Italy (see Chapter 10) is perhaps the best example that the Gerschenkronian insight could be pushed too far.

The role of ideology

Gerschenkron believed that ideologies favouring change, industrialization and modernization were themselves agents of industrialization. While present to an extent in every case of industrialization, such ideologies were more important and likely to be more 'virulent' as the degree of economic backwardness increased. The reason for ideological virulence was that the old vested interests in backward societies – the church, the old nobility, the landowning aristocracy, possibly even the conservative peasantry – were likely to be resistant to any change, such as industrialization, that brought forth new centres of power and threatened the relative, perhaps even the absolute, wealth, power and social standing of the old vested interests. These vested interests could be overcome only by new interests favouring modernization. Ideologies of industrialization were an independent force that moulded and gave energy to the modernizers.

In comparison with the clarity of his analysis of the mechanisms of capital supply to industrial firms as they varied according to degrees of backwardness, Gerschenkron's analysis of the role of ideology – as Parker notes in Chapter 5 – was less clear and precise. The British ideology of bourgeois democracy in general and free trade in particular was sometimes mentioned by Gerschenkron, but he did not dwell on it because Britain's advanced status meant that the role of ideology would not be important there. The German ideology of economic nationalism, stated at an early date in the writings of Friedrich List, was more important in Gerschenkron's scheme. Nonetheless, according to Parker and Tilly in Chapters 5 and 9, Gerschenkron's treatment was rather simplistic. Parker argues that economic nationalism and the corporatism to which it led had more negative aspects, in the short run and in the long run, than Gerschenkron seemed to realize. Tilly sees shifts over time in both German interest groups and their ideologies; an aggregative concept such as economic nationalism leaves out too much of the historical detail that shaped ideology. In Russia, a Marxist ideology of industrialization appealed to the intelligentsia because it would hurry along the inevitable processes and outcomes of history; in a curious way this Marxist thought dovetailed with the economic nationalist interest of the absolute state in increasing its political and military power by industrializing the Russian economy. But it is not clear what difference Marxist ideology made in Russia's spurt.

In other national cases, Gerschenkron, if anything, is even less clear on the role of ideology. He viewed the Saint-Simonian ideology of modernization in France as significant, but only for a limited period. From his treatment it is not clear whether France's rather advanced economic conditions limited the role of ideology, or whether the limited role of ideology accounted in some way for shortcomings of French industrialization.

Lévy-Leboyer and Lescure, in Chapter 8, lean toward the former view. The same ambiguity infuses Gerschenkron's treatment of Italy; Federico and Toniolo in their chapter here parallel Tilly in suggesting that there were more complexities in ideology than implied by Gerschenkron. As for Austria-Hungary, Gerschenkron argued that the failure to develop an effective ideology of industrialization, while obviously a difficult task in a multinational empire, contributed to the weakness of industrialization. If, as Good suggests in Chapter 11, Austria's path to modernization was different from what Gerschenkron expected but not as inadequate as he implied, Gerschenkron's analysis of ideology becomes even more problematical.

Ideology is not a 'comfortable' concept for economic historians. Gerschenkron placed it on the stage in the drama of economic modernization, although not in the centre of the stage; it played a supporting role. Parker in his essay here affirms the importance of ideology, but he views it as much less of a positive force, actually and potentially, than Gerschenkron did. Other studies here, directly or implicitly, question its relevance, at least in the ways Gerschenkron developed it in particular cases. There is a danger, possibly, that the role of ideology in modernization will be ignored not because it is irrelevant but because it is intractable.

GERSCHENKRON AND THE STATE OF THE ART

Since Gerschenkron produced his overall approach to European industrialization during the nineteenth century, research in the field has made considerable progress. Some results have been reviewed in the preceding sections. A more detailed survey of the 'state of the art' for individual countries and for some of the topics dealt with by Gerschenkron is embodied in each chapter of this book.

Aggregate statistics, particularly for national accounts, are now more abundant and of better quality than they were twenty years ago. Individual sectors, firms and banks have been more thoroughly researched, in part because of the recent development of historical consciousness among business enterprises which has led to establishment or reorganization of their archives. On the whole, research in the field of European industrialization is making slow but steady progress. Several projects, as we have repeatedly pointed out, have been stimulated directly or indirectly by Gerschenkron's approach to the pattern of European industrial growth. The following chapters will discuss in some detail which of his findings and insights have so far been confirmed and which of them today's scholars find difficult to accept. However, since each chapter debates and reviews individual issues, they say relatively little about the most important part of Gerschenkron's contribution to our understanding of nineteenth-century Europe, namely his comprehensive general view of the Continent's industrialization as a pattern that can be described and understood by appropriately arranging a set of variables.

We have seen that Gerschenkron's appraisal of the relative backwardness of individual European countries around the middle of the nineteenth century is consistent with more recent attempts at comparing GNP per head. Other indicators of living standards – including some favoured by Gerschenkron, e.g. literacy – seem to confirm these findings, although research in the field is still in progress (see Chapter 10). The time-pattern of industrialization in individual countries may, therefore, be framed within a continental setting characterized by the increasing degrees of economic backwardness a nineteenth-century traveller would have met when moving from the northwest to the east and the south.

Recent research has strengthened the perception of Britain as following the expected pattern of an early-comer. Rates of growth of industrial output were low relative to the experience of most latecomers and acceleration was slow. Advances in agricultural productivity played a major role both in increasing per capita income and in making resources available to manufacturing production. Fixed capital formation in industry never rose to a large relative or absolute share of national product. With an early diversification and specialization of inter-mediaries, British financial markets acquired a sophistication not found on the Continent. There was neither adequate demand nor, indeed, a supply-side push for industrial banking to rise to noteworthy importance.

The time-pattern of French industrialization now accepted by scholars of that country differs from the perceived wisdom of Gerschenkron's times. The acceleration that took place in the 1850s was preceded by non-negligible increases in industrial output taking place from the time of the Restoration in 1815. Gerschenkron, as we noted earlier, was not particularly at ease with the case of France, since neither banks nor government seemed to him crucially important in the process of industrialization of that country. Although he saw France as the least backward among the continental powers, as does recent research, perhaps Gerschenkron overestimated the economic gap between France and Britain during the first half of the century. If we accept the opinion of a number of scholars that such a gap was not particularly pronounced, then France would fit the pattern of an early-comer, once allowance is made for the impact of such an exogenous factor as the Napoleonic wars.

The pattern of industrialization of the other countries described in this volume does not seem to support Gerschenkron's approach in its precise original formulation. Particularly, it is difficult to detect those short periods of rapid growth beginning with discontinuities (or kinks) in indices of industrial production that were defined as 'great spurts'. Both industrial statistics and methods of analysis (see Chapter 7) may improve in the future. For the time being, however, the prevailing view of the processes of industrial development in Germany, Austria, Hungary, Italy and Russia is one of fluctuations around trends that do not show sharp discontinuities. It may be argued, therefore, that a strictly 'orthodox' Gerschenkronian view of the process of industrialization in con-ditions of backwardness is at odds with the most up-to-date empirical findings.

We remain convinced, however, that a 'loose' version of Gerschenkron's approach is helpful in explaining the overall pattern of European industrialization during the nineteenth century. The concept of relative backwardness in particular provides a powerful way of synthesizing a number of factors that are crucial in explaining specific features of industrialization in European countries. Moreover, in discussing 'prerequisites' as seen by Marx and Toynbee, and in introducing the idea of substitutes for such prerequisites, Gerschenkron provides an approach that is appealing both to the economist and to the historian. The questions he asked are among the most important ones to which today's scholars are trying to find answers. How powerful are market forces in promoting growth? Where and when are market failures more likely to arise? In what ways do institutions matter? What forces are likely to induce institutional changes better suited to serve the process of economic development? How does the transfer of technology take place and to what extent is technology adapted to relatively backward economic environments? Do financial institutions have allocative effects? Is the action of the government more effective in a given economic and social context than in another?

There are, in our opinion, good reasons for arguing that the answers to most of these questions may not be the same in the case of the early-comers (Britain and France) as in that of the latecomers (e.g. Russia). A narrow view of the 'big spurt', as we saw, does not find much support from empirical observation. The same empirical evidence, however, shows that an acceleration of growth took place in Germany during the 1840s, in Hungary during the 1870s, and in Italy and Russia during the 1880s. These industrial processes differed in many ways from those that led to the so-called first Industrial Revolution in Britain. Important differences relative to the British experience are found among latecomers in capital–labour ratios, in industry mix, in the size and organization of the firm, in the relations between entrepreneurs, bankers and governments, and in the role of agriculture. Can it be plausibly argued that such differences depended only on the fact that 'latecomers' were late in time? Are factors associated with time lags sufficient to explain the pattern of industrialization in the above-mentioned countries?

If one feels, as we do, that time is not a sufficient explanatory variable, country-specific variables should be included. And there is one important feature the latecomers discussed in this book have in common: namely, that for most of the nineteenth century they were more backward than Britain was a century earlier at the time of the 'Industrial Revolution'. Of all the backwardness-related economic and social variables, let us recall one, the ratio of agricultural labour force over total labour force. Wide differences in this ratio were related to differences in prevailing social values, the composition of the ruling class, the skills and education of the workforce, the savings and demand patterns, and the organization and efficiency of the market place for both real goods and financial instruments.

The discovery or rediscovery, almost in every country, of the eighteenth-century origins of industrial development does not change the overall importance of relative backwardness. Gerschenkron himself covered this topic at length in his courses at Harvard. He pointed out that handicrafts, artisans and small factories were instrumental in slowly producing a climate favourable to economic growth. But nineteenth-century industrialization could not and did not rely only upon small crafts. Alongside the traditional silk, wool and food-processing industries that enjoyed close links with agriculture, newer industries such as cotton textiles, steel-making, engineering and chemical industries had to be developed under less favourable conditions than those existing in Britain during the second half of the nineteenth century.

One may argue that Gerschenkron's selection of 'substitutes' for such favourable conditions is not entirely appropriate, that others should be added, that each of them individually did not matter much, and that a number of such 'substitutes' – perhaps more market-oriented or -induced – had to develop. All this will be, we hope, on the agenda for future research. But if this still seems a fruitful way of approaching the problem of European industrialization during the nineteenth century, then we may say that what we called the 'loose' version of Gerschenkron's paradigm still offers a good first insight into that problem and provides a powerful guide in framing the meaningful questions that scholars should ask.

ACKNOWLEDGEMENT

Financial support from Consiglio Nazionale delle Ricerche (CNR grant 87.01225.10) for the preparation of this paper is gratefully acknowledged.

NOTES

1   In fairness to Rostow, it should be noted that at the beginning of his *stages* he emphasized that 'the stages-of-growth are an arbitrary and limited way of looking at the sequence of modern history: and they are, in no absolute sense, a correct way' (Rostow 1961: 1). In the second edition (Rostow 1971) there is a 71-page appendix in which Rostow responds to his critics.
2   Komlos pushes back to the eighteenth century not only the roots of industrial growth but a relevant upswing that led to the development of the following century.

REFERENCES

Barsby, S.L. (1969) 'Economic backwardness and the characteristics of development', *Journal of Economic History* XXIX, 449–72.
Cameron, R. and Freedman, C.E. (1983) 'French economic growth: a radical revision', *Social Science History* 7, 3–30.
Carreras, A. (1982) 'La producciò industrial espanyola i italiana des de mitian segle XIX fins a l'actualitat', unpublished dissertation, University of Barcelona.
Crafts, N.F.R., Leybourne, S.J. and Mills, T.C. (1990) 'Measurement of trend growth in

European industrial output before 1914: methodological issues and new estimates', *Explorations in Economic History* 4.

Crouzet, F. (1966) 'Angleterre et France au XVIII^c siècle. Essai d'analyse comparée de duex conaissances économiques', *Annales* 21, 254–91.

Deane, P. and Cole, W.A. (1962) *British Economic Growth 1688–1959*, Cambridge: Cambridge University Press.

Feinstein, C.H. (1972) *National Income, Expenditure and Output in the United Kingdom 1855–1965*, Cambridge: Cambridge University Press.

—— (1978) 'Capital formation in Great Britain' in P. Mathias and M.M. Postan (eds) *Cambridge Economic History of Europe*, Cambridge: Cambridge University Press, vol. 7, part 1, pp. 28–96.

—— (1988) 'National statistics, 1760–1920: sources and methods of estimation for domestic reproducible fixed assets, stocks and works in progress, overseas assets and land', in C.H. Feinstein and S. Pollard (eds) *Studies in Capital Formation in the United Kingdom 1750–1920*, Oxford: Clarendon Press, pp. 259–471.

Fenoaltea, S. (1983) 'Railways and the development of the Italian economy to 1913', in P. O'Brien, *Railways and the Growth of Western Europe*, London: Macmillan, pp. 49–120.

Gerschenkron, A. (1962) *Economic Backwardness in Historical Perspective*, Cambridge, Mass.: Harvard University Press.

—— (1967) 'The discipline and I', *Journal of Economic History* 27, 443–59.

—— (1968) *Continuity in History and Other Essays*, Cambridge, Mass.: Harvard University Press.

—— (1970) *Europe in the Russian Mirror, Four Lectures in Economic History*, Cambridge: Cambridge University Press.

—— (1977) *An Economic Spurt That Failed*, Princeton: Princeton University Press.

Goldsmith, R.W. (1961) 'The economic growth of tsarist Russia, 1860–1913', *Economic Development and Cultural Change* 9, 460.

—— (1969) *Financial Structure and Development*, New Haven and London: Yale University Press.

Harley, C.K. (1982) 'British industrialization before 1841: evidence of slower growth during the Industrial Revolution', *Journal of Economic History* 42, 267–89.

Hoffmann, W.G. (1955) *British Industry, 1700–1950*, Oxford: Blackwell.

Huertas, T. (1977) *Economic Growth and Economic Policy in a Multinational Setting*, New York: Arno Press.

Istituto Centrale di Statistica (1957) 'Indagine statistica sullo sviluppo del reddito nazionale dell'Italia dal 1861 al 1959', *Annali di statistica*, Serie VIII, 9.

Komlos, J. (1983) *The Habsburg Monarchy as a Customs Union. Economic Development in Austria-Hungary in the Nineteenth Century*, Chicago: University of Chicago Press.

Kuznets, S. (1966) *Modern Economic Growth: Rate, Structure and Spread*, New Haven: Yale University Press.

Lévy-Leboyer, M. (1978) 'Capital development and economic growth in France 1820–1930', in *Cambridge Economic History of Europe*, vol. VII, Cambridge: Cambridge University Press.

Lévy-Leboyer, M. and Bourguignon, F. (1985) *L'économie francaise au XIXe siècle. Analyse Macroeconomique*, Paris: Economica.

Lewis, W.A. (1978) *Growth and Fluctuations*, London: Allen & Unwin.

McCloskey, D.N. (1970) 'Did Victorian Britain fail?', *Economic History Review* 23, 446–59.

McCloskey, D.N. and Sandberg, L.G. (1971) 'From damnation to redemption: judgements on the late Victorian entrepreneur', *Explorations in Economic History* 9, 89–108.

O'Brien, P.K. (1986) 'Do we have a typology for the study of European industrialization in the XIXth century?' *Journal of European Economic History* 15 (2), 291–333.

Roehl, R. (1976) 'French industrialization: a reconsideration', *Explorations in Economic History* 13, 233–81.

Rostow, W.W. (1961) *The Stages of Economic Growth – A non-Communist Manifesto*, Cambridge: Cambridge University Press.

Rosovsky, H. (1979) 'Alexander Gerschenkron: a personal and fond recollection', *Journal of Economic History*, December, 1009–13.

Rudolph, R. (1975) 'The pattern of Austrian industrial growth from the eighteenth to the early twentieth century', *Austrian History Yearbook* 11, 3–25.

Tilly, R. (1986) 'Alexander Gerschenkron – modern historian', unpublished paper.

Part I

European industrialization: institutions, ideologies and interpretations

Chapter 2

Substitution for prerequisites: endogenous institutions and comparative economic history

C. Knick Harley

Alexander Gerschenkron perceived European industrialization as a systematic whole that could only be understood by comparative analysis. However, he explicitly rejected Marx's dictum that 'the industrial more developed country presents the less developed country a picture of the latter's future' and insisted that a country's position within a typology of economic backwardness shaped its industrialization. Europe industrialized as a whole. Particular national experiences elaborated a general framework in which relative backwardness led to systematic differences. Substitution for prerequisites created endogenous institutional differences among national industrializations. Gerschenkron intertwined his broad insight of endogenous differences in institutions with a specific vision of European growth that focused on industrial production and predicted increasingly powerful industrialization spurts in economies whose growth started late. Big industrial spurts have proven elusive, but Gerschenkron's concept of 'substitution of prerequisites' continues to provide important insights for comparative economic history.

Substitution for prerequisites involved the creation of new institutional arrangements to direct economic activity. In Gerschenkron's typology, Britain's prototype industrialization occurred when prerequisite conditions of factor supply and market institutions led to capitalist development. Widely diffused accumulation and enterprise, an institutional framework supporting private property, and prosperous agriculture permitted Britain to industrialize by an atomistic process in which markets coordinated decisions of many individuals. More backward parts of Europe lacked Britain's prerequisites to various degrees and institutional substitution resulted in larger firms, investment banks and the state, and a different industrialization. Different institutions were endogenous; in more backward conditions, hierarchies increasingly substituted for markets.

The endogenous substitution of hierarchies for markets in backward areas followed a pattern recently analysed in the economics of industrial organization. Oliver Williamson, in particular, has analysed the competition between market and hierarchical organization in terms of transaction costs. Industrial activity may be organized by a variety of institutions which may be visualized as lying on a spectrum that run from small firms in competitive markets, to oligopolistic firms, to comprehensive economy-wide planning. In market economies, the organization in place arises from a competitive process of profit maximization by individual firms. Simple firms, whose owners exercise control, provide highly effective incentives and, in many circumstances, markets coordinate these firms efficiently and they are more profitable than complex firms. In other situations, hierarchies have lower transaction costs, because of the nature of technology or the size of the markets, and large hierarchical firms prove more profitable than simple firms. In certain environments, hierarchical organization above the firm level also has transactions cost advantages that encourage the development of cartels and powerful investment banks that are less useful in societies with well-developed markets.

Gerschenkron concentrated on the emergence of economic growth in European societies, but his insights on the endogeneity of institutions illuminate comparative history more generally. In particular, comparative institutional history has figured prominently in discussions of twentieth-century economic performance. The British economy, with its generally small firms and heavy reliance on market organization, performed poorly compared to the United States and Germany, whose economies were organized with greater emphasis on hierarchies, particularly larger firms and specialized industrial banking. Not surprisingly, a persistent line of historical analysis has attributed differences in performance to differences in organization. British industry failed to adopt the large modern corporation that arose first in the United States, and consequently failed to capture 'economies of speed' available from mass production of standardized products. British banking failed to provide the leadership to divert resources into strategic growth areas. The atomistic nature of British industry inhibited rationalization in the interwar years. In short, the British economy was fragmented and relied on the market for coordination when it is alleged that the economy would have benefited from more coordinated planning.

The argument that institutional forms explain differences in twentieth-century growth rests rather unsatisfactorily, however, on simple temporal association. Implicitly, the history of the most successful economy is seen to reveal a best institutional pattern, appropriate generally but not always adopted. Gerschenkron's and Williamson's insights suggest, however, that systematic differences in institutions arise from different objective circumstances. If institutions arise endogenously and systematically, comparative history must analyse the source of institutional differences and avoid facile *post hoc ergo propter hoc* arguments of cause. In particular, detailed consideration of the forces leading to institutional choice in the late nineteenth century suggests that Britain's institutions were appropriate to her circumstances.

SUBSTITUTIONS FOR PREREQUISITES: ENDOGENOUS INSTITUTIONS

Gerschenkron's schema

Gerschenkron rejected the idea that all development followed a pattern observable in the first industrializer, moving from a common stage of prerequisites into industrial growth. Britain, the first industrializer, experienced a long development of institutions – in a limited sense, prerequisites – that supported industrialization. A market economy had been created within a large unified state that replaced medieval restrictions with legal institutions specifying and enforcing property rights. Technological knowledge had been accumulated and regularly improved. Agriculture had been transformed from a manorial and customary basis, was incorporated into the market economy and experienced important productivity increases. Specialization and training had created a diversified and skilled labour force. Individuals and groups in British society took risks and innovated. They also channelled accumulated wealth into fixed capital.

Presenting Britain's development up to the mid-eighteeenth century as a model of necessary prerequisites, however, has 'rather discouraging implications as far as development of backward countries is concerned'. 'Prerequisites have been rather loosely defined', seeming, 'with a slight twist of the pen' to encompass the traits by which modern economies differ from pre-industrial. Many are not prerequisites at all but part and parcel of the development process (Gerschenkron 1966: 32–3). Gerschenkron emphasized that other European economies industrialized rapidly without Britain's rich prior institutional structure by successfully developing substitutes for Britain's prerequisites. Understanding historical industrialization requires exploration of the pattern of substitutions. Substitutions compensated for factor and product market differences between leader and follower economies. Followers used different production techniques, produced a different output mix, and relied on different governance structures. Larger decision units with hierarchical relationships substituted for market coordination because markets in backward economies were too thin and poorly organized to perform as they had in early industrializers.

Labour supply in backward economies was unsatisfactory. Firms had to recruit labour. Skill and industrial discipline were largely unattainable, so firms chose production techniques that economized on discipline and skill. Specialized machinery tended by unskilled or semi-skilled labour replaced skilled labour using general-purpose machines. The substitution, however, had additional dimensions because specialized machinery depended on high throughput of standardized products. Managerial firms arose to coordinate raw material supply, control production and market large, homogeneous output.

British firms had been financed by the mobilization of existing wealth, reinvestment of profits, and a well-developed short-term credit network based on mercantile credit, bills of exchange, and commercial banking. More backward areas could not duplicate this process; wealth was less easily mobilized and financial market traditions were scant or non-existent. In Germany, institutional innovation took the form of investment banks directly financing industry by accepting firms' long-term liabilities – a practice British banks regarded as unacceptably risky. German banks, unable to reduce risk by diversification on well-developed financial markets, sought alternatives. These banks favoured large firms and took positions in the hierarchical management of these firms to obtain information and influence that reduced the banks' risks. The banks also encouraged the formation of larger integrated firms and cartels to reduce risk by exploiting monopoly power. In Russia even greater backwardness precluded the use of German-type banks. Only the state had the power to mobilize savings and it came to play an important role in industrial finance, with guarantees of various kinds for firms and direct involvement in investment. Only large firms could engage in the political relationship crucial to success, so large firms possessed even greater advantages than in Germany.

Direction of economic activity – management and entrepreneurship – also adjusted to backward conditions. In Britain, alternative suppliers offered inputs and products sold easily on existing markets, so firms had little need for overall planning. Management could concentrate on details of efficient production. In more backward conditions, firms could not rely on poorly developed markets to provide alternative supply sources. The absence of well-developed markets for final goods serving a large and relatively prosperous public drove firms to systematic marketing, including perhaps even the creation of markets. Increasing industrial and economy-wide coordination were thrust onto managerial decision-making within large enterprises and cartels.

Gerschenkron's big spurt may also be viewed as substituting for insufficient markets. In his view, backwardness presented obstacles to the initiation of growth that could be surmounted by a rapidly growing industrial sector. The successful industrial sector, based on modern technology and supported by ideological commitment, overcame the inertia holding the backward economy in poverty. Successful exploitation of new technology involved capturing extensive economies of scale. Pre-existing consumer demand provided an insufficient market, so momentum for successful industrialization had to come from demand, within a 'development block' of producers' goods industries, generated by a major spurt of investment (Gerschenkron 1966: 35). The big spurt, the emphasis on producers' goods, and the pressure on the standard of living all emerged logically in Gerschenkron's pattern of backward industrialization.

Backward countries, of course, started with disadvantages, but there were some compensating advantages. The late industrializer could utilize the newest technology unencumbered by existing fixed capital and perhaps entrenched attitudes and institutions that constrained choices in more advanced nations. In iron and steel, for example, international comparative advantage and techno-logical evolution brought the world's most advanced plants to Germany and then to Russia at the end of the century. Furthermore, the creation of substitutions in the various successful backward states sometimes resulted in innovations that improved on existing best practice. Nonetheless, Gerschenkron felt that institutions created by latecomer substitution were usually inappropriate for more advanced economies. New institutions, in terms an economic theorist might use, were a substitution within a set of possible choices that maximized in the face of different constraints. Just as the neoclassical firm substitutes away from inputs that have risen in price, so the substitution of institutions for missing prerequisites represents an improvement over the adoption of the techniques and institutions of the advanced country. But substitution does not fully cancel the initial disadvantages, either of rising input prices or of economic backwardness.

Oliver Williamson's institutions of capitalism

Recent research in industrial organization illuminates the substitutions that Gerschenkron saw as central to European industrialization. Oliver Williamson's work, in particular, has focused on the benefits and limits of competitive markets and the rationale for complex contracting arrangements and hierarchical organizations. In fact, the title of Williamson's book, *Markets and Hierarchies* (Williamson 1975) provides a theme analogous to Gerschenkron's pattern of substitutions. Hierarchies become more important relative to markets, the more backward a country is at the time of its industrialization.

Williamson's analysis of hierarchical organizations is articulated in his recent work *The Economic Institutions of Capitalism* (Williamson 1985: 30). Economic organization emerges from the balance of positive and negative features of large organizations. Large hierarchical arrangements aid certain continuing relationships that increase efficiency by permitting specialization that requires special skills and capital. Hierarchical organizations, however, suffer from a dilution of incentives to efficient behaviour.

The advantages of hierarchical organizations arise from their ability to manage 'transaction-specific assets' (Williamson 1985: 30). Specialization of physical capital and human skill to a particular continuing transaction provides advantages but requires institutional support. In specialized arrangements at least one party has made a valuable commitment to a continuing transaction. Committed assets have reduced value in alternative uses, so adjustment within the continuing relationship raises problems of opportunism. Adjustment and problems of containing opportunism are unavoidable because anticipating future circumstances and specifying contingent actions prior to commitment is at best expensive, and at some point impossible. The role of opportunism constraining non-market adjudication is clearly summarized by Armen Alchian and Susan Woodward (1988). Two types of transactions are at the centre of the analysis: a spot market transaction, or exchange, that 'involves no promises or latent future responsibility', and a contract, that promises future performance. Contractual relationships present managerial difficulties not present in exchanges because 'typically one party makes an investment, the profitability of which depends on the other party's future behaviour'. Williamson focuses on the 'transactions cost' that

> includes, almost to the extent of ignoring the [costs of initial delineation of the contract], the costs incurred in making contracts enforceable by law or by self-enforcement, and extends to the precautions against potential expropriation of the value of investments relying on contractual performance as well as costs of informing and administering terms of contractual relations. These costs are associated with containment of opportunism.
>
> (Alchian and Woodward 1988: 66)

Adjustment in an unfettered market is very difficult, or costly, because the owner of transaction-specific assets, without comparably valuable alternative uses, finds his assets subject to threats of reneging or 'holdup'. Awareness of decisive disadvantage when circumstances require adjustment will lead to avoidance of commitment unless non-market adjudication rules are included in the initial agreement. Usually the non-market adjudication within a continuing transaction takes the form of a hierarchically managed firm (Williamson 1985: ch. 1–5).

Large hierarchial organizations, while reducing the costs of managing transaction-specific assets, have disadvantages because non-market adjudication loses the market's powerful incentives for efficiency. In market transactions each party benefits directly from actions that increase efficiency and thus has powerful incentives for efficient performance. Hierarchical organizations, designed to contain opportunism, must replace this direct payoff with rules that cannot fully duplicate these incentives. Hierarchy will be less efficient at tasks that both markets and hierarchy can perform (Williamson 1985: ch. 6).

An economy's institutions reflect, at least as a first approximation, an equilibrium of a competitive mechanism in which most profitable organizations survive. Alternative institutional arrangements, like alternative techniques in a simple production function, differ in their mix of costs. Cost depends both on factor inputs in production and the transactions, or governance, features associated with production and marketing. Complex organizations gain when planning and coordination present problems to be solved, but they lose from weakened incentives. The surviving mix of technique and management in a competitive environment will be the most profitable – usually the low cost mix, although market power of large organizations may offset inefficiency.

Williamson's analysis helps clarify institutional features Gerschenkron saw as central to late nineteenth-century industrialization. Backwardness – the poor development of market institutions – often shifts transactions from 'exchange' to more continuing 'contracts' in which 'profitability ... depends on the other party's future performance'. Hierarchial institutions arise when 'spot market transactions [become] less viable, and transactions governed by contracts more viable' (Alchian and Woodward 1988: 67). Williamson observes that '[t]o the extent that uncertainty decreases as an industry matures, which is the usual case, the benefits that accrue to internal organization (vertical integration) presumably decline. Accordingly, greater reliance on market procurement is commonly feasible for transactions of recurrent trading in mature industries.' Limited market size creates transaction-specificity that encourages hierarchical organization. Multiple suppliers and multiple markets reduce dependency on the actions of one, or a few, specific individuals or firms. The large firm's ability to manage 'contracts' has little value, and smaller more specialized firms, with high-powered managerial incentives, prove more profitable. The more backward an area, the greater the uncertainty, the smaller the market and the bigger the firms.

Transaction-specificity of assets may also arise from new technologies. At the end of the nineteenth century, high-throughput technologies and large firms emerged together in America. The affinity was natural. High-throughput production depended on specialized machinery and required the reliable presence of specific cooperating factors. Both features involved greater transaction-specificity than more flexible small-batch production. Britain, the most advanced industrial nation, adopted mass production and hierarchical firms more slowly than either the United States or Germany, not because of entrepreneurial failure but because of its advanced economy and its lack of America's advantages in raw material supply.

LATE NINETEENTH-CENTURY COMPARATIVE INSTITUTIONS AND PERFORMANCE

Mass production, endogenous institutions, and British failure

Gerschenkron's and Williamson's insights concerning institutional substitution should be near the centre of all comparative economic history. Comparative analysis of twentieth-century performance, however, suffers from failing to recognize that economic institutions were endogenous, not independent causes of performance. Recent literature (e.g. Elbaum and Lazonick 1986; Kennedy 1987) extends a long standing argument (see Landes 1969) that poor institutional choice caused poor British performance after 1870. Comparison of Britain with the United States, and often with Germany, underlies the indictment of British institutions. British institutions, it is alleged, delayed adoption of improved techniques, supported inappropriate old industries, and inhibited the adoption of improved organization. Alfred Chandler's (1977) notion that American success rested in large measure on the development of the large, horizontally and vertically integrated corporation lies at the base of this view. To Chandler, Americans innovated to create managerial structures capable of efficiently managing integrated production from raw material supply to final sale, thereby realizing the economies of mass production. Successful mass production required planning within giant firms to eliminate the uncertainties of spot markets. Americans developed new institutions and benefited; the British failed to adopt the new institutions and fell behind. From the perspective of institutional substitution, however, the sources of institutional differences also need to be considered.

At first glance, a comparison of Britain and the United States fits uneasily within Gerschenkron's relative backwardness framework. The apparent conflict disappears, however, when substitution of prerequisites is seen as a theory of endogenous institutions. Even Gerschenkron's specific comments regarding substitutions in response to backwardness illuminate the comparison. The concept of backwardness, as Gerschenkron often acknowledged, is multi-dimensional and not well specified when a consistent ranking fails to emerge in its various dimensions. By the end of the nineteenth century, Britain and the United States certainly differed in their rankings on different characteristics. For example, US per capita income probably exceeded that of Britain, but Britain's product and financial markets had attained greater sophistication than America's. The United States certainly led in some technologies; Britain in others. Comparison of Britain and the United States, nonetheless, reveals systematic differences that fit Gerschenkron's pattern of substitution. Many of the differences between the technologies and organizational forms of the two countries may be related, if not strictly to 'backward' conditions in the United States, at least to the newness of the economy. The industrial labour force was composed predominantly of immigrants from backward agricultural regions of Europe; in contrast, British labour had several generations of urban and industrial experience and industrial skills. The geographic 'newness' of the United States made resources abundant. Finally, the product market in the young United States accepted new, cheap, standardized products.

Britain relinquished its industrial leadership to the United States and Germany, not only by growing slowly but also by lagging in institutional change. Industry generally remained composed of small firms with transactions organized in markets rather than within large integrated corporations. British firms continued to rely on relatively labour- and skill-intensive methods, and they delayed adoption of 'high-throughput' techniques. Britain's financial institutions failed to promote the emergence of the integrated firms characteristic of German and American success. Naturally historians have suggested that institutional differences caused performance differences. The proposition that different techniques and institutions in Britain resulted from a matrix of rigid institutional structures that prevented the adoption growth-inducing change intuitively appeals. Temporal relationships, however, provide only weak *post hoc ergo propter hoc* arguments.

The institutional explanation of Britain's performance assumes an inherent superiority of large hierarchical organizations. Despite the appeal of the idea that a larger firm can do anything a smaller firm can do and benefit in addition from any scale economies, economic theory and evidence suggest otherwise for two long-discussed reasons. As Williamson (1985: 161) remarks, 'The market is a marvel ... because of its remarkable signalling properties (under the requisite preconditions), [and] also because of its remarkable capacity to present and preserve high-powered incentives.'

Proponents of hierarchical organizations, and planning in general, attribute efficiency to centralized information. Much of the intellectual appeal of economics since the time of Adam Smith, however, arises from a realization that the complexity of real economies precludes successful centralized planning. Under fairly realistic conditions, a competitive market achieves social optimality with information almost completely dispersed – each individual knowing only his own tastes and technology and market prices. The informational efficiency of this outcome is a marvel and goes far to explain the general success of market economies. Markets also provide superior incentives for efficient behaviour. A market linking small entrepreneurial organizations passes the benefits of efficient decisions to those who make them. Hierarchical organizations, on the other hand, require rules of distribution and status that cannot duplicate this market incentive (Williamson 1985: ch. 6). When conditions allow markets to work well, hierarchical planning generates inferior results. Hierarchical organization become superior when conditions for market coordination break down in the face of the possibility that transaction-specific assets may be opportunistically exploited.

Careful analysis within a framework of endogenous institutions suggest that institutional differences between Britain and the United States arose from differences in factor supply and 'preconditions'. Different institutions were appropriate to Britain's relative mature industrial economy and to the United States' relatively backward frontier economy. Raw materials were abundant in the United States. The industrial sector in the United States drew labour from a pool of recent immigrants who provided cheap but unskilled labour while skilled labour was scarce and expensive. Factor supply induced American firms to adopt high-throughput technologies using transaction-specific assets with associated hierarchical management before those techniques were profitable in Britain.

Early nineteenth-century engineering work in both Britain and the United States involved skilled machinists shaping metal on general-purpose machine tools (lathes, drill presses) and by hand with files. 'Fitters' assembled finished machines by shaping individual parts to fit tightly together in the final article. In mass production, as it evolved in America in the nineteenth century, special-purpose machine tools replaced much of the skilled manual shaping. Mass production altered the quantity and the nature of both the capital and the labour in the production process. Fixed capital equipment increased considerably. Equally important, machinery was specialized to perform specific production tasks. Labour costs fell in two ways. Labour time was reduced and relatively cheap, unskilled labour replaced expensive, skilled labour as subdivision of production and special-purpose machines eliminated much of the skilled metal working. Savings of labour also involved increased use of raw materials as well as the use of machinery. Special-purpose machinery lacked the finesse of skilled crafts-men and required larger, more wasteful work pieces and spoiled more of the work.

American factor supply particularly suited mass production. Raw material abundance encouraged resource-intensive industrial techniques (see Rosenberg 1972). Alfred Chandler emphasizes the high throughput of fuel and raw materials as key to savings of labour and capital in the new American organizations. Recently, Gavin Wright (1990) has shown that America's late nineteenth-century and early twentieth-century industrial success appears related closely to raw material abundance. Much of America's labour supply also favoured the use of special-purpose machinery. American industrial labour came from the massive influx of new European immigrants without industrial experience (see, for example, Guttmann 1973). Over 50 per cent of the labour force in American engineering industries in the early years of the twentieth century were immigrants (Harley 1974). At Ford in 1917, immigrants consti-tuted 60 per cent of the labour force (Klug 1989: 54). The British industrial labour force, in contrast, had several generations of industrial experience and skill. The adoption of special-purpose machines and minimum skilled fitting in final assembly – that is to say interchangeable parts – in America was a process of substitution away from skilled labour toward the use of unskilled labour, raw materials and capital.

British and American manufacturing differences were not simply in the use of different techniques to produce identical products; mass production's economies of scale required a homogeneous product and a mass market (see Rosenberg 1972; Hounshell 1984: ch. 2). During the late nineteenth century, transportation improvements dramatically increased the effective markets of firms, particularly in North America. But a mass market also required consumers willing to purchase a homogeneous product designed to suit machine production – often an inferior product in terms of utility and aesthetics, but a much cheaper one. Even in the United States consumers were not always convinced that the lower price compensated for the changed product. Singer's experience with sewing machine cases demonstrated extensive savings in mass producing wooden furniture, but the American public did not switch (Hounshell 1984: ch. 3). Small firms with 'handicraft' techniques rather than machine production continued to dominate the industry.

In nineteenth-century America relatively high and equally distributed incomes, a large rural market, and a democratic ethos combined to create particular willingness to accept cheap, utilitarian, machine-made goods (see Boorstin 1965). In part, of course, the homogeneous market was a response to the inexpensive standardized products that mass-production technology made possible. Cost saving was greatest in America because cheap resources and relatively cheap, unskilled labour particularly favoured mass production. The American market was highly protected (the tariff revenue equalled some 40 per cent of the value of dutiable imports) so relative prices in the United States reflected American conditions. Cheaper mass-produced goods encouraged Americans to purchase products of the new technology faster than would have been the case under European conditions (or in an unprotected American market) where relative costs were less favourable to mass-produced goods.

Hierarchical firms emerged with American high-throughput techniques because the technology enormously increased specificity. Dedicated, specialized machine tools, adaptable to other uses only at major cost, with economies of scale up to the machines' capacities characterized the system. To be economical, production lines had to run at machine capacity. The vast output produced required marketing – the discovery, or creation, and maintenance of a market for mass-produced standardized products. The production line depended on the rapid flow of raw materials, often themselves specific. Hierarchial structures, which solved management problems created by the asset specificity of mass production, became appropriate for American industries. Factor costs and market conditions encouraged the adoption of high-throughput techniques in the United States sooner than elsewhere, and organizational innovations and techniques were adopted together.

The history of mass production in the United States, at the armories, in sewing machines, in automobiles and in textiles, demonstrates the incremental nature of the changes and the role of particular supply and market circumstances in the development and adoption of high-throughput technologies. Mass production with machinery-based techniques in the late nineteenth century did not possess universal superiority. The techniques were adopted only under favourable cost and marketing circumstances that did not exist in Britain. Since they did not adopt the new processes, British firms remained small. There is little evidence of failures that could be overcome by 'industrial planning by enterprise, financial institutions, and the state,' (Elbaum and Lazonick 1986: 16).

Finance and planning

Criticism of Britain's continued dependence on market coordination extends beyond failure to develop mass-production technologies and the managerial firm to the extent the United States did. British financial institutions are also seen as continuing to depend excessively on markets to intermediate and organize transactions. As a result, British banks failed to undertake planning and provide direction that the economy needed. There is an element of paradox here; few doubt that in the nineteenth century the British developed financial institutions and markets to an unprecedented level. Financial institutions elsewhere, most notably in Germany, however, are seen as late century innovations that significantly improved the allocation of capital to new industries. German banks financed industry and provided the direction necessary for rapid growth. Because Britain failed to adopt these new financial forms, investment opportunities in domestic industry created by technological advance were missed. Instead British institutions continued to channel funds into established paths of railroad and government finance, and, increasingly, into overseas investments rather than into British industry.

William Kennedy (1987: ch. 5 and 6) expresses this view most fully. Large

German banks collected deposits and utilized them aggressively to provide long-term industrial finance; British banks shunned such activity. German banks' positions as large lenders to industry gave them unexcelled information to compare investment opportunities throughout the economy. As a result the banks became planning agencies directing finance to its most advantageous uses. No such institutions existed in Britain. The banks chose not to play the role and no other institution could obtain the needed information. As a result the economy failed to exploit opportunities in new industries.

Kennedy and other institutional critics of late nineteenth-century Britain, hold the view that individual initiative coordinated by atomistic markets failed to transform the economy from its nineteenth-century industrial structure into one appropriate to the twentieth. The transformation required planning such as large American and German firms and banks provided but which Britain failed to obtain, inexplicable except by reference to 'a matrix of rigid institutional structures' (Elbaum and Lazonick 1986: 21). The superiority of planning over markets, however, cannot be taken as self-evident, independent of other circumstances. After all, as Gerschenkron emphasized in his discussion of the German banks, a cost of German bank planning was neglect of sectors of the economy in which large firms did not appear. A planned economy which tends to neglect activity occurring in small units and to concentrate resources on a small portion of the economy with large firms will fail to provide optimality from a social point of view (see Neuberger and Stokes 1974).

Economists have argued, and historians confirmed, that difficulties of information-gathering and -processing hinder planning whereas a market economy dispenses with the need to collect information centrally. A planner requires complete information about technologies and tastes to make efficient allocations; a market, in the absence of monopolistic distortion, allocates efficiently if each individual has precise knowledge only of information directly affecting himself or herself. Although Kennedy (1987: 111–15) argues otherwise, efficient arbitrage can occur in segmented financial markets so long as the market has enough breadth that many individuals can arbitrage between small market subsets.

British financial markets had sophisticated arbitragers. As a result, the inherent inefficiency of centralized information and bureaucratic control rendered the kind of planning undertaken by the German banks inefficient. Therefore, German-type institutions did not arise in Britain. As Gerschenkron emphasized, the German banks were a substitute for the missing prerequisite, namely the development of British-type financial markets. The German banks were appropriate for German circumstances but inappropriate to British. In Williamson's terms, the lack of a broad financial market in Germany led to specificity in financial relations. Firms and banks depended on continuing relationships with each other because there were few alternative sources of finance or reliable investment opportunities. Bank–firm relationships involved ex-post bilateral monopoly and required non-market arbitration; consequently hierarchical finance arose in Germany.

Examination of the financing of individual British industries confirms the doubt cast on British failure by theoretical argument. Lack of German-type banks did not inhibit industrial finance of either old or new British industries. Firms entered the cotton industry, representative of the old industries, easily and frequently before the First World War and the industry's markets offered favourable opportunities (Lazonick 1986: 31). Any British failure more likely would involve the financing of a new industry such as automobiles. There is consensus, however, that automobile firms easily found finance at favourable terms (Church 1986; Lewchuk 1986: 141–2). Lewchuk seems, in fact, to argue that this efficient access to finance hurt the industry by inhibiting the development of dominant firms. The argument that British financial markets failed to perform an integrating function at least comparable to that performed by the German banks remains unconvincing.

Historical legacy: institutions and capital

Historical legacy, an idea that occupies a major place in the argument on institutional failure in Britain, deserves careful attention. Study of the effect of institutions and past experience on economic performance must be the main task of historical economics. The institutionalists argue that a major part of Britain's legacy of nineteenth-century 'competitive capitalism' was 'a matrix of rigid institutional structures that reinforced [conservative cultural] values and obstructed individualistic as well as collective efforts at economic renovation' (Elbaum and Lazonick 1986: 2). Small firms, extensive and efficient markets, and accessible finance left Britain with institutions that inhibited 'industrial planning by enterprises, financial institutions, and the state that has become increasingly important for international competitiveness and economic growth' (Elbaum and Lazonick 1986: 16).

The role of historical legacy, particularly as it shapes a society's institutions, requires serious study. It is unfortunate that recent industrial studies have failed to distinguish carefully between the effect of institutional rigidity and that of the existing capital stock. Britain's traditional industries – particularly cotton and iron and steel – suffered from overcapacity in the interwar period; their capital stock was larger than would have been chosen for interwar conditions had it not already existed. Certainly, curtailing output to raise prices would have increased profits. Even more certainly, individual firms would have benefited if their rivals' capacity had been removed. A monopoly or a tight oligopoly would have been less influenced by 'excess' capacity and more profitable.

Institutionalists argue that 'rationalization' would have improved the productivity of British industry by scrapping excess capacity, generating higher profits and promoting investment in new, more productive capital. Excessive fragmentation of the market – too many small firms – prevented rationalization (Lazonick 1986: 30–6; Lewchuk 1986: 147; Tolliday 1986: 82–108). Consequently, monopoly power could not be exercised and new productive investment failed to occur. This argument, however, fails to consider the economics of sunk costs.

Critics of British performance correctly describe British industry's problem. Given the installed capital, individual firms made more profits producing with existing capital than they would have done by scrapping it. Furthermore, in this situation firms had no incentive to undertake new investment. Output levels, arising from independent firm's decisions to continue to produce, depressed prices to low levels at which new, more productive investment was unattractive even for dynamic entrepreneurs. Planning, however, either by a social planner or by a monopolized industry, probably would not have replaced existing capital with newer, more productive, plants. An optimal social plan would continue to use existing capital whose opportunity cost was very low, and to provide goods for consumers at very low prices. In fact, Britain's fragmented markets approximately reproduced this solution. Nor would a profit-maximizing monopoly necessarily have replaced existing capital with new. A monopoly or a tight oligopoly would have cut production to increase price. At monopoly price, new technology possibly could have been adopted without an actual loss. The monopolist, however, would have no incentive to invest in new technology so long as the marginal cost of using old capital was less than the total cost of using new. A monopoly or oligopoly would not have installed new capital that reduced profits.

A historical overhang inhibited the adoption of higher productivity techniques in many British industries during the interwar years. While the overhang may have had institutional components, existing fixed capital was its most obvious main feature. Institutional inertia certainly existed and may well have been stimulated by the politics of interwar Britain. However, inertia is general; merely documenting its existence does not establish failure. To suggest that the British economy would have been better off if it could have adjusted without cost is hardly a useful analytic contribution. Failure can only be defined by comparison with alternative institutions. Late twentieth-century American experience, for example, suggests that managerial hierarchic organizations also possess considerable inertia. In general, it seems likely that the inertia of hierarchies exceeds that of markets. Markets have a certain anonymous ruthlessness towards firms that fail to change when change is required to maintain profitability.

CONCLUDING REMARKS

Alexander Gerschenkron's approach to European industrialization recognized that efficient economic growth did not follow a single path revealed by the history of the first industrializer. Instead, substitutions were pervasive, not only in the choice of production techniques, but also in institutional arrangements. Successful comparative economic history needs to appreciate the nature of substitution from which institutional differences can arise endogenously.

Most of the substitutions Gerschenkron identified involved replacing market solutions, that had developed gradually in Britain, with planning and hierarchical structures in increasingly backward conditions where markets were less developed. Such hierarchical arrangements are analysed by Oliver Williamson with particular emphasis on the problems of organizing transactions that involve commitment of assets. In nineteenth-century growth, transaction specificity arose from two central sources: backwardness and the specific technology of mass production. Uncertainty and lack of alternative opportunities characterize backwardness and create specificity absent in more advanced conditions. The development of mass-production technology also created specificity that endogenously stimulated the emergence of larger hierarchical firms. Adoption of mass production had at least three dimensions. First, improvements in mechanical and metallurgical technology made mass production possible. Second, Alfred Chandler and others who have focused on the institutional changes associated with the rise of mass production argue that institutional innovations also played an initiating role in the successful adoption of high-throughput, mass-production techniques. Third, and somewhat overlooked, Gerschenkron appreciated that in some circumstances the adoption of mass-production technology emerged as part of a pattern of substitution in conditions of backwardness. Gerschenkron's insight suggests that Britain's delayed adoption of mass production with its associated institutions may have occurred because such a form of organization was inappropriate to British conditions.

Examination of the relationship between British institutions and performance applies Gerschenkron's insights in a reverse direction from his particular concerns. But after all, insights gained from considering later industrialization in terms of substitutions for prerequisites in earlier industrializations also provides insight into the nature of the leading economy. To Gerschenkron, Germany's large firms, capital intensity and universal banks compensated for Germany's lack of Britain's prerequisites for development. Similarly the differences both in technological choice and in institutional form between Britain and the United States appear to arise simultaneously from differing circumstances. Endogeneity of institutions challenges the view that failure to move from markets to hierarchical planning institutions caused Britain's disappointing growth performance in the twentieth century. The proposition that 'industrial planning by enterprise, financial institutions, and the state has become increasingly important for international competitiveness and economic growth' (Elbaum and Lazonick 1986: 16) is not established. The institutional failure school perceives a single path to economic success revealed by the history of the most successful economy, in this case, the United States. Failure to follow America's path is seen as evidence of failure. If substitutions in technique and institutions arise as responses to differing circumstances, this argument is seriously incomplete. Successful comparative economic history needs to exploit Gerschenkron's and Williamson's insights of systematic substitution in institutional arrangements, that is, endogenous institutions.

REFERENCES

Alchian, Armen A. and Woodward, Susan (1988) 'The firm is dead; long live the firm: a review of Oliver E. Williamson's *The Economic Institutions of Capitalism*', *Journal of Economic Literature* XXVl (March), 65–79.

Boorstin, Daniel J. (1965) *The Americans: The National Experience*, part 2, New York: Random House.

Chandler, Alfred D. Jr. (1977) *The Visible Hand*, Cambridge, Mass.: Harvard University Press.

Church, R.A. (1986) 'Family firms and managerial capitalism: the case of the international motor industry', *Business History* 28, 165–80.

Elbaum, Bernard and Lazonick, William (eds) (1986) *The Decline of the British Economy*, Oxford: Clarendon Press.

Gerschenkron, Alexander (1966) *Economic Backwardness in Historical Perspective*, Cambridge, Mass.: Harvard University Press.

Guttmann, Herbert (1973) 'Work, culture, and society in industrializing America, 1815–1919', *American Historical Review* 78 (June), 531–88.

Harley, C.K. (1974) 'Skilled labor and the choice of technique in Edwardian industry', *Explorations in Economic History* 11, 391–414.

Hounshell, David (1984) *From the American System to Mass Production, 1800–1932*, Baltimore: The Johns Hopkins University Press.

Kennedy, William P. (1987) *Industrial Structure, Capital Markets and the Origins of British Economic Decline*, Cambridge: Cambridge University Press.

Klug, Thomas (1989) 'Employers' strategies in the Detroit labor market, 1900–1929', in Nelson Lichtenstein and Stephen Meyer (eds) *On the Line: Essays in the History of Auto Work*, Urbana: University of Illinois Press.

Landes, David (1969) *The Unbound Prometheus*, Cambridge: Cambridge University Press.

Lazonick, William (1986) 'The cotton industry', in B. Elbaum and W. Lazonick (eds) *The Decline of the British Economy*, Oxford: Clarendon Press.

Lewchuk, Wayne (1986) 'The motor vehicle industry', in B. Elbaum and W. Lazonick (eds) *The Decline of the British Economy*, Oxford: Clarendon Press.

Neuberger, H. and Stokes, H.H. (1974) 'German banks and German growth, 1883–1913: an empirical view', *Journal of Economic History* 34, 710–31.

Rosenberg, Nathan (1972) *Technology and American Economic Growth*, New York: Harper & Row.

Tolliday, Steven (1986) 'Steel and rationalization policies, 1918–50', in B. Elbaum and W. Lazonick (eds) *The Decline of the British Economy*, Oxford: Clarendon Press.

Williamson, Oliver E. (1975) *Markets and Hierarchies*, New York: Free Press.

Williamson, Oliver E. (1985) *The Economic Institutions of Capitalism: Firms, Markets and Relational Contracting*, New York: Free Press.

Wright, Gavin (1990) 'The origins of American industrial success 1879–1940', *American Economic Review* 80, 651–68.

Chapter 3

The role of banks

Richard Sylla

The role of banks and, more generally, financial systems in promoting economic development is a perennial issue in discussions of economic history and economic policy.[1] Europe's industrialization in the nineteenth century has furnished much of the material for the discussions and debates of economic historians. At the extremes of the debates, banks that provided finance to industrial firms have been viewed as necessary and/or sufficient for industrial development to occur, or as passive and not particularly relevant responses to such development.

In his approach to European industrialization, Alexander Gerschenkron adopted a view between these two extremes. He argued that bank finance of industry was crucial to successful industrialization in conditions of moderate economic backwardness such as in Germany. Where there was no backwardness in his sense, such as in Britain, banks were helpful but not crucial to industrialization; industrialists could find other sources of finance. In conditions of extreme economic backwardness, such as he found in Russia, banking was too limited and feeble to play a role in meeting the capital needs of industrial firms; industrialists had to find other sources of finance. With this pattern in mind, when Gerschenkron found a spurt of industrial development in any European country between Britain and Russia, one of the first things he would look for in order to explain the spurt would be the activity of banks in industrial finance.

Why was Gerschenkron so fascinated by the role of banking? The answer is not obvious when it is considered that banking, after all, was only a part of a part of his complex approach to European industrialization. The seemingly small role of banking can be seen in what I believe to be the most succinct description of Gerschenkron's approach from his own pen:

> The basic proposition is that within each of the individual countries in Europe certain specific features of the industrialization process depended on the level of relative backwardness of the countries concerned on the eve of the period of great accelerations in their industrial growth. What was found to vary in direct relation to the degree of backwardness were: 1) the speed of industrial growth; 2) the stress on bigness of plant and enterprise; 3) the composition of the nascent output, that is, the degree to which 'heavy' industries were

favored; 4) the reliance on technological borrowing and perhaps financial assistance from abroad; 5) the pressure on levels of consumption; 6) the passive role of agriculture; 7) the role of banks and state budgets; 8) the virulence of ideologies, under the auspices of which the industrialization proceeded.

(Gerschenkron 1970: 98–9)

If this is Gerschenkron in a nutshell, banking would appear to be little more than a fragment of the nut.

There are two reasons, I think, why banking to Gerschenkron was much more than a fragment. The first is that although Germany was the centre panel of his triptych of European industrialization – and, of course, the one in which banks were the focal point – in Gerschenkron's thought it was by far the largest and most interesting panel. England was the subject of one end panel, and Russia, the other. It is arguable, I think, that Gerschenkron regarded every European nation between (in a geographical sense) England and Russia as a potential member of the large 'German' panel featuring banks. If any of these countries had a successful great spurt of industrial growth it was likely that German-type banks would have played a large role in financing industry. If any of them did not have a great spurt, it was likely that the nation's bankers were either timid and unenterprising, or that they were prevented from becoming the engines of successful industrialization by unwise governmental policies. The industrial history of every European nation from the Iberian peninsula to Bulgaria, which is nearly every European nation other than Britain and Russia, could be approached with these generalizations as a starting point by a Gerschenkronian.

The second reason for banking's importance in Gerschenkron's thought is essentially personal. Gerschenkron, like all of us, was a product of his time and place. Born in imperial Russia, he left his native land as a youth for reasons related to the revolutionary upheavals taking place there. His formative years as an intellect and scholar were spent at Vienna in the 1920s. In central Europe banks were important institutions both historically and contemporarily with Gerschenkron's young adult years there. Without question, in intellectual circles and at the University of Vienna the ideas contained in Hilferding's *Finance Capital* and Schumpeter's *Theory of Economic Development* – books in which banks and bankers were key players – were much read and discussed. But there was more than book learning to be had in Austria in those interwar years. In what turned out to be his last book, Gerschenkron, responding in his inimitable polemical fashion to criticism by Richard Rudolph, referred to a more direct form of learning he had experienced:

[H]ow do Rudolf's [sic] lighthearted cogitations stand up against the fact that ... in the First Austrian Republic the banks controlled almost 80 percent of total industrial capital? This fact does not seem to denote any 'wariness of industrial investment.' I might add that I have had a close personal opportunity of watching how, in the 1920s, the representatives of the *Credit*

Anstalt appeared weekly at two machinery factories in a little industrial town near Vienna. They participated most intimately not just in all entrepreneurial decisions, but in many managerial decisions, and their word was received as command by the directors of the two firms.

(Gerschenkron 1977: 55)

'Take that, young man! More than historical fact and interpretation is involved in our dispute. I know what and whereof I speak in a way that will never be available to you, for I was there and experienced it.' This is what Gerschenkron, it seems to me, is saying here. His personal experiences in life should not be discounted as a source of his interpretations of economic and other history. Banking may have been only a part of a part of Gerschenkron's approach to European industrial history, but it was a very special part, one that loomed larger in his thought than might be inferred from the nutshell version of that approach.

GERSCHENKRON ON BANKING

The part of Gerschenkron's approach of which banking itself is a part needs now to be developed. It is, in general terms and Gerschenkron's words, 'the problem of financing, that is, of providing capital, in the sense of capital disposition, to industry' (Gerschenkron 1970: 101). Every successful industrialization has to solve this problem, for modern industry – the expanding, technologically progressive industry of the last two centuries – requires capital investment on a scale that is unprecedented in history.

In the materials of economic history and economic theory Gerschenkron found three different solutions to the problem of financing. One of these was that of Karl Marx, whose concept of the original accumulation of capital as a prerequisite to industrialization Gerschenkron regarded as quite respectable, describing it as follows:

[O]riginal accumulation means storing up of wealth from previous national incomes – through very long periods – which accumulation at a favorable moment – when the hour of industrialization has struck – can be converted into claims against current national income, so that entrepreneurs can get the means to compete labor and materials away from consumption and old firms.

Gerschenkron 1970: 101)

Marx formed his concept of original accumulation from his English experience. Britain's long national history, and in particular its history of successful overseas commerce in the centuries before its industrial revolution, had made it a rich country at the time of that revolution in the latter half of the eighteenth century. The funds needed to finance Britain's first modern industrial firms could be had from the entrepreneur's own pocket, or from his family and friends. Moreover, to extend the model, the profits of the successful pioneers of English industry were both quick and large in relation to capital needs, and thus amply sufficient to sustain expansion after the initial phases of industrial development.

An alternative solution to the financing problem was provided by Schumpeter, who like Gerschenkron matured in Austria, albeit two decades earlier. The banker in Schumpeter's *Theory of Economic Development* is the source of finance for the other key actor in the drama, the entrepreneur. It is the banker who sorts out the many proposals of would-be entrepreneurs, decides which ones to back, and backs them by creating credit and placing it at the disposal of the successful applicants. The entrepreneurs then bid resources away from their current employments, implement their innovations, and repay the bankers with interest and society with more goods. Gerschenkron was a student (at least indirectly) of Schumpeter in Austria, and later his colleague at Harvard. He often expressed great admiration for Schumpeter as a human being and a scholar. But he was quick to point out that Schumpeter had gone too far in raising an excellent theory of how industrial development had occurred in the particular circumstances of central Europe in the nineteenth century to the plane of universal and eternal truth about economic development.

Still a third alternative to the financing problem Gerschenkron found in the theory and history of the mercantilist state, which he viewed as the logical sponsor of development efforts in the backward economic conditions most nations found themselves in prior to the industrial era. For that very reason of priority, however, the mercantilist state, on the wane by the time of the first stirrings of modern industry, could not provide an example of state-financed industrialization. But Gerschenkron's native Russia, which experienced a great spurt of industrial growth with primary sponsorship from the governmental budget and state economic policies, could and did provide the historical example he needed.

By the time Gerschenkron was formulating his approach, socialist theory and practice argued that state sponsorship, control, and ownership of industry was the path that ought to be taken in economic development. But Gerschenkron was not at all enamoured of socialism or normative historiography, and he often emphasized that his approach applied only to Europe before 1914. I suspect that this was done in an attempt to disassociate and protect himself from any inference that socialism was a natural, logical and progressive result of modern economic history. As evidence in support of my suspicion, I would refer the interested reader to Gerschenkron's negative reaction to E.H. Carr's twisting of his views into what Carr termed, 'the progression from the primitive British model of industrialization by the private entrepreneur through the more advanced continental model of financing and control by the banks to the still more advanced Russian model of financing and control by the State ...' (Gerschenkron 1970: 112, quoting Carr 1967).

Gerschenkron's scholarly achievement, of course, was to turn the three alternative models of the financing of industrial revolutions – the initial 'great spurts' – into complementary rather than competing explanations. Relative backwardness at the time of the great spurt was the organizing principle.

Advanced Britain could rely on direct sources of finance when it began its industrial spurt in the late eighteenth century because of earlier original accumulation and the appearance of quick and sustained factory profits. Moderately backward Germany had to find a substitute for the missing prerequisite of original accumulation when it began to industrialize in the middle of the nineteenth century; the 'mixed' commercial/investment bank came forward to provide the substitute. Extremely backward Russia had neither the original accumulation nor the banks to finance its industrial spurt in the 1890s, so the state treasury substituted for both missing prerequisites.

The three methods of financing initial industrialization movements make up only the first stage of Gerschenkron's thinking on patterns of financial development. The rest of his story as regards European industrial finance is that industrialization reduces the relative backwardness of the industrializing country and thus tends to eliminate the need to continue to rely on the specific financial innovations of the initial great spurt. Thus, by the end of the nineteenth century Germany had advanced so far industrially that it could no longer be regarded as moderately backward in an economic sense compared to Britain a century earlier. Hence, German industry reduced its reliance on the intermediated financing and tutelage of banks and relied more on self-financing through retained profits. Similarly, Russia in the years before 1914 began to rely more on its banks for industrial finance and less on the state treasury. Having reduced its extreme backwardness to more moderate proportions, it became like Germany was a half century earlier. Gerschenkron confirmed these German and Russian trends to his satisfaction. They are the main confirmations in Gerschenkron's thought of relative backwardness not only as a useful historical insight but also as an economic analytic concept of operational significance.[2]

THE CRITIQUE OF GERSCHENKRON ON BANKING

Gerschenkron's hypothesis on the importance of banking in the industrialization of moderately backward countries inspired a substantial amount of further research on the subject. Moreover, those scholars who were not directly guided by Gerschenkron's thought often found it necessary to comment upon it in their related work. Out of this body of scholarship there emerges a critique of Gerschenkron along the following general lines:

1. Gerschenkron argued that banking played an important role, either positively or negatively, in accounting for the degree of success of industrialization in conditions of moderate economic backwardness. One line of critique of this proposition argues that banking played this role in all cases, from the most advanced to the most backward, that is, that banking mattered everywhere. This critique essentially holds that a well-functioning banking system is an aid to economic development. Gerschenkron would not have disagreed with such a general contention, but his interest was more in a specific type of banking – entrepreneurial, industrial banking – that in his view was crucial to, not merely

facilitating of, industrialization in the specific circumstances of moderate backwardness. Another critical line argues that banking arrangements respond passively to demands for banking services, and that whatever industrialization occurred or failed to occur in a given country depended on retained profits and was unrelated to its banking, that is, that banking mattered nowhere. Gerschenkron would have disagreed with this critique as a general proposition, although he would agree that it could apply to the specific case of an advanced country.

2. Whereas Gerschenkron argued that dynamic banking in certain conditions could be a substitute for a missing prerequisite to industrialization, critics retort that banking was neither necessary nor sufficient for industrialization to take place. A moderately backward country with good banking might not in-dustrialize as early or effectively as it should have in Gerschenkron's scheme. Or a moderately backward country without good banking might nonetheless industrialize.

3. Gerschenkron's hypothesis about banking is tied to his fascination with great spurts of industrialization. Critics note that some moderately backward countries industrialized without anything resembling a great spurt.

4. Gerschenkron was off on his timing. The banks he cited as important in a moderately backward country's industrial spurt sometimes appeared only after the initial spurt of industrialization had occurred.

5. Gerschenkron's hypothesis is too general. Whether banking was effective or not effective in promoting industrialization depended less on the relative backwardness of a country and more on the specific details of its banking legislation and the non-banking forces acting to promote or retard its industrial-ization.

These several lines of critique are not altogether distinct and different. Most are different shadings of a more general critique of the pristine Gerschenkron banking hypothesis.

A survey of scholarship produced since Gerschenkron nailed his theses to the door of modern European economic historiography will illustrate the emerging critique(s). I begin with the paradigm countries (Britain, Germany and Russia), and proceed thereafter to the non-paradigm cases. The survey is hardly inclusive of all that has been written on the subject, but it will place most of the European countries within Gerschenkron's framework and the critique of that framework as set forth in general terms in the above five points.

Britain

The banking question is complicated, but not much, by the different traditions of England and Scotland. There seems to be no disagreement with a Gers-chenkronian view that Scotland before 1844, when legislation began to end the traditional differences, was a moderately backward area in which banking played a large role in reducing economic backwardness (see Cameron *et al.* 1967: ch. 3;

Checkland 1975). Gerschenkron did not devote much attention to Britain. If he had, he would have found support for his banking hypothesis in Scottish experience before 1844.

The real issue regards England, where original accumulation and profits retained in the early industrial firms were thought by Gerschenkron and many other writers to have made banking unimportant as a source of long-term finance for the first industrial revolution. The two chief contentions of this traditional view are that the financing needs of fixed capital formation in early English industry were small, and that plenty of non-bank sources of finance were available. Then why, one may ask, did the number of English country banks increase from a dozen or so in 1750 to more than 300 by 1800? (Cottrell 1980: 14). Peter Mathias, in two penetrating essays, reviews accumulating evidence from monographic histories of industrial enterprises and banks which suggests that the role of English banks in the first industrial revolution was far more crucial than the traditional view contemplated (Mathias 1973, 1989). According to Mathias, many English bankers were closely allied with industrialists, short-term bank credits became long-term credits either by design or by default, and the instability of English banking from 1750 to 1850 itself suggested involvement in long-term lending. Moreover, even if the banks lent short, there was a resulting freeing up of industrialists' own funds for longer-term uses. Rondo Cameron made similar points, and added that the English banks could have made a still larger contribution if English banking and company law had been less restrictive of the forms and functions of enterprises (Cameron *et al.*, 1967; Cameron 1972).

Of the nineteenth-century United States it was said that banks were not usually founded by persons having money to lend but rather by those who had a need to borrow. I suspect that this was also true of England in the previous century. If the needs to borrow were coming from industrialists in a significant way, as Mathias argues, then Gerschenkron was wrong to characterize England as so advanced that banks were not important to the first industrial revolution. A small twist of interpretation, however, would save Gerschenkron's essential banking point, although not his tripartite paradigm: Perhaps no European country was so advanced on the eve of successful industrialization that it could dispense with innovations in industrial finance. In this sense, eighteenth-century England was moderately backward compared to what it would later become, and possibly not so different from Germany at mid-nineteenth century. If so, the critique of Gerschenkron is that banking mattered everywhere, not merely east and south of the English Channel.

Germany

Gerschenkron's emphasis on the importance of German banking to its industrialization has survived, but not unscathed. Virtually all authorities agree with Gerschenkron that Germany's large joint-stock banks (also called *Gross-banken, Kreditbanken*, 'mixed' banks, and universal banks) provided capital and entrepreneurial or managerial guidance to important sectors and firms during the country's post-1850 industrial surge (see, in particular, Chapter 9). Gerschenkron's general approach to European industrialization calls, however, for close attention to the initial great spurt, which in Germany would be in the period between 1834 and 1870. Before 1848, there were no joint-stock banks; before 1870 there were fewer than a dozen. These observations led Cameron (1972: 13–14) to charge Gerschenkron with an error or anachronism. But it is a small error, for, as Tilly has noted, German private bankers were developing the techniques later called mixed banking as early as the 1830s, although with a concentration on railroad rather than industrial finance (Tilly 1986a: 129–30). Gerschenkron's mistake was to concentrate exclusively on a particular form of German bank, the joint-stock form, that flourished only after industrialization was underway.

A more specific criticism came from Neuberger and Stokes (1974), who employed econometric modelling and testing of their version of Gerschenkron's hypothesis to reach a conclusion that turned out to be the opposite of his, namely, that the *Kreditbanken* impeded economic growth. They found that German non-agricultural output was negatively related to the proportion of *Kreditbanken* lending that went into current account loans, which were made primarily to large industrial firms. Neuberger and Stokes conclude that the banks, in favouring large firms, probably misallocated investment in Germany and reduced non-agricultural output growth below what it would have been without the misallocation. This provocative result has been criticized by others, including me, on such grounds as model misspecification (Fremdling and Tilly 1976; Sylla 1977; Komlos 1978). Other work, notably by Tilly, indicates that although the banks did concentrate on lending to large firms, they did so with great efficiency through portfolio diversification (Tilly 1986b). It thus appears that the status of German banks in the Gerschenkronian framework remains intact. As the earlier discussion of England implied, however, it is still possible that Germany in 1850 was no more backward than England in, say, 1770.

Russia

Gerschenkron argued that Russia was so extremely backward that its banks were underdeveloped and incapable of playing a leading role in industrial finance. Therefore, the state had to step forward as a substitute for private finance. One must be careful in the case of Russia to delimit the problem with precision. Most authorities agree that industrialization, and therefore the banks' role therein, was limited before the great spurt of the 1890s. Most also agree that in the second and not-quite-so-great spurt after 1908, the banks' role in industrial finance increased and that of the state diminished. The real issue regards the first great spurt of the 1890s. Olga Crisp argued two decades ago that, 'from the 1890s onward, at first gradually, and then on an increasing scale', the joint-stock banks, especially those of St Petersburg which resembled the mixed banks of countries to the west, became involved in industrial finance (Crisp 1967: 219). How extensive was this involvement in the 1890s? V.I. Bovykin and B.V. Anan'ich (1991), in work drawing on Soviet archival materials, make two pertinent points. First, Russian banking grew vigorously in the 1890s, with capital stock and liabilities more than doubling in the decade. Second, the archival materials demonstrate extensive bank involvement in industry. For example, by the early 1890s, the St Petersburg International, Russia's largest bank, had ties with forty-eight joint-stock enterprises, thirty of which were industrial firms representing a wide range of manufacturing activities. Other Russian banks had similar, though less extensive, ties. Moreover, the banks cooperated rather than competed with one another in participating in the finance of industrial enterprises, and they formed alliances with leading Western and Central European banks. In related work, Anan'ich (1988) notes that private bankers anticipated the entrepreneurial activities of later joint-stock banks in Russia, just as they had done in Germany. This sort of evidence says little about the relative importance of Russian banks and the Russian state in industrial finance during the 1890s spurt. But it does raise doubts about the stylized Gerschenkronian view that state financing of industry was necessary because the banks were incapable of providing it. The banking evidence is also consistent with Chapters 4 and 12 in this volume by Gregory and Crisp, who argue that the Russian economy was not as backward as Gerschenkron thought.

As regards Gerschenkron's three paradigm countries, the critical line that comes through most strongly is that bank financing of industrial firms mattered in all three, not just in Germany. Schumpeter's theory of economic development is perhaps more general than Gerschenkron thought. If this suggestion of recent scholarship holds up, Gerschenkron's financing hypothesis is attenuated. The experience of the non-paradigm countries, to which I now turn, has an obvious bearing on the issue.

France

Was France a case of stagnant or retarded industrialization, as traditional interpretations held? Or was France the 'advanced' paradigm for European industrialization, with Britain standing apart as an aberrant case, as Richard Roehl (1976), for example, argued in a clever paper that, methodologically speaking, stood Gerschenkron on his head? (see also O'Brien and Keyder 1978). Today, scholars are less certain about the proper answers to these questions than they were twenty years ago. Gerschenkron had similar problems with France. Although he regarded France as falling between Britain and Germany on his advanced-to-backward scale, he appeared to subscribe to the traditional view of France as a case of retarded industrialization, which he attributed to such factors as the persistence of peasant farming and a relative lack of coal (Gerschenkron 1962: 65–6). Yet he found in the France of the Second Empire the germ of his banking hypothesis. The Crédit Mobilier showed how moderately backward continental countries might solve the problem of financing industrialization. But the Crédit Mobilier had its defects and failed. France did not have a great spurt. It was left to the Germans to perfect the banking technique with their mixed banks while France remained relatively stagnant (Gerschenkron 1962: 11–16).

Roehl reaches an opposed conclusion by reversing the way Gerschenkron put his hypothesis: A pioneer or a least backward industrializer will feature no or at best only minor roles for banks and state budgets in the finance of industrialization (Roehl 1976: 241–2). Much evidence, Roehl thinks, is consistent with France being advanced, not backward, on a Gerschenkronian scale. His point is that since France was advanced, there was no reason for banks to play a large role in industrialization. Further applying in reverse Gerschenkron's approach, Roehl says that the less backward a country is the less one should expect a great spurt. So France's lack of a spurt is not a problem to be explained in terms of retardation or stagnation, but a Gerschenkronian consequence of its advanced economic status as early as the eighteenth century. Others have joined in the argument that although France might have been different (presumably from Britain), it was not backward (O'Brien and Keyder 1978; Cameron and Freedeman 1983). But not everyone is persuaded (Kindleberger 1984b, reprinted in Kindleberger 1985: ch. 4).

If France was not backward, the failure of dynamic banking to take hold there becomes a non-problem for a Gerschenkronian, even though Gerschenkron himself did not view it that way. French banking in that case is irrelevant. If France was somewhat backward, the lack of dynamics in French banking – itself widely accepted – becomes an interesting Gerschenkronian problem. Considerable insight on these issues is contained in Chapter 8 by Lévy-Leboyer and Lescure. In general, their views are consistent with Roehl's: France was an advanced country that began gradually to industrialize well before the appearance of the Crédit Mobilier in the Second Empire. Moreover, the Crédit Mobilier in particular and large joint-stock banks in general did little directly to meet the long-term capital needs of French industrial firms. On the other hand, local and regional banks did aid industrial firms in parts of France that, one might say, were more backward than others. Although Gerschenkron's general approach thus receives some support, the timing and overall impact of the banks' contributions to French industrialization are hardly consistent with his analysis of the French case.

Belgium

Gerschenkron chose Germany as his example of a moderately backward country that employed dynamic banking to industrialize. He might better have chosen Belgium. Mixed banking came to Belgium in the 1830s, at least a decade before it came to Germany, and the dominant scholarly interpretation – that banks such as the Société Générale and the Banque de Belgique played a large role in financing Belgium's industrial upsurge in the 1830s and 1840s – has not changed in the last two decades (Cameron *et al.* 1967: ch. 5; Van der Wee and Goossens 1991). The dominant view is not a unanimous view, however, for a minority argues that external finance was not important in Belgium, and that retained profits supported much of the country's industrial growth (Mokyr 1977). Most analysts, however, appear to agree that Belgium in the Gerschenkronian framework represents a case of moderate backwardness.

The Netherlands

There are no references to the Netherlands or to Holland or the Dutch in either of Gerschenkron's two large volumes of collected papers, *Economic Backwardness in Historical Perspective* and *Continuity in History and Other Essays*. Although it is not clear that he was aware of this little fact, Kindleberger may have explained it:

> [T]he development of financial institutions may be necessary to economic development. It is not sufficient. The proof: the Netherlands in 1750 boasted the most highly developed financial institutions in the world, including such sophisticated features as future markets, but failed to make the transition from commercial preeminence to industrialization for more than 100 years.
>
> (Kindleberger 1984a: 81)

On the other hand, just how backward were the Dutch? Bairoch's per capita GNP data indicate that the Netherlands was 45 per cent above the European average in 1830 (and the highest of his fifteen countries), and 41 per cent above the European average in 1913 (and behind only Britain, Switzerland, Belgium and Denmark) (Bairoch 1976: 286, as reworked by Sandberg 1978).

Switzerland

Switzerland merits more study. Its economic growth was unusually rapid from 1840 to 1880, the period of the European mixed banking revolution (Bairoch 1976: 286, as reworked by Sandberg 1978). Kindleberger (1984a: 134–5) refers to some mixed bank formations in the 1850s. Were the Swiss, in banking, more German than the Germans?

Austria

Much has been written about the economic history of Austria (and Austria/ Hungary) during the past two decades, including the last book of Gerschenkron. There is general agreement on one element of Gerschenkron's approach, namely, that Austria had no great spurt. Gerschenkron sought to analyse this 'failure', which in his view resulted over time in Austria slipping further and further behind its neighbour, Germany (Gerschenkron 1977). Others, including Good in Chapter 11, deny that Austria failed; a slow but steady pace of development may have resulted in Austria falling relatively further behind Germany, but there was development (Komlos 1983; Good 1984). The modern discussion of Austria is similar to the modern discussion of France, referred to earlier. Gerschenkron thinks that Austria failed to develop as much as it might have in terms of industry, and that the failure can be traced to the doorstep of the Austrian banks, which were more cautious and timid than their German counterparts in the last decades of the nineteenth century (Gerschenkron 1977: 50). His critics deny there was any failure. The roles they ascribe to banks in the lack of failure range from passive and irrelevant to active and quite relevant (Rudolph 1972; März 1983; Good 1984).

Italy

Gerschenkron (1962: ch. 4) himself tested his approach to European industrialization in Italy, and found to his own satisfaction that it worked. Italy's great spurt began in the mid-1890s. At the time, Italy was more backward than Germany had been when it industrialized, but on the backwardness scale it was still closer to Germany than to Russia. A Gerschenkronian would therefore expect German-type banks to be active in the great spurt. That is what Gerschenkron discovered in the 1950s. It is what Jon Cohen confirmed in the 1960s and 1970s, and what Peter Hertner further confirmed in the 1970s and 1980s (Cohen 1967, 1972, 1964 [1977]; Hertner 1978, 1980, 1991). In Italy, moreover, the German-type banks were actually founded by Germans experienced in mixed banking.

On the other hand, as Federico and Toniolo argue in Chapter 10, the Italian evidence that has now accumulated is much more mixed on the role of banks than thought by Gerschenkron and his disciples. At a minimum, the entrepreneurial role of the German-type banks in Italy appears to have been less than it was for similar banks in Germany. The Banca Commerciale and the Credito Italiano may have aided Italy's major industrial spurt that began in the 1890s, but they were only one of a number of favourable developments in that era. If the view taken by Federico and Toniolo, based on the work of Confalonieri, is correct, a good question for future research is why German bankers in Italy were not as active in industrial firms as they were in Germany.

Sweden and Denmark

Sweden and Denmark, it is generally agreed, were moderately backward when they began to industrialize in the last decades of the nineteenth century. They also had, in the general sense, good banking systems (Sandberg 1978; Lundstrom 1991; Johansen 1991). It would seem, therefore, that they would provide favourable testing grounds for Gerschenkron's hypothesis, even though it relates to a specific type of bank that takes an active, entrepreneurial role in industrial development. The evidence, however, is inconclusive. Banks were active in trade finance in Scandinavia, but most industrial investment appears to have been financed directly rather than through intermediation by banks. These were small economies dominated by export demand. Previous accumulation from commerce and ties to foreign markets fostered domestic and foreign investment, both direct and portfolio. Banks were present but apparently not crucial for industrialization in such economies. Sweden might be an exception to this view if, as Lars Sandberg (1978) argues, good banking preceded and aided industrialization. Kindleberger (1982), however, questions Sandberg's evidence. It deserves to be emphasized that Gerschenkron's focus on the intimate involvement of banks in industrial firms is quite different from good banking in general. Such involvement could be present in situations that on other criteria might be viewed as bad banking, e.g. unstable banking.

Serbia and Bulgaria

Serbia and Bulgaria did not industrialize, despite some bank presence. They were probably too backward, if I read Lampe's and Gerschenkron's studies correctly, to have provided a propitious environment for bank-led industrialization (Gerschenkron 1962: ch. 8; Lampe 1972). Their failure to industrialize is therefore to be attributed in a Gerschenkronian approach to a failure of the state to do in Serbia and Bulgaria what it did in Russia.

Other European countries

Of the remaining European countries, none had what could be called successful nineteenth-century industrialization, with or without great spurts. All, therefore, fall into the category of negative cases as far as Gerschenkron's framework is concerned. Only one, Spain, has been addressed in that framework; there, according to Tortella (1972), weak entrepreneurship and government policies that were either uninterested in, or actually opposed to industrialization prevented what banking there was from having a positive influence on development. The other countries – Portugal, Norway, Finland, Greece and Romania – have not, to my knowledge, had studies which address their industrial development (or lack thereof) in an explicit Gerschenkronian framework.

Non-European cases

As a historian, Gerschenkron said more than once that his approach was designed for and applicable to nineteenth-century European industrializations. Without quite saying so explicitly, he hinted that application either to non-European cases or to times outside of the 'long' nineteenth century were not likely to be pertinent or illuminating. On the other hand, as an economist Gerschenkron certainly had to think that his ideas could potentially offer insights into cases lying outside of nineteenth-century Europe. Indeed, one valid lesson of Gerschenkron's work for the twentieth century is that it is perfectly understandable why the backward underdeveloped countries of the contemporary Third World tend to feature more state involvement than most European nations did in their programmes of economic modernization. To be sure, twentieth-century trends away from *laissez-faire* in economic ideology as well as conditions of extreme economic backwardness could have led to this result. A Gerschenkronian, of course, would have no trouble with the ideological point; Gerschenkronians regard ideologies of industrialization as active forces working to overcome backwardness.

The United States and Japan were the two non-European industrializers before 1914. Each has been studied from a Gerschenkronian perspective. For the United States, my own treatment suggests that the perspective works too well: original accumulation, the banks, and the state all contributed to industrialization (Sylla 1972, 1975). In the initial phases of industrialization before the Civil War, mercantile capital and ploughed-back profits were the main sources of industrial finance. In this case, the United States fits the pattern of an advanced country in Gerschenkron's scheme. In later phases, however, US bankers such as J.P. Morgan were as intimately involved with industrial firms as their contemporary German counterparts, and the US government with its land grants to railroads and its budget surpluses fed into the capital markets through public debt retirement acted to promote industrial investment in a manner similar to that attributed by Gerschenkron to the contemporary Russian state. A construction of these American parallel behaviours that was favourable to Gerschenkron might be possible: the early and sustained industrial growth at relatively high rates in the case of the United States is perhaps better understood if all of Gerschenkron's financing mechanisms contributed. A negative construction is also possible: Gerschenkron's hypothesis is designed to distinguish between modes of financing depending on a country's position on the relative backwardness scale, but it fails to do so in the case of the US.

Work on Japan also has produced mixed results. Economic historians of Japan usually accord the state a large role in the initial phases of modernization after centuries of isolation. This much accords with Gerschenkron's ideas about the influence of backwardness on development strategies. But Japan modernized rapidly, and Japanese banks, therefore, have also been viewed as agents of industrialization. Hugh Patrick (1967) argued that post-restoration Japan showed a remarkable willingness to experiment with banking and that Japan's banks did, in fact, play a large role in the early industrial upsurge. Kozo Yamamura (1972, 1978), in contrast, contends that in a Gerschenkronian financing framework Japan was more like England than like Germany. He also argues that Japanese banks became more important for industrial finance later, after the initial upsurge, a point confirmed by Neuberger and Stokes (1975) when they applied their econometric testing procedures developed to study Germany to the Japanese case. The latter result is distinctly non-Gerschenkronian: as industrialization reduces relative backwardness, bank financing is supposed to become less, not more, important for further industrial growth.

Gerschenkron's analysis of the European experience of industrialization in the nineteenth century thus raises interesting questions about non-European experiences and brings considerable comparative perspective to the study of countries such as the United States and Japan. Only in a limited way, however, do these non-European cases fit into the pattern Gerschenkron found in Europe. Once one moves beyond the initial phases of industrialization, the US and Japanese cases do not conform to the sequences that would be expected as backwardness was reduced. This may help to explain why Gerschenkron was sceptical about the applicability of his approach outside of the context of nineteenth-century Europe.

GENERAL CONCLUSIONS

From the foregoing survey I conclude:

1. Gerschenkron's banking hypothesis or, more generally, his tripartite view of the ways in which industry could be financed in nineteenth-century Europe has been enormously influential. For much of the work on the history of industrial finance after his own he provided the questions, set forth the range of tentative answers, and determined the terms of debate. Some writers agree with him. Others do not. But most of them are aware of his presence. Surely this is a triumph of individual scholarship.

2. The problem of how the capital requirements of industrialization were financed is obviously an important one for economic historians. But neither the evidence nor the theory brought to bear upon the problem is very good. What was the share of bank-financed investment in total industrial investment during the industrial revolutions of Britain, Germany, Russia, and other countries? We still do not know. If we did, do we have a theory implying say, that a 25 per cent share made a difference whereas a 5 per cent share did not? David Good (1973), using perhaps less relevant measures than this (for example, the bank asset to GNP ratio) once attempted to test Gerschenkron's hypothesis, with mixed results. Good's approach to a general test of the hypothesis is easier to criticize than to improve upon (Sylla 1977). Gerschenkron's hypothesis about the role of banks remains influential in part because it was powerfully argued by its originator and in part because no one has produced the evidence to refute it across the board, even though strong doubts have been raised about particular cases. See, for example, the Chapters 8 and 10 on France and Italy.

3. A part of Gerschenkron's banking hypothesis is qualitative. Although Schumpeter's theory clearly demarcated the entrepreneurial and banking functions, Gerschenkron's best bankers were ones who supplied healthy doses of entrepreneurship along with finance. This aspect of his hypothesis is not amenable to quantitative testing. It would be useful, however, to know the extent to which successful industrial entrepreneurs were intimately associated with

banks. The accumulating business histories of Britain, referred to by Peter Mathias (1973, 1989), indicate that these associations were more common than Gerschenkron would have expected in an advanced country.

4. In emphasizing the entrepreneurial aspects of investment banking in moderately backward countries, Gerschenkron paid insufficient attention to the quality and efficiency of the entire banking systems of those countries. Banking systems are composed of different types of banking institutions, not just investment banks, and they are conditioned by laws, regulations and customs that varied from country to country. The work of Rondo Cameron and his many collaborators has done much to fill in the gaps that once existed in our comparative knowledge of banking systems. That work could well be extended to encompass financial systems as a whole, including such topics as the efficiency of primary and secondary markets, the effects of central banking, and the role of company law – in particular, limited and unlimited liability – as it applied to bank and non-bank enterprises. Across countries, differences in the financial and legal environment in which bankers and industrial entrepreneurs functioned may well have been as important as their individual characteristics in determining economic outcomes. These important issues were slighted by Gerschenkron when he focused his attention on a particular type of banking that he thought could have made a crucial contribution to the initial phase of industrialization in a particular setting along the scale of economic backwardness.

ACKNOWLEDGEMENTS

I thank Sheila Stone for research assistance and stimulating discussions on the topic of this paper, and Charles P. Kindleberger, John Komlos, and Gianni Toniolo for helpful comments on the draft.

NOTES

1   The World Bank, for example, devoted the major portion of its *World Development Report 1989* to 'Financial systems and development'. One chapter traces the history of financial development.
2   Gerschenkron's analysis of financial development anticipated later writings on the 'convergence' of industrializing economies – in his case, their financial systems – toward broadly similar characteristics.

REFERENCES

Anan'ich, Boris V. (1988) 'The Russian private banking houses, 1870–1914', *Journal of Economic History* 48 (June), 401–7.
Bairoch, Paul (1976) 'Europe's gross national product, 1800–1975', *Journal of European Economic History* 5 (Fall).
Bovykin, V.I. and Anan'ich, B.V. (1991) 'The role of international factors in the formation of the banking system in Russia', in V.I. Bovykin and Rondo Cameron (eds)

International Banking, 1870–1914, New York: Oxford University Press.

Cameron, Rondo (ed.) (1972) *Banking and Economic Development*, New York: Oxford University Press.

Cameron, Rondo, and Freedeman, Charles E. (1983) 'French economic growth: a radical revision', *Social Science History* 7, 3–30.

Cameron, Rondo, *et al.* (1967) *Banking in the Early Stages of Industrialization*, New York: Oxford University Press.

Carr, E.H. (1967) 'Some random reflections on Soviet industrialization', in C.H. Feinstein (ed.) *Socialism, Capitalism, and Economic Growth*, Cambridge: Cambridge University Press.

Checkland, S.G. (1975) *Scottish Banking: A History, 1695–1973*, Glasgow: Collins.

Cohen, Jon S. (1967) 'Financing industrialization in Italy, 1894–1914: the partial transformation of a late comer', *Journal of Economic History* 27, 363–82.

—— (1972) 'Italy, 1861–1914', in Rondo Cameron (ed.) *Banking and Economic Development*, pp. 58–90, New York: Oxford University Press.

—— (1964 (1977)) *Finance and Industrialization in Italy, 1894–1914*, New York: Arno.

Cottrell, P.L. (1980) *Industrial Finance 1830–1914*, London: Methuen.

Crisp, Olga (1967) 'Russia, 1860–1914', in Rondo Cameron *et al. Banking in the Early Stages of Industrialization*, New York: Oxford University Press, pp. 183–258.

Fremdling, R. and Tilly, R. (1976) 'German banks, German growth, and econometric history', *Journal of Economic History* 36, 416–24.

Gerschenkron, Alexander (1962) *Economic Backwardness in Historical Perspective*, Cambridge, Mass.: Harvard University Press.

—— (1970) *Europe in the Russian Mirror*, Cambridge: Cambridge University Press.

—— (1977) *An Economic Spurt that Failed*, Princeton: Princeton University Press.

Good, David F. (1973) 'Backwardness and the role of banking in nineteenth-century European industrialization', *Journal of Economic History* 33, 845–50.

—— (1984) *The Economic Rise of the Habsburg Empire, 1750–1914*, Berkeley: University of California Press.

Hertner, Peter (1978) 'Banken und Kapitalbildung in der Giolitti-Era', *Quellen und Forschingen aus italienischen Archiven und Bibiotheken* 58, 466–565.

—— (1980) 'Das Vorbild deutscher Universalbanken bei der Grundung und Ehrtwicklung italienischer Geschaftsbanken neuen Typs, 1894–1914', in F.W. Henning (ed.) *Entwicklung und Aufgaben von Versicherungen und Banken in der Industrialisiering*, Berlin: Duncker und Humblot.

—— (1991) 'Foreign capital in the Italian banking sector, 1860–1914', in V.I. Bovykin and Rondo Cameron (eds) *International Banking, 1870–1914*, New York: Oxford University Press.

Johansen, Hans Chr. (1991) 'Banking and finance in the Danish economy 1870–1914', in V.I. Bovykin and Rondo Cameron (eds) *International Banking 1870–1914*, New York: Oxford University Press.

Kindleberger, Charles P. (1982) 'Sweden in 1850 as an "Impoverished Sophisticate": Comment', *Journal of Economic History* 42, 918–20.

—— (1984a) *A Financial History of Western Europe*, London: George Allen & Unwin.

—— (1984b) 'Financial institutions and economic development: a comparison of Great Britain and France in the eighteenth and nineteenth centuries', *Explorations in Economic History* 21, 103–24.

—— (1985) *Keynesianism vs. Monetarism and other Essays in Financial History*, London: George Allen & Unwin.

Komlos, John (1978) 'The *Kreditbanken* and German growth: a postscript', *Journal of Economic History* 38, 476–9.

Komlos, J. (1983) *The Habsburg Monarchy as a Customs Union*, Chicago: University of Chicago Press.

Lampe, John R. (1972) 'Serbia, 1878–1912', in Rondo Cameron (ed.) *Banking and Economic Development*, New York: Oxford University Press, pp. 122–67.

Lundstrom, Ragnhild (1991) 'Sweden', in V.I. Bovykin and Rondo Cameron (eds) *International Banking, 1870–1914*, New York: Oxford University Press.

März, Edward (1983) 'The Austrian Credit Mobilier in a time of transition', in John Komlos (ed.) *Economic Development in the Habsburg Monarchy in the Nineteenth Century*, Boulder, CO: East European Monographs, pp. 117–36.

Mathias, Peter (1973) 'Capital, credit and enterprise in the industrial revolution', *Journal of European Economic History* 2, 121–43.

—— (1989) 'Financing the industrial revolution', in P. Mathias and J.A. Davis (eds) *The First Industrial Revolutions*, Oxford: Basil Blackwell, pp. 69–85.

Mokyr, Joel (1977) *Industrialization in the Low Countries, 1795–1850*, New Haven, Yale University Press.

Neuberger, Hugh, and Stokes, Houston H. (1974) 'German banks and German growth: an empirical view', *Journal of Economic History* 34, 710–31.

Neuberger, Hugh, and Stokes, Houston H. (1975) 'German banking and Japanese banking: a comparative analysis', *Journal of Economic History* 35, 238–52.

O'Brien, Patrick K. and Keyder, Caglar (1978) *Economic Growth in Britain and France, 1780–1914: Two Paths to the 20th Century*, London: Allen & Unwin.

Patrick, Hugh (1967) 'Japan, 1868–1914', in Rondo Cameron *et al. Banking in the Early Stages of Industrialization*, New York: Oxford University Press, pp. 239–89.

Roehl, Richard (1976) 'French industrialization: a reconsideration', *Explorations in Economic History* 13, 233–81.

Rudolph, Richard L. (1972) 'Austria, 1800–1914', in Rondo Cameron (ed.) *Banking and Economic Development*, New York: Oxford University Press, pp. 26–57.

Sandberg, Lars G. (1978) 'Banking and economic growth in Sweden before World War I', *Journal of Economic History* 38, 22–41.

Sylla, Richard (1972) 'The United States, 1863–1913', in Rondo Cameron (ed.) *Banking and Economic Development*, New York: Oxford University Press, pp. 232–62,

—— (1975) *The American Capital Market, 1846–1914*, New York: Arno.

—— (1977) 'Financial intermediaries in economic history: quantitative research on the seminal hypotheses of Lance Davis and Alexander Gerschenkron', in Robert E. Gallman (ed.) *Recent Developments in the Study of Business and Economic History*, Greenwich, Conn.: JAI Press.

Tilly, Richard (1986a) 'Financing industrial enterprise in Great Britain and Germany in the nineteenth century: testing grounds for Marxist and Schumpeterian theories?' in H.J. Wagener and J.W. Drukker (eds) *The Economic Law of Motion of Modern Society*, Cambridge: Cambridge University Press.

—— (1986b) 'German banking, 1850–1914: development assistance for the strong', *Journal of Economic History* 15 (Spring), 113–52.

Tortella, Gabriel (1972) 'Spain, 1829–1874', in Rondo Cameron (ed.) *Banking and Economic Development*, New York: Oxford University Press, pp. 91–121.

Van der Wee, Herman, and Goossens, Martine (1991) 'Belgium', in V.I. Bovykin and Rondo Cameron (eds) *International Banking, 1870–1914*, New York: Oxford University Press.

World Bank, International Bank for Reconstruction and Development (1989) *World Development Report 1989*, New York: Oxford University Press.

Yamamura, Kozo (1972) 'Japan, 1868–1930: a revised view', in Rondo Cameron (ed.) *Banking and Economic Development*, New York: Oxford University Press, pp. 168–98.

—— (1978) 'Entrepreneurship, ownership, and management in Japan', in Peter

Mathias and M.M. Postan (eds) *Cambridge Economic History of Europe*, vol. 7, *The Industrial Economies: Capital, Labour, and Enterprise*, Cambridge: Cambridge University Press, pp. 215–64.

Chapter 4

The role of the state in promoting economic development: the Russian case and its general implications

Paul R. Gregory

INTRODUCTION

This chapter studies the role of the state in dealing with Russian relative backwardness. Russia is used as a case study because of Alexander Gerschenkron's view that the Russian state substituted for missing preconditions. The chapter considers three forms of state involvement: constitutional change in agriculture, monetary and fiscal policy, and direct entrepreneurial activities. The chapter concludes that Gerschenkron's assessment of constitutional change in agriculture has proven to be seriously flawed and that the Russian state's entrepreneurial activities were minimal. The major success of Russian industrialization was the attraction of sufficient foreign investment to achieve high investment rates for a low-income country. While the state provided a stable monetary and fiscal framework, foreign capital was attracted principally by the private profit opportunities in Russia.

In assessing the role of the Russian state, Gerschenkron assumed that the provisions of the 1861 peasant emancipation would be adhered to even though they violated private profit incentives. He also assumed that the 'enlightened industrial policy' strategy outlined by Witte was actually implemented by the Russian state.

THE GERSCHENKRON PARADIGM

Alexander Gerschenkron sought to explain what he perceived to be an empirical regularity of the nineteenth century. Latecomer countries, such as Germany, Russia, Japan and Italy, experienced rapid spurts in their rates of economic growth that exceeded those of the countries that had industrialized before them. Gerschenkron used the theory of relative backwardness to explain why economies that had previously languished should suddenly experience growth accelerations (Gerschenkron 1962: essay 1, 1963, 1965).

As modern economic growth spread from England to Germany, France, the United States, and elsewhere, countries with development potential that failed to participate in modern economic growth became relatively backward. In 1850

Russia's per capita income was about half that of France and Germany and about one-quarter of England's. Some thirty years later, Russia's per capita income had dropped to one-third that of France and Germany and to about 15 per cent of England's. During the same period, Italy declined from per capita income parity to around three-quarters of the level in France and Germany (from Mitchell 1976: B1, K1; Gregory 1982: 155).

Gerschenkron felt that economic slippage in countries that had been competitive with now more-advanced rivals made them ripe for growth acceleration. Countries newly caught in a state of relative backwardness were under pressure to close the economic gap between themselves and their rivals.

Those countries that first experienced modern economic growth did so because of favourable preconditions (Rostow 1965). England experienced modern economic growth first because it had built up a constitutional democracy, a social infrastructure, an entrepreneurial middle class, and a track record of domestic capital formation. Almost by definition, relatively backward countries were backward because they lacked the preconditions for modern economic growth.

Gerschenkron sought to explain why nineteenth-century follower countries such as Germany, Russia and Italy – countries that lacked many preconditions – began to experience growth accelerations. After all, preconditions cannot be created overnight. Gerschenkron argued that relatively backward countries can create conditions for rapid growth by *substituting* for missing preconditions. If there is no middle class to supply entrepreneurs, foreign entrepreneurs can be used. If a skilled labour force is lacking, capital-intensive machinery can be substituted. If domestic capital formation is deficient, state capital formation or foreign saving can be used in its place (Gerschenkron 1968, 1970, lecture 4).

Nineteenth-century Russia was Gerschenkron's example par excellence of how relatively backward countries can use *and* misuse the state to accelerate economic development. He believed that although the Russian state achieved notable successes in promoting industrial growth, its failure to create an appropriate constitutional framework in agriculture caused the overall failure of Russian industrialization.[1]

The about-face of Russian state policy

Gerschenkron believed that the Russian state actually sought to impede economic development prior to its 'about-face' in the 1850s. In the Russian feudal autocracy, power was exercised by the tsar through advisors, relatives and ministers. The affairs of state were entrusted to a bureaucracy that was large for a relatively backward country but often lacking in professional competence.[2] Russian bureaucrats issued patents and licences, collected sales and excise taxes, managed the affairs of the court, supervised state and crown lands, ran the legal system, levied tariffs, collected statistics, and managed state enterprises.

The ruling élite was convinced of the virtue of feudal agriculture. The feudal lord used the village commune to police the unruly peasantry, restrict peasant mobility, collect agricultural taxes, and provide military recruits. Prior to the about-face of the 1850s, the Russian state feared that industrialization and modernization would concentrate revolution-minded workers in cities, railways would give them mobility, and education would create opposition to the monarchy.

Russia's backward feudal system served the ruling élite well until the 1850s, despite massive peasant uprisings. Russia's manpower advantage and vast territories had repelled Napoleon. The lack of railroads made it difficult for foreign invaders to penetrate the Russian homeland, and Russia's artillery was not notably inferior to Western Europe's at the turn of the nineteenth century.

Gerschenkron dates the about-face of Russian state industrial policy to the loss of the Crimean war (1853–6) to France, England, Turkey and Sardinia. The accession of Tsar Alexander II in 1855 and the capture of Sevastopol led to the Treaty of Paris that ended the dominant role of Russia in southeast Europe. The Crimean war confronted the Russian leadership for the first time with its economic inferiority *vis-à-vis* France and England.

The shock of relative backwardness forced the Russian state to turn its attention to catching up with Western Europe before Russia became a second-rate power in Europe. According to Gerschenkron, the about-face of state policy created new industrialization opportunities. With a powerful state bureaucracy dedicated rather than opposed to industrialization, Russia had – for the first time – a real opportunity to deal with its relative backwardness.

Gerschenkron looked at three types of state action that were available to the Russian ruling élite to overcome Russia's growing relative backwardness: (1) constitutional changes to provide appropriate property rights for economic development; (2) monetary and fiscal actions to create a financial and trade climate for economic development; and (3) state entrepreneurial actions to substitute for missing entrepreneurship. He concluded that the Russian state failed in the area of agrarian property rights, whereas it achieved notable successes in the other two areas. It was the failure in the constitutional area that caused Russian development to be halted by revolution and recession at the turn of the century, at which time more appropriate agrarian property rights were adopted.

Constitutional changes in property rights

England's head start in modern economic growth was aided by the early creation of a legal and constitutional framework that supported private property rights and sanctity of contract. Prior to the about-face of the 1850s, Gerschenkron felt that Russia's constitutional framework actively inhibited economic development. The vast majority of Russia's population lacked juridical freedom. Serfs could be bought and sold; they lacked the basic personal and economic rights that were taken for granted in Western Europe. Russian serfdom was based on compulsory labour obligations in the richer agricultural regions and on quit-rents in the steppes. The Russian village was run by a village self-government that handled matters of policing, tax collection, land distribution, family disputes and military recruitment. The three major owners of land – the gentry, the church, and the crown – all relied on serf labour to farm their lands. Private small-scale agriculture was lacking except on the periphery.

The about-face of the 1850s forced the Russian leadership to conclude that constitutional changes in agriculture were necessary. The tsar concluded that the initiative had to come quickly from above (in view of the strength of gentry opposition to emancipation) before the peasants took matters into their own hands from below.

The emancipation mistake

Gerschenkron felt that, if serfdom could have been replaced by private farming in Russia, the major obstacle to Russia's long-term economic development would have been removed, and Russian history would have been altered. It was the failure to create private peasant property rights in 1861 that doomed the state's other actions to overcome relative backwardness.

In an autocracy dominated by landed interests, serf emancipation required compensation not only for the land ceded to former serfs but also for lost labour services or quit-rents. The 1861 emancipation granted the gentry such compensation with an implicit payment for lost labour services in the form of overvalued land prices. The peasants, who had expected outright ownership, were saddled with redemption payments that were to amortize the land over nearly a half century's time. Moreover, the peasants ended up with less land, on average, than they had cultivated under feudal arrangements.

The 1861 Emancipation Act decreed that land be distributed to the village commune, not to individual peasant families. The emancipation retained the village commune to manage land allocation and redistribution, policing, and tax collection. Peasant families were made collectively responsible for the debts of the commune. Responsible households had to step in to cover for free-riders.

The peasants received their juridical freedom but not their economic freedom. They could not withdraw their land from the commune without paying off their share of the debt, and as long as their land remained within the commune, peasants could not make their own resource allocation decisions. Moreover, with periodic redistributions of land, adult family members had to stay in agriculture to ensure the peasant family's share of communal land. Furthermore, periodic redistributions penalized families that had made capital improvements on their plots of land.

The formal provisions of the 1861 Emancipation Act were not promising judged from an economic point of view. Gerschenkron concluded that the 1861 emancipation made balanced growth of the Russian economy an impossibility. The commune tied labour to agriculture and created the paradox of a labour-rich country starved for industrial labour. The inadequate land distribution of the emancipation left peasant families with inefficiently scaled plots. The retention of communal agriculture – and the lack of development of private farming – meant that productivity advances in agriculture would be minimal. The debt burden placed on the peasantry by the overstated land prices meant that there would be insufficient private demand to support industrialization.

Monetary and fiscal policy

Russia's monetary and fiscal policies were to a great extent dictated by the desire to join the international gold standard. In Russia's case, a remarkable series of influential finance ministers pursued a consistent fiscal policy of budgetary surpluses and limited monetary growth to create a stable currency on international currency markets. After more than two decades of stringency, the Russian credit ruble was trading at a fixed rate of exchange to the gold ruble, and Russia officially went on the gold standard in 1897.

The Russian state was not alone in directing its monetary and fiscal policies to the international gold standard. It appeared to be the thing that respectable countries did at the end of the nineteenth century (Yeager 1984: 651–70). The peculiar significance Gerschenkron attaches to Russian monetary and fiscal policies of the last quarter of the nineteenth century was that monetary stability was deliberately pursued to attract foreign capital. In a famous policy paper, Finance Minister Sergei Witte spelled out the importance of foreign capital in light of Russia's deficient domestic saving capacity (Von Laue 1954, 1963). Unlike other countries that pursued monetary stability and accumulated gold reserves to achieve convertibility, Russia did so expressly to substitute for a missing precondition – the lack of domestic saving.

According to Gerschenkron, Russia's monetary and fiscal conservatism paid off handsomely. Prior to the turn of the century, considerable direct foreign investment was attracted, bonds were successfully floated in the European money markets to finance railroad construction, and foreign entrepreneurs were attracted to Russia in large numbers. The Russian investment rate was pushed up by an influx of foreign saving and also by public saving from the state budget.

The state as entrepreneur

Constitutional and monetary and fiscal policy actions are common to all states. They do not involve an unusual substitution of the state for missing preconditions. Gerschenkron saw the unique state role in the Russian case to be the substitution of the state bureaucracy for missing entrepreneurship.

According to Gerschenkron, the Russian state followed what would now be called an enlightened 'industrial policy' which he felt contributed significantly to

Russian industrialization. The state managed construction of state-owned railroad lines and guaranteed loans to private railway lines. The state assisted in floating foreign-currency loans in European credit markets. The state reserved steel, military and railway equipment contracts for domestic industry, while pursuing anti-union policies. The state erected tariff barriers that increased the demand for domestic goods and attracted foreign direct investment behind Russian tariff walls. Moreover, the state engaged in a public relations campaign to attract Western entrepreneurs and craftsmen to Russia. The state granted licences to foreign companies that wished to do business in Russia.

Gerschenkron felt that the Russian state had to substitute its own demand for private demand. The backwardness imposed on Russia by communal agriculture meant that domestic demand for the products of Russian industry was deficient. By directing state purchases to domestic producers, the Russian state substituted state demand for private domestic demand. By placing a heavy fiscal burden on the peasantry and by generating surpluses from state-owned monopolies, state budgetary surpluses compensated for deficient private saving. By creating a stable environment for foreign investment, state monetary and fiscal policies attracted foreign saving to serve as a further substitute for deficient domestic saving.

The outcome according to Gerschenkron

The outcome of state activities was a spurt in the rate of industrial growth beginning in the mid-1880s.[3] While industrial growth was proceeding at a rapid pace, agriculture remained in an 'agrarian crisis'. Per capita agricultural output was actually declining. The tying of peasants to the land created rural over-population. Russian industry was forced to adopt capital-intensive factor proportions to make up for the scarcity of labour in a labour-rich country. Peasant 'land hunger' was evidenced by soaring land prices and land rents. The Russian agrarian crisis exhausted the tax-paying capacity of the Russian peasant, and the state system of generating fiscal surpluses could not be maintained.

The Russian agrarian crisis, coupled with world recessions, culminated in the 1905 revolution which shook both agriculture and industry. The 1905 revolution finally convinced the Russian leadership that the commune had to be abandoned in favour of private agriculture. The Stolypin Reforms of 1906 and 1910 cancelled peasant tax obligations and gave peasant families freedom to withdraw from the commune. These favourable changes set off a new wave of more balanced economic development. The outbreak of the First World War interrupted this second advance. No one knows what would have happened had Russian economic development been allowed to proceed on this more solid footing without interruption by the First World War.

The appeal of the Gerschenkron model

Gerschenkron's analysis of the economic development of tsarist Russia after the 1861 emancipation remains the most widely accepted version of Russian industrialization. What explains its continuing popularity? First, it offers a feasible explanation for the acceleration in Russian industrial growth in the 1880s. Second, it offers an optimistic view of the role of the state – the view that a state can use industrial policy to substitute for missing preconditions. Third, it offers a plausible explanation of political events. The Gerschenkron model explains the 1905 revolution in terms of the growing disequilibrium between industry and agriculture and the exhaustion of the Russian peasantry, drowning under the burdens imposed by the disastrous peasant emancipation. Fourth, it offers an appealing view of an alternate democratic Russian society in the twentieth century – a society that had finally found the key to pluralistic economic development based on private agriculture and enlightened state industrial policy.

GERSCHENKRON AND THE TEST OF TIME

Gerschenkron set the research agenda for economic historians studying the follower countries. Much scholarly effort has gone into examining his propositions. Students of Russian economic history have engaged in considerable research on Gerschenkron's interpretation of Russian economic history, especially his view of the state and Russian economic development. Some of Gerschenkron's insights have withstood the test of time. Others have not.

Overestimation of the effect of constitutional rules

The Gerschenkron model emphasizes the long-run damage inflicted by the 1861 emancipation. The retention of communal agriculture combined with the oppressive peasant debt burden meant that agriculture could not contribute to economic development either through productivity or demand increases.

Gerschenkron interpreted the emancipation law literally. He assumed that the state through its national and local representatives enforced rules that reduced profit opportunities in both agriculture and industry. Subsequent research has called this assumption into serious question.

Research on the post-emancipation period concludes that Russian peasant agriculture operated with much more flexibility than allowed by the formal letter of the law. Internal passport data and industrial labour force statistics reveal that the Russian peasant moved rather freely between agriculture and industry, despite the commune's restrictions on such mobility (Gregory 1974a; Crisp 1976). Despite their nominal rural ties, peasants several generations away from the countryside were engaged in work in Russian factories (Gatrell 1986: ch. 3 and 4). The growth of the industrial labour force in the 1880s was equal to or exceeded that of the United States during its period of most rapid expansion. Gerschenkron had argued that communal restrictions on peasant mobility forced the substitution of artificially capital-intensive factor proportions on Russian industry. This argument appears to be supported by Lenin's statistical study of Russian large-scale industry.[4] Olga Crisp has shown that the apparent high capital intensity of Russian industry may be the consequence of the peculiar reporting system of Russian factory statistics. Recent Soviet studies of industrial concentration may ultimately shed light on this issue, but we lack a comparative basis for judging relative capital intensity.[5]

The key point remains that Gerschenkron's justification for excessive capital intensity – the freezing of labour on the land – appears to be absent.

The most convincing evidence against Gerschenkron's agricultural stagnation thesis is the relatively rapid per capita growth of Russian agriculture from 1885 to 1913. Productivity advances achieved by Russian agriculture were equivalent to those of Western Europe – as shown by different studies of Russian agriculture (Liashchenko 1908; Gregory 1982: ch. 6, 1984: 21–31; Gatrell 1986: ch. 4; Goldsmith 1961). Moreover, peasant real living standards advanced at a rate comparable to the rest of Western Europen (Gregory 1980: 135–64).

Why did Gerschenkron miss the mark with respect to his assessment of Russian agriculture? First, the central black earth region on which much attention focused was definitely in a state of long-term decline. In this area, agricultural output per capita was likely declining, and former peasants were turning from agriculture to industrial and handicraft pursuits. Yet much of the contemporary statistical work of the *zemstvos* and anecdotal evidence were being drawn from these declining regions.[6] Moreover, nineteenth-century observers were convinced that an agrarian crisis was in progress, despite contemporary aggregative statistics that showed nationwide per capita agricultural growth.

Gerschenkron's interpretations of rising land prices and of rising marketings appear curious. He argued that rising land prices were a sign of peasant distress because of the cost pressure they placed on peasant households. Similarly, he interpreted rising peasant marketings as being 'forced' from the peasants by their high tax burden. I view both phenomena differently: Rising land prices and rising land rents, as rent theory would assert, are more suggestive of rising marginal revenue product than of agricultural stagnation. Rising marketings are more a sign of market integration and of rising peasant prosperity than of oppressive taxes (Gregory 1987).

If post-emancipation agriculture had adhered strictly to the formal emancipation provisions, agricultural stagnation would indeed have been a likely result. It appears that Gerschenkron underestimated the ability of Russian peasants to circumvent the anti-productivity provisions of the emancipation. Evidence suggests that peasants adjusted their tax payments to harvests. Commune taxes were dealt with on an ability to pay principle, and a series of side payments were instituted to compensate for productivity improvements and land transfers.[7] Although the emancipation act did not give formal property rights to peasant households, it appears that informal property rights emerged. Moreover, the land market showed considerable fluidity with substantial changes in land ownership during this period (Gatrell 1986: ch. 4).

When peasants were given the opportunity to leave the commune in 1907, the rate of departure was surprisingly slow as noted by Gerschenkron. It may well be that the changes in state policy towards communal agriculture (which Gerschenkron pictured as forced upon the leadership by the agrarian crisis) were *de facto* recognition of the informal arrangements that were increasingly practised in Russian peasant agriculture. Even Lenin (1977: ch. 2) emphasized the great diversity of arrangements in Russian agriculture.

Gerschenkron also underestimated the strength of the Russian empire's agricultural periphery. Since the eighteenth century, agriculture had been relatively free of feudal restrictions on the rapidly expanding periphery, leaving Russian peasants free to 'vote with their feet' against the Russian commune (Kahan 1985: ch. 2). Agricultural growth on the periphery exceeded growth in the fifty European provinces, thereby pulling up total agricultural output (Gregory 1982: app. D; Gatrell 1986: ch. 3 and 4).

Gerschenkron's assumption of declining per capita output caused him to anticipate the substitution of state demand for the declining private demand of peasant agriculture. Despite Gerschenkron's claims that Russia's industrial structure was 'top heavy' in favour of heavy industry, comparative statistics reveal that Russian industry was actually 'top heavy' in light industry (particularly textiles) for a country of Russia's size and resource base (Gregory 1974b; 520–7). The lack of substitution of state for private demand is what one would expect if per capita income was growing in agriculture, as the aggregative statistics show.

Monetary and fiscal policy role

Gerschenkron's conclusion that monetary and fiscal policy contributed appreciably to Russian industrial growth has withstood the test of time better than his propositions concerning the effects of constitutional change or agriculture. By comparative standards, Russia attracted an unusually high proportion of domestic capital formation through foreign saving. Indeed, the two unusual features of the composition of Russian national income were its high rate of capital formation and its high rate of foreign saving (Gregory 1976a, b). With Russia's limited domestic capital markets, it is unlikely that Russia could have achieved its relatively high rates of domestic capital formation without foreign saving.

Little attention has focused on the role of state saving, especially during the period of railroad construction. Gerschenkron felt that budgetary surpluses were substituted for deficient personal saving. Russian budgetary practices of the period are difficult to follow, but the 'extraordinary expenditures' devoted to railroad and port construction can be construed as in-kind public saving. Using this accounting procedure, public saving accounted for slightly less than 10 per cent of net investment in both 1885 and 1897.[8] While public saving accounted for some 10 per cent, foreign saving accounted for 15–20 per cent during the same period (Gregory 1982: table 3–2).

Gerschenkron's favourable assessment of Russian monetary and fiscal policy has been challenged by Arcadius Kahan (1967) and Haim Barkai (1973: 339–71), who have emphasized the high opportunity costs of monetary stringency. Yet evidence on the growth of foreign investment that accompanied conservative monetary and fiscal policies, combined with the fact that price flexibility was sufficient to neutralize the real effects of monetary stringency, suggests that the benefits of monetary and fiscal conservatism outweighed their costs (Gregory and Sailors 1976).

One of Gerschenkron's minor assertions appears not to have withstood the test of time. There is little evidence of the shift from direct to portfolio investment after the turn of the century that Gerschenkron had perceived (Gregory 1976b).

It is impossible to estimate how large foreign savings would have been to a Russia whose exchange rate was subject to large fluctuations. Whether foreign investors were sufficiently sophisticated at hedging in foreign exchange markets is not known. It may be that the major benefit of monetary and fiscal conservatism was that it gave the appearance of political stability to a regime that – as events demonstrated – was not stable.

State as entrepreneur

Gerschenkron's true interest in the Russian state was in the state as an ersatz entrepreneur. In the Russian case, the secret memorandum of Witte spells out a coherent entrepreneurial role for the Russian state. As in the case of the 1861 emancipation, I believe that Gerschenkron erred in mistaking intent for actual policy.

Arcadius Kahan (1967), in his noted analysis of Russian state budgets, has ably pointed out that there was a notable lack of industrial subsidies in Russian state budgets. An active industrial policy calls for subsidies of industries selected by the state for development. In the Russian budget, there are no notable industrial subsidies. The only 'industrial policy' items that show up in the state budget are loan guarantees for private railway construction and some minor expenditures on ports and military equipment. State expenditures for military hardware made up such a small proportion of the total that the military budget could not have served as a significant vehicle for hidden subsidization (Gregory 1982: app. F).

State enterprises, which could have served as vehicles for state entrepreneurship, did not appear to play an important role in Russian industrialization. State budgets identify state-owned railroads, the postal and telegraph systems, and the state spirit monopoly as the only significant state enterprises. Although railroads played a key role in Russian industrialization, it is not clear that the role of the state was more prominent in the Russian case than elsewhere.[9] With the exception of national railroads, Russian state enterprises were either those that were typically state-owned or, such as the spirit monopoly, were not the 'high-tech' industries associated with enlightened industrial policy.

Moreover, there appears to be a consensus that Russian state tariff policy was dictated by revenue needs rather than by a coherent industrial policy. There is no evidence of discretionary tariffs to favour specific industries or to encourage foreign industries to locate behind Russian tariff walls (Pokrovsky 1902; Kahan 1967; Gatrell 1986: 165–7). Manufacturing inputs were taxed at the same rates as manufactures. In fact, foreign manufacturers, seeking to penetrate Russian markets, paid remarkably little attention to lobbying for tariff reductions on the grounds that revenue requirements made changes impossible. Foreign manufacturers appeared to be more interested in their monopoly power in Russian markets, which would allow them to pass the tariff on to the Russian consumer (Kirchner 1986).

The role of state officials in attracting foreign capital is another entrepreneurial function emphasized by Gerschenkron. The image of political and financial stability engendered by Russian officialdom was indeed important to attracting foreign capital, but there is disagreement on its effect on foreign capital. John McKay (1970) has demonstrated that foreign capital was attracted primarily by higher rates of return, not by lobbying efforts of Russian bureaucrats. Interest rate differentials do indeed appear to explain capital movements into Russia (Gregory 1976b). Russia in the late nineteenth century was regarded as a land of unlimited economic opportunity, albeit a market with considerable risks.

Case studies of foreign investments in Russia show that the Russian state was regarded more as an impediment than as a source of assistance (see, for example, Kirchner 1986). Foreign concerns had to learn how to deal with the Byzantine Russian bureaucracy. Bureaucrats had to be bribed as a matter of course, and learning how to deal effectively with the bureaucracy and to find important patrons could take years of effort. In the German case, few companies earned quick and easy profits (Kirchner 1986). Primarily those companies that made long-term investments were those that earned long-term profits in Russian markets.

In defence of the Russian state bureaucracy, it should be noted that the bribes paid to Russian officials did not appear to be very significant. Moreover, the Russian bureaucracy appeared to grant licences primarily on the basis of merit. Companies that were the world leaders in their industries were typically licensed by the Russian bureaucracy, who may have been playing a conservative game by going with proven concerns. A listing of foreign concerns licensed to operate in Russian markets would include an honour roll of the best European and American firms of the day. It does appear that the Russian bureaucracy failed to engender competition by restricting licensing to single companies rather than using multiple licences to promote competition.

The legal role that Gerschenkron failed to deal with adequately was the gradual emergence of the limited liability corporations, a development that made industrial capital formation possible and served to attract foreign capital. Many fortunes were lost prior to limited liability, and risks to Russian entrepreneurs were exceptional in the eighteenth and early nineteenth centuries. Thomas Owen (1983) has chronicled the gradual changes in Russian commercial law and the ambivalent attitude of the Russian bureaucracy towards the corporation.

RETROSPECTIVE ASSESSMENT

Gerschenkron's main error in his assessment of Russian state involvement was his equation of intent with reality. Gerschenkron was fascinated by the coherent statement of industrial policy presented to the tsar by his top economic official, Count Witte. Gerschenkron was also perturbed by the anti-productivity features of the 1861 emancipation, which he interpreted literally. Gerschenkron overestimated the ability of the Russian state to enforce laws and constitutional rules in agriculture. Despite a large bureaucracy, it would nonetheless have been a notable achievement if this bureaucracy could have enforced provisions that worked against the economic interests of both peasants and industrialists. The credible performance of Russian agriculture in the post-emancipation era represents the major source of evidence against the Gerschenkron Russian model.

Subsequent research has failed to uncover significant direct entrepreneurial substitutions of the state for missing private entrepreneurs. On close inspection, one cannot find well-defined entrepreneurial activities of the state. Tariffs were set for revenue purposes, not by enlightened industrial policy. State involvement in railroad construction and management was, of course, a vital state activity, but it remains to be demonstrated that Russian state involvement was significantly different from state involvement in other countries.

The striking feature of Russian industrialization was the importance of foreign saving and foreign entrepreneurship. The influx of foreign saving allowed the achievement of relatively high investment rates in a country in which a domestic capital market was largely lacking. The influx of foreign entrepreneurs undoubtedly had a significant positive effect on technological progress in industry. Yet the Russian state's contribution to attracting foreign capital is unclear. It is clear that fiscal and monetary conservatism created a stable currency. The evidence, however, is persuasive that foreign capital was principally attracted by higher rates of return in private markets. Preliminary analysis of Russian state budgets suggests that public saving was indeed a source of investment finance, accounting for approximately 10 per cent of net investment during the 1880s and 1890s. The Russian state was indeed able to substitute public saving for private saving.

IMPLICATIONS FOR OTHER EUROPEAN COUNTRIES

Gerschenkron's analysis of the Russian case provides the most detailed case study of the role of the state in nineteenth- and early twentieth-century European economic growth. What lessons are to be learned from Gerschenkron that apply to the other European follower countries?

First, Gerschenkron's writings show the pitfalls of confusing intent with the reality of state economic policy. Although the Russian state enacted constitutional changes designed to create a desired set of organizational arrangements in agriculture, profit-oriented individuals were able to circumvent these provisions and create organizational arrangements that differed from the state's intent. The contemporary economic literatures on regulation and public finance show the ease with which laws and regulations that work counter to the profit interests of individuals can be circumvented. The Russian economic bureaucracy operated in a world of primitive information, vast distances, and inadequate official rewards. For laws and legislative intent to find actual translation into economic reality would have been a remarkable achievement for this bureaucracy.

Second, Gerschenkron's model of the state carries with it the intellectual imprint of the late 1940s and early 1950s. To an extent, it reflects the dominant belief expressed in the development literature of the 1950s that the state must assist follower countries in overcoming their relative backwardness. Private markets had 'failed' to create economic development; therefore, the state had to step in to replace private markets. The imprint of Keynes is also clear: inadequate demand was viewed as a source of relative backwardness, and state expenditures could serve as a substitute for inadequate private demand.

Modern public choice literature supplies a more sceptical view of the state's potential role in promoting economic development. Bureaucrats are viewed as self-interested individuals; political coalitions strike deals that are contrary to the national interest and so on. Moreover, even in cases where the state truly desires to promote general economic welfare – through an optimal tariff – the information requirements of devising optimal state policy are overwhelming.

My own research points out that the application of the Keynesian model to nineteenth-century European economies is invalid due to the considerable wage and price flexibility of this era (Gregory and Sailors 1976). The classical model would appear the more legitimate model than a Keynesian model for nineteenth-century Europe, and concerns over inadequate demand should be accorded less importance than concerns over capital formation and productivity improvements. Moreover, the Russian state indeed showed clear signs of the modern public choice model of state behaviour. The drafters of tariff policy considered only the revenue implications of tariffs; little or no thought was given to optimal tariffs or to tariff policies designed to implement specific industrial policies. State purchasing policies were tailored to favour vested political interests.

Third, the Gerschenkron model of the state consistently failed to recognize that the search for private profit opportunities dominated the effects of state activities. Studies of international capital flows during the nineteenth and early twentieth centuries agree that rate-of-return differentials were the dominant force in dictating capital flows. Any model that argues otherwise – namely that international capital flows depend upon state identification and recruitment – misses the mark.

Fourth, the Russian case prior to the 1850s probably was a unique example of a state policy designed to impede rather than promote economic development. If Gerschenkron's assessment of Russian state policy is accurate – particularly the state's anti-education stance and its opposition to railroad construction – then likely the most important state role in Russian industrialization was the abandonment of its anti-industrialization stance. This passive view of the Russian state's role differs dramatically from Gerschenkron's emphasis on the active role of the state in promoting industrialization.

Fifth, Gerschenkron's emphasis on state monetary and fiscal policy should have broad applicability to other European countries. The creation of a stable monetary and fiscal framework provided public capital for railway construction and foreign capital for industrial investment. In the Russian case, the long-run effects of a stable monetary and fiscal framework can be roughly estimated in terms of the increment to domestic capital formation. Similar studies should be done for the other European follower countries to assess the roles of monetary and fiscal policy in domestic capital formation.

NOTES

1   This view is expressed most forcefully in Gerschenkron (1965).
2   Surprisingly little information is available on the size and composition of the Russian bureaucracy. For the best source, see Zaionchkovski (1978).
3   This growth spurt has been found both by Alexander Gerschenkron (1947) and by Raymond Goldsmith (1961).
4   Crisp (1976) disputes Gerschenkron's interpretation of Russian industrial concentration statistics.
5   Bovykin (1984) provides valuable new data on industrial concentration that are suitable for international comparison. This work remains to be done but should shed light on Gerschenkron's hypothesis.
6   For a discussion of regional differentiation, the use of anecdotal evidence, and the consensus concerning an agrarian crisis, see Gregory (1987).
7   The assumption that Russian peasants were not economically rational has its tradition in the writings of Chayanov on peasant economy. See Chayanov (1966). Evidence on the ability of the Russian commune to respond rationally to economic conditions is presented in Gregory (1987).
8   These data are from official budgetary sources summarized in *Statisticheski sbornik svedenii po Rossii za 1884–1885*, Petersburg, 1887, pp. 183–184; *Entwurf des Reichsbudgets für das Jahr 1898*, Petersburg, 1897; Gregory (1982: table 3–2).
9   Crisp (1976) argues that the railroads were much more important to Russian industrialization than the peasant emancipation or other factors.

REFERENCES

Barkai, Haim (1973) 'The macro-economics of tsarist Russia in the industrialization era: monetary developments, the balance of payments, and the gold standard', *Journal of Economic History* (June), 339–71.

Bovykin, V.I. (1984) *Formirovanie finansovogo kapitala v Rossii*, Moscow: Nauka.

Chayanov, A.V. (1966) *The Theory of Peasant Economy*, edited by Daniel Thorner *et al.*, Homewood, Illinois: Irwin.

Crisp, Olga (1976) *Studies in the Russian Economy Before 1914*, New York: Barnes & Noble.

Gatrell, Peter (1986) *The Tsarist Economy 1850–1917*, New York: St Martin's Press.

Gerschenkron, Alexander (1947) 'The rate of growth of industrial production in Russia since 1885', *Journal of Economic History* 7 (Suppl.).

—— (1962) *Economic Backwardness in Historical Perspective*, Cambridge, Mass.: Harvard University Press.

—— (1963) 'The early phases of industrialization in Russia: afterthoughts and counterthoughts', in W.W. Rostow (ed.) *The Economics of Takeoff into Sustained Growth*, London: St Martin's Press.

—— (1965) 'Agrarian policies and industrialization: Russia 1861–1917', *Cambridge Economic History of Europe*, vol. 6, part 2, Cambridge: Cambridge University Press.

—— (1968) *Continuity in History and Other Essays*, Cambridge, Mass.: Harvard University Press.

—— (1970) *Europe in the Russian Mirror*, New York: Cambridge University Press.

Goldsmith, Raymond (1961) 'The economic growth of tsarist Russia, 1860–1913', *Economic Development and Cultural Change* 9 (3), April.

Gregory, Paul (1974a) 'Some empirical comments on the theory of relative backwardness: the Russian case', *Economic Development and Cultural Change* 22 (4), July, 654–65.

—— (1974b) 'A note on relative backwardness and industrial structure', *Quarterly Journal of Economics* 88 (August), 520–7.

—— (1976a) '1913 Russian national income: some insights into Russian economic development', *Quarterly Journal of Economics* 90 (3), August.

—— (1976b) 'The Russian balance of payments, the gold standard, and monetary policy: a historical example of foreign capital movements', *Journal of Economic History* 39 (2), December, 379–99.

—— (1980) 'Grain marketings and peasant consumption: Russia 1885–1913', *Explorations in Economic History* 17 (2), 135–64.

—— (1982) *Russian National Income, 1885–1913*, New York: Cambridge University Press.

—— (1984) 'The Russian agrarian crisis revisited', in Robert C. Stuart (ed.) *The Soviet Rural Economy*, Totowa, NJ: Rowman & Allanheld.

—— (1987) 'Rents, land prices, and economic theory: the Russian agrarian crisis', paper prepared for Conference in Honor of Olga Crisp, London, July.

Gregory, Paul and Sailors, Joel (1976) 'Russian monetary policy and industrialization', *Journal of Economic History* 36 (December), 836–51.

Kahan, Arcadius (1967) 'Government policies and the industrialization of Russia', *Journal of Economic History* 27 (4), December.

—— (1985) *The Plow, the Hammer, and the Knout: An Economic History of 18th Century Russia*, Chicago: University of Chicago Press.

Kirchner, Walther (1986) *Die Deutsche Industrie und Industrialisierung Russlands 1815–1914*, St Katarinen: Scripta Mercaturae.

Lenin, V.I. (1977) *The Development of Capitalism in Russia*, Moscow: Progress Publishers.

Liashchenko, P.I. (1908) *Ocherki agrarnoi instorii Rossii*, Petersburg.

McKay, John (1970) *Pioneers of Profit: Foreign Entrepreneurship and Russian Industrialization*, Chicago: University of Chicago Press.

Mitchell, B.R. (1976) *European Historical Statistics*, New York: Columbia University Press.

Owen, Thomas C. (1983) 'Entrepreneurship and the structure of enterprise in Russia, 1800–1880', in Gregory Guroff and Fred C. Carstensen (eds) *Entrepreneurship in Imperial Russia and the Soviet Union*, Princeton: Princeton University Press, pp. 59–83.

Pokrovsky, V.I. (ed.) (1902) *Sbornik svedenii po istorii i statistike vneshnei torgovli Rossii*, Petersburg: Department tamozhennykh sborov.

Rostow, W.W. (1965) *The Stages of Economic Growth*, Cambridge: Cambridge University Press.

Von Laue, Theodore H. (1954) 'A secret memorandum of Sergei Witte on the industrialization of imperial Russia', *Journal of Modern History* 26 (1) March.

—— (1963). *Sergei Witte and the Industrialization of Russia*, New York: Columbia University Press.

Yeager, Leland (1984) 'The image of the gold standard', in Michael Bordo and Anna Schwartz (eds) *A Retrospective on the Classical Gold Standard*, Chicago: University of Chicago Press.

Zaionchkovski, P.A. (1978) *Pravitel'stvenny apparat samoderzhavnoi Rossi v XIX v*, Moscow: Mysl'.

Chapter 5

Europe in an American mirror: reflections on industrialization and ideology

William N. Parker

DEMOCRACY AND CAPITALISM

The term 'an old-fashioned American' – and almost every American who has passed a certain age finds moments when he claims to be one – contains, as an Hegelian would suspect, an internal contradiction. An old-fashioned American likes things big, and done in a big way. But in the nineteenth century this was a vice shared with the entire élite of Europe in that period, in politics, in business enterprise, even in literature. What else was the unification of Italy and Germany but a tidying up of the history of those peoples into nation states, the sweeping away of ridiculous, fussy, 'petty' principalities, of lesser and impotent local sovereignties? How else to explain the death-grip of the Hapsburg Monarchy on southeastern Europe, the determined, ruthless power of the tsarist army and bureaucracy over the peoples of Eurasia, the imperialism – cultural and political – of a centralized French Republic, and of course, Britain.

> Wider still and wider
> Shall thy bounds be set;
> God who made thee mighty,
> Make thee mightier yet.

goes the patriotic British song, as law, Christianity, morality, and free trade were carried by the British navy and regiments to the five continents and most of the intervening islands (except, significantly, the Japanese archipelago).

In North America, between Canada and Mexico – those outposts, respectively, of Scotland and Spain – the experiment of government in a republican form, extending itself to the continental scale without fragmentation and without collapse, like its Roman predecessor, into absolutism, continued to be played out past one successive meridian after another westward to the Pacific. Its presidents from Jefferson, Polk, Lincoln, to the Roosevelts with the intervening Wilson, and the succeeding Truman and Johnson continued the vision and the thrust of its manifest destiny.

In American history, this intangible impulse appears indeed as the only plausible answer to the question: 'Why did the North fight the Civil War?' The answer was Lincoln's: that a government of the people, by the people, and for the people should not perish from the earth – and not only not perish from the earth, but should extend itself out over the earth. Old-fashioned, nineteenth-century America came out of the twentieth-century's two world wars with that dream still intact – a dream of making the world safe, first for a republic as against monarchy and aristocracy, then for bourgeois democracy as against Fascist corporatism, Nazism, and, on a world theatre, against Marxian socialism. It had a culture ensconced behind the social machinery of a nation state's three means of protecting and extending itself: (1) through enlightenment (called education and communication); (2) through trade and trade policy; (3) through diplomacy and force of arms. Europe's 'long nineteenth century' of expansion within and beyond national boundaries by all three means began, according to one's perspective, in 1763, or 1789, or 1815, or 1848, or 1870 – and ran to 1914. America's twentieth-century began in 1940, with the fact and date of its termination a matter, at the moment, of partisan dispute into which the mere economic historian is perhaps unwise to enter.

But for an old-fashioned American, with mind, heart, culture, and even costume established before 1940, the contradiction lies just here, in all this imperialism. For alongside the admiration of large-scale accomplishment – the spanning of a continent, the ploughing of the Plains to wheat, the assembly line that turns out a million cars, Texas, New York, Chicago, California, with everything that is the biggest and the best, and best because it is biggest and biggest because it is best (a simple re-statement of the law of natural selection) – the old-fashioned American as a political animal, revealed a deep mistrust of concentrated power.

Perhaps it began with the Revolution, which was really not very revolutionary, except from the point of view of King George and a few thousands of his officials and the Tory adulators of monarchy. The seventeenth-century's established colonial churches, Episcopal and Congregationalist, were already unravelling by 1750, and the whole power and prestige structure – the structure of deference to which John Adams was still wedded but from which Jefferson and Franklin, in their different ways, were half-emancipated – had fallen apart in the back-country, that is, 30 miles beyond the coast. Only in the tidewater and plantation South did it maintain its hold, though it threw long shadows up into the Southern hills and gave a colouration of residual deference or of outlandish, intensely individualistic or clannish localism to the social democracy of the up-country. After the brilliant and violent outbreak of democracy from Jackson through Polk, when the expansion of the political system of the United States reached its continental limits, and once and for all (we used to be taught) with Lincoln's noble words, and (we now say, also) his ruthless politics, democracy and capitalist economic organization based on personal, individual liberty – a legal freedom of thought and person and even more, of thoughtless action within the social sanctions of the local community, together with governance not by an executive, but by law-makers and judges – became established alongside private property, which as its elder brother among American freedoms, still kept pride of place.

Democracy and 'wealth' (called 'prosperity' when used without perjorative connotation and considered as a 'flow' rather than a stock) maintained their dialectic struggle through the decades 1870–1930, when the great American industrial region – the Northeast and the eastern Middle West – experienced modern industrial growth. The absolutely equal joint position of these two principles in the American public pantheon was confirmed in the presidential election of 1896, when the nation was made safe for the gold standard and the fundamental rights of capital were written in stone in the bland visage of William McKinley by the exercise of the ballot. The contradiction between property and democracy was sealed over by the concordat of 'Progressivism' in both political parties and across all the Wests – Middle, South and Far. The arrangement included the charade of anti-trust, the token federal regulatory commissions, the rather appreciable regulation and licensing of public utility monopolies at the state level, and sporadic intrusions of the law in matters of worker safety, health standards, weights and measures, and the like. Through the strong rising tides of prosperity from 1896 to 1929, in the boom of 1896–1903, the First World War, and the twenties between 1922 and 1928, the Emersonian observation of nearly a century earlier was applicable once again: 'Things are in the saddle and ride mankind'. For 'things' to be in the saddle meant in the American ideological context, economic, and in this earlier period particularly industrial, growth.

That democracy, or at least a perception of the ultimate possibility of democracy, could make large-scale capitalist organization work was shown by the behaviour of the industrial labour force as it grew by leaps and bounds. A quick summary has room to mention only three features in the formation of an industrial culture of proletarians and petty bureaucrats: (1) the conversion of a generation of farm and small-town native youth to the jobs and life of urban and suburban cultures – an army of tens of thousands pouring in every year from the countryside; (2) the Americanization of 25 million European immigrants, both of the 'old' immigration from Germany, Scandinavia, and the British Isles, and after 1880 the 'new' immigration from Italy and Central Europe; (3) the taming of the labour movement by political bossism and the courts. In these respects and in many others – particularly by the action of rising wages and the provision of public education – liberal democracy strengthened the workings of capitalism. This is not surprising except to those who see the history backwards from the present. Democracy and capitalism grew up hand in hand as prosperity diffused the evidences of material improvement, and the promises of still more, widely enough to strengthen their marriage, despite fears of monopoly, dehumanizing routines, bosses, and the capital's frequent ruthless use of its superior legal position. Despite – or perhaps because of – some growth in scale and discipline in plants and a surge of financial and organizational concentration in firms, the system worked through the 1920s to produce continuous rises in the production and productivity indexes in agriculture as well as manufacturing. A third essential element in the American ideology – pragmatic materialism – gives meaning to the phrase 'the system worked'.

The violent withdrawal of public confidence in the 'conservative–liberal', or traditionally progressive, programme in the election of 1932 struck at both its ideological bases in the interests of just such a pragmatism. Unrestricted control over labour, finance and capital was withdrawn from the private sector and the skittishness about concentrations of public power in a central authority away from the local community suddenly evaporated in the sunshine of a president's winning smile. That the system and the ideology could support such legalized violence against its principles in the interest of getting fast results in a new and threatening situation had already been shown in Wilson's drastic war prepared-ness measures in 1916–18. The New Deal programme at first sought only immediate results in a dozen different directions which, though in fact closely interrelated, were dealt with by various and, to a degree, mutually contradictory laws. The third 'leg' of the ideology, which was in effect to have no ideology at all except action directed by a striving for 'prosperity', had survived the collapse of the other two.

The period over which the old-fashioned American ethos worked and was valid thus showed a way around what an Hegelian might have seen as its fatal contradiction. Liberty and prosperity could both be preserved by a convincing show of government, by the fostering of homogeneity of goals – even of character structures – in the population, all if done in an atmosphere of high economic opportunity and continued growth in jobs, output, and welfare. Like a bicycle, the two wheels of the American system – democracy and property – could keep the rider balanced and whizzing forward if he carried his weight right, had a smooth road, and pedalled like hell. When the road got rocky in the 1930s, the bicycle wobbled. And when it righted itself after 1948, it was – to change the sports metaphor slightly – a decidedly different ball game.

EUROPE AND AMERICA

Most Americans know nothing of European history. There are indeed no historians of Europe, as such, in America or even in Europe. Imagine such a one, all-seeing, all-wise, who knows the geography, the culture, the technology, the tastes, and the behaviour of the people over long spans of time, one who like Fernand Braudel can speak of 'the Mediterranean' as a unit or, in one breath, of the fishing and shipping cultures from the North Sea coasts, the British Isles, and the Atlantic coastline, as D.W. Meinig (1986) has done for colonial North America, who at first glance into the interior sees not feudal fiefdoms, boundaries and wars but the great central European plain broken by the Rhine, as the Mississippi breaks the Mid-West, and sees in the cities, not provincial and national capitals, but trading points, nodes of economic activity and social communication. Such a one (it would have to be an American to have so broad a continental perspective and so deep a detailed ignorance) would view nineteenth-

and twentieth-century European industrial history rather differently from even the widest views of Europe-born historians.

Yet the histories of the two continents are not so different after all. In both, in the late eighteenth and early nineteenth century, several regions of intense mercantile activity entered into light industry – textiles, metalworking and machine tools – located in relation to water power, the markets and commercial facilities of ports, and pre-existing supplies of some skilled rural and craft labour. The phenomenon first appeared along the west coast in England, then in the iron and coal lands of the Midlands, South Wales and southern Scotland; on the continent it began to occur along the Seine, the Meuse, the Rhine and its tributaries and in some of the ancient craft cities along the North Sea and Baltic coasts, in southern Germany and northern Italy, in Alsace and along the Rhône at Lyon. Northeastern United States is but another example, at the commercial centres located on the Delaware and the Hudson (Philadelphia and New York), from Boston in a semi-circle 40 miles to the west from Providence to southern New Hampshire and in the Connecticut valley as far north as southern Vermont.

By mid-century, after accumulation of both real and financial capital, and with the experience of financing governments and wars (which in the United States meant the Civil War), banking and capital markets weighed in in time to help create the railroads and large-scale processes which a common industrial technology made available. On both continents, coal played its agglomerating and concentrating role from the 1840s on. After 1850, the huge steel plants burst from the ground, like giant mushrooms, in the valleys of the Rhine and the Ohio Rivers and their tributaries: the Ruhr, the Saar, the Moselle, the Allegheny and the Monongahela, the Mahoning and the north-emptying Meuse (Maas), Sambre, Scheldt and Cuyahoga. Both along the Rhine, its tributaries and canals, and down the Great Lakes, the systems of water and rail transport moved ores, coal, coke, heavy equipment, and iron and steel products to and from remote sources of minerals and dense industrial districts – the fast-multiplying sites of machinery manufacture, the railroad shops and marshalling yards, and the coastal centres of shipping, banking, and the earlier light industrial manufacture. The growth and diffusion of the market for manufactures over wide areas, the proliferation and exchanges of a common technology, the mobility of inter-national capital – all in all the continuous spread of a modern, successful, bourgeois culture, like a sheet of water over Western Europe and Northeast and North Central United States – drew one region, one state, one national unit, one local culture after another into the whirl. In the careful tracing of each nation's history by Alan Milward and Berek Saul (1977: ch. 3–5, 10) nothing is more impressive than the record of smaller nations – Switzerland, Sweden, Belgium, Norway, Denmark, finally the Netherlands and in Germany, Saxony and Würtemburg/Baden – areas all vastly different in resources, access to transport, industrial history and in many details of agrarian culture. All between 1850 and 1900, found something to do so as to produce national income growth rates of between 15 and 25 per cent per decade.[1]

Even more astonishing from an Anglocentric economist's view are the areas deep in Central Europe that come to life, both the old mining centres of the sixteenth century and those that had experienced the eighteenth-century textile industrialization – Saxony, Silesia, Bohemia. The spilling of this over the Alps into the northern Italian lands of the Renaissance completes the nineteenth century's series of 'spurts' of modernization in Western Europe. It is paralleled in a small way in the United States by the outcropping, and eventual in-migration from New England, of the major part of the textile manufacture in the southeastern Piedmont, the echo effect of the northern heavy industry growth at the Birmingham coal and ore deposits, and some modern urbanization in the rail terminal city of Atlanta. Then beginning in the 1880s, what Schumpeter termed the 'Third Kondratieff' – the burst of new technology in electricity and chemical processes, including in the latter the internal combustion engine, carried large-scale industry into the twentieth century.

The history, then, is that of the growth, like the tangled grasses, vines, bushes and trees in a fertile river valley (in this case an ocean valley), of one huge, inter-communicating capitalist culture. In all the basic components of a growing economy, similar trends and tendencies manifest themselves. The characteristic Western demographic pattern begins to appear; death rates fall toward a lower asymptote of 15–20 per thousand, the falling urban middle-class birth rate infects the whole income distrubution, above and below. Differences in the timing create local or national population bulges, to which for some areas migration provides an adjustment in local factor proportions over the whole two-continent space. Educational systems, state-controlled and financed, are erected, literacy increases, and new structures of scientific and technical training and discovery are superimposed on the ancient ecclesiastical centres of humanistic and theological learning. The scientific theories and knowledge underlying modern technology are elaborated along a common front from Moscow to Berkeley, California, and the specific arts of intervention develop, coloured by local cultures, individual mental sets, and economic opportunities. Ideas and inventions wherever created are readily picked up and carried to points of advantageous application.

This mass of innovation, of creativity, of industrial and agricultural production was mediated, as it were, by the human organizations through which individual men, alone and in associated groups, dominated, persuaded or purchased the services and allegiances of others in what was in effect, if not in spirit, a cooperative social enterprise. But the forms of organization and their modes of operation and control required, and ordinarily exhibited, the finest of adjustment to techniques, materials, products and market on the one hand, and to the social characteristics of the local regional human environments on the other. Until late into the nineteenth century, on both sides of the Atlantic, an intensely competitive business atmosphere prevailed; entrepreneurs and rentiers followed Marx's 'law of Moses and the prophets' – to accumulate, and to exploit and expand. After 1880 at many points, private entrepreneurs banded together, to shelter themselves from one another's competition, in syndicates, cartels, and large financial combinations and structures. This was a universal tendency in Europe and the United States. In America, a 'progressive' ethos produced the idea of 'anti-trust', enforcing competition in manufacturing and where competition did not promise to work, the idea of state regulation and control. Perhaps the very fractionation of sovereignty, the strength of individual states as organizational units in America favoured this. Many progressives too displayed a technocratic mentality, and revealed a bias toward professional government, a government by experts. In Europe the state in this period behaved somewhat differently. The consciousness of social subordination, remaining, no doubt, from the imprinting of a thousand years of feudalism and Catholic doctrine, had not died. The Church and large sections of the peasantry were fundamentally and philosophically not liberal and not at all capitalistic in attitudes and values. European capitalism had not had its slate wiped as clean as in America, of what had been written on the board hundreds of years before – a close sense of community, of social interdependence. Socialism was an important counterforce, and governments were pushed to develop worker welfare programmes. Labour parties formed in a futile effort to bring to pass democratic socialism as the means to harness the expansive and exploitative power of capital.

The political response of continental national societies to this international subversion by liberal capitalism and socialism alike was the idealization of the nation. This gave Europe a collection of strong and varied cultures and an exciting body of literature and art. But in the end, the word 'nation' served conservative politicians and, later, Fascist demogogues, as ultimately 'race' served the politicians of the American South, as a point around which to rally the conservative fears and hatreds of the 'little people'. The simultaneous growth of socialist and nationalist emotion after 1900 produced in the political crisis of 1914 the enlistment of the German, British and French socialist parties under the flags of their respective empires. The enemy was not within, but across the Rhine, and out of that mind-set, in the 1920s (which from 1923 to 1928 in Germany were a time of brilliant technological achievement), National Socialism was born. The progressivist, experimental, energetic New Deal in America in the 1930s was matched in Europe by the immersion of large-scale industry in the totalitarian state in Central Europe and the breakdown into impotence of the governments of France and Britain.

In the end, an economic historian must bring 'ideology' back on centre stage. It is not a word that an old-fashioned American liberal can admire. It is a European word, and has a nasty polemical ring. The role of the ideology of nationalism can be indeed most clearly seen by looking at the European developments not from the West looking east, but from the East looking west, i.e. by looking at Europe in a Russian mirror. One of Alexander Gerschenkron's last books – the penultimate effort of that remarkable émigré scholar to present and explain his vision of European industrialization – bears in fact this title and makes this effort (Gerschenkron 1970).[2] His schema can be shown as follows, with the addition of a column on an aspect on which he is not very precise, i.e. ideology:

Country	Source of capital and management	Presumed political ideology
Britain	Small-scale 'original accumulations', factor markets	'Bourgeois' democracy
Germany and mid-continent	Large credit banks, firms, and combines	Corporatism
Russia	Centralized state, mercantilism	Absolutism

Industrialization, he says, was achieved by each of these routes sequentially in Europe, a nation's particular history depending on the time, circumstances, posture, and especially on its state of 'relative backwardness', on the eve of its 'great spurt'.

Now this schema had a certain interest at the time and place at which it was advanced, i.e. the Harvard Department of Economics in the 1950s. It emphasized that a national production index could 'spurt' under several different organizational forms and in a variety of cultural and historical contexts. It threw off a coloured light from the complex, many-sectioned crystal of Europe's national histories and it put in the shade the simpler models of development then in vogue and in use. At points, Gerschenkron's schema invites comparison in scope and 'scientific' pretension with that of Schumpeter, his immediate predecessor and evident model in the role of great European scholar in the Harvard Department. But Schumpeter's attitudes and sweep were essentially aristocratic and imperial; he took all economic thought, and the whole dynamic capitalist world, as his oyster. Gerschenkron's focus throughout was on the national economy, *its* power structure, *its* organization, *its* controls, *its* position as a mercantilist power relative to its rivals. This is a richer view than one which considers all states or social structures to have been alike at all places and all times. It explains the specific patterns of institutional 'substitution' that evolved in different states as the formation of modern industry took shape. But the emphasis is on the formal style and organization of leadership under which a country's 'great spurt' occurred when its time had arrived. It is a notion that might have been evolved in the mind of a rather enlightened, but essentially authoritarian-minded Russian bourgeois, one who had stared too long perhaps at the blinding mercantilist achievements of Peter the Great.[3] It leaves no room to consider the profound questions of the relation within the capitalist culture as a whole between the growth of knowledge of techniques and resource supplies on the one hand and the expansion and focus of final demand on the other, a relationship which sets the limits of opportunity for entrepreneurs, however organized, and determines for a given region a zone of time within which its D-day can take place. Certainly in the growth of the various European industrial regions, these fundamental elements of production and trading opportunities – technological change, resource availabilities, population growth through natural increase and through net migration – weigh more heavily in setting the timing and extent of a 'spurt' than does the 'relative backwardness' of the various nation states that defined the political map of the Continent. The resounding 'theses' of Gerschenkron tell the size and shape and weave of the stockings the family hangs out on Christmas eve, but say nothing of when or why Santa Claus comes down the chimney. 'Relative backwardness' is thus a feature of almost no value in explaining the economic rise of a whole interconnected continental culture. It has no interest for American economic history, and this means that, taking a continental view, it has very little for Europe either.[4]

The political and cultural forms and relationships by which labour and enterprise are organized within the system of ideas and values by which men live, i.e. their ideologies, have, of course, when the chips are down, the greatest importance and interest for social life. They create not simply, or even principally, the economy, but the society which operates, with whatever results in terms of human happiness, as the technical wonders and miseries of modern industrialization unfold. The political and ideological accompaniments of Gerschenkron's three paths to a spurt of industry are by no means mere indifferent, value-free substitutes. He recognized this and wrote about it with passion in the case of the Soviet path. But nowhere in his writings did he dwell on the blank that is left under the heading of political economy in the second 'big bank' form, i.e. the German form, centralized and planned without the overlordship or ownership of assets by the state. Yet the preservation of the social and cultural values of liberal, market capitalism under twentieth-century production conditions has been the agonizing task of twentieth-century political and social organization, in America and Europe alike.

By Europe in an American mirror, then, I have meant European history as seen by an old-fashioned American liberal, one who clings to the idea that freedom and plenty, rather than power and plenty, are indissolubly linked. From such a view, the history of the nation states, their forms and their rivalries are a distracting nightmare. The common progress and the common confusion and disaster on both sides of the Pond are the imperfect products of liberal thought and attitudes, when pursued within the binding limits of national cultures. The important lesson of nineteenth-century history is the general growth of income and wealth over Western Europe and North America, when markets opened, factors gained mobility, technology became continuously fertile, and enterprise ceaselessly active. The fumbling fingers of the nation states, ancient and monarchical or newly-formed, even under bourgeois domination, sometimes pushed development along within national boundaries but as often interfered out of local, particularistic or military interests, and ended in disaster when the states themselves, like the early modern absolutist and bureaucratic empires to the east, became too centralized, too powerful, too far distanced from their base in liberal democracy. No doubt a truly common market would have been better. Even such a continent-wide arrangement, which America acquired in 1789, demands the encouragement, enforcement and monitoring of a body of officials themselves responsible to an electorate. The social effects of unbridled capitalism, and the long-run social interest in the environment, and in the care and preservation of the mind and the arts against the rude force of unrestricted democracy, still requires organizational structures that command respect and power equivalent to those of the economy. But all this is what Europe between today and 1992, and beyond, is trying to achieve. A new 'new economic history', written in a United Europe, or a United West, or a United Great Power World, will focus on and reveal the structures and motions of life both below the level of the nation and above it, far more than the national case histories of the 1950s and 1960s, whether examined alone or comparatively within Gerschenkron's curious model of relative backwardness.

But this is a dream not only for Europe but for America as it fumbles its way into the twenty-first century. Here it is a harder job since the simple goal of creating a homogeneous common market has long been attained. The 'problem' has been rather how to create a common society which is not a steamroller, one which can pass over the ground efficiently and still leave some varied life. Part of the problem lies in the educational system where today America seems sometimes simply to have given up. It is as one does with one's lawn sometimes: weary of trimming and rolling and endlessly mowing, one sits on the front porch and watches the grass and shrubs revert to the tangled wilderness. More immediately it concerns the relation of the culture to a vast and potentially powerful federal state, lurching in convulsive spurts from one social problem to another, rushing to fires indeed, but better equipped with TV cameras to capture the headlines than with hose and hook and ladder to put the fire out. It is not individual geographic entities that America must consolidate into an ordered union; it is individual interest groups, localities, classes, networks of associations, professions, age groups. The solution is not to abolish that state, but to make it responsible to social interests other than national defence and national aggression. America, as always, presents what a United Europe might become – the same possibilities, the same risks and the same dangers. Which continent today, one may ask, has the happier prospects ahead?

The principal source of America's and Europe's economic and political disasters of the interwar period lay outside the boundaries of any one nation, in a wholly ungoverned world of national individualisms, in the variety of sovereignties, and their uneven states of economic development and their discordant governmental forms. There is now a chance for perhaps half a dozen superpowers to form: America, Europe, Japan, China, possibly India, and whatever will lie within the boundaries of the Soviet Union. Africa, Latin America, the Middle East will still presumably remain 'trouble spots' in organizational chaos, still with the potential they showed in the nineteenth century for luring the 'Great Powers' into conflict on their terrain. The great power blocs today in relation to one another really are powerless since no one can dominate the others without destroying itself. A form then of social order imposed in each of them is ultimately the model for peace, order and amity among them all. American history shows a society forming within such a federal model, expanding for seventy years, then blowing apart, only to re-form as the frame for an industrializing expansion – again of vast dimensions – which ran another seventy years before a crisis. God forbid that anyone should suggest yet another cycle – a seventy-year cycle, say – which would predict yet another dissolution of the unity forged originally by the New Deal and the Second World War in the year 2000. But whether extended decades of hard times and ghastly internal political misery do come again to the industrialized West depends now not only on the behaviour of its own national entities, either individually or as a corporate group, but also on the course of history of the other of today's and tomorrow's great powers, both individually and in the development of a world order resting on structures and purposes in common. Perhaps, with eternal American optimism, and less than usual American egotism, we may feel that that is a cause, not for despair, but for hope.

ACKNOWLEDGEMENTS

I am much indebted to Professor Sylla for some frank and timely comments and criticisms. I doubt, however, that my corrections will have wholly satisfied him.

NOTES

1   See Kuznets (1965: table 2.5). See also my tabulation of these data in Parker (1968), especially table 2.
2   The book also offers a backward look into the body of Gerschenkron's thoughts and attitudes as they crystallized in the 1950s and 1960s in his concept of 'relative backwardness' and its application to the cases of the various Western European nations.
3   Gerschenkron (1970: lecture 3, 62–96). Unlike the acceptance given to these ideas by Gerschenkron's students, who sat in his lectures and directly felt the force of his personality and his learning, my own attitude to his work and influence, based on his writings, is decidedly ambivalent. These views, which are not appropriate to be aired in this space, are elaborated in a separate essay, 'European industrialization: The perspective from the East and from the West', presented to the Social Science History Association at its meetings in Washington, DC, in November 1989.
4   This is clearly an overstatement. The division of an area into separate political sovereignties has both retardative and stimulating effects on its rate of economic growth. The retardative effects are those dwelt on in all the economics descended from Adam Smith's original insight about the division of labour and the extent of the market and Ricardo's model of the gains from trade and international specialization. Free product and factor flows, equalization of marginal costs and marginal revenues, free exchanges of information within a single state – all these features contribute to the formation of an efficiently functioning capitalistic economic machine. This is the

positive side to political unification on a continental, or a world, scale. This analysis, however, neglects important features of the historical development of industry within a multinational world capitalism of the past two hundred years. In particular, it neglects, as Gerschenkron emphasized, the incentive effects of the nations' competitive mercantilisms and the value of a variety of separate local sources of creative innovation. These are indeed 'powers of production' spoken of by Friedrich List in *The National System of Political Economy* (1904). They must develop within a specific environment before their more generalizable features can be extracted and disseminated throughout the world. Like the varieties of vegetation and wildlife, much is lost by cultural homogenization in the interests of a narrowly conceived engineering efficiency passing itself off as a set of prices and economic values.

The subject is too grand and complex to be treated in a footnote. A very suggestive treatment of the economic significance of a customs union for the political unification of an area is offered by Hubert Kiesewetter for the German Zollverein in the national unification of the German states under the Prussian-led empire, in 1870. (Kiesewetter 1987).

REFERENCES

Gerschenkron, Alexander (1970) *Europe in the Russian Mirror*, Cambridge: Cambridge University Press.

Kiesewetter, Hubert (1987) 'Economic preconditions for Germany's nation-building in the nineteenth century', in H. Schulze (ed.) *Nation-Building in Central Europe*, Leamington Spa, Hamburg, New York: Berg, pp. 81–105.

Kuznets, Simon (1965) *Modern Economic Growth: Rate, Structure, Spread*, New Haven, Conn.: Yale University Press.

List, Friedrich (1904) *The National System of Political Economy*, trans., London: Longman.

Meinig, D.W. (1986) *The Shaping of America*, vol. I, *Atlantic America, 1492–1800*, New Haven, Conn.: Yale University Press.

Milward, Alan and Saul, S.B. (1977) *The Development of the Economies of Continental Europe, 1850–1914*, Cambridge, Mass.: Harvard University Press and London: George Allen & Unwin.

Parker, William N. (1968) 'Economic history seen through the national income accounts', *Zeitschrift für die Gesamte Staatswissenschaft* 124 (1), 148–58.

Chapter 6

Kinks, tools, spurts, and substitutes: Gerschenkron's rhetoric of relative backwardness

Donald N. McCloskey

Alexander Gerschenkron, one of the thin, bright stream of historical economists before the name, was educated as an economist and then used his education on historical questions. Economists believe in numbers. Gerschenkron the economist became a master of numbers in the 1930s and 1940s, when national income accounting and index numbers were on the frontier of statistical economics.

What made Gerschenkron and his work peculiar is that unlike most economists he also believed in words. He believed in them not merely the way any good writer does, or any widely read person who went to school in Mitteleuropa before its fall. He believed in words the way a literary critic does. His theory of relative backwardness rested on the theory of index numbers, true, with all its scientific authority, but it also rested on wordlore from novels and plays and poetry.

This peculiarity shows up best, perhaps, in comparison with another great student of European industrialization, Walt Rostow. Both started as statistical experts, Gerschenkron more penetrating; both wrote well, Rostow better; both thought in terms of grand theories of economic growth. It is no disrespect to Rostow, however, to observe that he uses a phrase like 'take-off into self-sustained growth' without irony or self-reflection, the way most economists use their words. A literary analysis of Rostow's work would show the master using metaphors and storylines without recognizing that he was using metaphors and storylines. Gerschenkron, by contrast, was obsessively interested in watching himself use words. Both men were wordspinners, of course, but Gerschenkron was also a critic.

His work invites rhetorical criticism. One cannot look at Gerschenkron's theory innocently, as a thing in itself. One places some sort of grid over it, and measures it along the notches cut into the grid.

The usual grid is a folk philosophy of science. Historians and especially economists share a grid marked by the positivism of the 1930s. Gerschenkron might be said to have offered a 'hypothesis', itself properly part of a 'hypothetico-deductive system', which can be 'falsified' by 'empirical testing' against 'observable implications'. His own words sometimes evoked these popular misunderstandings of scientific method, as near the beginning of 'Economic

Backwardness in Historical Perspective' (1952, when he was 48 years old (reprinted 1962)):

> Historical research consists essentially in application to *empirical material* of various *sets of empirically derived hypothetical generalizations* and in *testing the closeness of the resulting fit*, in the hope that in this way certain *uniformities*, certain typical situations, and certain *typical relationships among individual factors* in these situations can be ascertained.[1]
>
> (Gerschenkron 1962: 6)

And elsewhere he would say repeatedly that the concept of relative backwardness ('concept' and 'process' were favourite placeholders in Gerschenkron's prose) is 'an operationally usable concept' (Gerschenkron 1962: 354).

The words did not, in his practice, carry the freight they usually do in economics. He used Russian novels as a source for economic history and he recognized that his statistical work had normative content. In using the resources of language to argue his case he did not suggest that verbal evidence is necessarily less conclusive than statistical evidence. He wrote on the Soviet novel as historical evidence and contributed to literary journals. He used the absence of accounting terms in the Russian language of the eighteenth century to indicate the absence of commercial attitudes (Gerschenkron 1968: 449; 1970: 81). This early exponent of historical statistics, Paul Gregory notes, used mainly literary evidence to claim that Russian agriculture stagnated after emancipation.

The grid of folk philosophy does not recognize much subtlety. Its demarcations go some way towards classifying science: scientific/non-scientific, objective/subjective, positive/normative, observable/non-observable, justification/discovery, but they do not go very far. They cannot show science in detail. Furthermore the received demarcations are normative rather than positive but give no guidance on how to reason about norms. An observer of science using them cannot see, for instance, why scientists disagree, since every scientist claims stoutly to operate on the good side of each demarcation – scientific, objective, positive, observable, and justificatory. The grid therefore worsens disagreements. It leaves scientists to conclude that if another scientist disagrees with him the other must be incompetent. The grid of folk philosophy is itself unscientific, a bad description, and a bad moral theory of scholarship.

More often Gerschenkron applied another grid, the practical philosophy of the scholar, an older ethic than the positivism of the mid-twentieth century. Gerschenkron exhibited to a high degree the values of Continental scholarship. In a way that contrasts with British and some American traditions, he practised, as he affirmed, 'a program of research' – not a method of scholarship but a plan of life. His range as a scholar – at ease with mathematics, history, statistics and a dozen languages – was subordinated to the programme.

The programme was to yield not sharp or mechanical 'tests of the theory', but mature judgements, satisfying, as he frequently put it, 'the sense of reasoned adequacy'. This phrase itself is not without mystery, but he did not intend the historical reasoning to be kept mysterious. Doubtless some matters of scholarship would need to remain tacit, but Gerschenkron had no patience with the unfootnoted *argumentum ex cathedra*, even from eminent scholars. Repeatedly he advocated and exhibited explicitness in argument. His enthusiastic review in 1953 of Franco Venturi's *Il Populismo russo* (Gerschenkron 1968: 455) congratulates Venturi for a 'mature understanding': 'And yet one cannot but wish that the author had decided to share his thinking more fully with his readers'. Twelve years later he warmly praised his student Albert Fishlow for 'the statistical appendixes in which the author offers a full insight into his laboratory and without which no real appreciation of the importance of the study and of the validity of its interpretative results is possible' (Gerschenkron 1965: viii).

The scholarly ethos of care is prominently commended in Gerschenkron's reviews and in his footnote polemics. It has two parts: avoidance of error in the details and modesty in the putting forward of conclusions. We stop believing someone who makes little errors ('Bad spelling, bad reasoning') or who draws conclusions hastily ('How can she say such a thing?'). Gerschenkron here does not inhabit the world of modern economics, in which theory provides a check on facts and in which a blackboard exercise is said to have 'policy implications'. He detested theories of history that can in their rigidity supply bridges across evidential voids – Marxism most notably, of course – and favoured theories (such as Arnold Toynbee's) that provided merely a way to shape the facts into a story. The good theories, he said, were 'fruitful' in the sense of suggesting new enquiries; they did not close the conversation. In this he was a modern professional historian, whose discipline is not economic or historical theory but the shaping of tales constrained by fact.

But neither the folk's philosophy of science nor the scholar's credo of virtue is much of a grid for measuring Gerschenkron. They cannot register his peculiarly literary bent. A better grid is the ancient discipline of rhetoric, that is to say, the study since the Greeks of the available means of persuasion. As Paul Hohenberg has put it, we need a way of understanding 'how we experience Gerschenkron's writing', to better understand the meeting of number and word in the mid-Atlantic.

For instance, *ethos*, character, the implied author figures heavily in Gerschenkron's writing. Gerschenkron wrote judgementally about scholarly discourses, raising up or breaking down the *ethos* of other scholars. Most scientific prose suppressed such judgements. In a few pages early in *Europe in the Russian Mirror* Gerschenkron admired Marc Bloch and Max Weber and Tugan-Baranovskii – of the last, 'valuable contribution', 'probably the most original Russian economist, ... amazingly broad in his interests', 'a serious scholar', his greatest compliment (Gerschenkron 1970: 6ff). Such compliments serve more to honour the author than the subject. The author exhibits the good taste to admire good work. And the old Russian economist's 'amazingly broad interests' turn out to be various subjects within economics; whereas the author himself, also a

Russian economist, ranges over statistical theory, Greek poetry, and the Boston Celtics basketball team.

Part of his *ethos*, of course, was his style of writing, the most obviously 'rhetorical' part of anyone's rhetoric. Gerschenkron delighted in obscure but fine words in English, such as 'flummox', a special favourite. He spoke mainly in the idiom of cultivated Europe, which made some sentences pure Latin, especially in earlier writings. Most of the prose in his most famous and earliest article on the subject, 'Economic backwardness in historical perspective', though lucid, is undistinguished. He appeared to be playing the sober scientist, and waxed eloquent only when the subject turns to ideology ('Ricardo is not known to have inspired anyone to change "God Save the King" into "God Save Industry"' (Gerschenkron 1952 (1962), 24f)).

Beyond *ethos* and style, Gerschenkron recognized that social theories are metaphors. He recognized that words are not mere tags for things behind them but have an intent to persuade in the scholarly forum. When Gerschenkron speaks of the 'tensions' produced by economic backwardness he was aware that this was a manner of human speaking constrained by the facts of the world, not a raw fact in itself. If the Russian aristocracy used the condition of its serfs as a symbol of Russia's shameful backwardness, as Olga Crisp argues so persuasively, then the words have political and then economic consequences. The ideology of economic development resides in the metaphors used, whether of 'nation-building' or 'development' or 'backwardness'. One might ask whether Gerschenkron thought of the state as a Good Tsar or as an Ivan the Terrible; it is not clear. The nation itself is a metaphor; 'Germany' does not literally do anything, individual Germans do, as Gerschenkron pointed out, when they export bullion or banking to Italy. The very word 'growth' embodies a biological metaphor, which could be specialized, as Paul Hohenberg has observed, to tropical growth (a capitalist view that growth is hard to kill) or sub-arctic growth (a socialist view that growth is hard to sustain, and must therefore have the attention of the state).

Gerschenkron's chief scientific accomplishment was to undermine the metaphor of social stages which had dominated nineteenth-century and much twentieth-century thought. Henry Maine, Auguste Comte, Friedrich List, Karl Marx, Werner Sombart, Bruno Hildebrand, and latterly Walt Rostow thought of a nation as a person, with predictable stages of development from birth to maturity. If the stage theorists viewed the child as the father of the man, Gerschenkron was a new Freud, noting the pathologies arising from retarded growth.

He favoured his own metaphors of 'spurt' and 'relative backwardness' as against 'take-off' or 'absolute prerequisites', but not because he believed his to be less metaphorical. Wordlore was no ornamental appendage to the real work. European philology knew that the work was the word. Gerschenkron was aware in particular of the economistic character of his metaphors, especially the notion of 'substitutes' for prerequisites. 'The German investment bank was a substitute for the missing or inadequate available prerequisite' (Gerschenkron 1970: 103).

The word might be interpreted in the illuminating jargon of neoclassical economics as the speed of industrialization arising from a 'production function' with 'sustainable inputs' of demand, finance, entrepreneurship, disciplined labour, and so forth. Or it might be interpreted, as Paul David argues persuasively, as the substitute paths in a branching process of choice. In any case it is a metaphor with consequences. The size of the spurt, for example, has consequences: 'along with differences in the vehemence of the process were the differences in its character' (Gerschenkron 1970: 72). The argument persuades economists in part because it relies on their master metaphors. In the neoclassical interpretation, at greater speed of industrialization certain inputs would rise in marginal product, and the Soviets would naturally build giant factories and crush a complaining peasantry. In the branching interpretation, greater speed would require a choice of quick-but-centralized branches.

Gerschenkron justified his economistic metaphors in a mainly Kantian rather than a Baconian way. Like many scholars as they get older, he appears to have become more Kantian and less naively Baconian, becoming more convinced, as Kant said, that concepts without perceptions are empty and perceptions without concepts are blind. The classic essay on 'Economic backwardness' was first published in a volume edited by Bert Hoselitz in 1952. It is thoroughly Baconian and British. Things were as they were. The 'story of European industrialization' (Gerschenkron 1952 (1962): 26) is a 'story' only incidentally; really it is a scientific compound 'synthesized from the available historical information' (Gerschenkron 1952 (1962: 7). There is no trace here of 'story' as a shaping fiction, disciplined by the facts of matter but underdetermined by them. By 1962, however, at the age of 58, Gerschenkron is speaking of his argument in a different way. The 'Postscript' to the first collection of essays, in 1962, speaks of '*viewing* European history as patterns of substitution' (Gerschenkron 1962: 359). Failures of such a view 'may be such as to require and perhaps suggest an *organizing principle* very different from the variations in the degree of backwardness' (Gerschenkron 1962: 364). And likewise in similar words.

These are points of view, weights so to speak in a statistical index of industrial output. That is, they are human choices, not things-in-themselves. As William Parker has argued, Gerschenkron's experience as a double refugee from Russia and then Austria appears to have led him to thinking hard about points of view, relative backwardness, and translation.

Typologies or categories are points of view. In 'The typology of industrial development as a tool of analysis' (Gerschenkron 1968: 77–97), which was first published in 1962, Gerschenkron makes assertions about the uses of typologies that would be unintelligible to a true Baconian or to his positivist descendents. His placing of the extremes of stage theories and uniqueness theories into a unified pattern

> does not at all mean that the extreme approaches are necessarily 'wrong' in any meaningful sense of the term. Since any approach of this kind ...

inevitably deals not with the unmanageable and incomprehensible 'totality' of
the phenomena but with sets of abstractions, different approaches yield
different insights, and it is in terms of those insights that the value of an
individual approach must be judged. The results need not be commensurate.

(Gerschenkron 1968: 79)

And later: 'Historical generalizations are not universal propositions that are
falsified as soon as a single black swan has been observed. Our hypotheses are
not "lawlike"' (Gerschenkron 1968: 97).

Or consider the repeated images of visualizing in two pages of *Europe in the
Russian Mirror*, published in 1970 (the very title and theme of the book, of
course, mirrors an active vision): 'Once we *view* the industrial development of
Europe *in this fashion, it appears as* a unity ...' '[C]apital disposition is only one
of very many examples of *an orderly pattern* ...' Relative backwardness 'gives us
first of all *an opportunity to bring some order* into the apparent chaos, to
establish, that is, a morphology or typology of the development' (Gerschenkron
1970: 104, italics added). Or elsewhere, on applying it to mercantilism, 'it
conceives of Russia as a part of Europe' (Gerschenkron 1970: 87; and 'regarded',
'arraign', 'picture', and 'conceived' on the same page). Most Kantian of all, after
quoting Goethe to the same effect: 'What we call facts or reality, including
Colbert or Napoleon, are just phenomena of a low degree of abstraction'
(Gerschenkron 1970: 63). The scientist here is no passive observer of nature. He
chooses his ways of worldmaking.

Facts passively observed constrain what can be seen, of course, and
Gerschenkron drew willingly on the rhetoric of British empiricism when it suited
the rhetorical situation. At the end of the passage just quoted (Gerschenkron
1970: 104) he recurs to the nature of things (as against our way of seeing them):
'the degree of backwardness becomes then a causal principle, explaining for us
the nature of the process of industrial change'. Even in this, however, he is
pointing to the active observer, with the phrase 'explaining *for us*'. In the
sentences leading up to the assertion of how things are (as distinct from how they
seem) Gerschenkron insists on the shaping of the observer, who 'sees' a 'pattern',
a morphology 'temporally seen'. And the paragraph following returns to how we
see the matter: '[T]he more backward a country, the more barren *appears* its pre-
industrial landscape.... This then is ... my *picture* of European industrialization'
(Gerschenkron 1970: 104).

Gerschenkron drew on the doctrines of British empiricism to attack other
theories, but again with Kantian supplementation. The trouble with stage
theories, he says, is that '[t]hey are not very consistent with crude empiricism,
and are damaged seriously when confronted with the relevant facts as we know
them' (Gerschenkron 1970: 101). He appeals here to what 'we', the scientific
community, know; and to the vocabulary of 'consistent with ... empiricism' and
'confronted with the relevant facts', fragments of positivist dogma. Yet he injects
the 'not very' consistent and the 'crude' empiricism, urbane ironies distancing

him from a positivism that would forget Kant. Gerschenkron was, of course, an empiricist, but a sophisticated one, who understood that scientists do not merely tally up the world's noumena.

Gerschenkron's theory, then, is by his own description 'a way of looking' at the world. The metaphor of 'substitution' is useful because it is 'a construct that ... helps to conceive Europe as a graduated unit' (Gerschenkron 1970: 108). Note that the virtue claimed is conversational. Talking this way will be helpful to the historical conversation. He speaks frequently of the theory as a classification or typology, by which he means the classification of botanical species (Gerschenkron 1970: 96), with Russia the red butterfly at one end and Britain the blue one at the other. He is hostile to mathematical or logic metaphors to describe growth. Rostow's and other theories of prerequisites are described as 'beautiful exercises in logic' (Gerschenkron 1970: 101; cf. 101 middle) which 'have been defeated by history'.

Emphatically, to repeat, Gerschenkron did not view metaphors as mere ornaments. They are the stuff of thought. He was always reflecting on the aptness of the metaphors we live by. Consider, for example, his elaborate discussion of the metaphor of 'continuity' in history (Gerschenkron 1968). He noted that the continuity in question has often been misconstrued as philosophical. The philosophical difficulty was raised by Parmenides and Zeno: if everything is perfectly continuous, change is impossible. In a manner of speaking, things are packed so tightly that they cannot move. The economist will recognize the point as analogous to an extreme form of economic equilibrium; the physicist will recognize it as analogous to the maximum entropy of physics. If human nature does not 'really' change then history will be a string of weary announcements that the more things change the more they stay the same. More to the point in economics, if the economy is 'really' in equilibrium all the time, then nothing remains to be done. Gerschenkron (1968: 12) noted that such a metaphysics would close the book of history. A history or economics that began with the Parmenidean continuum would never speak.

For the purposes of social science Gerschenkron rejects the transition from the connectedness of all change to an absence of change. True, if you squint and fit a curve then no economic change looks discontinuous in the mathematical sense; but it is wrong then to deduce that 'really' there is no change at all, or that kinks don't happen. And here Gershenkron again criticizes alternative metaphors. 'Continuity' in the strict mathematical sense, he urged, must be kept distinct from 'continuity' in the storytelling sense.

Economists have often been muddled about this philosophical distinction, drawing surprising ideological implications from it. Alfred Marshall enshrined on the title page of *The Principles* his motto '*natura non facit saltum*' (nature does not make a jump; the phrase dates back through Linnaeus and Leibnitz to Jacques Tissot in 1613). Marshall himself perhaps believed that the ability to represent behaviour with differentiable functions implies that marginalism is a good description of human behaviour. It is less sure that he believed that the lack of jumps in nature (this on the eve of quantum physics), implies that people should not jump either, and should change society only gradually. Anyway, neither implication follows; though both have been attributed to neoclassical economics, neither is necessary for it. Much bitter controversy has assumed that neoclassical economics depends on smooth curves and in consequence must advocate smooth social policies. The peculiar alliance between discrete mathematics and Marxian economics has this origin, as does the enthusiasm of some conservative writers for continuities in economic history. Gerschenkron cursed both their houses; the social scientist should study change and continuity 'unbothered by the lovers and haters of revolutions who must find themselves playgrounds and battlegrounds outside the area of serious scholarship' (Gerschenkron 1968: 39).

The main problems of continuity and discontinuity, however, are not solvable in seminars on philosophy. They are practical problems in the uses of measurement, and must be solved in the workshop of the economic or historical scholar. When shall we say that the industrial revolution happened? Gerschenkron gives an answer confined to industry, for in common with most economic historians he regards agriculture and services as laggards in economic growth.

> In a number of major countries of Europe ... after a lengthy period of fairly low rates of growth came a moment of more or less sudden increase in the rates, which then remained at the accelerated level for a considerable period. That was the period of the great spurt in the respective countries' industrial development.... The rates and the margin between them in the 'pre-kink' and the 'post-kink' periods appear to vary depending on the degree of relative backwardness of the country at the time of the acceleration.
>
> (Gerschenkron 1968: 33–4).

The level at which such discontinuity is to be observed is at choice. As Gerschenkron remarks,

> If the seat of the great spurt lies in the area of manufacturing, it would be inept to try to locate the discontinuity by scrutinizing data on large aggregate magnitudes such as national income.... By the time industry has become bulky enough to affect the larger aggregate, the exciting period of the great spurt may well be over.
>
> (Gerschenkron 1968: 34–5)

The word 'inept' is notable here, speaking of seeing as a skill. In a footnote to these sentences he remarks that 'Walt Rostow's failure to appreciate this point has detracted greatly from his concept of the take-off, which in principle is closely related to the concept of the great spurt as developed by this writer'.

The point is a good one, and applies to all questions of continuity in aggregate economics. Small (and exciting) beginnings will be hidden by the mass until well after they have become routine. Joel Mokyr has put it as a matter of arithmetic: if the traditional sector of an economy is growing at a slow 1 per cent per annum, and starts with 90 per cent of output, the modern sector growing at 4 per cent per annum will take three-quarters of a century to account for as much as half of output (Mokyr 1985: 5). It can be called the weighting theorem (or the waiting theorem, for the wait is long when the weight is small to begin with), of which Harley's (1982) essay on cotton in the industrial revolution is a striking example.

In other words, the search for discontinuity in an aggregate time-series raises the question of the level at which we should do our social thinking, the aggregation problem. Yet Gerschenkron himself did not answer the question well, and was hoist by his own petard. For Italian industrial output he placed his 'big spurt' in the period 1896–1908, and wished to explain it with big German banks exported to Italy in the 1890s (the timing mattered because Gerschenkron was obsessed with the notion, as Federico and Toniolo have pointed out, that French or indeed Italian banks were utterly different in character from German banks; French and Italian banks were already there). Stefano Fenoaltea, once his student, anticipated the weighting theorem for the Italian case (Fenoaltea, forthcoming). Surely, Fenoaltea reasoned, the components of the industrial index – the steel output and the chemical output – are the 'real' units of economic analysis (note the similarity of this rhetoric to that advocating a micro-economic foundation for macro-economics). If the components started accelerating *before* the new banks appeared, becoming bulky only later, then the new banks could not have been the initiating force. Alas, the components did just this. They spoil Gerschenkron's bank-led story: the components accelerated not in the 1890s but in the 1880s, not after but before the banks. To paraphrase Gerschenkron on Rostow, by the time the progressive components of industry had become bulky enough to affect the larger aggregate, the exciting period was well over.

Yet the moral is still Gerschenkron's, or Kant's: that continuity and discontinuity are *tools* (a favourite word) 'forged by the historian rather than something inherently and invariantly contained in the historical matter.... At all times it is the ordering hand of the historian that creates continuities or discontinuities' (Gerschenkron 1968: 38). For the Italian case Homer nodded, but in nodding made the point. So does any choice of smoothness or suddenness in economic storytelling.

The point is that history, like economics, is a story we tell. Continuity and discontinuity are narrative devices, to be chosen for their storytelling virtues. Niels Bohr said once that 'It is wrong to think that the task of physics is to find out how nature is. Physics concerns what we can say about nature' (Moore 1966: 406). It is *our* say. We can choose to emphasize the continuous: 'Abraham begat Isaac; ... begat ... begat ... and Jacob begat Joseph the husband of Mary, of whom was born Jesus' (Matthew 1: 1–17). Or the discontinuous: 'There was in the days of Herod, the king of Judea, a certain priest named Zacharias' (Luke 1: 5). It is the same story, but its continuity is our creation, not God's.

Gerschenkron's hypothesis about European industrialization makes better sense if the language of 'hypothesis' is dropped and that of storytelling substituted. The Bulgarian experience, for example, 'rejects' the hypothesis, because Bulgaria's rate of industrial growth 'was obviously far below what one should expect in view of the country's degree of backwardness' (Gerschenkron 1970: 126; cf. 1962, 232). He notes that Bulgaria frittered away its governmental entrepreneurship on military adventures. In the 'failures' of the story one's attention is drawn to illuminating facts. In the peroration of *Europe in the Russian Mirror* he specifically rejects the language of hypothesis testing even while using it:

> For in trying to set up interpretative models [read 'stories'] historians do not deal in universal propositions which can never be verified and can only be refuted [a direct attack on positivist dogma]. We deal in particular or existential propositions. It is the very nature of an historical hypothesis [back to positivism: read 'plot'] to constitute a set of expectations which yields enlightenment ... within a spatially and temporally limited zone. To determine the delimitations of that zone does not mean at all a refutation of a hypothesis [if 'hypothesis' is not understood in its positivistic sense], but on the contrary its reinforcement as a tool of historical understanding.
>
> (Gerschenkron 1970: 130)

The last sentence makes no sense if relative backwardness is a 'hypothesis' like the inverse square law (incidentally, the *Oxford English Dictionary* gives the method-of-science definition as its third; none of its definitions fits Gerschenkron's usage exactly; his usage plays off the third definition, but is not identical with it). If planets were attracted inversely in proportion to the *cube* of the distance between them, that would be that. There would be no sense in which such a finding 'would not necessarily detract from my approach' (Gerschenkron 1970: 130). Relative backwardness, however, is not a scientific hypothesis in the usual sense. It is a device for telling a story, like the frontier in American history or the bourgeois in revolutionary France. It can be proven wrong (in fact these two have been) if it violates the sense of reasoned adequacy.

There is, of course, nothing unscientific about a story. Plate tectonics in geology is a story, not a universal hypothesis like the inverse square law or the Shrödinger equation. Better yet, and more conformable with Gerschenkron's delight in botanical analogies, the theory of evolution is a story. Determining the delimitations of evolution does not refute the hypothesis. Anti-evolutionists refute evolution by taking the falsificationist claims of folk philosophy seriously. The scientists who have mixed bad philosophy with their science deserve what they get from the fundamentalist preachers. As 'hypothesis' (*Oxford English Dictionary* definition 3) evolution is a failure because it is in positivistic terms 'meaningless'. But by the standard of reasoned adequacy it is, of course, a spectacular and continuing success.

The question is whether one can take as seriously in economics as in, say, the criticism of novels an assertion by Peter Brooks, in his *Reading for the Plot*: 'Our lives are ceaselessly intertwined with narrative, with the stories that we tell, all of

which are reworked in that story of our own lives that we narrate to ourselves. . . .
We are immersed in narrative' (Brooks 1985: 3). I would say yes, uncontro-
vertibly, for economic and other history. As the historian J.H. Hexter put it,
storytelling is 'a sort of knowledge we cannot live without' (Hexter 1986: 8).
This telling of stories was Gerschenkron's main project. Economists and
historians have not lived without it, ever. It is no accident that European
economics and the European novel were born at the same time. We live in an age
insatiate of plot.

Good empirical work in economics is like good history, in being realist fiction.
An historical economist such as Gerschenkron can be viewed as a realistic
novelist or a realistic playwright, a Balzac or a Strindberg. His work claims to
follow all the rules of actual worlds. (Well . . . all the *important* rules.) But of
course realism too is fictional. The evasion is similar in history: 'the plot of a
historical narrative is always an embarrassment and has to be presented as
"found" in the events rather than put there by narrative techniques' (White 1981:
20; cf. Megill and McCloskey 1987).

Constrained by evidence, we tell the stories about French coal mines or the
battle of Borodino as economic historians or as novelists. We do not find the
stories ready made. John Keegan has nicely illustrated the point in his book, *The
Face of Battle*. He speaks of the 'rhetoric of battle history' (Keegan 1977: 36) as
demanding that one cavalry regiment be portrayed as 'crashing' into another, a
case of 'shock' tactics. Yet an observant witness of such an encounter at
Waterloo reported that 'we fully expected to have seen a horrid crash – no such
thing! Each, as if by mutual consent, opened their files on coming near, and
passed rapidly through each other' (Keegan 1977: 149). A story is something
told to each other by human beings, not something existing ready-told in the very
railways or cavalry regiments or mute facts themselves.

As Piero Bolchini has pointed out, for example, Gerschenkron's telling of
industrialization on the Continent uses Britain as the mirror, always present if
seldom mentioned, the standard by which the story is told. The hypothetical
happy family in Anna Karenina likewise serves as an anti-plot to the dismally
unhappy one in the story. The anti-plot gives the target plot a meaning. The slow
and voluntaristic story of British industrialization, more implied than told in
Gerschenkron's writing, gives political meaning to the hurried and authoritarian
story of Russia.

The story of arriving at full industrialization, again, follows the storytelling in
psychology, which 'must first establish a goal state or valued endpoint. . . . [It
must] then select and arrange events in such a way that the goal state is rendered
more or less probable' (Gergen and Gergen 1986: 25f). So it is in history, most
self-consciously in the great nineteenth-century exponents of the science. In the
Preface to his mighty *History of the Conquest of Peru* (1843/48) William Prescott
justified carrying the story beyond the adventures of Pizzaro, down to the
integration of Peru into the Transatlantic empire: 'fixing the eye on this remoter
point, the successive steps of the narrative will be found leading to one great

result, and that unity of interest [will be] preserved which is scarcely less essential to historic than dramatic composition.'

Gerschenkron told the story of Petrine Russia by 'fixing his eye on the remoter points' in the time of Count Witte or Joseph Stalin, and on the one great result of forced industrialization, preserving thereby a unity of interest. (Paul David has noted too that his story puts more weight on individuals than do the stories by Marx or Rostow.) Gerschenkron's story, like that of Freud or Sophocles, is the story of a tragic flaw, a curse of relative backwardness damning the generations. That does not make it literature rather than science. As Gergen and Gergen (1986: 31) remark, in developmental psychology the good scientific 'narrative is likely to draw from the pool of commonly accepted narratives within the culture. To do less would fail to participate in the communal practices of making sensible accounts.'

There is more than prettiness in such matters of plot. There is moral weight. Hayden White has written that 'The demand for closure in the historical story is a demand ... for moral reasoning' (White 1981: 20). A monetarist is not morally satisfied until she has pinned the blame on the government. The historical economist says, Do not be fooled about Russian history; wake up; act your age; look beneath the surface; recognize the dismal tragedies of life. Stories impart meaning, which is to say worth. A *New Yorker* cartoon shows a woman looking up worried from the TV, asking her husband, 'Henry, is there a moral to *our* story?'

That the humanities can read the sciences should be no surprise. After all, reading is their job. I think it would have pleased Gerschenkron to see the sciences and humanities back on speaking terms this way. He too would have found the rhetorical grid better than the usual ones.

Applying such a grid, you can see, does not necessarily produce a hostile judgement. Rhetoric is not a mask to be stripped away to reveal the bare Logic and Evidence beneath. Rhetoric, like any tool, can be dishonestly used, as the best tools can be misused to greatest effect. But viewed scientifically rhetoric is merely the art of argument, ranging from index numbers to literary parallels, and from the fourth digit of accuracy to the story of industrialization. A rhetorical reading of Gerschenkron does not reveal him as a non-scientist, a mere word-spinner. Master scientists are master rhetoricians, word-spinners in no dishonourable sense. Science is rhetoric, all the way down.

The rhetoric of economic history has continued to depend on the old verities of positivism. Gerschenkron's example was not followed. For the most part one does not see economic historians nowadays crafting their statistical stories with self-conscious care, combining number and word in the style of Bloch or Heckscher or Gerschenkron. One sees them emulating modern economics instead of instructing it, pursuing this or that five-year wonder of technique from across the hall. Gerschenkron sets a different standard, worth meeting. It would improve economics and would in any case result in better economic history: examine all the evidence, not merely the evidence that fits a quantitative or anti-quantitative epistemology; and argue the case fully aware of its fact and logic, its metaphor and story.

NOTE

1   Gerschenkron seldom required italics to make his points. All italics in quotations from his works are my own.

REFERENCES

Brooks, Peter (1985) *Reading for the Plot: Design and Intention in Narrative*, New York: Vintage.
Fenoaltea, S. (forthcoming) *Italian Industrial Production, 1861–1913: A Statistical Reconstruction*, Cambridge: Cambridge University Press.
Gergen, Kenneth J. and Gergen, Mary M. (1986) 'Narrative form and the construction of psychological science', in T.R. Sarbin (ed.) *Narrative Psychology: The Storied Nature of Human Conduct*, New York: Praeger, pp. 22–44.
Gerschenkron, Alexander (1952 (1962)) 'Economic backwardness in historical perspective', reprinted pp. 5–30 in Gerschenkron (1962).
—— (1962) *Economic Backwardness in Historical Perspective: A Book of Essays*, Cambridge, Mass.: Harvard University Press.
—— (1965) 'Foreword' to Albert Fishlow, *American Railroads and the Transformation of the Ante-Bellum Economy*, Cambridge, Mass.: Harvard University Press.
—— (1968) *Continuity in History and Other Essays*, Cambridge, Mass.: Harvard University Press.
—— (1970) *Europe in the Russian Mirror: Four Lectures on Economic History*, Cambridge: Cambridge University Press.
—— (1977) *An Economic Spurt That Failed: Four Lectures in Austrian History*, Princeton: Princeton University Press.
Harley, C.K. (1982) 'British industrialization before 1841: evidence of slower growth during the Industrial Revolution', *Journal of Economic History* 42 (2), June, 267–90.
Hexter, J.H. (1986) 'The problem of historical knowledge', unpublished manuscript, Washington University, St Louis.
Keegan, John (1977) *The Face of Battle*, New York: Penguin.
McCloskey, D.N. (1986) 'Economics as a historical science', in W. Parker (ed.) *Economic History and the Modern Economist*, London: Basil Blackwell, pp. 63–9.
—— (1986) *The Rhetoric of Economics*, Madison: University of Wisconsin Press.
—— (1987) 'Continuity in economic history', article in *The New Palgrave: A Dictionary of Economics*, London: Macmillan.
—— (1988a) 'The storied character of economics', for a special issue of *Tijdschrift voor Geschiedenis*, September.
—— (1988b) 'Thick and thin methodologies in the history of economic thought', in Neil de Marchi (ed.) *The Popperian Legacy in Economics*, Cambridge: Cambridge University Press, pp. 245–57.
—— (1990) *If You're So Smart: The Narrative of Economic Expertise*, Chicago: University of Chicago Press.
McCloskey, D.N., Klamer, Arjo and Solow, Robert (eds) (1988) *The Consequences of Economic Rhetoric*, Cambridge: Cambridge University Press.
Megill, Allan and McCloskey, D.N. (1987) 'The rhetoric of history', in Nelson John, Allan Megill and D.N. McCloskey (eds) *The Rhetoric of the Human Sciences*, Madison: University of Wisconsin Press, pp. 221–38.

Mokyr, Joel (ed.) (1985) *The Economics of the Industrial Revolution*, Totowa, NJ: Rowman & Allanheld.

Moore, Ruth (1966 (1985)) *Niels Bohr*, Cambridge, Mass.: MIT Press.

Nelson, John, Megill, Allan and McCloskey, D.N. (eds) (1987) *The Rhetoric of the Human Sciences*, Madison: University of Wisconsin Press.

Prescott, William H. (1843/48 (no date)) *History of the Conquest of Mexico and History of the Conquest of Peru*, New York: Modern Library.

Rostow, W.W. (1960) *The Stages of Economic Growth*, Cambridge: Cambridge University Press.

White, Hayden (1981) 'The value of narrativity in the representation of reality', in W.J.T. Mitchell (ed.) *On Narrative*, Chicago: University of Chicago Press, pp. 1–24.

PART II

European industrialization: country studies

Chapter 7

Britain

N.F.R. Crafts, S.J. Leybourne and T.C. Mills

INTRODUCTION

Cliometric research has led to a considerable revision of an earlier conventional wisdom concerning the pace and nature of economic growth during British industrialization. Britain is still very much an early industrializer and a country whose employment structure became non-agricultural to an unusual extent, but can now be seen as a case of relatively slow overall growth involving a gradual acceleration rather than a take-off in the late eighteenth and early nineteenth centuries (Crafts 1985a). These revisions to the quantitative record of British economic development make this an opportune moment to reflect on contrasts between British industrialization and that of later developers with reference to some of the themes brought forward by Gerschenkron's 'economic backward-ness' approach to nineteenth-century European economic history.

In the next two sections we review recent developments in the historiography of nineteenth-century British economic growth. Inevitably this survey relies quite heavily on already published work by Crafts. In the following sections we build on the improved time-series relating to industrial growth in Britain and Europe to reconsider the timing and extent of trend growth changes to develop an appropriate comparative perspective on Gerschenkron's notions concerning 'great spurts' of industrialization. These sections constitute new research based on quantitative techniques not used hitherto in this context.

OVERVIEW OF BRITISH GROWTH AND STRUCTURAL CHANGE 1700–1913

At the time when Gerschenkron's economic backwardness thesis achieved prominence Deane and Cole (1962) represented the best available estimates concerning British economic growth in the long run. Subsequent research has improved considerably on those estimates, although, given the problems of imperfect data, there will always be some room for disagreement and doubt. Thus, the Matthews *et al.* (1982) figures for growth in the late nineteenth century shown in Table 7.1 are based on an average of the somewhat discrepant

Table 7.1 Growth rates of real GDP, real industrial output and total factor productivity in Britain: old and new views (% per annum)

	GDP		Industrial output		TFP in whole economy		TFP by sector: new view	
	New	Old	New	Old	New	Old	Industry	Agriculture
1700–60	0.7	0.7	0.7	1.0	0.3	na	na	na
1760–80	0.7	0.6	1.5	0.5	} 0.2	} 0.2	} 0.2	} 0.2
1780–1801	1.3	2.1	2.1	3.4				
1801–31	2.0	3.1	3.0	4.4	0.7	1.3	0.3	0.9
1830–60	2.5	2.0	3.4	1.7	1.0	0.8	0.8	1.0
1856–73	2.2	3.0	2.8	2.8	0.8	1.6	1.0	0.9
1873–99	2.1	2.8	2.2	1.8	0.7	1.4	0.7	0.5
1899–1913	1.4	1.4	1.6	1.9	0.0	0.0	0.0	0.4

Sources: 'New' is based on Crafts (1985a) and Matthews et al. (1982); 'old' is based on Deane and Cole (1962) and for factor input growth to derive TFP growth uses Feinstein (1978) and Matthews et al. (1982). Feinstein's capital stock estimates in levels are superseded by his (1988a) estimates but growth rates and hence TFP growth are unaffected after rounding.

estimates produced by the output, income and expenditure methods, while the Crafts (1985a) figures for earlier growth are necessarily crude for parts of the services sector. Nevertheless, these 'best guess' estimates of growth appear to be more soundly based than was the 'old view'. They embody more detailed archival work by many different authors and, in particular, avoid errors made in earlier attempts to obtain constant price series by deflating current price series for output.

As far as rates of growth are concerned, the major differences between the Deane and Cole's view and that offered by the Crafts and Matthews *et al.* studies are, first, that acceleration in the trend rate of growth during the British industrial revolution was more modest and gradual than was widely believed in the heady days of the 'take-off' literature and, second, that the late Victorian climacteric seems to have been pushed forward to Edwardian times. It should be noted that it is possible to test both these claims more rigorously than did their proponents originally and we report results of these tests on pp. 125–41 where it is shown that the first appears to be valid but the second not so.

It has also been possible to quantify more firmly what has always been known in outline, namely that in a number of ways the British pattern of economic development differed strikingly from the experience of other European countries. Table 2 reports the results of a Chenery–Syrquin type investigation carried out by Crafts (1984, 1985a). Several aspects of Table 7.2 are of interest in the context of Gerschenkron's hypotheses. Britain is confirmed as a country whose labour force was particularly rapidly redeployed out of agriculture and into industry, which was relatively urbanized but in which home investment remained low and savings flowed abroad to an unusually high extent.

THE NEW VIEW OF BRITISH GROWTH AND GERSCHENKRON'S HYPOTHESES

With the broad outline of the previous section in mind it is now possible to examine Britain's development in the light of Gerschenkron's hypotheses in rather more detail. As will become apparent, there are in fact divergent paths which can be followed within the 'new view' which have rather different implications especially in this context for the first half of the nineteenth century.

Agriculture and British industrialization to 1860

Gerschenkron's approach to economic backwardness suggests that Britain, as the least backward industrializer, should have experienced a relatively large contribution to its growth and development from productivity increases in agriculture. Crafts (1985a) regarded this expectation as broadly fulfilled and stressed relatively high output per worker in British as compared with continental agriculture, a rapid rate of increase in total factor productivity in British agriculture (see Table 1), and the decline to very low levels in agriculture's share

Table 7.2 Britain's development transition compared with the European norm

Year	1700	1760	1800	1840	1870	1890	1910
Income level (1970 dollars)	333	399	427	567	904	1,130	1,302
Crude birth rate	33.1	33.9	37.7	35.9	35.2	30.2	25.1
European norm	38.0	36.5	36.0	33.7	30.0	28.2	27.0
Crude death rate	26.5	28.7	27.1	22.2	22.9	19.5	13.5
European norm	28.0	26.4	25.9	23.4	19.4	17.5	16.3
Urbanization	na	na	33.9	48.3	65.2	74.5	78.9
European norm			23.2	31.4	44.8	51.3	55.4
Percentage of labour force in primary sector	57.1	49.6	39.9	25.0	20.0	16.3	15.1
European norm	69.8	64.3	62.3	53.7	39.7	32.9	28.6
Percentage of male labour force in agriculture	61.2	52.8	40.8	28.6	20.4	14.7	11.5
European norm	72.0	66.2	64.0	54.9	40.0	32.8	28.3
Percentage of male labour force in industry	18.5	23.8	29.5	47.3	49.2	51.1	54.3
European norm	12.6	16.9	18.6	25.3	36.5	41.9	45.2
Percentage of income in primary sector	37.4	37.5	36.1	24.9	18.8	13.4	10.3
European norm	51.4	46.6	44.8	37.2	24.8	18.9	15.1

Percentage of income in industry	20.0	20.0	19.8	33.5	33.6	31.8
European norm	19.3	21.3	22.0	30.3	32.8	34.4
Consumption as % of national expenditure	92.8	74.4	76.8	80.5	81.6	73.8
European norm	82.7	81.5	81.1	76.2	74.8	73.8
Investment as % of national expenditure	4.0	6.0	7.9	8.5	7.3	7.0
European norm	11.1	12.2	12.6	17.2	18.6	19.5
Government spending as % of national expenditure	4.8	12.7	15.3	4.8	5.9	8.2
European norm	7.8	7.5	7.4	6.3	5.9	5.7
Foreign capital inflow as % of national expenditure	na	na	0.6	−6.2	−5.2	−11.0
European norm	na	na	0.5	−0.4	−0.7	−0.9
School enrollment ratio	na	na	na	0.168	0.385	0.542
European norm				0.514	0.582	0.626

Source: Crafts (1985a: 62–3) based on regression analysis reported in Crafts (1984); the European norm was obtained using a variant of the approach adopted by Chenery and Syrquin (1975). The table has not been revised to take account of the slight changes to I/Y arising from Feinstein's (1988a) estimates.

in the labour force by 1840 even prior to the abolition of the Corn Laws. This view has been challenged by Williamson (1985, 1987) and there have been some important recent publications by other writers. It seems appropriate to review the state of play.

Difficulties arise, of course, from the lack of direct data on agricultural output prior to the late 1860s. Inferences must be drawn from price information, trade data and labour force estimates backed up by the work of contemporary investigators such as Marshall or Young. The evidence is to an extent contradictory; in particular, estimates of total factor productivity growth for c.1780 or 1800–50 derived from price data appear to yield lower estimates than those Crafts obtained from Deane and Cole's work on agricultural incomes and labour force inputs (Mokyr 1987). Neither set of data is particularly well-suited to producing robust estimates of productivity growth.

Williamson (1985) offers a view of British productivity growth for the period 1821–61 quite different from that of Table 1; he uses estimates of total factor productivity growth of 1.05 per cent in manufacturing and 0.3 per cent in agriculture and this imbalance is indeed central to his vision of, and explanation for, rising differentials between skilled and unskilled workers related to the induced expansion of manufacturing and contraction of agriculture. This account of productivity advance with manufacturing dominant is distinctly less in accordance with Gerschenkronian expectations than is Crafts'. Subsequent research suggests that Crafts' view is nearer to the truth than Williamson's. Three points in particular should be noted.

1. Williamson's 'estimates' for sectoral productivity growth rates were in fact assumptions (Crafts 1987a: pp. 250–4). The a priori reasoning involved seems predicated on the need to explain a Kuznets Curve of rising inequality which Williamson claims to have found for Britain in the period 1815–c.1870. As Feinstein points out, however, the evidence for the pay ratio of skilled to unskilled workers, which is the key endogenous variable in Williamson's model, is that, contrary to Williamson's own calculations, over the period 1821–61 there appears to be little change (Feinstein 1988b: table 2). It appears likely that Williamson's own model would require reasonably rapid agricultural productivity growth if Feinstein's demolition of Williamson's pay-ratio calculations itself is robust.[1]

2. Wrigley's work in estimating labour force shares suggests relatively rapid increases in output per worker in British agriculture over the long run. He shows that trends in population and urbanization make it likely that output per worker in British agriculture rose by between 60 and 100 per cent over the period 1600–1800 compared with less than 20 per cent in France (Wrigley 1985: 720). Wrigley has also completed a full reworking of the early census estimates of the male agricultural labour force which shows a growth rate of only 0.26 per cent for 1811–51, an estimate he regards as very reliable, with 39 per cent of the male labour force in agriculture in 1811 and 25 per cent in 1851. As Wrigley (1986: 334) notes, on the assumption that demand for agricultural output grew only as

fast as population (a conservative estimate), given what is known about imports, output per worker grew about 1 per cent per year. Feinstein's estimates of capital stock growth per worker (1978: 42, 68) show only 0.35 per cent in agriculture and, with unimproved land per worker not rising, this makes a value for total factor productivity growth as low as 0.3 per cent incredible and tends broadly instead to support Crafts' 1985 estimates.

3. As a result of the research of Allen (1988), it now appears possible to clarify the sources of rising labour productivity based on micro-economic information. The fundamental changes in pre-1850 agricultural production functions are usually thought of in terms of improved crop rotations which reduced fallow land, introduced legumes and root-crops and permitted greater livestock herds sustained by the new fodder crops. A particularly influential article by Timmer (1969) used contemporary evidence to consider the effects on a 500-acre farm of a switch to these new farming methods and concluded 'the increase in output per worker was nearly nil. The English agricultural revolution increased land, not labour, productivity' (Timmer 1969: 392). This article is unfortunately seriously misleading. Work on probate inventories helps to confirm that yields per acre rose much more than Timmer supposed – for wheat from 10 bushels in medieval times to 27 or so in 1850; it is also true that Timmer's example revolves around turnips, a particularly labour-intensive but by no means universally adopted crop. Most importantly, about half the gain in output per worker in the South Midlands between 1600 and 1800 (an area which reflects Wrigley's view of overall advance) came from the rising size of farms. Whereas in the early seventeenth century only 12 per cent of farms exceeded 100 acres, by the early nineteenth century 57 per cent did. On both arable and pasture farms labour costs per acre for a 400-acre farm were about 40 per cent of the figure for a 25-acre farm. The ability to obtain greater output per worker in agriculture in Britain compared to elsewhere during the Industrial Revolution was crucially dependent on having much larger farms. In 1851 only 21.7 per cent of agricultural land was farmed in units less than 100 acres, whereas in Ireland 67 per cent was in this category. Average farm size in France was about 30 acres against over 100 acres in Britain (Crafts 1989a). On the basis of Allen's results for the South Midlands, the smaller size of farms relative to Britain would imply in both France and Ireland a difference of around 30 per cent in land- and capital-to-labour ratios (Allen 1988: 128–9). Comparisons of output per worker in mid-nineteenth-century agriculture suggest that Britain's lead of 40 per cent or so over her near neighbours comes mainly from differences in land and capital per worker rather than total factor productivity (Crafts 1989a).

Thus the large long-run increases in output per worker suggested by Wrigley's estimates appear fairly straightforward to account for on the basis of rising yields and bigger farms. Despite the high labour requirements of some new crops, the claim that the English agricultural revolution did not raise labour productivity should not be taken seriously. Substantial growth of overall output allowed absolute numbers employed in agriculture to rise slowly over time but there was a very substantial release of labour in the sense that many more urban/industrial workers could be fed by each agricultural worker (Crafts 1980). In assessing Britain's agricultural revolution it is essential to look at the effects of changing agrarian structure as well as those of new crop rotations.

It is easy to construct *arithmetic* examples which suggest that the key implication of Britain's unique agricultural history was a much greater industrialization of employment based on higher agricultural labour productivity than elsewhere (Crafts 1989a). Such examples are, of course, unsatisfactory and it is necessary also to explain why Britain's agricultural superiority did not lead to her becoming the granary rather than the workshop of the world. Indeed, it has been suggested that such would be the implication of Crafts' total factor productivity growth estimates as in Table 7.1 and that accordingly Britain's experience in international trade shows them to be unreliable (Williamson 1987: 275).

Only by considering developments in agriculture together with industrial advance in an international context can we obtain an adequate account of the redeployment of labour out of British agriculture. There is an obvious requirement to approach this question in a general equilibrium framework, but Williamson's model is clearly inadequate and the data requirements to find an appropriate specification are too severe to be met at present (Crafts 1987a; 248–56, 260–4; 1987b: 182–4; Feinstein 1988b). Nevertheless, the broad outlines of the process can be plausibly guessed at.

First, it is important to bear in mind that much of British 'industry' in the first half of the nineteenth century was traditional, small-scale and catering for local markets without entering into international trade – this sector was responsible for perhaps 60 per cent of industrial employment and probably experienced virtually no productivity growth at all during 1780–1860 (Wrigley 1986; 298; Crafts 1987a: 255). Second, by contrast productivity growth in exportable manufacturing was rapid. The most notable sector was cotton textiles, which accounted for over 40 per cent of British exports in the first half of the nineteenth century. Total factor productivity in British cotton spinning rose by 64 per cent and in weaving by 56 per cent between 1835 and 1856 (Von Tunzelmann 1978: 225), while between 1830 and 1860 labour costs fell by a half and two-thirds respectively (Merttens 1894: 128). Even in France, Britain's closest rival, despite wage rates more than a third lower, supply prices for cotton yarn and woven goods were about 25 per cent higher than in Britain in the 1850s (Rist 1956). Third, cotton textiles were very cheap to transport at a time when most goods were not; as a result they were a large part of world trade and completely dominated by one relatively efficient producer. At mid-century, exports were about 60 per cent of British cotton output and as late as 1882/4 Britain still held 82 per cent of the world market for cotton cloth (Sandberg 1974). Patterns of trade, as Ricardo noted,[2] are based on *relative* efficiency and, given the position in cottons, agricultural goods became importables much more quickly than elsewhere in Europe. Specialization in international trade contracted agriculture's share in output in Britain which, when combined with the effects of rising yields, farm size and investment on output per worker in the sector, promoted a low share of employment in agriculture.

In sum, our reading of the role of agricultural productivity growth in British industrialization would be as follows. Productivity levels in British agriculture were unusually high both before and during the Industrial Revolution. This was made possible in substantial part by the attainment of a capitalist, large-farm agrarian structure, which institutional arrangement could not be emulated in many other countries. Productivity growth in agriculture was relatively rapid during British industrialization and, in the context of the lead Britain achieved in cotton textiles, was conducive to the unusually rapid shift of labour into industry. This was very much an 'early-comer's' unique achievement (Pollard 1981: 176–82). This interpretation seems very much in keeping with the spirit of Gerschenkron's vision but at the same time would insist on giving patterns of comparative advantage a more explicit and prominent role than has been common in discussions of Gerschenkron's hypotheses.[3]

Consumption, investment and real wages during the Industrial Revolution

Gerschenkron's analysis of backwardness argues that latecomers to European industrialization could expect to experience most pressure on consumption standards during their growth spurt as perforce they emphasized capital accumulation. Yet the case where debate over standards of living has been the most bitter is Britain, where a strong pessimist tradition critical of the impact of the Industrial Revolution on the economic welfare of the working classes still exists.

On the whole, recent quantitative research has tended to favour a rather more optimistic view of living standards, particularly for the period after the French Wars when growth in the economy is now perceived first to have exceeded 2 per cent. At the same time, the over-enthusiastic pronouncement from Lindert and Williamson (1983: 11) that 'real wages ... nearly doubled between 1820 and 1850 ... a far larger increase than even past "optimists" had announced' can now be seen as a considerable exaggeration.

Revisions to earlier views of trends in real wages have come mainly from the construction of new cost-of-living indices. These are improvements on what was previously available as they include rent and have weights with some claim to represent workers' expenditure patterns. Earlier indices were, in fact, distinctly unsuitable for calculating workers' real wages. For example, although Phelps-Brown and Hopkins' index continues to be widely used, its weights are completely inappropriate, for it takes no account of rent, its cereals do not include bread or flour, and drink is very largely represented by beer (Phelps-Brown and Hopkins 1981: 28–44). No-one should use this index without first considering adjustments to remedy these deficiencies, which are certainly feasible for 1750–1850. Nevertheless, it must be recognized that we are still some way from obtaining a fully satisfactory cost-of-living index for this period; budget studies are of poor quality as regards information on purchases other than food or on differences in weights appropriate for different income levels, family sizes, regional tastes, etc., and price data are scarce for all services, rents and manufactured goods other than clothing.

Lindert and Williamson's (1985) index is the best available at present. This constitutes a major revision of their (1983) index, following a debate with Crafts (1985b), and remedies a highly unsatisfactory treatment of clothing prices in their earlier work. For the years 1750–80 Lindert–Williamson's index can be extended back by including available information on rent and reweighting the Phelps-Brown and Hopkins index (Crafts 1989b).

Table 7.3 shows that the outcome of the interchange between Crafts and Linde.t and Williamson is to provide a 'consensus' new view of real wage growth for all blue collar workers for 1780–1850, namely that it was virtually equal to overall personal consumption growth and quite modest prior to 1820. The revisions made by Lindert and Williamson in their 1985 paper are shown to be much larger than they admitted at the time. The divergence between estimates of

Table 7.3 Growth of real wages and real personal consumption per head: old and new views (% per annum)

New views

	Lindert–Williamson, real wages, 1983	Crafts, real wages, 1985	'Best guess' real wages	Real personal consumption/head	Real national output/head
1760–1800	−0.15	na	−0.17	0.25	0.18
1780–1820	0.28	0.71	0.56	0.47	0.42
1820–1850	1.92	0.94	1.27	1.24	1.19
1780–1850	1.00	0.80	0.88	0.80	0.75

Old views

	Phelps-Brown and Hopkins, real wages	Feinstein, real personal consumption/head	Deane and Cole, real national output/head
1760–1800	−0.57	0.23	0.52
1780–1820	−0.03	1.08	0.98
1820–1850	0.92	1.52	1.48
1780–1850	0.38	1.27	1.19

Sources: Lindert and Williamson (1983: table 5), Crafts (1985b: table 4), 'Best guess' is based on Lindert and Williamson (1985) extended to 1760 as described in the text, Crafts (1985a: table 5.2), Crafts (1985a: table 2.11) are the new views; the old views come from Phelps-Brown and Hopkins (1956), Feinstein (1981: 136) and Deane and Cole (1962: 78, 166).

real wage growth and per capita consumption and national output growth, apparent in the 'old views' part of the table, disappears by virtue of increases to the former and reductions in the latter of similar absolute magnitude for 1780– 1850. Slow growth in consumption and real wages thus appears very much as an outcome of slow growth in the economy as a whole rather than of a really major change in income distribution, as seemed possible to writers like Perkin (1969: 138).

It should be noted, however, that this macro view conceals substantial regional variation in real wage behaviour. Recent publications by Schwarz (1985) and Botham and Hunt (1987) have highlighted this point without being in any way inconsistent with the 'consensus' view despite their authors' rather emotive claims to the contrary, as is shown in Crafts (1989b: table 7). Indeed, given the unevenness of industrial output growth between sectors and the limited impact of technological progress, quite large regional divergences in real wage growth are to be expected (Crafts 1985a: 105–7). This means that there is certainly still life in a carefully stated pessimistic case emphasizing that, as far as unskilled workers are concerned, only those in the north can be regarded as certain gainers before the 1830s (Crafts 1987a: 265).

Despite the opening up of a north–south divide, the evidence is against a great surge in inequality during the period 1815–71, as argued by Williamson (1985). When the plainly unreliable evidence on civil servants is dropped from Williamson's calculations of the pay ratio of the wages of skilled to unskilled workers, Feinstein (1988b: table 2) concludes that it rose from 1.74 in 1815 to a peak of 1.92 in 1851, which then declined slightly to 1.86 in 1911, whereas Williamson's estimates (1985: 31, 48) were 2.56 in 1815, rising to 3.64 in 1851 and 3.44 in 1871, and falling to 2.64 in 1911. Similarly, Feinstein shows that the tax assessments available do not support Williamson's inequality surge when they are processed correctly; for example, dealing properly with the estimation of values of houses below £20 gives a best-guess Gini coefficient based on an Inhabited House Duty of 0.607 in 1830, rising to 0.667 in 1871, and falling to 0.553 in 1911 (Feinstein 1988b: table 5), rather than Williamson's estimates of 0.451, 0.627 and 0.328 respectively for the same years. Williamson's own estimates, based on the Social Tables of Colquhoun and Baxter for current incomes, show only a very modest rise in the Gini coefficient from 0.519 in 1801/3 to 0.551 in 1867 (Williamson 1985: 68).[4]

Thus the overall picture which emerges from this discussion is that the explanation for slow growth in real wages and workers' consumption reflects slow economic growth rather than a shift in income distribution. In the long run there was little change in the share of national expenditure going to consumption (Crafts 1985a: 95) and, as will be discussed more fully below, there was no surge in capital accumulation based on high taxation or profit retention in the style Gerschenkron associated with latecomers. It must, however, be noted that there is one piece of evidence which does not fit very easily into this account, namely Mokyr's (1988) investigation of the consumption of sugar, tea and tobacco in the period 1780–1850. His econometric estimates lead to an inference that, having allowed for price effects, slow growth in consumption of these imported goods implies little or no increase in workers' real incomes. Rightly he warns against over-confident acceptance of the 'consensus' view. We would be reluctant to give Mokyr's findings a heavy weight against the formidable array of other evidence at present.

Revisions to overall growth estimates for output in Crafts (1985a) can be combined with Feinstein's most recent revisions to his investment estimates (1988a: 462) to obtain estimates of the ratio of investment to gross national product in current prices. The results are shown in Table 7.4. The rate of increase is distinctly slower than the Rostow–Lewis hypothesis would predict or than Feinstein (1978) himself had believed, and a little less than in Crafts (1985a: 73), which used Feinstein's earlier investment figures. The picture, as indicated in Table 7.2, is of British home investment levels throughout the eighteenth and nineteenth centuries tending to be decidedly low relative to the European norm. It was only after the French Wars that capital stock growth moved appreciably ahead of population growth, although at its maximum, population growth was just less than 1.5 per cent. Thus relatively slow increases in output per head reflected capital stock growth and total factor productivity growth of 1.5 per cent and 0.7 per cent per year respectively in 1801–31 and 2.0 per cent and 1.0 per cent per year respectively in 1830–60 (Crafts 1985a: 81).

Williamson (1985: 178) has argued that had it not been for the French Wars, Britain would have had investment as a share of national expenditure about 6 percentage points higher, leading, on a neoclassical analysis of the sources of growth, to growth of real GNP about 0.8 percentage points faster from a capital stock growth up by 2.4 percentage points. In other words, but for the crowding out effects of government borrowing to finance military expenditure, Britain would have had a much more decisive growth spurt and an investment boom and would altogether have looked much less like a Gerschenkronian early-comer – in

Table 7.4 Revised estimates for I/Y in current prices (%)

1761/70	6.8
1771/80	8.1
1781/90	8.0
1791/1800	8.5
1801/10	8.4
1811/20	10.1
1821/30	10.7
1831/40	9.7
1841/50	10.8
1851/60	9.7

Source: see text.

this view much of the contrast between Britain and later developers would be no more than a fluke of political history. Williamson's position seems to be an extreme one, however, and unlikely to be accepted by many, based as it is on the heroic assumption that war debt crowded out private capital formation on a one-for-one basis – in current prices, investment in real capital used savings of £707.7 million over 1791–1820 while the increase in government debt was £594.3 million, which in Williamson's counterfactual would also have represented saving to have been invested in physical capital (Crafts 1987a: table 2). In particular, the absence of any rise in real interest rates during the wartime period (Heim and Mirowski 1987) and the availability of foreign funds (Neal 1985) both suggest the existence of an elastic supply of savings; moreover, the savings rates of 1791–1800 and 1811–20 were not observed again during the nineteenth century and the British economy did not achieve Williamson's counterfactual investment rate until after the Second World War. Investment rates in 1791–1820 were only about 1.5 percentage points lower than 1821–50, which includes the railroad boom. Williamson's argument, therefore, seems overstated, but it is important to recognize that war may have had a distorting effect on comparisons of the growth spurt with those of other countries.

The traditional picture in the literature which stresses the importance of ploughed-back profits in financing investment and points out the absence of investment banking institutions in Britain is also consistent with Gerschenkron's vision of early-comers compared with latecomers. This view is in need of some modification but still seems basically correct. Research has emphasized in recent years that, despite the small size of English banks and their proneness to fail, nevertheless the banking system did in various ways expedite the provision of what were in effect long-term loans to industry (Mathias 1973). Indeed, the most detailed recent research stresses the essential part played by long-term bank finance in the transition to factory production in the West Riding woollens industry (Hudson 1986). Nevertheless, legal restrictions kept English banks to a small scale prior to the mid-nineteenth century. Moreover, when the really large investment demands associated with railways came along, Britain was a relatively mature economy and invested £15 million a year for a decade without recourse to the institutional innovations related to railway building in Germany (Tilly 1986: 118). So despite the obvious weaknesses of the financial system, partially reflected in high rates of bankruptcy (Duffy 1985), in an era of family capitalism Britain at the middle of the nineteenth century, based on her early start, still had a capital-to-labour ratio in the economy as a whole some 12 per cent higher than that of the United States.[5]

Thus, as far as consumption and investment are concerned, in the main, recent research has suggested that the British Industrial Revolution can still be seen as broadly in line with Gerschenkron's expectations of an early-comer economy. Growth was not rapid enough to permit workers' consumption standards to rise much prior to the second quarter of the nineteenth century but there was only a modest increase in the investment ratio. Comparisons with other countries are complicated somewhat more than was once recognized by the counterfactual question of what would have happened in the absence of the Napoleonic wars.

Late Victorian economic failure?

The apparent slowing down in British economic growth somewhere in the later part of the nineteenth century has given rise to vigorous controversy. We defer discussion of problems of measurement later in this chapter and concentrate at this point on the debate concerning the extent of, and reasons for, any failure in growth performance and the links between this literature and Gerschenkron's hypotheses.

The widespread notion that Victorian Britain 'failed' was one of the earliest targets for attack by new economic historians, with the main thrust of the argument forcefully stated in McCloskey (1970) and McCloskey and Sandberg (1971). Earlier writers had accused entrepreneurs of failures in innovation, research and development, and marketing, had blamed capital markets for inefficient allocation of funds, notably an undue bias towards foreign investment, and had attributed to falling export growth a failure of the 'engine' of British growth, leading to actual growth falling behind potential. In one of the most popular versions of this view, Richardson (1965) developed the argument that Britain was 'overcommitted' to the old staples as a result of her early start in industrialization and the 'lop-sided' economic structure that was its legacy. By contrast, new economic historians examined choices of technique from a profit-maximizing criterion and found that British failures to adopt new technology in use abroad were typically rationally based on British cost conditions (Sandberg 1981), investigated home and foreign investment and found little evidence of bias in the London capital market (Edelstein 1982) and concluded that the idiosyncratic structure of the British economy reflected comparative advantage under free trade (Harley and McCloskey 1981) such that McCloskey's seminal paper argued that this was a case of 'an economy not stagnating but growing as rapidly as permitted by the growth of its resources and the effective exploitation of the available technology' (McCloskey 1970: 459).

Since the mid-1970s the pendulum has swung back towards a rather more critical view of the late nineteenth-century British economy even among the cliometrics fraternity.[6] Business historians have in any case continued to draw unfavourable comparisons between British firms and their Continental or American counterparts, particularly in respect of slowness to move to large-scale corporate capitalism, hostility to new methods and inability to develop strategies capable of handling industrial relations in a manner compatible with twentieth-century industrial leadership (Chandler 1980; Coleman and Macleod 1986; Lewchuk 1987). From the quantitative economic history literature the following points have emerged:

(1) Comparisons of productivity levels and rates of growth at the macro-economic level do not seem fully to justify McCloskey's optimism. Thus,

Feinstein's estimates show that while in 1870 GDP/hour worked in the United States was only 90 per cent of the British level, by 1890 it was 5 per cent and by 1913, 25 per cent, higher (Feinstein 1988c: 4). Over the period 1873–1913, American total factor productivity growth appears to have been about three times the British rate (Feinstein 1988c: 10) and Britain appears to have failed to participate in the American leap forward to total factor productivity growth rates of 1.5 per cent or so, characteristic of the early twentieth century but well ahead of anything Britain achieved until the post-1945 era.

(2) Micro-economic studies of productivity levels and entrepreneurial decisions have also become a little less favourable to the Panglossian view. In particular, in the much studied iron and steel industry Allen (1979, 1981) and Berck (1978) have produced evidence that innovation lagged and productivity fell below German and American levels (perhaps by 15 per cent c. 1910).

(3) There are reasons to be sceptical of the effectiveness of British education, training and research in an age when these factors mattered much more than earlier in the achievement of rapid productivity growth. Pavitt and Soete (1982) show that Britain's share of patents granted in the United States as a percentage of all foreign patents fell from 36.2 per cent in 1890 to 23.3 per cent in 1913 while Germany's share rose from 21.5 to 34.0 per cent over the same period. Crafts and Thomas (1986) showed that British comparative advantage was based on exports intensive in the use of unskilled labour while Williamson, noting growth in skills per worker over 1871–1911 at only 70 per cent of the American rate, concluded that 'it may well be said that the "failure" of British industry in the late nineteenth century can be laid at the doorstep of inadequate investment in human capital ... compared to her main competitors in world markets' (Williamson 1981: 28).

McCloskey, in seeking to exonerate the late nineteenth-century British economy, stressed the power of market forces in eliminating inefficient management and suboptimal performance – a theme which is developed particularly well in his study of the steel industry (McCloskey 1973). Certainly, earlier advocates of British failure had not adequately dealt with this line of argument, especially in proclaiming entrepreneurial failure. On reflection, however, McCloskey's position is itself vulnerable to counter-attack as has been implied in some of the subsequent literature. First, and most obvious, some of the alleged failings, particularly in education and training, are in activities where one would expect market failure and where the state was slow to develop appropriate remedies (Sanderson 1988). Second, the economy lacked the capital market institutions appropriate to effective monitoring and allowance of takeover threats to guarantee rapid exit of bad management (Hannah 1974). Indeed, in some cases such as chemicals, the capital market may have been instrumental in creating large barriers to entry (Kennedy 1987). Third, the laxity of disclosure requirements may have led to serious weaknesses in the market for new industrial issues, arising from problems of asymmetric information impeding the development of new industries such as electricity (Kennedy 1987: ch. 5).

In other words, it is no longer easy to believe that conditions of entry and exit into most industries were so easy as in effect to prevent managerial failure. Moreover, these lines of argument both make early-start hypotheses such as Richardson's potentially more plausible and also relate to Gerschenkron's ideas on backwardness. The reasoning would run that Britain's early start obviated the need to develop new forms of banking, for example, to construct a railroad network, or to legislate for appropriate reforms of financial markets. By contrast, the pressures of backwardness, it might be argued, led in Germany especially to the creation of investment banking in a form conducive to lessening inefficiencies resulting from problems of information flows, to reducing managerial in-competence and to promoting vertical integration and corporate capitalism. Something very much like this position can be found in both Kennedy (1987) and Tilly (1986).

It will be obvious that the Kennedy/Tilly view is at most an agenda for research, but nevertheless it should not be discarded a priori. Some support can be found in Cottrell (1980: ch. 7), who finds a tendency for British banks to *withdraw* from long-term industrial financing as amalgamations led to nationwide and conservative lending policies being established, and in Tilly's own calculations that the German bank portfolio was much closer to the efficient portfolio frontier than was a collective portfolio based on new capital issues in London, and that the contribution of the portfolio diversification achieved by the advent of superior financial intermediation in raising the supply of funds to higher risk, higher yield sectors could have been to raise the growth rate for the whole economy by 50 per cent (Tilly 1986: 130–9). On the other hand, calculations of counterfactual growth rates are fraught with difficulty and Kennedy's own attempt to justify a 2.9 per cent growth rate for Britain in 1870–1913, rather than the actual 1.8 per cent had capital markets been less inefficient (or more like Germany!), has been widely dismissed as arbitrary and un-convincing (Thomas 1988; Harley 1989).

In sum, there are grounds for suspecting that late Victorian and Edwardian Britain did fail. The extent of the failure is not entirely clear but its proximate sources seem to lie in poor productivity performance not prevented by the market institutions of the day. It is possible that Britain was more vulnerable to these problems by virtue of receiving the institutional legacy of a Gerschenkronian early-comer. Such a hypothesis may well appeal to followers of Mancur Olson (1982), but remains at the moment a very speculative proposition.

GROWTH AND FLUCTUATIONS IN BRITISH INDUSTRIAL OUTPUT IN COMPARISON WITH OTHER EUROPEAN COUNTRIES

The notion of 'great spurs' in industrial growth is central to Gerschenkron's approach to European industrialization. As is well-known, he argued that 'the more delayed the industrial development of a country, the more explosive was the great spurt of its industrialization, if and when it came' (Gerschenkron 1962:

44). This claim has been tested, albeit rather crudely, using rank correlations by Barsby (1969) and Trebilcock (1981), who both find support for it, although characteristically Trebilcock is no more than lukewarm.

More precisely, Gerschenkron provides the following description:

> after a lengthy period of fairly low rates of growth came a moment of more or less sudden increase in the rates, which then remained at the accelerated level for a considerable period. That was the period of the great spurt ... the phenomenon in its entirety was altogether different from the cycle.... The crucial observation, then concerns a specific 'kink' in the curve of industrial output (drawn on a semi-logarithmic scale).... The more backward the country, the sharper was the angle of the kink.
>
> (Gerschenkron 1968: 33–4)

Gerschenkron did not, however, offer any precise operational criteria for distinguishing the 'specific discontinuity of the kink', although he did advise that historians should work with 'appropriately selected periods' and not be put off by 'the fact that any curve can be "smoothed" by the use of an appropriate technique in such a way as to eliminate any sign of discontinuity' (Gerschenkron 1968: 34). Unfortunately, as O'Brien notes in his recent survey article, European economic historians have found that 'the statistical problems of delineating phases of trend acceleration are formidable' (O'Brien 1986: 306) and 'discussions of "decisive" upswings ... degenerate into semantics' (1986: 309).

Recent historiography reflects O'Brien's point only too well. In the British case, most recent writing has rather coyly tended to talk of a gradual acceleration in trend without giving any precise timing and has sheltered behind phrases such as 'rapid growth of the industrial sector ... became dominant after 1815' (Mokyr 1985: 4) when considering the question of a great spurt. Neither Crafts (1985a) nor Harley (1982) are able to throw much light on the issue as they both worked from benchmark years chosen for data availability. Thus, while few would any longer readily accept Hobsbawm's singling out of the 1780s as the point where 'all the relevant statistical indices took that sudden, sharp, almost vertical turn upwards which marks the take-off' (Hobsbawm 1962: 28), there is no detailed chronology with which to replace this description, merely growth rates calculated between 'convenient end-points'.

Similar tendencies appear in the historiography of other European countries as it has retreated from the Rostovian era. Thus for both France and Austria it has been strongly argued, by Marczewski (1963) and Komlos (1983), that there was no true take-off and no unambiguous discontinuity. For each country there is also a quite extensive literature pointing to unevenness in rates of growth over time and trying to read more or less significance into particular upturns. For Italy, Gerschenkron (1962: 76) isolated 1896–1908 as the years of the 'great spurt' but other writers have been less confident, for example, Cafagna (1973: 321) and Trebilcock, whose picture is of 'a series of jerks towards industrialization, each linked fairly closely to its predecessor, none of outstanding force, frequently interspersed with periods of hesitation' (Trebilcock 1981: 305). Tilly is similarly sceptical in the German case of the advisability of singling out a period of trend acceleration:

> It is both possible and theoretically plausible that German economic growth in the nineteenth century took the form of long swings and, furthermore, that the take-off of the 1840–73 period was little more than the sum of one complete long swing (from 1843 to 1861) plus the expansion phase of another (from 1861 to 1879), coupled to some historically unique railway investment booms.
>
> (Tilly 1981: 52–3)

There are important implications which arise from this review of the literature. In particular, it is clear that hitherto problems of measurement have bedevilled the identification and thus the international comparison of 'great spurts'. Thus the Barsby and Trebilcock rank correlations of backwardness and industrial output growth are undermined both by lack of agreement on the periods of growth to be compared in the test and also by uncertainty in distinguishing trend growth and actual growth. Many writers are justifiably worried that misleading inferences may be drawn from *ad hoc* approaches to the analysis of time-series of industrial output. Moreover, not only is it desirable that changes in the estimated rate of trend growth are the result of appropriate time-series decomposition procedures but also it would seem sensible to use techniques which do not rely on prior specification of points at which the trend shifted.

In the British case these remarks apply not only to the investigation of increases in growth in the Industrial Revolution period but also to the subsequent slowing down in the era when the alleged problems of the early start putatively made an impact. There has, of course, been a prolonged debate over the extent and timing of the climacteric in British growth which is well surveyed in Saul (1985). Saul, whose pamphlet is probably the most widely-read item in the literature on late nineteenth-century growth, in his second edition favoured placing the climacteric in the period after 1899, whereas in his first edition he preferred to date it in the 1870s. The issue is of considerable interest given the prominence which comparisons of growth trends have assumed in the British failure debate (Floud 1981).

DATA

For the purposes of our analysis of trends in growth of industrial output in different European countries we have attempted to select the best available series. It must be recognized, however, that the quality of data is somewhat variable and that the coverage of activities is inevitably not equally complete in every case. For Russia and Italy we relied on the series in Goldsmith (1961) and Fua (1966) respectively, although in the latter case Fenoaltea's forthcoming work will surely supersede what is currently available. For Austria-Hungary we used the indices constructed by Komlos (1983) and for Germany we based our work on Lewis's (1973) revision of Hoffmann's index. For France, discussion of acceleration and deceleration has involved indices with and without traditional handicrafts and accordingly we analysed both the series in Toutain (1987) and in Lévy-Leboyer (1978).

For Britain we require a series for industrial output free of the faults from which the Hoffmann (1955) index suffers. We have therefore prepared two revised series. Britain (1) seeks to embody the revisions proposed by Harley (1982) and Lewis (1973) and is set out in Crafts et al. (forthcoming (b)). Lewis's revisions, which were accepted by Feinstein (1972), are used from 1855 to 1913 and Hoffmann's original index for 1700–60 and 1801–54. For 1761–1800 Harley (1982: 277) pointed out that Hoffman's index is fatally flawed by virtue of giving much too high a weight to the atypically fast growth sectors of cotton and iron. The problem arose because Hoffmann was only able to obtain estimates for 56 per cent of industrial output which he then used to represent the whole. In effect this virtually doubled the weighting for cotton and iron, although calculations for benchmark years, where a fuller set of data can be constructed, suggest that Hoffmann's unobservable sectors grew at a rate similar to that of his observable sectors *minus* cotton and iron (Harley 1982: Crafts 1985a). We have therefore reweighted the Hoffmann index for 1761–1800 giving cotton and iron their 1783 weights of 6.7 and 6.5 per cent respectively and inflating the remaining observable sectors pro rata to represent the other 86.8 per cent of industrial output.

Britain (2) contains a more ambitious, but perhaps slightly more controversial, revision of Hoffmann for the period 1700–1801, after which it is the same as Britain (1). We have reweighted the index in accordance with Crafts (1985a) and extended its coverage to include all the now available customs and excise data. Full details are reported in Crafts et al. (1990). Both indices are similar in their growth rates between benchmark years to those for industry and commerce in Crafts (1985a: 32) and the low sensitivity of estimated growth rates to alternative weighting schemes provided Harley's correction for cotton and iron is retained is a reassuring feature. We would regard Britain (2) as now representing our marginally preferred estimate.

MODELLING TRENDS AND CYCLES IN ECONOMIC TIME-SERIES

In examining the behaviour of economic growth in nineteenth-century Britain and Europe, we make use of some recently developed techniques in the econometric analysis of macro-economic time-series. In particular, macro-economists are often concerned with 'decomposing' an observed time-series to isolate, for example, its trend (or secular) and cyclical components. The fact that the trend component is thought to be of importance necessarily implies that the series under examination is non-stationary, so that it has a tendency to depart even farther from any given value as time goes on. This leads to a number of statistical problems, brought about by the non-constancy of the series mean, variance and autocovariances. In applied work, a simple way of capturing trend is to attribute such movement to a functional dependence on time. Accordingly, non-stationary time-series are often 'detrended' by regressing the series on a function of time, the resulting residuals then being treated as a stationary time-series with well-defined variance and autocovariances. The implicit model underlying these procedures is

$$y_t = f(t) + u_t, \tag{1}$$

where $\{y_t\}$ is the observed non-stationary time-series and $\{u_t\}$ is the stationary series of residuals around the trend function $f(t)$, often taken to be the linear trend, $\alpha + \beta t$. These residuals can then be interpreted as the cyclical component to be explained by business cycle theory. Recent examples of this approach include Perloff and Wachter (1979), Hall (1980), and Blanchard (1981), while Nelson and Plosser (1982) provide a more extensive list of references.

As these last authors point out, secular movement need not be modelled by a deterministic trend. One alternative is that popularized by Box and Jenkins (1976), namely that y_t represents the accumulation of changes that are themselves a stationary time-series, so that

$$y_t = y_{t-1} + \beta + \varepsilon_t, \tag{2}$$

where $\{\varepsilon_t\}$ is a stationary, but not necessarily uncorrelated, series with mean zero and constant variance σ_ε^2, and where β is the (fixed) mean of the differences. Accumulating changes in y from any initial value, $y_0 = \alpha$, say, yields

$$y_t = \alpha + \beta_t + \sum_{i=1}^{t} \varepsilon_i, \tag{3}$$

which looks superficially like the linear trend version of equation (1), but has a fundamental difference. The disturbance is not stationary; rather, the variance and covariances depend on time. For example, if the $\{\varepsilon_t\}$ are serially random, then the disturbance variance is $t\sigma_\varepsilon^2$. Nelson and Plosser (1982) refer to models of the class (1) as trend stationary (TS) processes and those of the class (3) as difference stationary (DS) processes.

The distinction between these two types of process has important implications for both business cycle analysis and theories of economic growth. If output is of the TS class, then all variation in the series is attributable to changes in the cyclical component, whereas if output is a DS process its trend component must be a non-stationary stochastic process rather than a deterministic function of time, so that an innovation to output has an enduring effect on the future path of the series. Hence treating output as a TS process rather than as a DS is likely to lead to an overstatement of the magnitude and duration of the cyclical component and to an understatement of the importance and persistence of the trend component. Furthermore, as West (1987) points out, if output is DS then, since all innovations are permanent, the concept of a stationary natural rate will have little meaning, for an output shock will, on average, never be offset by a return to some trend growth rate.[7] In addition, if monetary shocks are typically thought to be transitory, such shocks must therefore be unlikely to be important sources of output fluctuations, which are thus dominated by variations in real factors.

STRUCTURAL TIME-SERIES MODELS

In Appendix 1 we present evidence to suggest that one European industrial production series (Austria) is best described as a trend stationary process, while the others appear to be difference stationary processes. This is an important result since it suggests that the conventional economic historians' approach to trend estimation which has assumed trend stationarity at least over specified intervals is not appropriate in general for the analysis of nineteenth-century European industrial output growth. Although the analysis in Appendix 1 contains useful information, neither of the models given by equations (1) or (3) is a particularly attractive specification in the context of Gerschenkron's theses. Both models imply that trend growth is constant while differing in how they allow (cyclical) innovations to affect the level of the series.

Economic historians have typically rejected the view that trend growth is constant through time, preferring models which allow for variable growth rates. Feinstein *et al.* (1982), for example, allow trend growth to vary across chosen phases, calculating growth trends as the average rates required to connect the actual values of the series in the chosen terminal years of two successive phases. A related approach, not favoured by Feinstein *et al.* but preferred by Greasley (1986), is to compute growth rates across chosen phases by semilogarithmic trend regression, i.e. by using the TS model (1), with $\{y_t\}$ measured in logarithms, in a piecewise fashion, thus allowing for abrupt jumps in trend growth across phases. The significance of these jumps can easily be examined by extending equation (1) with an appropriate set of intercept and slope dummies. If desired, continuity in trend growth can be imposed by using a cubic spline formulation, as carried out by Hausman and Watts (1980). While undoubtedly enabling non-constant trend growth rates to be examined, these approaches may be criticized as being essentially *ad hoc*, forcing trend growth to shift abruptly at discrete intervals whose exact timing must be agreed upon.

An alternative approach to trend estimation, usually employed for trend removal so that the cyclical component can be isolated, is to use some form of moving average as, for example, Aldcroft and Fearon (1972). While such techniques have long been used for trend estimation (see, for example, Macauley 1931) and are, indeed, the basis for the widely used X-11 seasonal adjustment programme, difficulties can arise if the chosen moving average, usually a simple

9- or 13-year filter, departs substantially from the optimal linear filter derived by signal extraction from the stochastic process actually generating the observed series, as the results for the X-11 filter obtained by Burridge and Wallis (1984) and the more general examples of Mills (1982) and Whiteman (1984) clearly reveal.

The approach to trend estimation that we favour here is to consider a *structural* time-series model. This has the advantage of enabling a wide range of trend and cyclical behaviour to be analysed while still remaining within a formal modelling framework that admits a clear interpretation of the evolution of the underlying, but unobserved, components. The model employed here is similar to that proposed by Harvey (1985) and, in fact, includes all of the models discussed above as special cases. Rather than the trend-cycle decomposition of equation (13) an irregular component is explicitly included for model identification, so that we have

$$y_t = \mu_t + \psi_t + \varepsilon_t \tag{4}$$

where, as before, y_t is the observed value (typically the logarithm) of output, μ_t is the trend, ψ_t is the cycle, and where ε_t is an irregular component. We assume that ψ_t is a stationary linear process, that ε_t is white noise with variance σ_ε^2, and that all components are uncorrelated with each other.

A *stochastic* linear trend can be modelled as

$$\mu_t = \mu_{t-1} + \beta_{t-1} + \eta_t \tag{5}$$

$$\beta_t = \beta_{t-1} + \xi_t \tag{6}$$

where η_t and ξ_t are uncorrelated white noise disturbance terms with variances σ_η^2 and σ_ξ^2 respectively. If $\sigma_\eta^2 = \sigma_\xi^2 = 0$, then μ_t reduces to a deterministic linear trend and the model is then of the TS form (1). When $\sigma_\xi^2 = 0$, equation (4) is stationary in first differences and provided $\sigma_\eta^2 > 0$, it is of the DS form (2) with $\beta_t = \beta$.

The cycle ψ_t, since it is assumed to be a linear stationary process, should be capable of displaying pseudo-cyclical behaviour. Harvey (1985) uses a sinusoidal process that explicitly exhibits such behaviour, but we prefer here to employ the second-order autoregressive (AR(2)) process (see also Clark 1987):

$$\psi_t = \rho_1 \psi_t - 1 + \rho_2 \psi_{t-2} + \omega_t \tag{7}$$

where ω_t is a white noise disturbance with variance σ_ω^2. This choice is made on two grounds. The first is that it is relatively easy to handle and to estimate; the second is that the presence of a business cycle in all the series under investigation has by no means been demonstrated convincingly. The condition under which ψ_t will display pseudo-cyclical behaviour is well known to be $\rho_1^2 + 4\rho_2 < 0$, in which case the fundamental period (in years) of the cycle is given by $\lambda = [2\pi/(\cos^{-1}(|\rho_1|/2|\rho_2|^{\frac{1}{2}})]$ (Box and Jenkins 1976: ch. 3).

Estimation of the model is best carried out through a state-space representation using the Kalman filter. Details are reported in Appendix 2. Three countries are indeed found to have stochastic trends in their industrial output growth and these are shown graphically in Figs 7.1–4. Our results are summarized and compared with standard OLS estimates in Table 7.5.

IMPLICATIONS OF THE RESULTS

In the preceding two sections we set out what we consider to be an appropriate methodology for investigating the behaviour of trend growth over time and have implemented it for seven nineteenth-century economies. It should be clear from our discussion that previous investigations of these questions in European economic history have been based on rather unsatisfactory and potentially misleading procedures. In particular, it is crucial in order to avoid biased measurement of trend growth, to distinguish between trend stationary and difference stationary series of output and, in order to do justice to the concerns of the historical literature, it is also necessary to go beyond the Beveridge–Nelson decomposition of difference stationary processes.

Our approach is based on unobserved components models in which both the trend and cycle components are stochastic and in which there is no ex-ante specification of dates at which the trend is hypothesized to have changed. Our approach is more general than the conventional approach to trend estimation used by economic historians, namely OLS equations of linear trends over predetermined intervals of time; this traditional method is, of course, a special (restricted) case of our general model. In terms of the underlying economic models, the conventional approach is akin to assuming a neoclassical growth model with a natural rate of growth exogenously given and which is to be estimated. Our methodology does not rule out this possibility but can also embrace models where technological progress is endogenous and the evolution of the economy is path-dependent, as envisaged for example in David (1975: ch. 1). The results obtained in some respects contrast markedly with conventional wisdom. We discuss first the implications for Gercshenkron's views on 'great spurts' and second the pattern of British industrial growth which emerges.

International comparisons of trend growth in industrial output

Table 7.5 provides a resumé of the results obtained by our preferred methodology for trend estimation and also reports, for comparison, the results obtained from conventional OLS estimation of the equation $y = \alpha + \beta t$ for discrete intervals whose timing, based on beliefs about the dates of business cycles, were chosen on the basis of the available historiography.

It is clear from Table 7.5 that estimates of trend growth are quite sensitive to

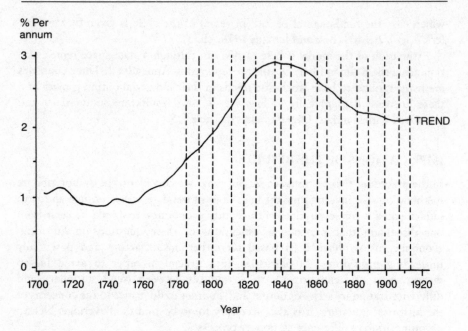

Figure 7.1   Britain (1): trend growth

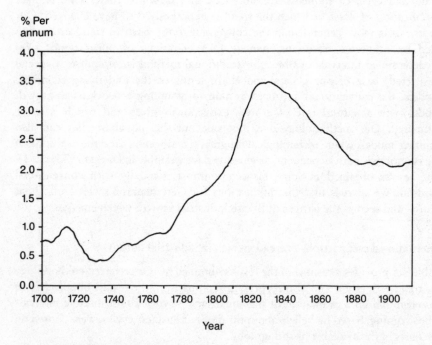

Figure 7.2   Britain (2): trend growth

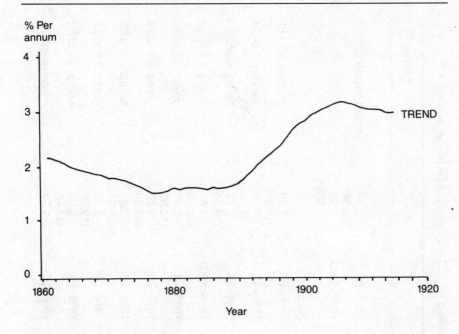

Figure 7.3 Italy: trend growth

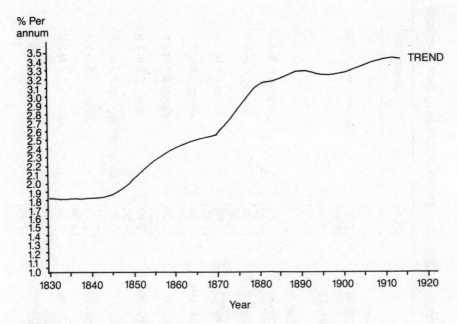

Figure 7.4 Hungary: trend growth

Table 7.5 Comparison of estimates of trend growth in industrial output obtained by OLS and Kalman filter (% per annum)

	OLS	Kalman filter		OLS	Kalman filter
Austria			*cont.d*		
1830–46	2.55 (16.93)	constant throughout: 2.9	1873–96	3.11 (23.98)	constant throughout: 2.9
1851–72	2.68 (6.18)		1897–1913	2.95 (13.23)	
Britain (1)			*Britain (2)*		
1700–25	1.71 (6.22)	varying: 0.9–1.2	1700–25	1.19 (6.02)	varying: 0.5–1.0
1726–45	0.34 (1.40)	varying: 0.9–1.0	1726–45	0.19 (1.67)	varying: 0.4–0.6
1746–83	0.63 (7.58)	rising: 0.9 to 1.6	1746–83	0.75 (16.40)	rising: 0.6 to 1.4
1784–1802	1.46 (9.67)	rising: 1.6 to 2.1	1784–1802	1.48 (13.93)	rising: 1.4 to 1.8
1803–18	2.09 (10.33)	rising: 2.1 to 2.6	1803–18	2.09 (10.33)	rising: 1.8 to 3.0
1819–36	3.93 (24.58)	rising: 2.6 to 2.9	1819–36	3.93 (24.58)	rising: 3.0 to 3.4
1837–53	3.21 (15.01)	falling very slightly: 2.9 to 2.8	1837–53	3.21 (15.01)	falling: 3.4 to 2.9
1854–74	2.79 (19.98)	falling: 2.8 to 2.4	1854–74	2.79 (19.98)	falling: 2.9 to 2.4
1875–99	2.09 (14.48)	falling: 2.4 to 2.2	1875–99	2.09 (14.48)	falling: 2.4 to 2.2
1900–13	1.52 (7.40)	constant: 2.2	1900–13	1.52 (14.48)	constant: 2.2

France (1)

Period		Kalman
1815–40	3.37 (60.36)	constant throughout: 2.7
1841–60	1.55 (9.84)	
1861–82	3.11 (23.89)	
1883–99	2.60 (17.32)	
1900–13	2.70 (8.76)	

France (2)

Period		Kalman
1820–40	1.68 (10.41)	constant throughout: 1.8
1841–60	2.09 (12.09)	
1861–82	1.23 (6.15)	
1883–99	1.54 (9.17)	
1900–13	2.88 (10.43)	

Germany

Period		Kalman
1850–7	2.70 (3.71)	constant throughout: 4.3
1858–74	5.31 (22.44)	
1875–99	4.51 (51.52)	
1899–1913	4.38 (31.33)	

Hungary

Period		Kalman
1830–47	1.42 (29.74)	constant: 1.8
1851–74	2.18 (9.61)	rising: 2.0 to 2.5
1875–96	4.93 (19.11)	rising: 2.5 to 3.3
1897–1913	3.53 (17.25)	rising: 3.3 to 3.5

Italy

Period		Kalman
1861–81	1.40 (9.56)	falling: 2.2 to 1.6
1882–96	0.35 (1.62)	constant to 1890: rising to 2.5 in 1896
1897–1908	4.98 (17.24)	rising to 1902: 2.6 to 3.1 then constant
1909–13	2.42 (3.56)	constant at 3.1

Russia

Period		Kalman
1860–84	4.93 (18.42)	constant throughout: 5.3
1885–99	6.54 (25.76)	
1900–7	1.18 (1.41)	
1908–13	6.26 (12.94)	

Sources: OLS regressions based on data series described in Section 5 and t-statistics reported in parentheses; Kalman filter estimates as presented in text.

the methodology employed. For example, in the cases where the Kalman filter estimates are of a constant trend rate of growth, in 50 per cent of cases that rate would not be in a 95 per cent confidence interval of the trend growth estimated by OLS. In the countries where Kalman filter estimates are of a variable trend rate of growth, the range of variation is substantially less than that obtained from the OLS procedure and there are some marked differences in the pattern of changes in trend growth. Although an important general message is that we believe economic historians have been prone to exaggerate the variability of trend growth, nevertheless three of the seven countries do exhibit stochastic trend growth and this supports economic historians in their insistence on considering models with non-constant trends.

Table 7.5 also makes interesting reading in the context of the historiography of individual countries. For Austria our results tend to confirm Komlos's view that 'the Austrian-Bohemian lands entered the modern industrial phase of economic development by 1825/30' (Komlos 1983: 16) and that he is right to insist on 'the absence of any unambiguous discontinuity in Austrian output' (1983: 91). In this case the picture derived from the OLS approach is fairly similar. We share in a consensus, including Gerschenkron (1977: 52–4) and Trebilcock (1981: 300–2), emphasizing the stability of long-run trends in industrial growth in Austria which has developed in the aftermath of an earlier search for a take-off.

For France our estimates are consistent with Marczewski's well-known view that 'there was no true take-off in France at all' (Marczewski 1963: 129). They do not, however, confirm the chronology promoted by Crouzet (1974) and accepted by Caron (1979) in his well-known textbook. Crouzet's character-ization was as follows – 1815–40: irregular, sometimes fast growth; 1840–60: fast growth; 1860–82: slowing down; 1882–96: stagnation; 1896–1913: fast growth (Crouzet 1974: 171). Although this account is broadly consistent with what would be obtained from the traditional OLS approach using France (2), which as the more comprehensive of the two French series we would prefer, our methodology suggests that as a picture of trend growth it is misleading.

Our estimates for Germany also indicate constant trend growth after 1850 but unfortunately we are unable to go back before that date when perhaps there were variations in trend. The chief contrast with the OLS results is that they suggest a slowing down in trend growth after the alleged take-off phase prior to 1873, albeit of a modest deceleration. The absence of any marked climacteric in German growth seems to be generally agreed (Trebilcock 1981: 48–9).

The remaining case of constant trend growth according to our estimates is Russia. There is a contrast here with what seems to be a generally accepted view in the literature that there was an upsurge in industrial output growth from the mid-1880s (Gregory 1982: 1), a spurt that is central to Gerschenkron's most famous example of backwardness. Even the OLS estimates and Goldsmith's original calculation (1961: 471) suggest that it would appear that trend growth of industrial output in the quarter-century or so after the emancipation was rapid and a division of the period 1860–1913 at 1885 reveals no structural break on a Chow test. It must be remembered that the series for industrial output prepared by Goldsmith, although the best available, is of rather dubious quality but on the present evidence it appears to us that acceleration in Russian industrial growth from the 1880s has been oversold.

Hungary we find to be a case of stochastic trend. The pattern is one of a fairly steady increase in trend growth from around 1.8 per cent in the 1830s and 1840s to around 3.5 per cent on the eve of the First World War. There is some support for Komlos's identification of a spurt in the late 1870s (Komlos 1983: 112) but there seems to be no particular reason to identify any short period as representing a decisive change. The OLS results, by contrast, would point to the twenty years from the mid-1870s as showing a marked jump in trend, whereas we would see Hungary's industrial advance as a gradual process.

Our estimates find that trend growth in Italian industrial output was both stochastic and highly volatile. For the OLS estimates our breakpoints were chosen on the basis of Gerschenkron (1962), whose discussion of the Italian great spurt is well-known and singles out 1879–1908; the OLS procedure appears to vindicate Gerschenkron. Figure 7.3 indicates clearly, however, that this pre-selection of turning points may be highly misleading; our estimates suggest that trend growth was generally declining from the early 1860s to the late 1870s, levelled off, and then increased from 1890 to 1902 by about 1.5 percentage points all told. This is a striking example of the difference between allowing the data to speak and imposing a priori notions on historical time-series.

Table 7.6 brings out some of the implications of our analysis for Gerschenkron's propositions concerning great spurts and backwardness. The countries are ordered according to Gerschenkron's own assessment of 'Backwardness' (1962: 44), with Hungary inserted between Italy and Russia.[8] Column 1 of the table reports the growth rate of industrial output over the first twenty years of the spurt periods proposed by Barsby (1969). On the basis of the now revised estimates for British growth a perfect rank correlation is observed on this test. The test can be refined somewhat by estimating trend growth either by OLS or Kalman filter methods and by choosing dates based on more recent discussions of possible 'take-off' periods. Columns (2) and (4) of Table 7.6 present the results of these refinements and reduce the rank correlations to 0.77 and 0.74 respectively. On reflection, however, this type of test does not really seem appropriate for Gerschenkron's hypothesis which, as set out earlier, actually concerns changes in the trend rate of growth.

Recognizing this point brings to the forefront questions of statistical methodology. Column (3) of Table 7.6 illustrates what might be obtained using a conventional OLS approach providing agreement could be obtained on the dates between which to compare growth trends and providing the date of the great spurt can be agreed upon a priori. The results are a little less favourable to Gerschenkron as a consequence of Russia's rather low change of trend ($r = 0.54$). As we have seen in the literature review, such a priori agreement is

Table 7.6 Great spurts compared using different methodologies (% per annum)

	Trebilcock/ Barsby (1)	OLS (2)	Δ OLS (3)	Kalman filter (4)	Δ Kalman filter (5)
Britain (1)	3.6/1.7 [a] (1780–1800)	1.5 (1784–1802)	0.8	1.6 to 2.1	2.0 (1760–1835)
Britain (2)	3.6/1.6 [a]	1.5	0.7	1.4 to 1.8	3.0 (1730–1830)
France	3.0 [b] (1829–49)	2.1 (1841–60)	0.4	1.8	0
Germany	3.2 (1850–70)	5.3 (1858–74)	2.6	4.3	0
Austria	3.3 (1880–1900)	2.6 (1830–46)	–	2.9	0
Italy	4.8 (1896–1916)	5.0 (1897–1908)	4.6	2.6 to 3.1	1.5 (1890–1902)
Hungary	–	4.9 (1875–96)	2.7	2.5 to 3.3	1.6 (1850–1910)
Russia	5.6 (1884–1904)	6.5 (1885–99)	1.6	5.3	0

Sources: 'Trebilcock/Barsby' is based on Barsby (1969: 456), an analysis which has been popularized by Trebilcock (1981: 429–31). Other columns are derived from Table 5.
[a] The Trebilcock/Barsby estimate based on Hoffmann (1955) was 3.6%; these are juxtaposed with the revised figures from the present indices.
[b] Trebilcock (1981: 430) suggests the spurt should be dated 1850–70 but does not supply an estimate of industrial growth over the period.

not always available and, as our discussion of Table 7.5 made clear, we ourselves are sceptical of many of the proposed chronologies of growth. The results of our methodology, which leaves the question of stochastic or deterministic trend to be decided on objective statistical criteria and which allows the data to reveal the dates of changes in trends, are much less favourable to the notion of the 'specific discontinuity of the kink'. In four cases, including Russia, we estimate trend growth to be constant; in two cases (Britain and Hungary), we find a prolonged period of increases in trend growth of unspectacular dimensions and only in Italy do we find Gerschenkron's expectations more or less fulfilled. It must be remembered, of course, that series for industrial output do not go as far back in time as we would like and that interesting changes in trend may well have occurred before the periods we are able to investigate.

We find therefore that the sympathy of writers like Barsby and Trebilcock for the proposition that backwardness is associated with great spurts in industrial output growth is misconceived and based on an inappropriate statistical methodology. This does not, of course, mean that the backwardness approach should be taken to be totally lacking in insights into nineteenth-century growth and the ways in which it was achieved. We would readily invoke Solow on this point:

> [T]o believe as many American economists do that empirical economics begins and ends with time-series analysis, is to ignore a lot of valuable information that cannot be put into so convenient a form . . ., information that is encapsulated in the qualitative inferences made by expert observers, as well as direct knowledge of the functioning of economic institutions.
>
> (Solow 1988: 311)

It follows, however, that we do not regard favourably Gerschenkron's suggestion that the search for discontinuities in industrial growth provides explicanda which will fertilize historical research in a fruitful way (Gerschenkron 1968: 36–7). In all cases but that of Austria, we have found that industrial production time-series are difference stationary processes and in three of the seven cases trend growth is stochastic. It could, therefore, be quite unfortunate only to concentrate on apparent upward moves in trend growth, as Gerschenkron suggested. The 'dog that didn't bark', i.e. the falling off in trend growth that could have but did not materialize may be just as important to consider.

Acceleration and slowdown in British industrial growth

The British experience is unlike that of any other country included in our analysis. The pattern revealed in Fig. 7.2 is of a long, slow acceleration in trend growth, a brief interlude around the peak of about 3.5 per cent, followed by a decline beginning before the middle of the nineteenth century and apparently completed by the end of the century. The estimates in Table 7.5 confirm that trend growth in British industrial output was slow relative to that in Germany or Russia, which Gerschenkron would have expected, of course, and even tended to be less than that of Austria during the nineteenth century, which he might have found a little more surprising.

Our results, which we discuss more fully in Crafts et al. (forthcoming (a)) also indicate that a number of beliefs among British economic historians will need to be revised. Partly this is a consequence of better indices of industrial output but mainly it is because the use of estimated trend growth rates over arbitrarily selected short periods has distorted general perceptions of the achievements of the economy over time; for example, our industrial production trend growth estimates suggest that growth during the so-called climacteric of the late Victorian and/or Edwardian periods was always greater than during the so-called 'take-off' period in the late eighteenth century.

Two points in particular stand out. First, it seems unreasonable to single out, as Hoffmann did (1955: 32) and many followed, a change at 1780 as clearly marking an epoch in the evolution of Britain's economy. Notwithstanding the adverse effects of war on the economy in the years 1793–1815, the trend rate of growth is estimated to have increased throughout the period 1760–1835, a finding which adds to the weight of evidence that Rostow's choice of 1783–1802 as the 'take-off' period (Rostow 1960: 38) was mistaken.

Second, in strong contrast with the views of Matthews *et al.* (1982), we do not wish to stress 1899–1913 as a climacteric – within this period any fall in trend growth of industrial production was extremely modest. We have shown elsewhere (Crafts *et al.* forthcoming (a)) that a similar result applies to real GDP. Controversy has existed, of course, with both the 1870s and 1890s seen as the onset of a climacteric. We find a declining trend rate of industrial output growth from the late 1830s, although this decline is initially very modest in the case of the Britain (1) series. This fall is distinctly earlier than has been suggested in most recent discussions, although interestingly Hoffmann (1955: 32) dated the slowdown from 1855. The value of allowing the data to speak unhindered by the preconceptions of recent historiography is again apparent.

Closer examination of components of industrial production reveals where the slowdown in trend growth was located. Figure 7.5 displays estimates of trend growth derived as in the previous section for British industrial output for sectors other than cotton, coal, and iron and steel. Exclusion of these export staples leaves roughly the same time pattern of acceleration and decleration of trend growth but greatly reduces their magnitudes. Thus the decline from the mid-nineteenth to early twentieth centuries is from 2.4 to 2.1 per cent rather than from 2.9 to 2.2 per cent as in the case of total industrial production.

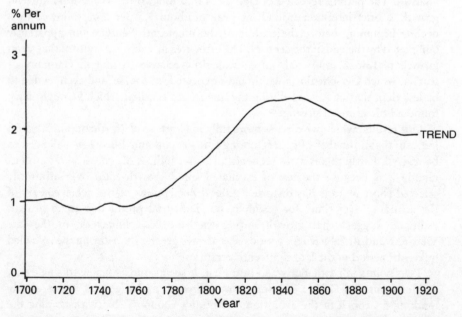

Figure 7.5 Britain (1): trend growth excluding cotton, iron, steel and coal

It must be stressed that the finding that British trend industrial output growth slowed from the mid-nineteenth century onwards does not of itself indicate that the economy failed. Certainly, as we argued earlier, we are sympathetic to the view that there were weaknesses in the late Victorian economy but it is much less clear that such failings mattered much at mid-century or that they inhibited the growth of the staples at that point. Moreover, our results suggest that any late Victorian/Edwardian failure is to be found in an inability to match American productivity growth acceleration rather than any marked British trend deceleration. Thus, although it is interesting to place the idiosyncracy of British industrial growth trends on a firm statistical basis, the British experience is one where paying undue attention to changes in the trend rate of growth is not necessarily particularly helpful as a starting point for analysis of economic performance.

SUMMARY AND CONCLUSIONS

Our main points can be briefly recapitulated as follows.

(1) It is still reasonable to regard Britain as fitting in most respects the pattern of a Gerschenkron early-comer: in general, recent research has strengthened this perception. Thus, the acceleration in economic growth in the Industrial Revolution was modest, agricultural productivity advance played a major part in the development process, investment never became a large fraction of national product and investment banking was unimportant.

(2) It is, however, important to recognize that British industrialization and, more especially agriculture's part in it, can only properly be understood in the context of comparative advantage and patterns of international specialization.

(3) It is extremely important to approach comparisons of growth rates over time or between countries using appropriate statistical techniques. We advocate the use of an unobserved components model with stochastic trend and cycle and with no prior selection of structural breaks.

(4) Application of our methodology gives results in key respects different from conventional wisdom. In particular, we find that British industrial growth entered its climacteric at the middle rather than the end of the nineteenth century and that discontinuities in trend growth in nineteenth-century Europe were less common and less dramatic than Gerschenkron imagined – or indeed than most of the historiography would suggest.

ACKNOWLEDGEMENTS

We are grateful to participants at the conference on 'Patterns of European Industrialization: Rethinking Gerschenkron's Hypotheses' for their helpful comments and are particularly indebted to Paul David and Vera Zamagni. Any errors are those of the authors.

NOTES

1 Feinstein provides an overwhelming case for rejecting Williamson's figures for middle-class and service-sector occupations. He does not, however, offer alternative estimates but rather shows that eliminating the unreliable series removes virtually all the movement in the pay ratio. It may be that further research will reinstate some of Williamson's claims by filling in gaps in the coverage of the present set of information on earnings. It should also be noted, however, that Williamson's assumptions on productivity growth are inconsistent with the estimates in his model for factor shares, output and input growth (Feinstein 1988b) and that his model contains a number of highly undesirable features notably with regard to the treatment of the tradables/non-tradables division and the use of a small-country assumption (Crafts 1987a: 248–56, 260–4).

2 Ricardo clearly foresaw the outcome of the discussion in this section as the following passage first published in 1817 shows: 'a country possessing very considerable advantages in machinery and skill, and which may therefore be enabled to manufacture commodities with much less labour than her neighbours, may in return for such commodities, import a portion of the corn required for its consumption, even if its lands were more fertile, and corn could be grown with less labour than in the country from which it was imported' (Ricardo 1971: 154).

3 As Gerschenkron himself put it, 'the Industrial Revolution in England ... affected the course of all subsequent industrializations' (1962: 41).

4 Williamson does suggest a lower Gini of 0.468 for 1688 at variance with Soltow's earlier estimate of 0.551 (Soltow 1968: 22), with the difference arising mainly from Lindert's work on occupations from burial register samples (Lindert 1980). It is possible, however, that this value is too low, first because lower wages in the north of England than in the south at this time are not allowed for and, second, because Lindert acknowledges that his occupations estimates are subject to large confidence intervals – allowance for these considerations leaves the distinct possibility that inequality in 1688 was much the same as 1801/3.

5 Based on Field (1985: 394) corrected on the basis of Feinstein's (1988a) capital stock estimates; the comparison is for 1860.

6 Perhaps at least partly because McCloskey has been otherwise occupied.

7 The use of the term difference stationary process is equivalent to the phrases 'random walk approximation' or 'unit root' for describing the evolution of output over time.

8 Other authors have adopted different rankings: Trebilcock (1981) and Barsby (1969) both use as one way of assessing backwardness the date of entry into the big spurt – as our discussion suggests, however, this is a dubious procedure.

REFERENCES

Aldcroft, D.H. and Fearon, P. (1972) 'Introduction', in D.H. Aldcroft and P. Fearon (eds) *British Economic Fluctuations, 1790–1939*, London: Macmillan, pp. 1–73.

Allen, R.C. (1979) 'International competition in iron and steel, 1850–1913', *Journal of Economic History* 39, 911–37.

—— (1981) 'Entrepreneurship and technical progress in the northeast coast pigiron industry: 1850–1913', *Research in Economic History* 6, 35–71.

—— (1988) 'The growth of labor productivity in early modern English agriculture', *Explorations in Economic History* 25, 117–46.

Barsby, S. (1969) 'Economic backwardness and the characteristics of development', *Journal of Economic History* 29, 449–72.

Berck, P. (1978) 'Hard driving and efficiency: iron production in 1890', *Journal of*

Economic History 38, 879–900.

Beveridge, S. and Nelson, C.R. (1981) 'A new approach to decomposition of economic time series into permanent and transitory components with particular attention to measurement of the "Business Cycle"', *Journal of Monetary Economics* 7, 151–74.

Blanchard, O.J. (1981) 'What is left of the multiplier accelerator?', *American Economic Review* 71, 150–4.

Botham, F.W. and Hunt, E.H. (1987) 'Wages in Britain during the Industrial Revolution', *Economic History Review* 40, 380–99.

Box, G.E.P. and Jenkins, G.M. (1976) *Time Series Analysis: Forecasting and Control*, San Francisco: Holden-Day.

Burridge, P. and Wallis, K.F. (1984) 'Unobserved-components models for seasonal adjustment filters', *Journal of Business and Economic Statistics* 2, 350–9.

Cafagna, L. (1973) 'Italy 1830–1914' in C. Cipolla (ed.) *The Fontana Economic History of Europe*, vol. 4, part 1, 279–328, London: Collins/Fontana.

Caron, F. (1979) *An Economic History of Modern France*, London: Methuen.

Chandler, A.D. (1980) 'The growth of the transitional industrial firm in the United States and the United Kingdom: a comparative analysis', *Economic History Review* 33, 396–410.

Chenery, H.B. and Syrquin, M. (1975) *Patterns of Development, 1950–1970*, London: Oxford University Press.

Church, R.A. (1975) *The Great Victorian Boom, 1850–1873*, London: Macmillan.

Clark, P.K. (1987) 'The cyclical component of U.S. economic activity', *Quarterly Journal of Economics* 103, 797–814.

Coleman, D.C. and Macleod, C. (1986) 'Attitudes to new techniques: British businessmen, 1800–1950', *Economic History Review* 39, 588–611.

Cottrell, P.L. (1980) *Industrial Finance, 1830–1914*, London: Methuen.

Crafts, N.F.R. (1980) 'Income elasticities of demand and the release of labour by agriculture during the British industrial revolution', *Journal of European Economic History* 9, 153–68.

―――― (1984) 'Patterns of development in nineteenth century Europe', *Oxford Economic Papers* 36, 438–58.

―――― (1985a) *British Economic Growth during the Industrial Revolution*, Oxford: Clarendon Press.

―――― (1985b) 'English workers' real wages during the Industrial Revolution: some remaining problems', *Journal of Economic History* 45, 139–44.

―――― (1987a) 'British economic growth, 1700–1850: some difficulties of interpretation', *Explorations in Economic History* 24, 245–68.

―――― (1987b) 'Cliometrics, 1971–1986: a survey', *Journal of Applied Econometrics* 2, 171–92.

―――― (1989a) 'British industrialization in its international context', *Journal of Interdisciplinary History* 19, 415–28.

―――― (1989b) 'Real wages, inequality and economic growth in Britain, 1750–1850', in P. Scholliers (ed.) *Real Wages during Industrialization*, pp. 75–95 Oxford: Berg.

Crafts, N.F.R. and Thomas, M. (1986) 'Comparative advantage in UK manufacturing trade, 1919–1935', *Economic Journal* 96, 629–45.

Crafts, N.F.R., Leybourne, S.J. and Mills, T.C. (1989a), 'The climacteric in late Victorian Britain and France: a reappraisal of the evidence', *Journal of Applied Econometrics* 4, 103–17.

Crafts, N.F.R., Leybourne, S.J. and Mills, T.C. (1989b) 'Trends and cycles in British industrial production, 1700–1913', *Journal of the Royal Statistical Society* 152, 43–60.

Crafts, N.F.R., Leybourne, S.J. and Mills, T.C. (1990) 'Trend growth of British industrial output, 1700–1913: some further estimates', mimeo, University of Warwick.

Crouzet, F. (1974) 'French economic growth in the nineteenth century reconsidered', *History* 59, 167–79.

David, P.A. (1975) *Technical Choice, Innovation and Economic Growth*, Cambridge: Cambridge University Press.

Deane, P. and Cole, W.A. (1962) *British Economic Growth, 1688–1959*, Cambridge: Cambridge University Press.

Dickey, D.A. and Fuller, W.A. (1979) 'Distribution of the estimators for autoregressive time series with a unit root', *Journal of the American Statistical Association* 74, 427–31.

Dickey, D.A. and Fuller, W.A. (1981) 'Likelihood ratio statistics for autoregressive time series with a unit root', *Econometrica* 49, 1057–72.

Duffy, I.P.H. (1985) *Bankruptcy and Insolvency in London during the Industrial Revolution*, London: Garland.

Edelstein, M. (1982) *Overseas Investment in the Age of High Imperialism: The United Kingdom, 1850–1914*, London: Methuen.

Feinstein, C.H. (1972) *National Income, Expenditure and Output of the United Kingdom, 1855–1965*, Cambridge: Cambridge University Press.

—— (1978) 'Capital formation in Great Britain', in P. Mathias and M.M. Postan (eds) *Cambridge Economic History of Europe*, Cambridge: Cambridge University Press, pp. 28–96.

—— (1981) 'Capital accumulation and the Industrial Revolution', in R.C. Floud and D.N. McCloskey (eds) *The Economic History of Britain since 1700*, Cambridge: Cambridge University Press, pp. 128–42.

—— (1988a) 'National statistics, 1760–1920: sources and methods of estimation for domestic reproducible fixed assets, stocks and works in progress, overseas assets and land', in C.H. Feinstein and S. Pollard (eds) *Studies in Capital Formation in the United Kingdom 1750–1920*, Oxford: Clarendon Press, pp. 259–471.

—— (1988b) 'The rise and fall of the Williamson Curve', *Journal of Economic History* 48, 699–729.

—— (1988c) 'Economic growth since 1870: Britain's performance in international perspective', *Oxford Review of Economic Policy* 4, 1–13.

Feinstein, C.H., Matthews, R.C.O. and Odling-Smee, J.C. (1982) 'The timing of the climacteric and its sectoral incidence in the UK', in C.P. Kindleberger and G. di Tella (eds) *Economics in the Long View*, Oxford: Clarendon Press, pp. 168–85.

Fenoaltea, S. (forthcoming) *Italian Industrial Production, 1861–1913: A Statistical Reconstruction*, Cambridge: Cambridge University Press.

Field, A.J. (1985) 'On the unimportance of machinery', *Explorations in Economic History* 22, 378–401.

Floud, R.C. (1981) 'Britain 1860–1914: a survey', in R.C. Floud and D.N. McCloskey (eds) *The Economic History of Britain since 1700*, Cambridge: Cambridge University Press, pp. 1–26.

Fua, G. (1966) *Notes on Italian Economic Growth*, Milan: Ciaffrè.

Fuller, W.A. (1976) *Introduction to Statistical Time Series*, New York: Wiley.

Gerschenkron, A. (1962) *Economic Backwardness in Historical Perspective*, Cambridge, Mass.: Harvard University Press.

—— (1968) *Continuity in History and Other Essays*, Cambridge, Mass.: Harvard University Press.

—— (1977) *An Economic Spurt That Failed*, Princeton: Princeton University Press.

Goldsmith, R.W. (1961) 'The economic growth of Tsarist Russia, 1860–1913', *Economic Development and Cultural Change* 9, 441–75.

Greasley, D. (1986) 'British economic growth: the paradox of the 1880s and the timing of the climacteric', *Explorations in Economic History* 23, 416–44.

Gregory, P.R. (1982) *Russian National Income, 1885–1913*, Cambridge: Cambridge University Press.

Hall, R.E. (1980) 'Labour supply and aggregate fluctuations', *Journal of Monetary Economics* 12, 7–33.

Hannah, L. (1974) 'Takeover bids in Britain before 1950: an exercise in business pre-history', *Business History* 16, 65–77.

Harley, C.K. (1982) 'British industrialization before 1841: evidence of slower growth during the Industrial Revolution', *Journal of Economic History* 42, 267–89.

—— (1989) 'Review of W.P. Kennedy, industrial structure, capital markets and the origins of British economic decline', *American Historical Review* 94, 1380.

Harley, C.K. and McCloskey, D.N. (1981) 'Foreign trade: competition and the expanding international economy', in R.C. Floud and D.N. McCloskey (eds) *The Economic History of Britain Since 1700*, Cambridge: Cambridge University Press, pp. 50–69.

Harvey, A.C. (1985) 'Trends and cycles in macroeconomic time series', *Journal of Business and Economic Statistics* 3, 216–27.

Hausman, W.J. and Watts, J.M. (1980) 'Structural change in the eighteenth century British economy: a test using cubic splines', *Explorations in Economic History* 17, 400–10.

Heim, C. and Mirowski, P. (1987) 'Interest rates and crowding out during Britain's Industrial Revolution', *Journal of Economic History* 47, 117–39.

Hobsbawm, E.J. (1962) *The Age of Revolution, 1789–1848*, London: Weidenfeld and Nicolson.

Hoffmann, W.G. (1955) *British Industry, 1700–1950*, Oxford: Blackwell.

Hudson, P. (1986) *The Genesis of Industrial Capital*, Cambridge: Cambridge University Press.

Kennedy, W.P. (1987) *Industrial Structure, Capital Markets and the Origins of British Economic Decline*, Cambridge: Cambridge University Press.

Komlos, J. (1983) *The Habsburg Monarchy as a Customs Union*, Princeton: Princeton University Press.

Lévy-Leboyer, M. (1978) 'Capital investment and economic growth in France, 1820–1930', in P. Mathias and M.M. Postan (eds) *Cambridge Economic History of Europe*, Cambridge: Cambridge University Press, pp. 231–95.

Lewchuk, W. (1987) *American Technology and the British Vehicle Industry*, Cambridge: Cambridge University Press.

Lewis, W.A. (1973) *Growth and Fluctuations*, London: Allen & Unwin.

Lindert, P.H. (1980) 'English occupations, 1670–1811', *Journal of Economic History* 40, 685–712.

Lindert, P.H. and Williamson, J.G. (1983) 'English workers' living standards during the Industrial Revolution, a new look', *Economic History Review* 36, 1–25.

Lindert, P.H. and Williamson, J.G. (1985) 'English workers' real wages: reply to Crafts', *Journal of Economic History* 45, 145–53.

Macauley, F.R. (1931) *The Smoothing of Time Series*, New York: NBER.

McCloskey, D.N. (1970) 'Did Victorian Britain fail?', *Economic History Review* 23, 446–59.

—— (1973) *Economic Maturity and Entrepreneurial Decline: British Iron and Steel, 1870–1913*, Cambridge, Mass.: Harvard University Press.

McCloskey, D.N. and Sandberg, L.G. (1971) 'From damnation to redemption: judgements on the late Victorian entrepreneur', *Explorations in Economic History* 9, 89–108.

Marczweski, J. (1963) 'The take-off hypothesis and French experience', in W.W. Rostow (ed.), *The Economics of Take Off Into Sustained Growth*, London: Macmillan, pp. 119–38.

Mathias, P. (1973) 'Capital, credit and enterprise in the Industrial Revolution', *Journal of European Economic History* 2, 121–43.

Matthews, R.C.O., Feinstein, C.H. and Odling-Smee, J.C. (1982) *British Economic Growth, 1856–1973*, Stanford: Stanford University Press.

Merttens, F. (1894) 'The hours and the cost of labour in the cotton industry at home and abroad', *Transactions of the Manchester Statistical Society*, 125–90.

Mills, T.C. (1982) 'Signal extraction and two illustrations of the quantity theory', *American Economic Review* 72, 1162–8.

Mitchell, B.R. (1981) *Abstract of European Historical Statistics*, London: Macmillan.

Mokyr, J. (1985) 'The Industrial Revolution and the new economic history', in J. Mokyr (ed.) *The Economics of the Industrial Revolution*, Totowa: Rowman & Allanheld, pp. 1–51.

—— (1987) 'Has the Industrial Revolution been crowded out? some reflections on Crafts and Williamson', *Explorations in Economic History* 24, 293–319.

—— (1988) 'Is there still life in the pessimist case? consumption during the Industrial Revolution, 1790–1850', *Journal of Economic History* 48, 69–92.

Neal, L. (1985) 'Integration of international capital markets: quantitative evidence from the eighteenth to twentieth centuries', *Journal of Economic History* 45, 219–26.

Nelson, C.R. and Plosser, C.I. (1982) 'Trends and random walks in macroeconomic time series: some evidence and implications', *Journal of Monetary Economics* 10, 139–62.

O'Brien, P.K. (1986) 'Do we have a typology for the study of European industrialization in the nineteenth century?', *Journal of European Economic History* 15, 291–333.

Olson, M. (1982) *The Rise and Decline of Nations*, New Haven: Yale University Press.

Pavitt, K. and Soete, L. (1982) 'International differences in economic growth and the international location of innovation', in H. Giersch (ed.) *Proceedings of a Conference on Emerging Technology*, Huburgen: Mohr.

Perkin, H. (1969) *The Origins of Modern English Society*, London: Routledge & Kegan Paul.

Perloff, J.M. and Wachter, M.L. (1979) 'A production function-nonaccelerating approach to potential output: is measured potential output too high?', *Carnegie-Rochester Conference Series on Public Policy* 10, 113–64.

Perron, P. and Phillips, P.C.B. (1987) 'Does GNP have a unit root? a re-evaluation', *Economics Letters* 23, 139–45.

Phelps-Brown, E.H. and Hopkins, S.V. (1956) 'Seven centuries of the prices of consumables compared with builders' wage-rates', *Economica* 23, 296–314.

Phelps-Brown, E.H. and Hopkins, S.V. (1981) *A Perspective of Wages and Prices*, London: Methuen.

Phillips, P.C.B. and Perron, P. (1988) 'Testing for a unit root in time series regression', *Biometrika* 75, 335–46.

Pollard, S. (1981) *Peaceful Conquest*, Oxford: Oxford University Press.

Ricardo, D. (1971) *On the Principles of Political Economy and Taxation*, R.M. Hartwell (ed.), Harmondsworth: Penguin.

Richardson, H.W. (1965) 'Overcommitment in British industry before 1930', *Oxford Economic Papers* 17, 237–62.

Rist, M. (1956) 'Une expérience francaise de libération des echanges au dix-neuviéme siécle: le traité de 1860', *Revue d'Economique Politique* 66, 908–61.

Rostow, W.W. (1960) *The Stages of Economic Growth*, Cambridge: Cambridge University Press.

Said, S.E. and Dickey, D.A. (1984) 'Testing for unit roots in autogregressive moving-average models with unknown order', *Biometrika* 71, 599–607.

Sandberg, L.G. (1974) *Lancashire in Decline*, Columbus: Ohio State University Press.

—— (1981) 'The entrepreneur and technological change', in R.C. Floud and D.N.

McCloskey (eds) *The Economic History of Britain Since 1700*, Cambridge: Cambridge University Press, pp. 99–120.

Sanderson, M. (1988) 'Education and economic decline, 1890–1980s', *Oxford Review of Economic Policy* 4, 38–50.

Saul, S.B. (1985) *The Myth of the Great Depression, 1890–96*, London: Macmillan.

Schwarz, L.D. (1985) 'The standard of living in the long run: London, 1700–1860', *Economic History Review* 38, 24–41.

Schwert, G.W. (1987) 'Effects of model specification on tests for unit roots in macroeconomic data', *Journal of Monetary Economics* 20, 73–103.

Solow, R.M. (1988) 'Growth theory and after', *American Economic Review* 78, 307–17.

Soltow, L. (1968) 'Long run changes in British income inequality', *Economic History Review* 21, 17–29.

Thomas, M. (1988) *The Edwardian Economy: Structure, Performance and Policy in Britain, 1890–1914*, Oxford: Clarendon Press.

Tilly, R.H. (1981) 'The "Take-off" in Germany', in E. Angermann and M.L. Frings (eds) *Oceans Apart?*, Stuttgart: Klett-Cotta, 47–59.

—— (1986) 'German banking, 1850–1914: development assistance for the strong', *Journal of European Economic History* 15, 113–52.

Timmer, C.P. (1969) 'The turnip, the new husbandry and the English agricultural revolution', *Quarterly Journal of Economics* 85, 375–95.

Toutain, J.C. (1987) 'Le produit intérieur brut de la France de 1789 à 1982', *Economies et Sociétés* 21, 49–237.

Trebilcock, C. (1981) *The Industrialization of the Continental Powers 1780–1914*, London: Longman.

Von Tunzelmann, G.N. (1978) *Steam Power and British Industrialization to 1860*, Oxford: Oxford University Press.

Watson, M.W. (1986) 'Univariate detrending methods with stochastic trends', *Journal of Monetary Economics* 18, 49–75.

West, K.D. (1987) 'On the interpretation of near random walk behavior in GNP', *American Economic Review* 78, 202–9.

Whiteman, C.H. (1984) 'Lucas on the quantity theory: hypothesis testing without theory', *American Economic Review* 74, 742–9.

Williamson, J.G. (1981) 'What do we know about skill accumulation in nineteenth century Britain?', University of Wisconsin Discussion Paper.

—— (1985) *Did British Capitalism Breed Inequality?*, London: Allen & Unwin.

—— (1987) 'Debating the British industrial revolution', *Explorations in Economic History* 24, 269–92.

Wrigley, E.A. (1985) 'Urban growth and agricultural change: England and the Continent in the early modern period', *Journal of Interdisciplinary History* 15, 683–728.

—— (1986) 'Men on the land and men in the countryside: employment in agriculture in early nineteenth century England', in L. Bonfield, R.M. Smith and K. Wrightson (eds) *The World We Have Gained*, Oxford: Blackwell, pp. 295–336.

APPENDIX 1

The testing of whether a time-series belongs to the DS class against the alternative that it belongs to the TS class is essentially one of testing whether $\{y_t\}$ contains a *unit root*. Thus, following Dickey and Fuller (1979), in its simplest set-up this requires estimating the model

$$y_t = \beta + \rho y_{t-1} + \gamma t + \varepsilon_t \tag{10}$$

by least squares and testing whether the estimate of ρ is significantly less than unity, for under the null hypothesis that $\{y_t\}$ belongs to the DS class, $\rho = 1$, whereas under the alternative of a TS class of model, $\rho < 1$. The usual 't-ratio' for $(\hat{\rho} - 1)$ is, however, not distributed as Student's t and, in the above case, the tables given in Fuller (1976: 373) must be used. When computing such tests, it is important to account for any serial correlation in ε_t, and two families of test statistics have been developed. Said and Dickey (1984) consider parametric variants, where the basic equation (10) is augmented by an autoregression in the lagged changes of y_t,

$$y_t = \rho + \rho y_{t-1} + \gamma t + \sum_{i=1}^{\ell} \delta_i (y_{t-1} - y_{t-i-1}) + \varepsilon_t \tag{11}$$

in which, after judicious choice of the lag length ℓ, ε_t is assumed to be serially independent. Again, the appropriate t-test on y_{t-1} can be used, and a second test statistic, the 'F-test' of the joint null hypothesis $[\gamma = 0, \rho = 1]$, denoted Φ and obtained in the conventional way from the regression of equation (11) may also be employed. For this joint test, the asymptotic distribution tabulated in Dickey and Fuller (1981) must be used.

The second family of tests has been proposed by Phillips and Perron (1988), in which the above test statistics are non-parametrically adjusted to account for both serial dependence and heteroskedasticity in $\{\varepsilon_t\}$. Details of these adjustments are presented in Phillips and Perron (1988) and Perron and Phillips (1987) and require an estimate of the variance of $\{\varepsilon_t\}$ based on sample autocovariances truncated at lag ℓ. These non-parametric statistics have the same asymptotic distributions as the parametric statistics presented above, and Phillips and Perron (1988) show that their use entails no loss of power over the parametric tests in spite of the fact that they allow for a more general class of error processes. The battery of test statistics applied to the logarithms of the European industrial production series are shown in Table 7.7. The statistics t_ρ and Φ are the Said and Dickey (1984) 't-ratio' and 'F' tests obtained from estimation of equation (11) while $Z(t_\rho)$ and $Z(\Phi)$ are their non-parametric counterparts calculated by adjusting the statistics obtained from the estimation of equation (10). Also shown is Phillips and Perron's (1988) 'normalized bias' statistic $Z(\rho)$. In both cases the lag length ℓ was set at 4, this choice being in accordance with the selection criteria used by Schwert (1987).

Before discussing these statistics, Schwert's (1987) important simulation findings must be taken into account. He found that if the series under investigation contain important moving average components, then the usual critical values (at the 5 per cent level, -3.41 for t_ρ and $Z(t_\rho)$, 6.26 for Φ and $Z(\Phi)$, and -21.8 for $Z(\rho)$) are too small in absolute value, so that the unit root hypothesis would tend to be rejected too often. Schwert thus recommends that, prior to testing for unit roots, the correct specification of the ARIMA process generating each series should be ascertained. On the assumption that each series contains a unit root, so

Table 7.7 Unit root test statistics

(a) Parametric test statistics

	$\hat{\rho}$	t_ρ	Φ
Austria	0.440	−4.75	11.29
Britain (1)	0.980	−1.59	4.68
Britain (2)	0.979	−2.15	10.42
France (1)	0.789	−3.10	4.89
France (2)	0.812	−2.03	2.13
Germany	0.790	−1.98	2.05
Hungary	0.903	−1.85	3.06
Italy	0.986	−0.18	1.28
Russia	0.595	−2.45	3.34

(b) Non-parametric test statistics

	$\hat{\rho}$	$Z(\rho)$	$Z(t_\rho)$	$Z(\Phi)$
Austria	0.689	−61.74	−3.45	13.82
Britain (1)	0.971	−11.78	−1.23	2.52
Britain (2)	0.780	−15.93	−1.66	5.61
France (1)	0.801	−43.69	−2.79	9.56
France (2)	0.725	−59.35	−3.28	12.89
Germany	0.777	−32.14	−2.50	7.12
Hungary	0.895	−19.01	−1.73	4.02
Italy	0.953	− 7.98	−1.27	1.49
Russia	0.507	−50.46	−2.90	12.11

that first differencing is required, the ARIMA specifications shown in Table 7.8 were arrived at. We see that many of the series do indeed have important moving average components. Since Schwert's simulations suggest that the parametric tests are less affected by the presence of such components, it may be wise to concentrate on these statistics in determining the presence of unit roots. From these, only Austria rejects the unit root null hypothesis and this conclusion is supported by the non-parametric tests, since both $Z(\rho)$ and $Z(\Phi)$ are highly affected by moving average behaviour.

The TS model fitted to the Austrian series is

$$y_t = 1.833 + 0.028t + u_t$$
$$\quad\ (0.044)\ \ (0.001)$$
$$u_t = 0.698u_{t-1} + a_t, \quad \hat{\sigma} = 0.0560 \tag{12}$$
$$\quad\ (0.080)$$

(standard errors in parentheses)

so that the series evolves as a deterministic linear trend, having a constant growth rate of 2.8 per cent per annum, upon which is a cyclical component that exhibits

Table 7.8 ARIMA specifications

Austria	$y_t - y_{t-1}$	$= 0.027 + \varepsilon_t \,; \hat{\sigma} = 0.0600$
Britain (1)	$y_t - y_{t-1}$	$= 0.019 + \varepsilon_t - 0.400\varepsilon_{t-2};$ $\hat{\sigma} = 0.0617$
Britain (2)	$y_t - y_{t-1}$	$= 0.024 - 0.134(y_{t-1} - y_{t-2})$ $- 0.196(y_{t-2} - Y_{t-3}) + \varepsilon_t \,;$ $\hat{\sigma} = 0.0451$
France (1)	$y_t - y_{t-1}$	$= 0.064 - 1.023(y_{t-1} - y_{t-2})$ $- 0.357(y_{t-2} - y_{t-3}) + \varepsilon_t$ $+ 0.754\varepsilon_{t-1}\,; \hat{\sigma} = 0.0356$
France (2)	$y_t - y_{t-1}$	$= 0.018 + \varepsilon_t - 0.241\varepsilon_{t-1}$ $- 0.321\varepsilon_{t-2}\,; \hat{\sigma} = 0.0470$
Germany	$y_t - y_{t-1}$	$= 0.043 + \varepsilon_t \,; \hat{\sigma} = 0.0354$
Hungary	$y_t - y_{t-1}$	$= 0.027 + 0.397(y_{t-2} - y_{t-3})$ $+ \varepsilon_t \,; \hat{\sigma} = 0.0648$
Italy	$y_t - y_{t-1}$	$= 0.020 + \varepsilon_t \,; \hat{\sigma} = 0.0438$
Russia	$y_t - y_{t-1}$	$= 0.046 + \varepsilon_t - 0.266\varepsilon_{t-2}\,;$ $\hat{\sigma} = 0.0789$

a first-order autoregressive structure, i.e. any innovation away from trend decays back exponentially, the decay factor being approximately 0.7, so that the mean and median lengths of decay are 2.3 and 1.0 years respectively. In terms of residual standard error, this model is superior to the ARIMA specification (a random walk with drift of 2.7 per cent per annum) shown in Table 7.8.

The remaining series are consistent with them evolving as difference stationary processes. Beveridge and Nelson (1981) show that, under rather weak assumptions, y_t can then be decomposed into trend and cyclical components,

$$y_t = \mu_t + \psi_t \tag{13}$$

such that, if y_t has the Wold decomposition

$$\nabla y_t = \alpha_0 + a_t + \alpha_1 a_{t-1} + \ldots$$

where $\nabla y_t = y_t - y_{t-1}$, α_0 is the mean of ∇y_t, and $\{a_t\}$ is a white noise series with zero mean and constant variance σ_a^2, then the trend component is given by

$$\nabla \mu_t = \alpha_0 + \left[\sum_{j=0}^{\infty} \alpha_j \right] a_t, \quad \alpha_0 = 1$$

and the cyclical component is

$$\psi_t = \left[\sum_{j=1}^{\infty} \alpha_j \right] a_t + \left[\sum_{j=2}^{\infty} \alpha_j \right] a_{t-1} + \ldots$$

Since a_t is white noise, the trend component is therefore a random walk with rate of drift equal to μ and an innovation equal to $(\Sigma_0^\infty a_j)a_t$. The cyclical component, on the other hand, is clearly a stationary process which may exhibit many patterns of serial correlation depending on the signs and pattern of the α's. It may be interpreted as representing the forecastable 'momentum' present at each time period but which is expected to be dissipated as the series tends to its 'permanent' level, given by the trend component.

Using the ARIMA specifications shown in Table 7.8 the Beveridge and Nelson decomposition implies that, since both Germany and Italy evolve as pure random walks, $\mu_t = y_t$ and $\psi_t = 0$, and hence they contain no forecastable momentum and no meaningful cycle. Britain, France (2), and Russia are all integrated moving average processes and hence cyclical components that are also (finite) moving averages, thus ruling out (pseudo-)cyclical behaviour. France (1) has a more complicated dynamic structure, being an ARIMA (2,1,1) process. The autoregressive polynomial has complex roots, and thus the cyclical component does exhibit pseudo-cyclical behaviour. Hungary too has an autoregressive structure having complex roots, so that pseudo-cyclical behaviour is again implied for the cyclical component.

Beveridge and Nelson (1981) provide estimators of the trend and cyclical components that are based simply on the present and past observations of the series, so that they are estimated by *one-sided filters*. This is very convenient for assessing current business cycle developments, but is less attractive in historical exercises, for the known 'future' observations are ignored. Perhaps more appropriately in this context, Watson (1986), for example, considers estimators based upon this extended information set, and which use *two-sided* filters.

APPENDIX 2

The model can be written in state-space form by defining the state vector to be

$$\alpha_t = (\mu_t, \beta_t, \psi_t, \psi_{t-1})'$$

The measurement and transition equations can then be written as

$$y_t = A\alpha_t + \varepsilon_t$$

and

$$\alpha_t = M\alpha_{t-1} + u_t$$

where

$$A = (1,0,1,0)$$

and

$$M = \begin{bmatrix} 1 & 1 & 0 & 0 \\ 0 & 1 & 0 & 0 \\ 0 & 0 & \rho_1 & \rho_2 \\ 0 & 0 & 1 & 0 \end{bmatrix}$$

Table 7.9 Maximum likelihood estimates of parameters from structural time-series models

	σ_ε^2 $(\times 10^{-5})$	σ_η^2 $(\times 10^{-3})$	σ_ζ^2 $(\times 10^{-5})$	σ_ω^2 $(\times 10^{-3})$	ρ_1	ρ_2
Austria	1.41	0	0	2.99	0.78	−0.12
Britain (1)	0.03	0.81	0.02	1.47	0.25	−0.11
Britain (2)	0.32	0.12	0.27	1.34	0.49	−0.12
France (1)	79.30	0.80	0	0.05	−1.09	−0.80
France (2)	24.58	1.44	0	0	−1.19	−0.96
Germany	0.06	1.07	0	0	−0.09	−0.94
Hungary	1.40	2.32	0.47	0.46	−0.31	−0.75
Italy	0.11	1.45	1.16	0	0.05	−0.83
Russia	0.02	3.75	0	0	−0.99	−0.86

respectively, with

$$u_t = (\eta_t, \xi_t, \omega_t, 0)'$$

The disturbances η_t, ξ_t and ω_t are assumed to be normally distributed with zero means and the assumption that the components are uncorrelated implies that the disturbances will have a diagonal covariance matrix.

Maximum likelihood estimates of the unknown parameters σ_ε^2, q_t, σ_ξ^2, σ_ω^2, ρ_1 and ρ_2 can be obtained numerically via the application of the Kalman filter algorithm. Conditional upon these, optimal estimates of the components of the state vector a_t are then obtained by smoothing (running the Kalman filter forwards and backwards through time). Further discussion of this smoothing procedure and details of maximum likelihood estimation are given in Crafts *et al.* forthcoming (a).

The parameter estimates obtained for each series are shown in Table 7.9.

Chapter 8

France

Maurice Lévy-Leboyer and Michel Lescure

Gerschenkron did not devote as much research to the economic development of France during the nineteenth century as he did to the cases of Russia, Austria, Germany and Italy. This is hardly surprising given his interest in the specific features of industrialization in conditions of economic backwardness; in spite of all her 'failures', in the middle of the century, France was the most advanced of the large continental countries (Gerschenkron 1962: 44).

Gerschenkron's appraisal of French economic growth reflects what was probably the mainstream view among scholars in the 1950s. 'The period of both the Bourbon Restoration and the so-called Bourgeois Monarchy,' he says, 'must be regarded as one of relative stagnation' (Gerschenkron 1968: 265). Thereafter, he pinpointed a 'spurt' during the 1850s which, however, 'could not be sustained and the French industrial economy continued at a rather slow pace until some acceleration occurred in the years immediately preceding the outbreak of war in 1914' (Gerschenkron 1968: 266). Over the whole of the century, French economic performance is judged as 'unimpressive'. Among the various retarding factors that were then discussed by the literature on the subject, Gerschenkron stresses the character of the 'French family farms' and an ill-advised tariff policy (Gerschenkron 1968: 268).

The 'spurt' of the 1850s is linked by Gerschenkron to a number of factors that include a very liberal tariff policy and an ideological climate stressing the advantages of industrialization created by the followers of Saint-Simon (Gerschenkron 1962: 11–26). Moreover, 'French industry received a powerful positive impetus from ... the development of industrial banking under Napoleon III' (Gerschenkron 1962: 12). At the same time, 'the French failure to reimport the French innovation in banking in the creatively adjusted form of the mixed bank' (Gerschenkron 1968: 391) seems to Gerschenkron to be partly responsible for the fact that the 'spurt' was exceptionally short-lived.

In the last twenty years or so, research on the process of early French industrialization has made substantial progress both at the macro and micro levels. As a result of research at the macro level, neither the periodization proposed by Gerschenkron nor his overall impression of sluggish growth, particularly during the first half of the century, seem tenable today (Table 8.1).

Table 8.1 Growth rates of French real output and capital formation, constant boundaries (% per annum)

	Agriculture	Non-agricultural sector		GDP	GDCF	Investment level (%)
		industry	total			
1826–46	0.7	1.8	1.6	1.3	2.0	8.1
1846–56	1.1	2.0	2.3	2.0	2.0	8.2
1856–66	2.5	1.3	1.3	1.6	1.1	7.4
1866–75	2.0	1.3	1.5	1.7	1.0	5.4
1875–82	−0.7	2.6	3.1	2.0	4.9	9.1
1882–92	0.2	0.8	1.0	0.8	−1.3	6.4
1892–1900	2.4	1.4	1.9	2.1	2.2	8.2
1900–13	0.4	2.5	2.2	1.7	2.5	8.8

Source: Lévy-Leboyer and Bourguignon (1985: app. A-IV): and Lévy-Leboyer (1978: table 60) for column 5. The 1866–75 rates, if uncorrected for the 1871 change in territory, would have been 1.7 per cent, 0.8 per cent, 1.1 per cent and 1.3 per cent. Investment levels in terminal years (1846, 1856, and so forth) are the ratios of net domestic capital formation to NNP.

Industrial output grew on average by 1.9 per cent a year up to 1860. During the first half of the century new industrial structures were developed in various parts of the country by merchants and local manufacturers. The two central decades of the century witnessed major technical and organizational progress that slowed down in the late 1860s. Between 1860 and 1890 the rate of growth of industrial output fell to a yearly average of 1.2 per cent because of sluggish demand for consumers' goods, exports and investment.

Moreover, recent research has strengthened whatever doubts Gerschenkron himself seems to have had in applying his analytical framework to the French case. The resource endowment of France was not that of a backward country. Unlike other countries, it could not draw a significant impulse from the use of large and indivisible investments, the borrowing from abroad of the most modern and efficient equipments, with their skilled labour-saving effect, and from the setting up of banking institutions expected to bring about forced saving by their money-creating activities. The labour force was neither scarce nor uneducated in France when the industrialization process was starting. The widespread use of the domestic system in the rural districts of the country (some 75 per cent of total population lived outside the cities) gave an opportunity for merchant-manu-facturers to use a well-trained and rather abundant work force. Further, in order to raise labour's technical level and make it more suitable for employment in factories, some of the large manufacturing enterprises, especially in the east and the centre of the country, set up technical and elementary schools that took in workers and their children. These schools improved the level of literacy in the country (30 per cent of men among married couples were able to read by 1860).

Similar improvements were registered in the field of savings, as one could guess by taking into account the fact that real income per head rose by more than 1.2 per cent per annum from 1840 up to 1880 (Table 8.2).

In the countryside the fall in birth rates coupled with a substantial increase in real agricultural prices provided for a rising standard of living for rural people, especially in the 1840–80 period. And even though there were important groups that did not share in the general prosperity (particularly the working class up to the 1850s), most of the people in the cities saw their situation improve. The rise in wealth-holding per inhabitant was 3 per cent per annum in Lille during the first half of the century and 2 per cent in Paris. Coming along with the growth of the National Debt (to some 20 billion francs in 1875–9, i.e. ten times the figure of 1815–19), these developments were to modify the allocation of funds by savers. The shares of real and personal property in Paris, according to a sample of estates, were in a ratio of 52:48 in 1820, and of 45:55 in 1847. To some extent, the holding of public bonds (as high as 37 per cent among financial assets) was a preliminary step toward a greater diversification of private savings. In France, therefore, the need for institutional arrangements to make up for a deficiency in skills and savings cannot be considered so stringent a precondition for growth as in other countries.

However, this is not to deny any utility to the account Gerschenkron gave of the key factors that bear on industrial development. Backward countries were not the only ones that could expect to benefit from the impact of the railroads and the setting up of large universal banks. We agree with Gerschenkron that these factors were important in the case of France, but we think that his analysis and interpretation of the French evidence has to be modified in the light of recent research. Therefore, we shall review the findings of this research and reinterpret the role of French railways and banks.

THE STATE AND THE RAILROADS

Even though one would not find a special section devoted to French public works in any of Gerschenkron's writings, those who heard his lectures will recall that he

Table 8.2 Real income per head in England and France (US dollars)

| | A. Maddison | | | | | P. Bairoch | | N. Crafts | |
	1840	1860	1880	1900	1912	1860	1913	1870	1910
England	612	863	1051	1366	1455	600	1070	904	1302
France	467	605	747	949	1149	380	670	567	883
Ratio	76	70	71	69	79	63	63	63	68

The estimates are either in 1970 US dollars, as in the case of Maddison (1979) and Crafts (1983), or in 1960 dollars in that of Bairoch (1981).

drew attention to the importance of Napoleon III's railroad policy: First, France needed to enlarge its market base – the high cost of transport being as detrimental to growth, in Gerschenkron's account, as the French tariff, which by contrast he discussed at length. Second, railroad construction required heavy capital investments and the need to develop a producers' goods sector, which, Gerschenkron thought, was to play a major role in the initial stages of any industrialization process. It is obvious that on both accounts the building of French railroads answered these purposes. The deficiencies in the density of the network were swiftly overcome. Rail tracks (measured on a per capita basis), which were in a ratio of 1:5 in 1840 (France: Belgium, England and Germany), levelled off to near equality, at 1:1.25 in 1869 and 1880. By 1913, the positions came to be reversed with 104 km of tracks (per 100,000 inhabitants) in France, against 89 km in the three other countries and 54 km in Italy, equivalent to the French position in the 1860s.

The diversification of industries followed in step. Building up from Walther Hoffmann's findings, Gerschenkron used estimates showing that the ratio of consumers' to producers' goods moved in a steady fashion in favour of capital equipments. According to him, modern industry was limited in France before the 1820s, but the ratio was already at about 4:1 in 1860–5, obviously as a result of the boom in railroad construction. It fell to 2.3:1 in 1896, and 1.5:1 in 1921, bringing France to parity with England and other industrial countries. One should also add that these figures are broadly in line with more recent estimates (Table 8.3).

Further, in conformity with Gerschenkron's 'big spurt' concept, growth accelerated twice, with railroads and the state both acting as moving forces. In fact, French national income and capital formation series, now available for the nineteenth century, present two long waves of 20–25 years, with peaks in 1856 and 1882 that coincide with those of railroad investments. At each of these upper turning points, the amount invested in new tracks and rolling stock amounted to some 20–29 per cent of the net capital formation; and the capital flow fell back at the end of the downswing, to 16 per cent in 1867–74 and to 12 per cent in 1894–7, a fact that confirms the importance of railroads in accelerating and retarding the growth process.

France, moreover, was spared the many crises that often plagued railroad construction in other countries, very much because of the state's numerous initiatives. From the very start, public engineers supervised the concessions and in some cases the material building of the lines. They sketched out the first national network that received parliamentary sanction in 1842, and also the two next systems that were planned in response to economic slowdowns in 1857–9 and 1876–8. Financial aid was granted for the building of some of the main lines and also to subsidize companies in difficulty; eventually, some twelve railroads were taken over and amalgamated into a state company in 1876–8 and in 1908. In short, public funds allocated to the whole system increased over time from 1.4 billion F in 1823–75 to 4.5 billion F in 1876–1913, i.e. one-third of the 18.5

Table 8.3 Industrial production: value-added (%)

	1840	1860	1880	1900	1910	1922	1930
Consumers goods	65.3	61.7	64.7	61.0	58.9	56.7	53.2
Producers goods	9.1	12.0	16.9	22.2	24.5	29.2	31.2
Basic industry	7.5	10.1	12.6	16.3	17.8	18.5	22.1
Mechanical engineering	1.6	1.9	4.3	5.9	6.7	10.7	9.1
Building, etc	25.6	26.3	18.4	16.8	16.6	14.1	15.6
Total	100.0	100.0	100.0	100.0	100.0	100.0	100.0
Ratio (consumer: producer)	7:1	5:1	4:1	3:1	2:1	2:1	1.7:1

Source: Markovitch (1966: appendix, table 4).
All data are ten-year averages (1835–44), 1845–54, and so forth, except 1910 (1905–13)
and 1922 (1920–4). As in Gerschenkron's calculations, producers' goods include basic
industries, machinery and engineering (lines b and c).

billion F that were required to open up the roads (what is called '*les dépenses de premier éstablissement*') throughout the country.

But even if the French case seems to give validity to Gerschenkron's general account, one may still question the extent, the duration, and the ultimate results of a policy that moved so many resources for the benefit of a single sector. Early in the century, transports occupied a strategic position to create a market, and the massive investments they required could have only positive results for the economy during some 10 or 20 years. But the analysis of their longer-term effects is lacking. In spite of the interrelatedness that is said to exist between industries, it is a fact that French mechanical and engineering industries were slow to reach maturity: as may be seen from Table 8.3, the sector did not contribute more than 20–25 per cent of the value added by producers' goods up to the 1880s, their share increasing only after the turn of the century, conspicuously under the impact of war demand. In 1913, French production of machinery represented only 6 per cent of the combined output of England and Germany, and less than 5 per cent of that of the United States. Obviously, the backward linkage did not operate in the way Gerschenkron suggested.

Similarly, in the forward sectors, the effects of a more unified market are still uncertain. Jean Toutain has made estimates showing that transport activity, over the 1840–1913 period, increased at a rate of 3.3 per cent per annum, almost twice the 1.4 per cent registered for commodity output. But there are no criteria to assess the value of such a performance, and, for instance, no way to determine whether the state controls that were imposed upon the companies as a substitute for their outright purchase in 1848 and again in the 1870s, had positive or negative effects. Thus, it is necessary to re-examine Gerschenkron's hypothesis to give more specific answers to the three problems raised by the advent of the railroads: Did they contribute to improving the integration of the French market? Its capital equipment? And, as a side aspect, the quality of French business management?

Market integration

The first major lines that were built up to 1856, from the borders to the capital, and some of the feeder lines added in the 1860s had beneficial effects. With the fall in freight rates, remote agricultural regions, among others, were given access to Paris and northern export markets, and, with it, the possibility to break in new lands, increase their grain and wine crops, and improve their terms of trade. There was a consensus in 1876–8, when a state network of 17,000 km of low-traffic lines (a near doubling of the existing system) was being contemplated by Freycinet, that the social profit coming from the railroads had been substantial. According to L. Marchal, an engineer writing in 1880, the extra cost of using railroads instead of waterways (a difference of some 1 billion F, or 4 per cent of current production) was more than made up for by the speed and regularity of the new transport, by the reduction in the volume of stocks, and by the rise in prices and output. It was often held that the opening of new local lines at a cost of some 150,000–200,000 F per km would necessarily bring returns, since that had been the case in the past with the trunk lines that had required three times that amount to build.

But some civil servants and company managers were more sceptical. They highlighted the poor design of the first networks, and the fact that they had been drawn to cover equally the different regions without due attention to the inequalities of their traffic potential. As early as 1869, only 5,380 km out of a total of 15,480 km, and only one single company out of six brought some profit; as much as 72 per cent of the lines were operated at a loss by the Eastern, the Western and the PLM companies. Further, even if many railroad directors had displayed commercial skills in the 1850s, for instance, by opening branch offices to by-pass other shippers and control the market–traffic expansion was at its peak in 1846–56 (Table 8.4) – the trend quickly turned around: (1) Travelling by rail remained of limited use; at the end of the 1860s, with networks of equal length, British companies had three times more third-class passengers and 25–30 per cent more gross income, all categories included, than the French ones; and (2) freight shipments became scarcer – in the 1860s probably because the substitution effects due to the railroads were almost exhausted, and from the 1870s because coal and primary metals, cash crops and building materials were hit by the general depression that slowed down activity. Competition also worked in reverse, as water transports, which had the benefit of free way, new government subsidies, and a greater flexibility in pricing, were able to attract a greater share of the traffic. They handled 24 per cent of the combined shipments by water and rail in 1895, against 16 per cent in 1880.

Eventually, a revival set in during the 1890s, bringing increased activity on the

Table 8.4 Main transport indicators, 1826–1913

	Transport volume growth rates (% pa)			Freight rates c. per t/km		Railroad product 1000 F p. km		Ratio
	Total	Canals	Rail	Canal	Rail	Gross	Net	%
1826–46	2.5	–	–		11.4	39.3	20.7	52.7
1846–56	4.5	–	20.6	–	7.6	54.7	30.7	56.1
1856–66	3.7	2.3	9.7	6.4	6.0	44.8	23.9	53.4
1866–75	2.7	−1.2	3.7	6.6	6.1	44.6	21.9	49.1
1875–82	3.7	2.0	4.4	7.1	5.9	44.1	20.9	47.4
1882–92	2.2	4.6	1.3	5.7	5.4	33.9	14.9	44.0
1892–1913	2.3	2.4	3.8	5.3	4.1	50.5	18.4	36.4

Source: Annuaire statistique (1947); Toutain (1967); Merger (1979).
Data for freight rates and railroad product are those of the terminal years (1846, 1856, 1866, and so forth).

roads, new shipments (more diversified products from southern agricultural, iron ore from Briey, and so on), and a definite improvement in the financial position of the Eastern, the PLM, and some other companies.

In spite of these more favourable developments, however, the French network could not overcome its major weakness, namely the fact that it had been overbuilt almost from the start. Whatever the reason, public constraints or unrealistic expectations, railroads receipts in 1869 were 59,700 F per km, against 75,130 F for the British railroad lines. And the gap kept increasing with the construction of the third network, so that average products, still on a per km basis, were some 42,600 F and 78,060 F in the two countries in 1908, and 60,100 F in Germany. On social or moral grounds, extension of the network may have been justified, but it proved harmful for the companies because it lowered the net product – to 4,350 F per km in the pre-war years on the third network, against 51,000 F and 14,000 F in Britain and Germany. It also penalized the country as a whole, since people living in remote regions were offered artificial marketing conditions that saved them the trouble of moving to the cities. The near stoppage of internal migrations in the 1880–1905 period – of which railroad policy was only one factor among others – contributed in a major way to slowing down the growth of the economy. France at the end of the century was still a rural country, with 65 per cent of its population living in small villages, 15 per cent in sixteen large cities (of more than 100,000 inhabitants), and 20 per cent dispersed in some 700 towns. It was still without the densely populated urban base that was required to make a modern market economy viable.

Industrial capacity

When the first railroads were constructed, some major advances were realized in the basic industries. Obviously, the negative expectations that had hampered investments in earlier periods were no longer justified. Actually, over the century as a whole, track construction and replacement required some 15 million tons of rails, one-fifth of France's metal output, hastening the use of new technology: railroad orders averaged 40 per cent of the coal-processed iron in the 1850s, when British methods were coming into general use, 65 per cent of Bessemer and Siemens steel in 1866–75, and as high as 22 per cent of Thomas steel in the pre-war years, in spite of the greater diversification of demand. Similarly, French mechanical industries were developed with the financial aid and direct orders that locomotive builders received from railroad companies. Even if their production never matched that of their British colleagues, the five leading French firms were able to export in the 1860s as much as 40 per cent of their production, a real achievement in a country where, as a consequence of poor mineral resources, alternative markets were limited.

But the success was short-lived. Steel production, which had reached in the 1870s a level equivalent to 15 per cent of European output, fell to less than 10 per cent, and did not regain its past position until the pre-war years. French mechanical industries also lost ground, and, strange as it may seem, never managed to reassert themselves. Locomotive building, in particular, which had grown at a time of peak capacity at a rate of 500 engines a year, recovered somewhat, after a break, to only 150–200 units (of higher power standards) in 1900–4, and 600–700 on the eve of the war. This did not amount then to more than 5 per cent of the combined output of England, Germany and the United States, and only some 20–25 per cent of what a strong American firm could distribute in a year. To explain this loss in competitiveness and the industry's poor adaptation to market changes, one may be tempted to use what was said formerly of the conservative attitudes and values of French entrepreneurs. But business studies have brought a revision of such negative appraisals. It seems fair to say that the blame should be laid not with the firms that supplied railroad equipment but rather with the railroad companies.

The demand for metals in the 1850s had remained high because, apart from laying the tracks, railway engineers had to replace them frequently because of the poor quality of the materials used and the unanticipated increase in the traffic once networks entered service. But in the 1870s and early 1880s, the whole process grew out of proportion for three main reasons: (1) the need to repair damage on the lines after two periods of heavy traffic resulting from the Prussian War in 1870–2, and to the closing of canals during the winter of 1879–80; (2) a general policy applied simultaneously from 1872–3 to substitute steel for iron rails, the companies being led by the sharp fall in the price of steel and its greater durability to re-lay large sections of lines and give orders in advance of normal replacement so as to forestall shortages; and (3) in the early 1880s, after three years of preparatory studies, the start of building operations on the new state lines under the Freycinet plan. All told, 4 million tons of rails were brought into the market in some thirteen years, one-quarter of the total production of that century. Abnormal industrial investments followed. Hence, in 1882 when a monetary panic broke out and imposed abrupt curtailments on all expenditures including those of the state, a sharp recession set in that almost destroyed the steel industry in central France where firms were too heavily indebted. In 1886, Terrenoire, the leading and most modern firm, was sold for scrap, and others followed. In fact, the whole episode slowed down production and technical progress in every region, including the new Lorraine Basin where Thomas steel reached its first million tons only in 1907. The mishandling of rail orders in a crucial period had cost the French industry 10–15 years of steady growth.

Firms that supplied rolling stock fared better in the crisis. Orders had been more evenly distributed over time and between countries (some 20 per cent to foreign industry in 1880–4), and a diversification of markets and products remained possible. But the fall in transport activity that ensued imposed new guidelines among railway managers, and their impact proved harmful in the long run for the French mechanical industries. First, reversing their past investment policies, the railways reduced all expenses, paying greater attention to labour productivity, train loads and turnover, and maintenance and repair, in order to extend the lifespan of equipment and postpone replacement expenditure. From almost 350 units a year in 1875–86, new orders for locomotive engines averaged less than 90 in the late 1880s and 1890s, a fall of 75 per cent. Further, since the state was called upon to assist the companies once they had taken charge of the Freycinet lines, its engineers brought pressure upon railway managers to exact lower prices from industry, to set higher standards, and also to divide orders between firms, a policy that hampered productivity gains in the mechanical industry sector.

In a way, all this proved successful; current expenditures on the French railroads were kept to a minimum, at 23,700 F per km in the pre-war years, against 42,000–49,000 F in England and Germany (or 56 per cent versus 63–70 per cent of current receipts). But this was achieved to the detriment of industrial performance: French exports of machinery were outpriced from the 1870s; and when new railroad orders for replacement and extension were at last issued in 1900, and with greater regularity after 1906, almost 30 per cent of the locomotives (and in fact more than half the machinery used in the country) had to be imported. There had been no spin-off from the gains that were secured earlier in the century.

Business management

The railroads were the first large-scale corporations to operate at a national level. As such, they were used in many countries to teach how to build managerial hierarchies, control and coordinate operations, allocate responsibilities over large territories, keep accounts, issue stocks and plan investments. These functions were performed effectively in France, a fact that should have built, in contemporary opinion, a positive image of the services railroads could achieve. In practice, however, the outcome was not favourable, probably because the public resented the assumption by profit-seeking individuals of a public service, against all past traditions. Further, there was resentment of the monopoly position railroads held once the twenty-eight existing railways were merged into six major companies, and of the many privileges that were granted them, including state guarantees of their bonded debt (as part of two agreements for taking over the construction of the second and third networks in 1859 and 1883). In short, public opinion was alerted by the fact that the private firms had assumed a power that could lead to abuse and ought to be regulated. Thus, instead of taking the emergence of railroad companies as a unique experience that could bring an improvement in business practices, a movement developed through the chambers of commerce and other local authorities requesting a reinforcement of public controls and disregarding the contra-productive effects these controls might have on the economy at large.

Among the questions that were submitted by statute to official commissions, tariff rates came up early as one of the most sensitive issues. At first, the railways adopted flexible schedules; they tried to apply favourable treatment to the large, regular, long-distance shipments so as to reach fuller utilization of their lines and to reduce prices. But this entailed some discrimination against the smaller shippers and a possible displacement of trade routes. Therefore, under the influence of local pressure groups, the advisory commission stepped in and imposed, from 1854 to 1857, a policy of strict uniformity; freight rates were made equal for all, whatever the volume, the distance, and the firm, under what was called 'the rule of the unspecified station' (any rebate on a line being immediately published and made the general case). But even if the principle seemed justified in equity, it probably neutralized some of the productivity gains that could have been expected from the fall in freight rates and an early redistribution of trade. The financial accounts also became a major issue once the state stepped in to cover the deficit. The problem raised was to improve control of railways and perhaps limit their spending. Thus, in the 1880s, the balance sheets and book-keeping methods used in the public sector were adopted, although they often ran against current accounting practices. For instance, industrial amortization ceased to be applied to the railroads, since the jurisprudence set by the Council of State was that all equipment should be written off in one lump sum the year it had to be scrapped or sold, and this at the price that had been paid for the equipment in the past.

Actually, the problem was not limited to the fact that market prices and normal accounting procedures could not operate in an efficient way. Risks and profit also lost their proper functions, in part because industry and foreign interests initially had supplied the equity capital (20 per cent of the 1.5 billion F in 1850 were British and Swiss). Later, once the state guarantee had generalized the use of bonds for the construction of the track, and after 1883 for all current operations, there was no need to increase the capital at risk. In 1900, it did not amount to more than 1.4 billion F, while the bonded debt had been raised to 16 billion F, almost 30 per cent of the French securities listed on the stock market. And profits also were foregone because, as an offset for the public funds that were advanced to service the debt, the companies were compelled to set aside part of the expected incomes coming from the first network in order to finance the second and, eventually, the third networks. As a consequence, profits were capped, the shareholders renouncing their claim to increased dividends. From 1864 to 1908, some 5.1 billion F (or 3.6 billion in net terms when state advances are deducted) were 'diverted' internally between the three networks.

In other words, if the allocation of funds had functioned properly during the first decades of railroad operations, the change of procedure that was imposed upon the companies by the convention of 1858 blurred the issues. New stations, new lines, and new services were developed in the second half of the century at steadily reduced prices for passengers and shippers, giving the impression that there was no limit to demand and progress. The state itself received transport services at free or reduced rates that amounted over the century to 3.2 billion F of foregone incomes. But these developments also had their costs, namely, (1) excessive capital outlays – 21.3 billion F of private savings were sunk in the railroads; (76 per cent in bonds, 6 per cent in shares, and 17 per cent in foregone dividends); (2) low earnings for the bond- and shareholders – they amounted in 1900 to some 650 million F a year, or 3 per cent of their market value; and (3) on the part of the railroads, some lack of response to market demand once growth had recovered: In the absence of true productivity gains, expenses on the lines increased after 1892 at a higher rate than receipts, leaving a net product per kilometre equivalent to 36.4 per cent of gross income in 1913, against 48.1 per cent in 1866–92, and 54.1 per cent earlier in the century.

THE BANKS

Even more than railroads, Gerschenkron emphasized the role of the Saint-Simonian banks set up during the Second Empire period. 'Designed to build thousands of miles of railroads, drill mines, erect factories, pierce canals ...', the new joint-stock industrial banks (Crédit Mobilier of the Pereires was the paragon) were said to have given 'a powerful positive impetus' to French industry.

Although there are few recent studies devoted to these banks, it is obvious that such an appraisal is in line neither with the views of many contemporaries nor with some major historical hypotheses. On the one hand, these banks have been charged with wasting national savings through urban speculations and foreign investments. As a result of the development of public works and the railroadization of the southern and eastern European countries in the 1850s and the 1860s, most of the new universal banks turned to speculative urban ventures and looked abroad for investment opportunities. In the following decades, when the deficit in both the state budget and the balance of trade curtailed the range of these opportunities, banks were led to prospect more actively in the markets by setting up building societies and foreign branches, which made their role if not more important, at least more visible.

On the other hand, it has been argued that, along with these conspicuous activities, the domestic productive operations of the banks developed rather slowly. During a first period, running from the foundation years through the early 1880s, when most of the banks patterned on the Pereire bank were thought by Gerschenkron to have encompassed a wide range of operations, the business of these banks seems to have been confined to the narrow circle of the founders' groups (such as the companies of Talabot for Société Générale) or to firms and sectors spared from market constraints by concessions (transport businesses and public utilities), by positions of monopoly (in the case of Crédit Mobilier), or by patents (in that of Crédit Lyonnais). As a general rule, enterprises and sectors that were more exposed to the pressure of competition remained on the fringes of the large banks' interests. In the 1860s, for instance, less than 3 per cent of the manufacturers and merchants of Paris were customers of Comptoir d'Escompte de Paris. Although these banks progressively lowered the scale of their transactions in order to enlarge the scope of their business, the average size of the bills they discounted in the later 1870s remained 62 per cent higher than that of all bills issued at this time. In the ensuing period (1880–1914), when large joint-stock banks gave up their universal-bank pattern to be turned into deposit banks (designed to serve exclusively as a source of short-term capital), it has been argued that the search for liquidity was pushed too far. As demonstrated by several surveys, small and middle-sized manufacturing enterprises in financing their long-run investment needs as well as craftsmen and tradespeople in financing their short-term transactions did not make much use of the joint-stock banks.

The share of the largest banks in total lending provides further evidence that they did not succeed in expanding their relative position in the domestic market (Table 8.5).

Far from increasing their sway over the corporate banking sector, the largest banks tended to lose ground at the turn of the century. This was a rather unexpected result. These banks had been launched by the most important financial and industrial groups of the country and with state involvement, which enabled them to be large corporations from the start. In the following, we shall discuss the reasons for the large banks' failures to attain their destinies.

Universal banks as substitutes for the lack of investment opportunities (1850–80)

Rather than playing a central role in processes of forced saving, French universal banks can be said to have attempted to overcome the deficiency of home

Table 8.5 Four largest banks' advances and deposits as percentage of banks publishing their balance sheets

	1891	1901	1911
Total assets	60.2	65.8	51.5
Securities holding	50.4	42.5	22.3
Advances	57.5	65.2	45.2
Commercial portfolio	66.3	70.7	64.5
Deposits	68.4	72.1	57.6

Source: J.L. Billoret, 'Systeme bancaire et dynamique économique dans un pays à monnaie stable, La France de 1816 à 1914', doctoral diss., Université de Nancy, 1969. The four largest banks are Crédit Lyonnais, Société Générale, Comptoir Nationale d'Escompte de Paris, Crédit Industriel et Commercial.

productive investment opportunities. As often recalled, these banks came into being when growth slowed down after a thirty-year period of economic progress. The buoyancy of the early railroadization period was gone. Gross domestic investment as a proportion of GNP remained stable at 12–13 per cent from 1845–54 to 1875–84. Relative economic stagnation along with the growing integration of firms curbed the growth of commerical transactions: growth in the issue of bills of exchange from the late 1850s was much lower than in the previous period.

New factors, however, were at work on firms' side. The period running from the 1860s to the early 1880s experienced a major shift in the process of industrialization. Operating as driving forces, the rise in real wages (from the 1850s), market integration (from the 1860s), and the growth of external competition (in the 1870s) compelled firms to reduce their costs both to maintain their profit levels and to make their products more suitable to international demand. Certain types of investment goods also received powerful impulses from these circumstances. The rate of growth of gross domestic investment in tools and machinery (as a proportion of GNP) rose to 3.3 per cent annually from 1845–54 to 1875–84; this is 2½ times the rate reached during the thirty previous years. But these developments were not to provide many additional opportunities to new large banks for three reasons:

(1) Long-term investment came not so much from banks as from firms themselves or from private persons with money available. In the northern woollen industry, for instance, the mechanization of combing from 1852 was partially financed by local trade; that of the silk-weaving in Lyon after 1876 was provided by the 'Fabrique'. Even in the most capital-intensive industries, self-reliance through retained profits remained a general rule. As shown from the example of metallurgy in the centre of France, which spent large sums from 1860 to 1873 in order to develop coke equipment and set up Bessemer converters, the call to the banks to provide financing was rather meagre. And to meet any serious

emergencies resulting from the shortage of liquid funds (a frequent problem with self-financing practices), firms could rely on the large current accounts of the partners or staff (39 per cent of the floating debt, for instance, at Société de Terrenoire in 1884) or they could require more financing facilities from their suppliers or from their customers. Railway companies, for instance, offered large instalments and advances to their contractors (for raw materials and sometimes for new equipment), especially when demand for rails or locomotives tended to exceed supply.

(2) The rise in stock market operations provided new financing opportunities for large firms. As the French capital market became more mature, the corporate sector of the economy tended directly to discharge its debts and to do without financial intermediaries. In the six years from 1867 to 1872, Schneider et Compagnie, a top-ranking enterprise, issued 14 million F of securities in order to be less dependent on its bankers.

(3) This is not to deny that banks played a role in the process of economic growth. Rather, it is to affirm that local banks, not the large national banks, were to have the more important role. By contrast with Saint-Simonian views, the French banking system was not underdeveloped at mid-century. According to a recent survey (Plessis 1987), there were 2,000 or 3,000 unit banks by 1870; this is four or six times more than Cameron (1967) estimates. Some of these banks date back to the first half of the nineteenth century, but encouraged as they were by economic growth and the setting up of numerous branches by Banque de France (which carried benefits for local bankers), many banks came into existence during the Second Empire period. Most of them were small local private banks, but as they had been launched by merchants and manufacturers to respond to local needs, they enjoyed advantages in meeting competition from the new large banks. Until the latter extended their branch networks (by 1872, Société Générale had less then thirty-seven permanent offices throughout the country and Comptoir d'Escompte had no more than five), the local banks were able in their decentralized positions to draw the custom of local enterprises. They offered these enterprises facilities to buy raw materials and to meet the cost of holding the finished goods; they cashed their cheques and they discounted their bills. They were so successful that many branches of Banque de France (such as in Lyon or Grenoble) complained that discount was lacking. Large corporations themselves resorted to them; Chatillon-Commentry, the fourth largest metal-lurgic firm in France in 1880, financed its several plants through half a dozen local bankers led by Moussy and Armetz of Montluçon.

Local bankers were not merely suppliers of short-term self-liquidating credits. The intimacy of the relationship between banker and local industry and trade allowed more significant commitments from the banks. In the north, for instance, banks such as L. Dupont or Caisse Commerciale du Nord provided sugar and textile industries with long-term capital. As shareholders or managers, local bankers in Lyon (Aynard, Guérin, Veuve Morin-Pons) were present in all the regional activities (mining, metallurgy, textiles), and their influence spread far beyond the city. Where industrial and financial traditions were not so ancient, local bankers supported regional development by taking up parcels of shares in new companies and by channelling local savings to enterprises. In Lorraine, for instance, the iron and steel industry began with an active role of banks such as Weill Levy et Compagnie, Banque Lenglet or Banque Thomas.

All things considered, a banking system based on local units proved quite adequate for economic structures in which small and middle-sized enterprises were the prominent figures. This made the role to be played by the new large joint-stock banks less crucial than Gerschenkron, among others, implied.

The universal banks at the regional level (1880–1914)

The balance between national and local banks was not immutable. By 1880 or so, both supply and demand factors ought to have enlarged the role of national banks.

During the late 1870s and the early 1880s, the national banks considerably extended their branch networks (the number of offices increasing, for instance, by about 34 per cent at Société Générale), and their resources rose by some 44 per cent between 1872 and 1882. Furthermore, a more efficient banking system as a whole could be expected from the new guidelines followed by large banks, which served to increase the specialization of financial institutions. Three waves of bankruptcies that took place in 1867, 1876 and 1882, with their harmful effects on the economy, had enlightened banks' managers on the difficulties of matching the two sides of the mixed banks' balance sheets, especially when industrial production turned down. As a result of both the growth of their branch networks and the disappointing performance of the French economy, large banks severely curtailed their illiquid transactions. Crédit Lyonnais in the 1880s, Comptoir d'Escompte in the 1890s, and Société Générale in the 1900s cut off their investment portfolios and checked their long-term lending activities. Credits were divided up and shortened (discounts and advances rising from 56.9 per cent of the banking assets in the 1870s to 69 per cent in the closing decade of the nineteenth century), and financial expenses cut down by reducing savings accounts. More significant industrial commitments were left to the 'Old Banks' (particularly active in petroleum and electrical industries) and to new financial corporations specially designed to provide long-term loans and to control industrial operations through shareholdings and 'participations' in other firms. In 1913, for instance, the investment portfolio of Banque de Paris et des Pays-Bas, an investment bank launched by private bankers in 1872, amounted to 160 million F (more than 20 per cent of its assets), which allowed the bank to be related with 120 large companies.

On the firms' side, the second stage of industrialization in France, from the 1880s, was to provide new opportunities to the banking system. For historical reasons (such as the loss of the Alsatian pole of mechanical industries) as well as for economic ones (such as the overcommitment of many ancient corporations with unprofitable investments), new enterprises in France assumed a larger role than in other countries in the start of new industries such as motor cars and steel. Even though capital requirements remained generally modest, fast-growing young firms were likely to turn to banks for financial facilities.

Nevertheless, it was the country banks rather than the large national banks that appear to have been more successful in taking advantage of these new opportunities. Changes were also under way on their side. From the crowd of local unit banks some regional joint-stock banks progressively emerged; the shift went along with the change of scale in economic structures. Some of these banks which had been launched with the support of Parisian banks (namely the Crédit Industriel et Commercial group) now went their own way and made their status more suitable to local needs. By doing so, banks such as Crédit du Nord, Société Lyonnaise de Dépôts or Société Marseillaise de Crédit steadily moved towards favouring regional industrialization. Furthermore, country joint-stock banks benefited by the decentralization of economic initiatives allowed by the emergence of new regional industries (such as hydroelectricity in the Alps), the new wave of urban equipment (electric lighting and tram), and the narrowness of the new liquidity rules followed by national banks. While the commerical portfolio/advances ratio rose from 0.87 in the 1880s to 1.3 in 1913 at the four largest banks, it fell from 2 and 3 at Crédit du Nord and Société Marseillaise de Crédit in the 1860s to 0.62 in 1910–13. In the north and the east of the country as well as in cities such as Lyon, Grenoble, Marseilles and Bordeaux, current account loans (most of them without any security) and credits, even though they were disguised as short-term advances, were in fact often long-term loans. The basic nature of country banks was the rolling over of formerly short-term advances. When designed to serve new investments, advances were usually coupled with further securities issues. Country banks were in charge of connecting firms' demands for capital with the regional supply of loanable funds. A broad indication of their efficiency in this business is provided by the fact that Stock Exchange transactions increased by 68.3 per cent in the country between 1897–1901 and 1909–13, but only by 54.8 per cent in Paris.

The involvement of the country banks with local trade and industry was the consequence of the growing worry of the large banks over their liquidity and that of the policy of Banque de France. Just like regional banks, Banque de France faced serious competition from large banks for discount. The growing amount of their deposits made these banks more reluctant than before to discount their bills at Banque de France. Their commercial portfolio increased by six times from 1884 to 1906, while that of Banque de France fell behind by 1,000 million F. As an attempt to overcome this decline in traditional business, Banque de France turned to the country banks. By discounting their bills, Banque de France enabled the country banks to extend their long-term current account credits without their liquidity being threatened. In order to increase the amount of their transactions, several branches of Banque de France (especially in Lorraine) began to discount bills issued for long-term loans. Thus, far from being the prelude to the death of the country banks, the emergence of a branch banking system enhanced their position. Through a new division of banking work (now a technical division rather than a geographical one), the country banks tended to enlarge their share within the banking system, particularly in the opening decade of the twentieth century.

Some distinctive features of the regional banking system, however, are consistent with Gerschenkron's hypotheses. Three kinds of regional banking practices can be distinguished that to a considerable extent can be regarded as reflecting the specific conditions of regional industrialization. The first pattern, illustrated in Table 8.6 by Crédit du Nord, is that of the old industrial regions. In the north of France, but also in Rouen or Lyon, regional banks gave the same extent to their commercial portfolio as to their advances (the ratio was 48:52 for the seven main northern banks in 1900). As securities-issuing houses, it was only for bonds that these banks played a part of some account. The relative passiveness of these banks was the result of the early start of industrialization in their regions, the small-scale size and the family character of most of the enterprises, and the importance of the textile industry with its relatively high requirements for cash funds rather than for fixed capital.

Quite different were the functions that banks were expected to fulfil in the new industrial areas such as in Lorraine or in Dauphiné. Discount remained an important business for banks (at Société Nancéienne de Crédit, its amount rose from 100 million F to 1,000 million F between 1884 and 1908), but bills were promptly rediscounted at Banque de France. As a result of the specific needs brought by the process of industrialization, the heavy nature of the industries, and the youth of the firms, advances and current account loans represented, for

Table 8.6 Assets and resources structure of corporate banking sector, 1900–9

	% of total assets				
	Four largest banks	Other banks publishing their balance sheet	Crédit du Nord	Société Nancéienne de Crédit	Société Marseillaise de Crédit
Commercial portfolio	47.6	30.3	43.5	11.3	32.5
Advances	38.5	46.9	41.6	82.1	45.8
Securities	3.0	9.0	2.1	2.8	9.6
Capital and reserves	15.6	24.3	15.0	19.9	30.5

The four largest banks are Crédit Lyonnais, Société Générale, Comptoir Nationale d'Escompte de Paris and Crédit Industriel et Commercial. Data are ten-year averages (1900–9) except for columns 1 and 2, where data are two-year averages (1901 and 1911).

instance, 62 per cent of the total banking assets in Lorraine in 1909 against 37 per cent in the north. The consequence was that an important share of deposits (42.5 per cent at Société Nancéienne de Crédit against 10.7 per cent at Crédit du Nord) had no liquid counterpart. The flotation of industrial securities was another means of supporting regional development, an all the more helpful means, as stock exchange facilities were lacking in Lorraine; the issue of bonds and shares amounted to 152 million F from 1899 to 1908 (35 per cent coming from metallurgy, 22 per cent from banks, 13 per cent from electrical industries). The intimacy between banks and industry was both a reason for such an involvement of banks with securities flotations and its consequence. Manufacturers and merchants accounted for 60 per cent in the boards of the four banks of Nancy, so that industrial representatives played a major part in banking behaviour. Similarly, bankers were present on the management boards of 143 firms, so that banks acquired an important degree of ascendancy over industrial enterprises.

These close relationships, however, never turned into 'commandite' from the banks. Ample supplies of savings in their regions allowed these banks to limit their role to that of an intermediary. 'Commandite' was reserved to a third kind of regional bank, illustrated by Société Marseillaise de Crédit. In addition to an important lending activity, this bank held a considerable amount of securities (14 per cent of its assets in the 1890s). Through advances and 'participations' the bank helped to finance the modernization of old industries (such as the sugar industry) and promoted the start of new ones (e.g. public utilities, electrical industries).

This deliberate policy on the part of the bank reflected the scarcity of capital available for industrial purposes rather than the specific conditions of a relatively backward economy. Savings were not lacking in Marseilles, but as a reaction to the speculative character of the local economy (which prevented the bank from making advances without security), savers there were prone to invest in the most secured way (Table 8.7). Houses and public securities represented two-thirds of the private investment in Bouches du Rhône against half in North and in Rhône. By holding shares and bonds of regional (and other) companies, the banks came to be a substitute for the lack of dynamics in local savings.

If the differences within banking practices can be said to have reflected several stages and specific patterns of industrialization, it should be added that they were also to influence further regional banking developments. In contrast to the active role of the eastern and southern banks of the country, most of the regional banks in Lille or Lyon were absent when new industries were launched. Their overcommitment with ancient industries (75 per cent of the board of Crédit du Nord, for instance, came from textiles by 1890) coupled with their role as short-term credit suppliers did not predispose these banks to take a leading part in the start of new industries. Because their practices were not so different from those of large banks, country banks in old industrial regions had little choice but to meet the competition from the large banks by using their methods and to turn into

Table 8.7 Distribution of private investments in 1898

	France	Rhône	Nord	Meurthe et Moselle	Bouches du Rhône
% of total wealth					
Real estates	46.7	38.9	46.1	35.4	57.5
Personal property	53.3	61.1	53.9	63.6	42.5
(securities only)	30.0	32.9	23.6	42.0	22.1
% of securities					
French securities	77.8	69.3	85.9	82.5	76.4
Foreign securities	22.2	30.7	14.1	17.5	23.6
Shares	28.1	33.9	40.5	27.1	20.8
Bonds	37.7	36.8	41.3	39.6	40.3
Public bonds	34.2	29.3	18.2	33.3	38.9

Source: L. Salefranque, 'La fortune privée en France', Congrès international des valeurs mobilières, 1900.

deposit banks. The northern country banks had twenty-four branch offices as early as 1900 and ninety-nine in 1914.

Two factors, however, increased the tendency for passiveness in country banks: (1) The renewal of the extension of their branch networks by national banks after 1894 (the number of offices rising from 258 in 1890 to 1,519 in 1912 for the three largest banks) urged every kind of regional bank to preserve its further development possibilities (particularly with regard to the amount of deposits) by setting up its own branch network. Through amalgamations with small local banks or creation of branch offices, Société Nancéienne de Crédit launched twenty-three branches from 1894 to 1910. But the consequence was the same as for national banks and an increase in cash ratios followed in step. At Société Nancéienne de Crédit, for instance, the amount of short-term current account credits, a new item published in the balance sheet from 1893, usually exceeded that of long-term loans after 1907. (2) Speculative excesses, frequent problems resulting from the tendency for raw materials import prices to rise disproportionately in periods of prosperity, and the magnitude of short-term fluctuations that marked the twenty years of French economy recovery (1895–1913) had similar effects on the banks' behaviour. Facing the same difficulties as those encountered by large mixed banks in the last decades of the nineteenth century, regional mixed banks were included to reverse their policy and become more passive. As a reaction to the important losses registered in 1907–12 on some large advances and financial operations, Société Marseillaise de Crédit, for instance, decided that any further growth of its investment portfolio was to be checked (this item dropping from 14 per cent to 8 per cent of its assets from the 1890s to the 1910s); thereafter, a merger with two local banks brought a welcome twenty-nine offices.

Thus, in France, it was not only the growing influence of national banks over the banking system that led banking away from significant industrial commitments, it was also the successful endeavour of regional banks to defend their liquidity and to slacken their links with regional industries. On the other hand, their rise involved the decline of the private local bankers who remained active through the end of the century. Restrained as they were by the branch network of Caisses d'Epargne from 1875 to 1881, that of national banks from 1894, and that of Banque de France (trying from the late 1890s to increase the number of its direct discounters), local banks had fallen back on 'commandites' and other entrepreneurial functions. The lowest rated in terms of liquidity, these high-risk operations enabled the local banks to find a good return for the deposits they could not afford to lose. Many of them went bankrupt in the 1900s when regional banks joined the ranges of their competitors. These developments were to give new impetus to the debate on the ability of the French banking system to promote economic growth.

CONCLUDING REMARKS

It would be unfair to conclude without mentioning that, beyond the details of his historical account, Gerschenkron's lectures and most of his writings were delivered in the postwar years when the future of Europe, the reconstruction, and the possibility of a new depression such as that of the 1930s were at stake. His ideas and the audience he managed to command had a special value. It came from the fact that he was able to call upon history, as he wrote it, to fit in with ideas prevalent in those days, in particular about investment, as a means not simply to maintain full employment, but also to retrieve backward (or war-damaged) economies and put them back on the path of growth. He addressed himself to problems that were the real concern of the time, and his ideas seemed to be confirmed by contemporary achievements.

But with the passing of time, and a better and more quantified knowledge of the past, it is quite natural that some of his hypotheses, when applied to the French case, should require amendments. First, Gerschenkron's concept of a 'big spurt' provides a good narrative, but has too short a horizon. It is not enough for an economy to begin to industrialize. Industrialization once under way, may go astray. Poverty, inadequate consumption patterns, misguided allocations of capital and labour, slow adaptations to technical change and international competition are issues that were sometimes left out of the picture. They require further analysis.

Moreover, his idea of a 'central push', and the emphasis he laid on Saint-Simonian élites and state bureaucracy, even if they are consistent with French tradition, should not lead to oversimplifications: the state did assist major projects and big banks, but innovations were often carried on by small entrepreneurs who gave flexibility and drive to industry.

And last, one should not take the state as a neutral entity, dedicated solely to the public good – an idea Gerschenkron developed in his treatment of the eighteenth-century enlightened despots. Public works such as the railroads were overextended in the latter part of the nineteenth century under the influence of local interests, and they became themselves a major pressure group when they had to face in the interwar period the competition of air-carriers, trucks and other coal-saving devices. Obviously missing from Gerschenkron's account beyond the initial stages of industrialization is an appreciation of the un-certainties of history that give rise to differences among industrial societies that are almost as great as the differences they exhibited before their industrializations began.

REFERENCES

Bairoch, P. (1981) 'The main trends in national economic disparities since the industrial revolution', in P. Bairoch and M. Lévy-Leboyer (eds) *Disparities in Economic Development since the Industrial Revolution*, London: Macmillan.

Bouvier, J. (1961) *Le Crédit Lyonnais de 1868 à 1882. Les Années de Formation d'une Banque de Dépôts*, Paris: SEVPEN.

—— (1973) *Un Siècle de Banque Française. Les Contraintes de l'Etat et les Incertitudes du Marché*, Paris: Hachette.

Cameron, Rondo (1967) 'France', in R. Cameron *et al.* (eds) *Banking in the Early Stages of Industrialization*, New York: Oxford University Press.

Caron, F. (1973) *Histoire de l'Exploitation d'un Grand Reseau. La Compagnie des Chemins de Fer du Nord, 1846–1937*, Paris: C. Mouton.

Chaline, J.P. (1974) 'La banque à Rouen au XIXe siècle,' *Revue d'Histoire Economique et Sociale* 3, 384–420.

Charpenay, G. (1939) *Les Banques Régionalistes, leur vie, leur mort*, Paris: Editions de la Nouvelle Revue Critique.

Collot, C. (1973) 'Les banques d'affaires meusiennes de 1871 á 1914', *Revue d'Histoire Economique et Sociale* 4, 552–77.

Colson, Cl. (1910) 'Question des transports', *Revue Politique et Parlementaire* X, 381ss.

Crafts, N.F.R. (1983) 'Gross national production in Europe, 1870–1910: some new estimates', *Explorations in Economic History* 20, 387–401.

Crouzet, P. (1977) 'Essor, déclin et renaissance de l'industrie française des locomotives, 1838–1914', *Revue d'Histoire Economique et Sociale* 55 (1–2), 112–210.

Franqueville, Ch. de (1873) *L'Etat et les Chemins de Fer en Angleterre*, Paris.

Gerschenkron, Alexander (1962) *Economic Backwardness in Historical Perspective*, Cambridge, Mass.: Harvard University Press.

—— (1968) *Continuity in History and Other Essays*, Cambridge, Mass.: Harvard University Press.

Hoffmann, Walther (1956) *The Growth of Industrial Economies*, Manchester: Manchester University Press.

Jacquemard, P. (1911) *Les Banques Lorraines*, Paris.

Laloux, J. (1924) *Le Rôle des Banques Locales et Régionales du Nord de la France dans le Développement Industriel et Commercial*, Paris: GIARD.

Leclerc, Y. (1982) 'Les transferts financiers. Etat et compagnies privées de chemin de fer d'intérêt général, 1833–1908', *Revue Economique* 5, 896ss.

Lescure, M. (1982) *Les Banques, l'Etat et la Marché Immobilier en France à l'Epoque Contemporaine 1820–1940*, Paris: Editions de l'EHESS.

—— (1985) 'Banques régionales et croissance économique au XIXe siècle. L'exemple de la Société Marseillaise de Crédit', in *Banque et Investissements en Méditerranée à l'Epoque Contemporaine*, Marseille: Editions de la Chambre de Commerce et d'Industrie de Marseille.

Lévy-Leboyer, M. (1964) *Les Banques Européennes et l'Industrialisation Internationale dans la Première Moitié du XIXe Siècle*, Paris, PUF.

—— (1976) 'Le crédit et la monnaie', in F. Braudel and E. Labrousse (eds) *Histoire Economique et Sociale de la France*, vol. 3, Paris, PUF.

—— (1978) 'Capital investment and economic growth in France, 1820–1930', in *Cambridge Economic History of Europe*, vol. VII, *The Industrial Economies: Capital, Labour and Enterprise*, Cambridge: Cambridge University Press.

Lévy-Leboyer, M. and F. Bourguignon (1985) *L'économie Française au XIXe Siècle. Analyse Macro-économique*, Paris: Economica.

Maddison, A. (1979) 'Per capita output in the long run', *Kyklos* 32 (1–2), 412–29.

Marchal, L. (1880) 'Etude sur la mesure d'utilité des voies de communication', *Journal des Economistes* X.

Markovitch, T.J. (1966) 'L'industrie française de 1789 à 1964: analyse des faits', *Cahiers de l'ISEA*, série AF 6, no. 174 (June).

Merger, M. (1979) *La politique de la IIIe République en matière de navigation intérieure de 1870 à 1914*, PhD thesis, Paris, 451 pp.

Plessis, A. (1985) *La Politique de la Banque de France de 1851 à 1870*, Genève: Droz.

—— (1985) 'Les concours de la Banque de France à l'économie (1842–1914)', in J. Bouvier and J.C. Perrot (eds) *Etats, Fiscalités, Economies*, Paris: Publications de la Sorbonne.

—— (1987) 'Le "retard français": la faute à la Banque? Banques locales, succursales de la Banque de France et financement de l'économie sous le second Empire', in P. Fridenson and A. Straus (eds) *Le Capitalisme Français, 19e–20e Siècles. Blocages et Dynamismes d'une Croissance*, Paris: Fayard.

Pouchain, P. (1986) 'Banque et crédit à Lille de 1800 à 1939', *Revue du Nord* 270, 635–61.

Toutain, J.C. (1967) 'Les transports en France de 1830 à 1965', *Cahiers de l'ISEA*, série AF 9, no. 8 (September–October).

Chapter 9

Germany

Richard Tilly

Germany played an important role in Gershchenkron's work: it supplied the subject of his first major book, *Bread and Democracy* (1943) and subsequently served in his celebrated typology of industrialization[1] as the principal case of 'moderate backwardness' – in which banks supply crucial financial and entrepreneurial inputs. In addition, frequent references to Germany, to German industrialization, and especially to the German universal banks – which he at one point described as an innovation comparable in importance to the steam engine (Gerschenkron 1968: 137) – are scattered throughout his writings. These are grounds for expecting to find important connections between the historiography of German economic history and Gerschenkron's work.

The connections, however, reflect a kind of historiographical multicollinearity. For Gerschenkron's reception in German economic historiography was part of the latter's interest in two major paradigms: (1) The 'growth paradigm' of economics came to dominate European economic history in the 1950s and 1960s, and suggested that German industrialization and its causes – capital accumulation, technical innovation, labour force growth, etc. – represented a species of a larger genus encompassing many, if not all, countries of the world. For this purpose Gerschenkron proved relevant, though not more so than, say, W.W. Rostow or Simon Kuznets (Tilly 1977). (2) The 'Sonderweg' paradigm stressed the need to interpret recent German history as a special case of political, socio-economic and cultural development (or 'modernization') occurring in many countries, but marked in Germany by a sharp discrepancy between successful economic and incomplete political modernization. The norm here is the strong positive correlation between industrialization and democratization – Hobsbawm's 'Dual Revolution' seems apt here – observed for such Western countries as Great Britain, the United States and France. In this 'Sonderwegdebatte', as with Rostow or Gerschenkron, concern with Marxist interpretations of general history in terms of economic classes is paramount. Perhaps H.-U. Wheler's writings offer the best recent example of German work dealing with this triangle of issues: the general relationship between economic and political change in modern history, the challenge of improving upon Marxist versions of that connection, and the fitting of German history into the discussion of both (Wehler 1987).

In the following, I discuss Gerschenkron mainly in association with the first paradigm, but some passing remarks are directed to the second as well. We ask: to what extent does the history of Germany's industrialization reflect, confirm or refute Gerschenkron's view of Europe's modern economic growth. Our answer adopts the primitive approach of running down a checklist of the major elements of his 'syndrome of backwardness'.

THE TIMING OF GROWTH AND THE 'BIG SPURT' DISCONTINUITY

Over the last ten years or so the view that Germany's industrial breakthrough – in Gerschenkron's terminology, its 'big spurt' – came in the 1840s has increasingly dominated the country's economic historiography (Lee 1988). This view supports Gerschenkron since it involves not only the notion of a clear acceleration of industrial production concentrated in producers' goods, but also the successful borrowing of technology from abroad, e.g. in ironmaking and railroad organization, and the unprecedented large-scale development of investment banking. The empirical basis of this view derives from Spree's study of German growth cycles and from a number of studies of heavy industry. The former stresses the cycle-making role of railroad investment and heavy industrial growth from 1840 to 1880, the latter the backward and forward linkages generated by railroad expansion beginning in the 1840s and rising dramatically in the 1850s (Fremdling 1975, 1977; Spree 1977). As Fremdling has shown, thanks to a combination of tariffs and technological progress, continued growth of the German network in the 1850s induced rapid growth of iron output, leading in turn to increasing domestic coal production. We may see this as a case study in successful German borrowing of technology and import substitution aided by tariff policy (Fremdling 1977, 1986; Henning 1973; Holtfrerich 1973).

Nevertheless, it is a case of successful adoption tied to the leading sector, domestic railway expansion. Further studies of the relations between railway demands for equipment and iron materials and the iron and metal-working firms show that railroad orders were a significant source of income for the largest and technologically most progressive firms, and undoubtedly a major cause of their investment programmes (Wagenblass 1973; Krengel 1980). And work on early railroad finance shows that universal banking originated here – modernization of German banking thus being a kind of backward linkage derived from railroad-building (Fremdling 1975: 150–8; Steitz 1974; Spree 1977: 267–73). But perhaps the clearest expression of this view is in Hans-Ulrich Wehler's modern classic volume II of *Deutsche Gesellschaftsgeschichte*. Here, the expansion of heavy industry in the 1840s marks the beginning of Germany's 'industrial revolution' and of the end of the period of her tutelage based on imitation of British industrial technology (Wehler 1987: vol. II, 614).

In my opinion this has been a useful way of looking at German in-dustrialization. However, it has deficiencies, some of which are inherent in the

Gerschenkronian idea of industrialization via a 'big spurt' discontinuity. First, and least important, if one adheres to Gerschenkron's definition of a 'big spurt' as an extended phase of expansion of industrial output covering at least two major business cycles which do not reflect international cyclical downturns, then Germany experienced no 'big spurt' in the nineteenth century (Spree 1977; Gerschenkron 1962: 77, 203).

Second, and more important, the 'big spurt' view is based mainly on empirical study of German heavy industry and railroads, coupled to the leading sector theory of industrialization; it is *not* based on firm quantitative evidence covering other sectors and the *pre*-1840 period. Although the latter period is largely *terra incognita* from the econometric point of view, some quantitative data are available which raise doubts about the uniqueness of the 1840s: (1) Schremmer's recent reworking and extension of Hoffmann's series on industrial investment back to 1815 shows a slowdown in investment in the 1840s relative to the 1820s and 1830s. (2) The same holds for my own estimates of total net capital formation in Prussia over the 1816–49 period. (3) Agricultural output estimates for the entire 1800–60 period identify the 1840s as a time of marked slowdown or even collapse, preceded and followed by respectable growth trends. (4) A careful re-estimation of Spree's industry and social product series using 1850–4 weights (instead of 1913 ones) reversed the ordering of the 1840s and 1850s: the new estimate has the 1840s growing only slightly more than half as much as the 1850s.

Third, and most important, even if the quantitative underpinning of the 'big spurt' of the 1840s were unambiguous, a case could be made for seeing the latter as the result of gradual, cumulative changes in previous decades. An interesting indication of this possibility can be found in recent analyses of the German railroads, already referred to. The weakest link in the argument connecting railroads with the 'big spurt' is the explanation of railway investment itself. Time-series analyses show the latter to depend largely upon previous profits and profit expectations. Studies of the early companies, moreover, suggest that they were generally responses to pre-existing transportation demands; for this reason

Table 9.1 Estimated annual rates of growth (%)

| Net investment levels | | | Agricultural output | | Net domestic product | | |
Schremmer	Tilly		Helling			Spree	Tilly
1815–30	4.68	3.72	1820–30	1.32	1840–50	3.43	1.74
1831–40	3.17	2.20	1830–40	2.58	1850–60	2.03	2.70
1841–50	1.46	1.72[a]	1840–50	0.12	1860–70	−2.02	
			1850–60	1.72	1870–80	2.21	

Sources: Helling (1965); Schremmer (1987); Spree (1977); Tilly (1985).
[a] 1840–9.

they yielded above average returns to their owners – virtually as soon as they began operation (Fremdling 1977: 132–63). According to these findings, the restrictive policies of the German states towards railways in the 1830s held up development, for such profits represented demands which could have been realized earlier. If that is so, we need to explain the emergence of those demands. That is, we need to explain pre-railway, pre-1840 development.

This need enhances the importance of a number of recently revised chapters in the history of Germany's early industrialization. One such chapter concerns the spread of export-oriented rural industry in various parts of Germany since the sixteenth century. This 'protoindustrialization' involved the relative growth of proletaroid strata dependent on non-agricultural wage incomes, the development of supraregional markets for agricultural and protoindustrial products such as cloth, and the accumulation of capital in the hands of merchants creating new needs as well as providing the basis for further expansion of rural industry. Thanks to the work of such scholars as Kriedte, Medick, Schlumbohm, Mager, Schultz or Kisch, we are able to identify dynamic centres of craft-type, industrial development clearly emerging as early as the eighteenth century in such Rhenish centres as Krefeld, Elberfeld and Barmen, or in Saxon regions such as the county of Zwickau. Such regions not only produced the labour surpluses and merchant capitalists characteristic of 'protoindustrialization', but also the cadres of skilled craftsmen and innovative industrial entrepreneurs which introduced factory-type industrial growth in the nineteenth century. Although research on this problem has not yet reached the point where quantitative evidence on the contribution of craft-type development (textiles and iron wares) to German industrialization can be easily summarized, it is clear enough that (1) individual, local examples of rapid industrial growth occurred commonly long before 1840, and that (2) their cumulative effect could conceivably have been weighty enough to have induced the investment of the 1840s (Kriedte *et al.* 1977; Kisch 1981; Schultz 1984; Mager 1988).

A second chapter focuses directly on agriculture – seen by Gerschenkron to play only a minor role in cases of backwardness. Most of the new contributions unfortunately continue to build on the older estimates of von Finckenstein, Helling and Hoffmann, and can only partially overcome the basic uncertainty surrounding them (particularly with respect to estimates of the total area under cultivation and of fallow land). On the one hand, a visible expansion of agricultural production (and of land, seed and labour productivity) can be traced, with interruptions, back to the eighteenth century. Indeed, for the first half of the nineteenth century one can identify productivity gains which could have contributed significantly to economic growth before the take-off ('big spurt') (Finckenstein 1960; Helling 1965; Franz 1976; Rolffs 1976; Dipper 1980). One important source has argued – on the basis of largely non-quantitative evidence – that agrarian households were far and away the most important source of increased demand for domestically produced non-agricultural goods and services in Germany in 1800–50 (Harnisch 1977). This view is supported by old and new estimates of the demand of agricultural producers for iron products (implements, machinery) – a demand which turns out to be approximately equal in aggregate to that of the railroads in the 1840s and 1850s (Fremdling 1986: 335–7; Müller 1987). And further support comes from a recent reassessment of users of early pre-railway nineteenth-century transportation facilities: agricultural products clearly dominated (Kunz 1989). These are grounds for encouraging more work on German agriculture in the early period of industrialization.

The third relevant chapter takes up the growth and structure of German foreign trade and links it to the development of the country's internal trade. It first notes the structure of foreign trade (documented by Borries 1970; Kutz 1974; Dumke 1976): imports of intermediate and colonial products and exports of primary and manufactured goods. It then discusses a triangular trading pattern. The Prussian eastern provinces enjoy a primary goods export surplus *vis-à-vis* Britain, Britain an export surplus with western Germany dominated by intermediate goods (such as iron and yarn), and western Germany enjoys an export surplus *vis-à-vis* the eastern provinces dominated by final manufactured goods. High transportation costs limit east–west trade to relatively high-value commodities. Dumke attempts terms of trade and trade volume comparisons to show that this 'system' is determined by British demand for primary products: an expansion of export of primary goods raises eastern incomes and stimulates eastern German demand for western German manufacturers, while this expansion of sales stimulates, in turn, imports of intermediate goods from Britain. Exports of manufactured goods, particularly textiles and iron goods produced to a large extent under protoindustrial conditions, expand little before 1850, mainly due to British competition. The gradually rising level of internal trade draws attention to the need for internal transportation improvements, which are then carried out, beginning with the road investments of the 1820s and culminating with the railroad projects of the 1830s. The significance of this 'model' is – apart from its interpretation of regional differences – that it offers an explanation of how a virtually stagnating export in manufactures is consistent with a gradually expanding internal trade leading to, indeed, inducing, investment in transportation improvements. It thus offers German industrialization as a case in which export-led growth of one kind gradually turns into rapid industrial growth carried forward by investment and import substitution (Dumke 1979).

These strictures raise the more general question of the timing and character of German industrialization. As suggested, Gerschenkron's 'model' seems to best fit the 'take-off' period from the 1840s to the 1870s. As already noted, that implicitly downgrades the importance of prior changes. It has another defect, however. It obscures the subsequent changes in German economic life which were also part of the industrialization process. Historians have argued that German industrialization entered its 'second phase' sometime around the 1870s. This 'second phase' – some have called it 'high industrialization' – describes the period to 1914 and encompasses a number of important changes: the political organization of agriculture in response to its decline as the principal sector of the

German economy; the related decline in economic liberalism as the dominant ideology of the country's economic policymakers: the related increase in state intervention designed to soften some of the effects of market competition on the less well-to-do population, e.g. social insurance; the development of scientific knowledge as a factor of production and its encouragement by government institutions; and the absolute and relative growth of very large industrial enterprises.

Some historians have found that the 'second phase' of industrialization came quite abruptly, initiated by the crisis of the 1870s which, in attenuated form, lasted until the mid-1890s and has been called the 'great depression' (of 1874–94). Most economic historians, however, have resisted this notion of a 'great depression' twenty years in length, some of them on the grounds that the 'great depression' was largely a price phenomenon – a 'great deflation' – while the existing output data show no marked decline in volume well-correlated with the relevant period (Borchardt 1966). In this view, sustained real output growth as observed in Germany is semantically inconsistent with the term 'great depression'. Although I sympathize with this position and fully accept dismissal of the term 'great depression', something with analogous connotations may be needed to replace it, e.g. the 'prolonged slowdown'. There are three reasons for this. First, Rainer Fremdling's recent work casts doubt on the reliability of Hoffmann's index of industrial production for the period, mainly its probable sensitivity to weighting assumptions (Fremdling 1988). Second, the Hoffmann or Hoffmann-based data *do* show a slowdown in real output even if one adjusts for position within the business cycle to obtain fully comparable periods (see Table 9.2). Note the sharp contrast obtained by adhering to the older ('Contrast Maximizing') periodization. I am not convinced that this is illegitimate practice. Third, some

Table 9.2 Comparable growth cycles and periods in Germany, 1850–1913 (real output, annual rate of growth)

Industry and crafts				Net domestic product	
Trough-to-trough	Growth rate	Contrast maximising	Growth rate	Peak to peak	Growth rate
1848–66	0.0294	1850–74	0.0441	1857–64	0.0261
1866–79	0.0380			1864–74	0.0250
1879–91	0.0338	1874–94	0.0262	1874–84	0.0127
1891–1901	0.0364			1884–90	0.0283
1901–8	0.0406	1894–1913	0.0416	1890–1900	0.0339
1908–13	0.0497			1900–7	0.0268
				1907–13	0.0321

Sources: Hoffmann *et al.* (1965); Solomou (1987).

other indices of industrial activity also reflect a slowdown from the late 1870s to the mid-1890s, namely Hoffmann's estimates of net investment in crafts and industry and, moreover, an independent estimate of industrial fixed investment based on the experience of large enterprises confirms the periodization suggested by Hoffmann's investment estimates (Rettig 1978).

The upshot of these observations is that one can make a case for a slowdown phase – possibly a transitional phase? – followed by a phase of re-acceleration around the mid-1890s. This latter period, however, has also been seen as sufficiently unique to deserve its own name, the 'rise of organized capitalism'. This involved big business and oligopoly, cartels, organized labour and strikes, increased government regulation and intervention which was seen in part as 'stabilizer' of a system otherwise prone to anarchy and breakdown. This notion has not found favour with most economic historians, but it does raise the question of swings in industrialization which would not seem to fit in with the idea of relative backwardness as the 'master process' driving economic development.

THE ROLE OF THE BANKS

Gerschenkron's well-known emphasis upon Germany's universal banks as developmental instruments was built on an historiographical tradition going back to the beginning of this century and including such names as Hilferding and Schumpeter – illustrious names, I might add, strategically placed, as it were, to make an impression on Gerschenkron. The continuing flow of publications on the subject is thus obviously more than a response to his work (Tilly 1986).

In general, the notion that these banks – at first private firms and from the 1850s increasingly joint-stock companies – provided much entrepreneurship and risk capital and thus positively contributed to industrial growth and especially to the growth of large-scale industrial enterprises in Germany has stood the test of time quite well. The contrast to the role of banks in Great Britain – Gerschenkron's basic standard – has been confirmed. The consensus can be described in the following four propositions:

First, despite some dissent, the historical literature generally attributes to the banks a positive and significant contribution to Germany's economic development in the nineteenth century. This contribution consisted in the financing of risky investments, particularly in heavy industry, and included entrepreneurial feats such as the formation of new enterprises, the implementation of mergers, and the organization of cartels (Tilly 1982; Kennedy and Britton 1985; Wengenroth 1986). It is unsurprising, but nevertheless interesting, that recent work – including some application of modern portfolio theory – suggests that the German institutional arrangements for capital market finance of risky industrial investments were significantly more effective in the 1870–1913 period than those of Great Britain at this same time (Kennedy and Britton 1985; Tilly 1986).

Second, there is more dissent but on balance a clear preference in the literature for the view that these 'great' banks and their executives exercised considerable power in German economic life, power indicated by the large number of banks they took over and the resultant increase in their share of total bank deposits, by the large number of directorships they occupied in German business corporations, by their well-known ability to control strategic decisions through the institution of proxy voting in shareholders' meetings, by the close links between leading bankers and the political élite of the German Kaiserreich, and by a number of well-documented concrete cases of enterprise decision-making in which conflicts resolved themselves in favour of intervening banks (Jeidels 1905; Witt 1970; Feldenkirchen 1982; Wengenroth 1986; Pappi *et al.* 1987). This is related to the first point about financing risky investments, for such power reflected banker access to information which could lower their ex-ante risk assessment.

Third, the literature agrees that by concentrating on the financing of small numbers of relatively large-scale projects and established enterprises, the 'great banks' neglected large segments of the country's financial business: agricultural credit, housing, small business (especially new business enterprises), small savings were all fields left to the municipal savings banks, the credit cooperatives, local small private bankers – so far as these fields attracted financial intermediaries at all. After all, then, as later, most industrial investment was self-financed (Rettig 1978; Pohl, M. 1986). It was only in the 1890s that the large credit banks, spurred by the expansion of the savings banks and the credit cooperatives, began to utilize their branch systems to attract small savings and finance smaller business (M. Pohl 1986). This is significant for two reasons: 1) the relatively élite character of their business operations, in fact, explains much of their willingness to engage in fairly risky investment finance and also the low cash reserves they maintained, and (2) the overall effectiveness of Germany's financial institutions in promoting industrialization was by no means solely a function of the activities of universal banks.

Fourth, much of the vitality of the universal banks rested on the complementary relationship developed between their own activities and those of the government institutions regulating the payments system, above all the central bank of issue. By the early 1860s note issue was virtually a government monopoly. The result was a division of labour which left most pure payments and short-term trade credit business of the economy to the government bank of issue and most of the industrial credit and security issue business to the private bankers and their protégés, the corporate 'mixed banks'. In addition, the latter found themselves increasingly able to turn to the former for payments services, cash, and for short-term discount credits when the need arose. By establishing a thick network of branch offices covering most of Germany, the Prussian Bank contributed to a significant reduction in transaction costs of trade and finance, illustrated, for example, through the setting of one rate of interest and fixed exchange rates for bill payments anywhere in Prussia as early as 1848. Thus, to some extent, even before the 1870s, the 'mixed banks' could build their growing business upon the security that the bank of issue could and would supply it with liquidity, if necessary.

However, from 1876 the powerful support universal banks gave German industry and trade rested in part on the payments network and liquidity guarantee provided by the Reichsbank. By the 1880s this government institution (with its more than 200 branches) dominated the country's payment business. The credit banks used it extensively, eventually even when they were transferring funds between offices of their own systems. But most important in the present context was the virtually unlimited access to the Reichsbank's discounting facilities which the credit banks came to enjoy. The German banks could get by with less liquidity and 'lend to the hilt' if demands warranted, because the Reichsbank provided extremely liberal rediscounting facilities. In fact, they were so liberal – though not cheap – that bills of exchange held by the banks or their acceptances could be seen as substitutes for central bank notes. This was in contrast to the Bank of England, which frequently resorted to credit rationing.

The behaviour just described tended to stabilize the business cycle in Germany, for at least since the 1880s, through its discount policy, the Reichsbank tended to attract business in upswings and repel it in downswings, which meant a substitution of central bank money or gold coin for short bills, or what was, in effect, potential central bank money. (The reason for this was that the Reichsbank discount rate was generally higher than the market rate, but it rose and fell proportionately less than the latter.) With this stabilizing guarantee behind them, the German banks did not have to live with the fear of illiquidity which combining commercial and investment banking activity might otherwise have dictated (as, for example, under the British set of arrangements).

Of course, the 'take-off' phase of German industrialization from the 1840s to the 1870s had in fact evidenced considerable instability. The crises of 1847–8, 1857–8 and 1873–6 brought down large numbers of firms and especially banks. The crisis of the 1870s was particularly severe, as noted above. It forcibly called attention to the need for more comprehensive controls of financial activity. No doubt the Reichbank's subsequent policies reflected this.

Nevertheless, the Reichsbank remained a gold standard creature to 1914, and it did not underwrite more 'on-trend' credit expansion than its gold reserve position allowed. Its contribution to the 'German system' lay in the flexibility/elasticity of its rediscount policy, especially in times of 'liquidity pressure'. The universal banks, in consequence, could hold more risky portfolios than would have otherwise been the case.

Explaining this connection, however, involves a good deal more than Gerschenkron's summary references to Germany's industrial backwardness and capital scarcity relative to Great Britain. It requires going back to the early nineteenth century and examining two related questions: (a) the precarious fiscal position of most of the German states (especially Prussia) and its connection with internal political and class conflict on the one hand, and with monetary and banking policy on the other; and (b) the relationship between those fiscal needs and the development of the German customs union, on the one hand, and the need to coordinate currency policies among the several states, on the other. Briefly, the story is this. Its first part concerns the metallic currency. In the first half of the nineteenth century metal monies dominated Germany's currency stock. Owing to the historical heritage of multiple governments a wide variety of coins circulated, and fluctuations in their value are alleged to have hampered intra-German trade and capital flows. For rulers in some of the German states, the coinage was seen as a sovereign monopoly right and valuable independent source of revenue worth defending. However, given the initial difficulties, the problem was overcome with astounding speed. The catalyst was the Prussian government's customs union policy of the 1820s leading to the Zollverein. Here, the Prussian government built on the success of its own customs union of 1818, which had already proven to be a useful generator of revenues. Its offer of a substantial share in anticipated customs revenues to the rulers of the smaller German states proved irresistible to a decisive number of them, for it promised tax revenues free from parliamentary restraints or concessions. But the practical problem of revenue collection and redistribution required agreement on the value of different monies and on exchange rates. Negotiations on these matters received legal expression in treaties of 1837 and 1838, later again in 1857 (Holtfrerich 1989). Formally, two currency areas emerged from this: the Thaler and the Gulden areas. However, the Thaler dominated (and became the standard) and it is important to note that power politics – particularly the struggle between Prussia and Austria – and parochial fiscal interests had a powerful influence on this institutional change, not the needs of 'the economy' – which appears to have adjusted to the change readily.

The second part of the story builds on the first and concerns the handling of paper money and note-issuing banks. As suggested elsewhere, in Prussia, fiscal needs and commitments supplemented aristocratic-agrarian suspicions about private business aims, leading to the decision (in 1846) in favour of a government monopoly of paper money and note issue. This was related to the Zollverein question, for negotiations about the metallic currency had not regulated paper money, while some German states permitted private banks of issue, which began to circulate their notes in Prussia. Prussia's answer to this was to impose penalties on the use of such money and to expand her own note-issuing bank. This worked. By the 1860s the Prussian Bank's circulation dominated in most parts of Germany. By this time, also, a Zollverein treaty prohibited the issue of non-convertible paper money. This was one of the foundations for the development of German banking system as already discussed.

Reviewing this evidence, one is forced to conclude that in order to explain the evolution of banking structures and institutions in countries like Germany, one must devote considerable attention to political forces and institutions. Economic backwardness *per se* certainly seems inadequate to the task and that is one important limitation of Gerschenkron's model as originally formulated.

THE STANDARD OF LIVING

Gerschenkron's model suggests that economically backward countries experience falling consumption levels and living standards during their early stages of industrialization – well into and possibly beyond their 'big spurt' of growth. This is due to the stress in such countries on investment goods and possibly 'forced savings' associated with credit creation and inflationary price increases for consumption goods. Such a characterization would seem to fit German experience as rendered by recent research. For a consensus has emerged that in that phase of Germany's development which most closely corresponds to the 'big spurt' – from the 1840s to the 1870s – rapid industrial growth dominated by investment goods production went hand in hand with virtually stagnating living standards. The latter were also associated with food prices which tended to rise over the period and which accompanied a considerable rise in the terms of trade of agricultural vis-à-vis industrial prices.

It is only in the 1880s that a clear and widespread rise in real incomes and living standards can be documented. Here, the consensus is equally strong: living standards rose. Our knowledge of these changes stems from (a) general studies of wages and living standards (Gömmel 1978, 1979; Saalfeld 1984), from special sectoral and regional studies by Kirchhain (1977) on the cotton industry, by Holtfrerich (1973) and Tenfelde (1977) on Ruhr coal miners, by Fremdling (1975) on railroad workers, by Borscheid (1976) on Württemberg textile workers, or by Fischer (1968) and Noll (1976) on artisans ('Handwerker'), and from (b) direct examination of consumption standards themselves, e.g. by Teuteberg and Wiegelmann (1971) on food and nutritional standards or by Niethammer and Bruggemeier (1976) and also by Teuteberg (1986) and Wischermann (1983) on housing (Saalfield 1974; Gömmel 1978, 1979). One must concede that huge gaps in our knowledge remain, especially for the considerable number of self-employed households in agriculture and (mainly rural) domestic industry. However, all recent work on this group points to average levels of income considerably below those enjoyed by employed labour in the 1840s and 1850s and to a noticeable decline in their number over the 1860s and 1870s (Henning 1975). This supports the periodization on living standards just outlined.

One needs to stress the distributional aspects involved, however. To reiterate: what we have is the disproportional growth and leading cyclical role of the heavy-investment goods sectors of the economy. For the German economy as a whole this was accompanied by a clear rise in per capita incomes. The estimated annual increase in real per capita income of 1.6 per cent probably exceeded the growth rate in the previous period. However, it was not remarkable when compared with later periods and – most important for our present purposes – it was not matched by increasing real wage income, which rose hardly at all over the period (roughly zero from 1850 to 1873 and about 0.35 per cent per annum, 1844–80). Moreover, this stagnation in real wage income was accompanied – at least until 1873 – by a clear rise in the degree of inequality of personal income distribution (as reflected in the Prussian data) and a probably related decline in the share of labour (or wages) in aggregate social product (from about 0.82 to 0.77). At the same time, we may note that both levels and growth rates of wages in the heavy industrial sectors stood well above the overall average and above the average of those in cotton textiles – a branch probably representative of the consumption goods sectors (see Table 9.3).

Given this pattern, and also the relatively constant and high share of foods and beverages in German consumption patterns over the period we have, I believe, some strong arguments for speaking of a 'capital-oriented' growth process during the take-off era.

This took place at the cost of virtually stagnating domestic wage incomes, whose distribution, however, made possible substantial gains not only to owners of property but also to sellers of agricultural products, and less substantial gains to the workers of the expanding heavy industrial sector. It was this kind of squeeze on overall living standards – with a hierarchy of exemptions running from 'substantial' for property holders to 'modest' for workers in the favoured growth sectors – which lay behind the period of the 'big spurt'. It was a squeeze which augmented agricultural and industrial profits and, in all probability, the investment financed out of them. This is not to claim, I should add, that the German working class achieved no improvements in their standard of living during the take-off period, for there were modest gains in real wages – supported, moreover, by some reductions in hours of work and in the mortality rate. Nevertheless, these gains did not lead to a pattern of growth which assigned a leading role to workers' purchasing power. This picture corresponds to Gerschenkron's typology, I believe.

German historiography, however, has repeatedly drawn attention to a dimension of the question of living standards poorly handled in Gerschenkron's basic model: the role of demographic change. According to currently standard versions (Dickler, Harnisch, Hohorst, Knodel, Köllmann, Lee, etc.) Germany's population growth accelerated in the second half of the eighteenth century and remained high, though unstable, until the end of the nineteenth century. German

Table 9.3 Wages in selected industries, 1840–80

Annual growth rates, wages 1840–80 in sectors (%)		Ratio of wages engineering/cotton textiles	
Cotton	1.3	1850/54	1.7
Coal (Prussian)	3.1	1860/64	1.5
Railways (German)	2.4		
Iron	1.5	1870/74	1.8
Engineering	1.4	1875/79	1.8

Source: Tilly (1985).

experience seems to confirm the idea that children are the poor man's capital, for population growth resulted primarily from increased nuptiality and fertility among the rural poor as a response to the demand for labour, in rural domestic industry as well as in agriculture. Shifts in labour demands and restrictions on child labour associated with urban living conditions weakened this nexus from the 1860s. High and unstable child and infant mortality rates are also seen as determinants of fertility, with overshooting and externalities of reproduction decisions dominating population growth rhythms. When these mortality rates fell, beginning in the 1870s, family planning became possible and fertility decline set in. There is some debate about which of these two forces weighed more heavily in explaining German population growth, but the importance of the question for my purposes here is that, whatever the reason, it resulted in a labour surplus economy in Germany for much of the nineteenth century. This view is implicitly supported by dozens of collections of contemporary descriptions of underemployment, living conditions, and work-seeking migration among the poor, by the gap, already noted, between growth of aggregate real income per capita and real wages, and by a number of studies suggesting that wage rates – especially for unskilled labour – tended to respond more to migration from rural areas and shifts in economic opportunities there than to productivity and demand shifts in the industrial centre (Köllmann 1974; Saalfeld 1974; Fremdling 1975; Kirchhain 1977; Gömmel 1978, 1979; Hohorst et al. 1979; Fischer et al. 1982; Lee 1988).

There may thus be sense in viewing German industrialization as a case of rapid industrialization with abundant, elastic labour supplies, as well as the scarcity of capital stressed by Gerschenkron. For an evaluation of this part of Gerschenkron's typology, however, it is useful to refer back to the periodization argument raised in the first section of the paper. In the period up to the 1870s, institutional change tended to strengthen the pressure on living standards just described. The capital accumulation and growing inequality which accompanied the early phase of industrialization reflected more than differential fertility among social strata; it reflected the highly unequal distribution of property and property incomes. This was largely a result of market forces in the nineteenth century. But these market forces operated on the basis of institutions which strengthened and supported owners of capital relative to labourers, e.g. the rules governing conversion of feudal claims and obligations upon peasant land and labour into private property, the laws weakening the guilds, the regressive taxes and the defences against labour organization.

The situation changed in the 1870s, to be sure. From the 1870s onward, collective official concern for workers' employment and living conditions grew. Due to urbanization and growing urban concentrations of working-class populations those problems become highly visible to public opinion and policymakers. Real wages and living standards begin to rise significantly in this period. This rise did not result solely or even primarily from mounting public concern, but a positive connection doubtless existed.

Does this fit in with Gerschenkron's views? Perhaps one could argue that public concern for the workers resulted from collective recognition that further German industrialization depended crucially on the country's human capital resources and hence, on related investments in health, education and welfare: Bismarck's social legislation was an essential part of the 'second phase of industrialization'. Certainly, Germany's industrialization pattern here did diverge significantly from that of Great Britain, and there may be something in the idea of a link to the backwardness syndrome. But the issue is by no means clear-cut. It would seem panglossian to believe that such institutions came when the country's development 'needed' them. And it would be ahistorical to ignore the fact that, for example, Germany's educational institutions had powerful non-industrial features – and could thus be considered 'dysfunctional' – or that social legislation was hotly contested and only gradually came to be a significant socio-economic factor in German daily life. Thus, an attempt to link living standards and the German 'social question' to industrial backwardness alone would seem to be guilty of gross oversimplification.

THE ROLE OF IDEOLOGY

According to Gerschenkron the degree of economic backwardness is generally reflected in a country's dominant ideology. In the German case, that was the kind of economic nationalism articulated by Friedrich List. No doubt, economic nationalism – giving priority to national over international or individual interests – is more visible as a professed creed among political and business leaders in Germany in the nineteenth century than in Great Britain. But on the whole, I do not find this interpretation too helpful. It has two related weaknesses: (1) it overlooks change over time; and (2) it is excessively aggregative, i.e., it neglects class differences and the structure of organized interests. These deserve brief discussion.

I begin by asserting that ruling élites are identifiable in nineteenth-century German history and that the ideologies these espoused shifted over time. If my assessment of the literature is correct, the middle decades of the nineteenth century are seen as witness to a shift in attitudes among Germany's ruling élite – particularly among the publicly articulate – in favour of capitalist industrial growth, and individualist, competitive economic activity. This shift accompanied a liberalization of economic policy – not least a remarkable shift in the sphere of commercial policy which had very important long-run political consequences – and was no doubt reinforced by the ongoing strength of the economic growth of the 1850s. But in the course of the depression of the 1870s a remarkable shift in this élite's ideology against economic and political liberalism took place. Most authors have seen the shift as a response to the threat posed to East Elbian owners of agricultural estates by intensified international and national com-petition in grain markets, to the desire of industrialists and their bankers to stabilize their shares in a shrinking national market, and to the interest of both and of the bureaucracy in combatting the growing socialist labour movement. It is important to note, however, that this shift was not complete. In many areas of public policy involving housing, trade unions, voting rights, etc., the debate between liberals and conservatives – or reformists – went on. Moreover, – and this takes us the second point referred to above – it goes without saying that the Marxist programme of the socialist labour movement represented yet another and highly distinct position within the German ideological scene. In short, it seems unhelpful to look for a dominant ideology directly connected with a country's level of backwardness, not least of all since such a procedure begs the important question of whether or not ideologies are dysfunctional. I think there is a need here to tie up ideologies with analyses of interest group organization and political change on a more general level. That is, the links between ideologies and backwardness should be seen as *indirect* ones.

REGIONAL DIFFERENCES

An obvious and frequently noted defect of Gerschenkron's 'model' is its aggregative, national orientation, its failure to account for or even interpret regional differences. In the light of the previous discussion of ideology it is interesting to note a recent suggestion that the strength of nationalism as an ideology in Germany has to do with the strength of regional differences in development levels – seen as a political problem which must be overcome (Lee 1988). In fact, Gerschenkron himself pointed out this possibility, though he drew no consequences from it for his basic model. In any case, German economic historiography is clear on this issue. For one of the clearest results of recent work into regional dimensions of industrialization is the stress on its unevenness. There are leading regions – such as parts of Saxony or the Rhineland – as well as leading sectors. However, growth in one region need not and did not automatically contribute through trade, factor movements or the diffusion of technical knowledge to growth in another. This work shows that developmental differentials were (a) a pre-industrial phenomenon which (b) industrialization failed to remove, mainly because the east had remained largely agricultural (Borchardt 1966; Hesse 1971; Hohorst 1977; Fremdling and Tilly 1979; Lee 1988). It is thus possible that the temporal and sectoral shape of German industrialization could have varied substantially from region to region, so much so, in fact, that 'German industrialization' could turn out to be a phrase denoting an average or artifact including highly diverse components. Explanation of German industrialization, in such a case, might require (a) explanation of regional changes and (b) explanation of how the weights of regions changed over time, as well as (c) explanation of linkages between regions. Under extreme assumptions – factor immobility, internal trade barriers and impotent national policy – the development of national economies depends on these regional changes and not at all on policy. But most important, regional differences may have powerful consequences for the development of the national economy and polity. Tipton (1974, 1976) has used his own study of Germany's regional differences to raise this question, focusing particularly on the well-known east–west differential and on the response of agricultural protectionism and the problem of migration and labour supply. Ongoing industrialization shifted the economic centre of gravity in Prussia – Germany's dominant state – westward and away from the agricultural regions. As Tipton puts it, 'The eastern landlord class achieved and maintained an important political position, but the economic basis of that position eroded as their region began to drop behind the urban and industrial centers of central and western Germany'. This erosion threatened to accelerate in the agrarian depression of the 1870s, which concentrated strongly upon the East Elbian grain producers. Tariff protectionism was the political response engineered by Bismarck, but this penalized labour-intensive mixed farming and taken together with the competition which continued despite the tariff, could not slow down and may have even encouraged the massive emigration out of the agrarian east which had begun in the 1860s. By the 1890s, this made recourse to seasonal immigrant labour a necessity for the East Elbian grain producers and the result was that peculiar labour market which maintained, just as it reflected, the continued power of the eastern landlords. This further retarded any attempt to industrialize the east. Given the Prussian-German political structure and the disproportionate weight it gave to the eastern landlords (and the Conservative Party) in national questions, democratic change in the country as a whole proceeded more slowly than a regionally balanced industrialization would probably have allowed (Tipton 1974, 1976; Bade 1982).

THE ROLE OF THE STATE AND ITS POLITICAL ECONOMY

To some extent this section is a residual. In the previous sections much of our topic has already been covered, for 'the state' is virtually omnipresent in German economic historiography. A few remarks will suffice. To begin with, there is no question but that the state's direct role was greater in Germany's industrialization than in Great Britain's. A number of relevant areas can be cited: there is government's direct support for, even entrepreneurial involvement in, the creation of social overhead capital (e.g. railroads); the agrarian reforms involved setting up government banks which facilitated the conversion of previously feudal claims into private property rights; there was commercial policy involving selective tariff protection and easing national economic integration; an ambitious programme of social insurance; and so on. On the other hand, in the case of 'moderate backwardness' (Germany's) Gerschenkron's model 'predicts' the rapid development of private business entrepreneurship, and is thus consistent with a literature full of observations of inefficient government policies, such as those restraining entrepreneurs in banking, transportation, etc. This obviously differs from cases of extreme backwardness such as Tsarist Russia (where government policy might be inept but without alternatives). The trouble with Gerschenkron's formulations, however, is that they do not offer an adequate explanation of changing levels of state action. His references to military priorities, while pertinent, certainly fall short of the mark, for the state is more than the collective national interest in military power. And the level of backwardness is not the only other conditioning factor. National governments or polities are coalitions of regional, sectoral and class interests which mobilize political resources and contend for control of the polity.

In fact, the economic history of German industrialization is full of government actions, economic policies, decisions having at most an indirect connection with economic backwardness and military considerations. I conclude this section by briefly mentioning one set of actions which illustrates an alternative approach: it concerns the Prussian and German customs unions: Ohnishi's well-documented study of the Prussian commercial union, 1818–33, demonstrates the strong, positive fiscal motivation and positive revenue effects of the union, but also surprisingly significant (and rising) protective effects as well. R. Dumke's work extends the discussion. First, he shows that the Zollverein was an extension of the Prussian commerical union in the sense that (a) the latter's relatively high rates became the norm for the former and, more significantly, that (b) the revenue motive was of decisive importance, since Prussian statesmen, drawing on their own experience, could offer the rulers of small and poor states the prospects of revenues free of the necessity for democratic-parliamentary concessions as enticement to joint the Zollverein. Parochial interests – including those of the civil servants in the several German states – explain commercial policy and not economic backwardness or military needs. The history of German state activity contains many chapters into which an approach stressing micro interests and political bargaining might be extended.

CONCLUSIONS

The main body of this chapter offers quite a few generalizations about the appropriateness of Gerschenkron's basic model for the study of European industrialization. For this reason, these conclusions can be brief. They make only three points.

First, criticism and suggestions for revision are directed toward Gerschenkron's basic model (as developed in Gerschenkron 1962), not toward his life's work as a scholar. That work is a treasure trove of differentiated knowledge about European history, even about German history, and contains numerous valuable insights into the process of economic development generally. And one must add that it also contains observations which qualify and even contradict the basic model. Nevertheless, it is the basic model – which necessarily suppressed much differentiated knowledge – which is on trial here, not Gerschenkron the scholar.

Second, Gerschenkron's fundamental insight – the importance of relative levels of backwardness as a determinant of industrialization patterns – automatically produces a significant deficiency in his model: the model's premise is that it makes sense to 'tune in' on the industrialization drama of a country on the 'eve of its initiation' – a point in time (or period?) determined by ex-post knowledge of a great spurt which subsequently took place. But this way of formulating the problem begs the question of why a given country is backward in the first place and precludes discussion of factors present in 'earlier developers' but not in their backward rivals. His model focuses on the successful followers, and neglects the failures or partial failures (with slow growth). Revision here implies at least three modifications of the basic model.

1   There is a need to distinguish between relative backwardness and absolute levels of development, a need which calls for an extension of what we wish to explain beyond the rate of industrial growth and the share of industry in total output and employment to more general measures of economic welfare.

2   A more general model should include factors generally – at least potentially – relevant for all countries; natural resources, labour supply, the levels of human and non-human capital, the level of technological knowledge, communications and mobility, the distribution of wealth and income and so on.

3   There is a need to relax (or forget) the assumption that modern·economic growth takes the form of a 'big spurt' discontinuity associated with rapid, dramatic industrial changes, and a need to see modern economic growth as a more gradual, longer-run process extending well into the pre-industrial period.

Third, as suggested throughout the paper, Gerschenkron's basic model implicitly assigns great importance to the state but fails to develop an explanation of state behaviour and changes in it. More generally, modern economic growth depends on the state, not only or even primarily as a source of specific services (financial and otherwise), but as the social arrangement through which the general rules and especially the legal framework of economic activity are negotiated, established and enforced. Explaining the role of the state means developing an appropriate model of political change. This is not the place to attempt to sketch out such a model, but in order to be useful as part of an explanation of the modern economic growth of nations it should probably cover at least the following needs:

1   the need to explain how regional, sectoral and socio-economic class interests are mobilized and organized and what determines their effectiveness at the national level. It is the economic weight of their basic constituencies, their social homogeneity, the particular kinds of coalitions they enter into, ideology, or some combination of all of these?

2   the need to see the state as more than the collective expression of organized interest groups but as an autonomous actor (or collection of autonomous actors) pursuing independent aims. Autonomy may have a purely traditional

base, which may correspond to no more than the inherited prerogatives of a small but highly cohesive minority. On the other hand, autonomy can be maintained by the adept exploitation of differences among contending socio-economic interest groups. What explains autonomy and with what kinds of state behaviour is it associated? That leads directly to

3   the obvious need to monitor the 'output' of the state action, to assess its efficiency in promoting or hindering modern economic growth in nations. This has been a traditional field of work for economic historians, so little more need be said. Nevertheless, if more attention is paid to the relationship between the political bases of government – the kinds of coalitions and bargaining its stability depends on – and the contribution of state activity to modern economic growth (net of resources absorbed by government), that work will doubtless yield higher returns.

NOTE

1   In the following 'industrialization', 'modern economic growth' and 'economic development' are used interchangeably; the same applies to the terms 'typology' and 'model' with respect to Gerschenkron.

REFERENCES

Bade, Klaus (1982) 'Transnationale Migration und Arbeitsmarkt im Kaiserreich: vom Agrarstaat mit starker Industrie zum Industriestaat mit starker Agrarbasis', in T. Pierenkemper and R. Tilly (eds) *Historische Arbeitsmarktforschung. Entstehung, Entwicklung und Probleme der Vermarktung von Arbeitskraft*, Göttingen.

Beyer, P. (1978) *Leipzig und die Anfänge des deutschen Eisenbahnbaus*, Weimar.

Borchardt, Knut (1966) 'Regionale Wachstumsdifferenzierung in Deutschland im 19. Jahrhundert unter besonderer Berücksichtigung des West-Ost Gefälles', in W. Abel *et al.* (eds) *Wirtschaft, Geschichte und Wirtschaftsgeschichte. Festschrift zum 65. Geburtstag von Fr. Lütge*, Stuttgart.

Borries, Bodo von (1970) *Deutschlands Aussenhandel 1836–1856*, Stuttgart.

Borscheid, Peter (1976) *Textilarbeiterschaft in der Industrialisierung*, Stuttgart.

Dickler, Robert A. (1975) 'Organization and change in productivity in eastern Prussia', in W.N. Parker and E. Jones (eds) *European Peasants and their Markets*, Princeton, pp. 269–92.

Dipper, Christoph (1980) *Die Bauernbefreiung in Deutschland, 1790–1850*, Stuttgart.

Dumke, Rolf (1976) 'The political economy of economic integration: tariffs, trade and politics of the Zollverein era', PhD thesis, University of Wisconsin.

—— (1979) 'Anglo-deutscher Handel und Frühindustrialisierung in Deutschland, 1822–1865', *Geschichte und Gesellschaft 5*, 175–200.

Feldenkirchen, Wilfred (1982) *Die Eisen- Und Stahlindustrie des Ruhrgebiets, 1879–1914*, Wiesbaden.

Finckenstein, Graf Finck von (1960) *Die Entwicklung der Landwirtschaft in Preussen und Deutschland, 1800–1930*, Würzburg.

Fischer, Wolfram (1968) 'Die Rolle des Kleingewerbes im wirtschaftlichen Wachstumsprozess in Deutschland, 1850 bis 1914', in F. Lütge (ed.) *Wirtschaftliche und soziale Probleme der gewerblichen Entwicklung im 15./16. und 19. Jahrhundert*, Stuttgart.

Fischer, Wolfram, Krengel, Joachim and Wietog, Jutta (eds) (1982) *Sozialgeschichtliches Arbeitsbuch I*, Munich.

Franz, Günter (1976) 'Landwirtschaft, 1800–1850', in W. Zorn (ed.) *Handbuch der deutschen Wirtschafts- und Sozialgeschichte*, Klett, Stuttgart.

Fremdling, Rainer (1975) *Eisenbahnen und deutsches Wirtschaftswachstum, 1840–1879*, Dortmund.

—— (1977) 'Railroads and German economic growth: a leading sector analysis with a comparison to the United States and Great Britain', *Journal of Economic History* XXXVII, 583–604.

—— (1986) *Technologischer Wandel und internationaler Handel im 18. und 19. Jahrhundert. Die Eisenindustrien in Großbritannien, Belgien, Frankreich und Deutschland*, Berlin.

—— (1988) 'German national accounts for the 19th and early 20th century. A critical assessment, in *Vierteljahresschrift für Social- und Wirtschaftsgeschichte* 75, 339–54.

Fremdling, Rainer and Tilly, Richard (eds) (1979) *Industrialisierung und Raum. Studien zur regionalen Differenzierung im Deutschland des 19. Jahrhunderts*, Stuttgart, pp. 27–53.

Gerschenkron, Alexander (1943) *Bread and Democracy in Germany*, Berkely.

—— (1962) *Economic Backwardness in Historical Perspective*, Cambridge, Mass.: Harvard University Press.

—— (1968) *Continuity in History and Other Essays*, Cambridge, Mass.: Harvard University Press.

Gömmel, Rainer (1978) 'Wachstum und Konjunktur der Nürnberger Wirtschaft (1815–1914)', in H. Kellenbenz and J. Schneider (eds) *Beiträge zur Wirtschaftsgeschichte*, vol. I, Vortragsreihe Univ. Köln.

—— (1979) *Realeinkommen in Deutschland. Ein internationaler Vergleich (1810–1914)*, Nürnberg.

Harnisch, Hartmut (1977) Die Bedeutung der kapitalistischen Agrarreform für die Herausbildung des inneren Marktes und die Industrielle Revolution in den östlichen Provinzen Preussens in der ersten Hälfte des 19. Jahrhunderts', *Jahrbuch für Wirtschaftsgeschichte*, 4, 63–82.

Helling, Gertrud (1965) 'Berechnung eines Index der Agrarproduktion in Deutschland im 19. Jahrhundert', *Jahrbuch für Wirtschaftsgeschichte*, 4, 125–43.

Henning, Friedrich-Wilhelm (1973) 'Eisenbahnen und Entwicklung der Eisenindustrie in Deutschland', *Archiv und Wirtschaft* 6, 1–20.

—— (1975) 'Industrialisierung und dörfliche Einkommensmöglichkeiten. Der Einfluß der Industrialisierung des Textilgewerbes in Deutschland im 19. Jht. auf Einkommensmöglichkeiten in den ländlichen Gebieten', in H. Kellenbenz (ed.) *Agrarisches Neben-Spätmittelalter und 19./20. Jahrhundert*, Stuttgart.

Hesse, Helmut (1971) 'Die Entwicklung der regionalen Einkommensdifferenzen im Wachstumsprozess der deutschen Wirtschaft vor 1913', in W. Fischer (ed.) *Beiträge zu Wirtschaftswachstum und Wirtschaftsstruktur im 16. und 19. Jahrhundert. Schriften des Vereins für Sozialpolitik*, N.F., vol. 63, Berlin.

Hoffmann, W.G., Grumbach, F. and Müller, J.H. (1965) *Das Wachstum der deutschen Wirtschaft seit der Mitte des 19. Jahrhunderts*, Heidelberg, Berlin: Springer NY.

Hohorst, Gerd (1977) *Wirtschaftswachstum und Bevölkerungsentwicklung in Preussen von 1816 bis 1914*, New York.

Hohorst, Gerd; Kocka, Jürgen and Ritter, Gerhard (eds) (1979) *Sozialgeschichtliches Arbeitsbuch. Materialien zur Statistik des Kaiserreichs 1870–1914*, Munich.

Holtfrerich, Carl-Ludwig (1973) *Quantitative Wirtschaftsgeschichte des Ruhrkohlenbergbaus im 19. Jahrhundert*, Dortmund.

—— (1989) 'The monetary unification process in nineteenth-century Germany.

Relevance and lessons for Europe today', in M. de Cecco and A. Giovannini (eds) *Monetary Regimes and Monetary Institutions: Issues and Perspectives in Europe*, Cambridge: Cambridge University Press.

Jeidels, Otto (1905) *Das Verhältnis der deutschen Großbanken zur Industrie, mit bes. Berücksichtigung der Eisenindustrie*, Leipzig.

Kennedy, William P. and Britton, Rachel (1985) 'Portfolioverhalten und wirtschaftliche Entwicklung im späten 19. Jahrhundert. Ein Vergleich zwischen Großbritannien und Deutschland. Hypothesen und Spekulationen', in Richard Tilly (ed.) *Beiträge zur quantitativen vergleichenden Unternehmensgeschichte*, Stuttgart.

Kirchhain, Günter (1977) *Das Wachstum der deutschen Baumwollindustrie im 19. Jahrhundert*, New York.

Kisch, Herbert (1981) *Die transindustriellen Textilgewerbe am Niederrhein vor der industriellen Revolution*, Göttingen.

Köllmann, Wolfgang (1974) *Bevölkerung in der Industriellen Revolution*, Göttingen.

Krengel, Joachim (1980) 'Zur Berechnung von Wachstumswirkungen konjunkturell bedingter Nachfrageschwankungen nachgelagerter Industrien auf die Produktionsentwicklung der deutschen Roheisenindustrie während der Jahre 1871–1882', in W.H. Schröder and R. Spree (eds) *Historische Konjunkturforschung*, Stuttgart.

Kriedte, Peter, Medick, Hans and Schlumbohm, Jürgen (1977) *Industrialisierung vor der Industrialisierung. Gewerbliche Warenproduktion auf dem Land in der Formationsperiode des Kapitalismus*, Göttingen.

Kunz, Andreas (1989) 'Die Verknüpfung von Märkten durch Transport, Verkehrsstatistik und Marktintegration in Agrarregionen', in Toni Pierenkemper (ed.) *Landwirtschaft und Industrielle Entwicklung – Zur ökonomischen Bedeutung von Bauernbefreiung, Agrarreform und Agrarrevolution*.

Kutz, Martin (1974) Deutschlands Aussenhandel, 1789–1834, Wiesbaden.

Lee, W.R. (1988) 'Economic development and the state in nineteenth-century Germany', in *Economic History Review*, 2nd series, vol XLI, pp. 346–67.

Mager, Wolfgang (1988) 'Protoindustrialisierung und Protoindustrie. Vom Nutzen und Nachteil zweier Konzepte', *Geschichte und Gesellschaft* 14, 275–305.

Müller, Hans-Heinrich (1987) 'Anfänge der deutschen Landmaschinenindustrie. Beispiele aus den 30er bzw. 50er Jahren des 19. Jahrhunderts', in *Jahrbuch für Wirtschaftsgeschichte* 3, 169–194, esp. 172.

Niethammer, Lutz and Bruggemeier, Franz (1976) 'Wie wohnten Arbeiter im Kaiserreich?', *Archiv für Sozialgeschichte* 16, 61–134.

Noll, Adolf (1976) *Sozioökonomischer Strukturwandel des Handwerks in der 2. Phase der Industrialisierung*, Göttingen.

Ohnishi, T. (1973) 'Zolltarifspolitik Preussens bis zur Grüdung des Deutschen Zollvereins', dissertation, University of Göttingen.

Pappi, F.U., Kappelhoff, P. and Melbeck, C. (1987) 'Die Struktur der Unternehmensverflechtung in der Bundesrepublik', *Kölner Zeitschrift für Soziologie und Sozialpsychologie*, 39, 693–717.

Pohl, Hans (1986) *Form und Phasen der Industriefinanzierung bis zum 2. Weltkrieg, Bankhistorisches Archiv 9, Beiheft*, Frankfurt.

Pohl, Manfred (1986) *Entstehung und Entwicklung des Universalbankensystems*, Frankfurt.

Rettig, Rudi (1978) 'Das Investitions- und Finanzierungsverhalten deutscher Großunternehmen, 1880–1911', dissertation, University of Münster.

Rolffs, M. (1976) 'Landwirtschaft, 1850–1914', in W. Zorn (ed) *Handbuch der deutschen Wirtschafts- und Sozialgeschichte*, vol. 2, Stuttgart.

Saalfeld, Dietrich (1974) 'Lebensstandard in Deutschland, 1750–1860', in I. Bog et al. (eds) *Wirtschaftliche und soziale Strukturen im säkularen Wandel. Festschrift für W.*

Abel zum 70. Geburtstag, 3 vols, Hannover, vol. II, pp. 417–43.

—— (1974) 'Lebensverhältnisse der Unterschichten Deutschlands im 19. Jahrhundert', in *International Review of Social History* XXIX (2), S219.

Schremmer, Eckhard (1987) 'Die Badische Gewerbesteuer und die Kapitalbildung in gewerblichen Anlagen und Vorräten in Baden und in Deutschland, 1815 bis 1913', *VSWG* 74, 18–61.

Schultz, Helga (1984) *Landhandwerk im Übergang von Feudalismus zum Kapitalismus*, Ost Berlin,

Solomou, Solomus (1987) *Phases of Economic Growth, 1850–1973. Kondratieff Waves and Kuznets Swings*, Cambridge.

Spree, Reinhard (1977) *Die Wachstumszyklen der deutschen Wirtschaft von 1840 bis 1880*, Berlin.

Steitz, Walter (1974) *Die Entstehung der Köln-Mindener Eisenbahn*, vol. 17, *Schriften zur rheinisch-westfälischen Wirtschaftsgeschichte*, Cologne.

Tenfelde, Claus (1977) *Sozialgeschichte der Bergarbeiterschaft an der Ruhr im 19. Jahrhundert*, Bonn-Bad Godesberg.

Teuteberg, Hans-Jürgen (1986) *Stadtwachstum, Industrialisierung, Sozialer Wandel. Beiträge zur Enforschung der Urbanisierung im 19. und 20. Jahrhundert*, Berlin.

Teuteberg, Hans-Jürgen and Wiegelmann, Günter (1971) *Der Wandel der Nahrungsmittelgewohnheiten unter dem Einfluß der Industrialisierung*, Göttingen.

Tilly, Richard (1977) 'Das Wachstumsparadigma und die europäische Industrialisierungsgeschichte' (Fontana Economic History of Europe), *Geschichte und Gesellschaft* 3, 93–108.

—— (1982) Mergers, external growth and finance in the development of large-scale enterprise in Germany, 1880–1913', *Journal of Economic History* XLII, 629–58.

—— (1985) 'Some problems in the measurement of economic growth in Germany in the nineteenth century', paper presented at Workshop on Quantitative Economic History, University of Groningen.

—— (1986) 'German banking, 1850–1914: development assistance to the strong', *Journal of European Economic History* 15 (Spring), 113–52.

Tipton, F.B. (1974) 'Farm labor and power politics: Germany 1850 to 1914', *Journal of Economic History* XXXIV, 951–79.

—— (1976) *Regional Variations in the Economic Development of Germany during the Nineteenth Century*, Middletown.

Wagenblass, Horst (1973) *Der Eisenbahnbau und das Wachstum der deutschen Eisen- und Maschinenbauindustrie, 1835 bis 1860*, Stuttgart.

Wehler, Hans-Ulrich (1987) *Deutsche Gesellschaftsgeschichte*, vol I, *Vom Feudalismus des alten Reiches bis zur Defensiven Modernisierung der Reformära, 1700–1815* vol. II, *Von der Reformära bis zur Industriellen und politischen 'deutschen Doppelrevolution' 1815–1848/9*, München.

Wengenroth, Ulrich (1986) *Unternehmensstrategien und technischer Fortschritt, Die deutsche und britische Statlindustrie 1865–1895*, Göttingen, Zürich.

Wischermann, C. (1983) *Wohnen in Hamburg vor dem ersten Weltkrieg*, Münster.

Witt, Peter Christian (1970) *Die Finanzpolitik des Deutschen Reiches von 1903 bis 1913*, Lübeck/Hamburg.

Chapter 10

Italy

Giovanni Federico and Gianni Toniolo

'Clio is not a tidy housewife'

(A. Gerschenkron)

ALEXANDER GERSCHENKRON ON THE ECONOMIC DEVELOPMENT OF ITALY

Italy takes an important place, second only to that of Russia and possibly Austria, among the individual countries specifically investigated by Gerschenkron within the framework of his general approach to European industrialization during the nineteenth century. To the Italian case he devoted three important papers (Gerschenkron 1962: 52–89, 90–118, 1968: 98–127) and the effort of constructing an *ad hoc* index of industrial production (Gerschenkron 1962: 367–421).

To use his own words, Gerschenkron 'approached the Italian material with a series of historical questions or expectations in mind' (Gerschenkron 1962: 73) reflecting his own generalizations about the features of the industrialization process in a relatively backward European country. Typically, he expected to find a 'big push' of considerable intensity and length favouring the 'output of producers' goods as against that of consumers' goods' (Gerschenkron 1962: 73) and inducing various forms of industrial concentration. Moreover, he expected these 'basic features of delayed industrialization to be reinforced by the use of specific institutional instruments, such as the investment policies of banks and various policies of the state' (Gerschenkron 1962: 73).

In order to test the consistency of the Italian case with his general view of European industrialization during the nineteenth century, Gerschenkron set out to build his own index of industrial growth covering the period 1881 to 1914. This was, at the time (1955), a pioneering work and a very welcome addition to the paucity of quantification in Italian economic historiography. The results allowed Gerschenkron 'to locate the period of great push between the years 1896 and 1908' and to see that it was, as he expected, characterized by a rapid increase in the share of producers' goods in total output (Gerschenkron 1962: 77). At the same time, comparing Italy's performance with that of other countries during their own 'spurts', Gerschenkron found that 'the industrial growth in Italy, while free from any severe setbacks, seems to have proceeded in a less uniform and more jerky fashion, denoting perhaps a more delicate state of public confidence and greater entrepreneurial uncertainties and hesitations' (Gerschenkron 1962: 79). The reasons listed for Italy's relatively poor industrial performance are: (a) inept government policies, (b) a supposed time inconsistency between railroad building and the 'spurt' (c) a political situation around the turn of the century 'not propitious to quiet economic growth' (Gerschenkron 1962: 85), and (d) 'the absence of any strong ideological stimulus to industrialization' (Gerschenkron 1962: 86). On the other hand, 'if one were to look for a single important factor that succeeded in offsetting at least some of the great obstacles to the country's industrialization, one could not fail to point to the role performed by the big Italian banks after 1895' (Gerschenkron 1962: 87). Gerschenkron is therefore able to conclude that 'in this respect at least, the Italian case fits well into the general pattern of European industrialization in varying conditions of economic backwardness' (Gerschenkron 1962: 89).

This chapter discusses Gerschenkron's appraisal of Italian industrialization before the First World War in the light of the later literature. The first section deals with measures of Italy's backwardness relative to other European countries, and is followed by a section reviewing the existing indices of industrial production. The role of such 'agents of industrialization' as the German banks, the state and ideology are then discussed. The last part of the chapter is devoted to a summary of the main points and to some general conclusions.

THE BACKWARDNESS OF THE ITALIAN ECONOMY

When asked about the operational value of the concept of backwardness Gerschenkron replied that no precise answer was possible because one could define the degree of backwardness in several ways and, while granting that 'this might seem discouraging and clumsy', he added that 'it was true of 19th-century Europe at least that, whatever measures used, individual countries were fairly easy to arrange in order of backwardness' (Rostow 1963: 385).

Gerschenkron's well-known concern with index number problems made him reluctant to suggest per capita output as a fully operational measure of backwardness. He also suggested that, in any event, information deriving from output levels should be used together with other parameters – such as literacy or the prevailing ideology – that 'would involve asking to what degree a country at a certain moment had developed the preconditions for subsequent economic development' (Gerschenkron 1962: 43).

How backward was Italy, in Gerschenkron's eyes, around the middle of the nineteenth century? The most important suggestion comes from the following passage:

Few would disagree that Germany was more backward than France; that

Austria was more backward than Germany, that Italy was more backward than Austria and that Russia was more backward than any of the countries just mentioned. Similarly, few would deny England the position of the most advanced country of the time.

(Gerschenkron 1962: 44)

Does research carried out in the last quarter of a century confirm at least this ranking? Measures of economic backwardness explicitly related to Gerschenkron's hypotheses were first provided by Barsby (1969). Relying on Colin Clark's pioneering work, he sees Italy's GNP per capita around 1890 to be equal to that of Russia and less than one-fourth that of Britain.

Subsequent work has considerably revised Colin Clark's estimates. We may refer directly to Crafts (1983) since this article takes into account the most relevant previous contributions (particularly Bairoch 1976), producing the least unreliable estimates of nineteenth-century per capita product to date. They are reproduced in Table 10.1 for the countries mentioned by Gerschenkron and for Spain. As regards Italy in the third quarter of the nineteenth century, Gerschenkron's appraisal of Italy's relative position seems to be confirmed for 1910 but not for 1870, when Austria displays a per capita income approximately equal to that of Italy. What is striking, and somewhat puzzling, in Table 10.1 is the relatively high level of Italy's income at about the time of its political unification, as well as the stagnation in the subsequent thirty-odd years which resulted in its slide down the rankings.

These data rest on two assumptions: (a) that we accept Kravis's (1982) purchasing power parities and relative income levels for 1970, and (b) that we

Table 10.1 Crafts' estimates of per capita national product (US dollars of 1970)

	1870	1890	1910
Great Britain	904	1130	1302
Germany	579	729	958
France	567	668	883
Northwestern Italy			(810)
Italy	466 (513)	466 (513)	548 (603)
Austria	466	664	802
Spain	391	554	547
Southern Italy			(450)
Russia	252	276	398

Source: Crafts (1983: 389, 394).
Italian data in parenthesis derive from the recent official upward revision by 10% of current (1980s) GNP estimates and their backward extrapolation, according to Crafts' methodology.
Italian regional estimates from Zamagni (1978).
Northwestern Italy includes Lombardy, Piedmont and Liguria.
Southern Italy includes the former Kingdom of Naples plus Sardinia.

believe long-term growth rates implicit in the existing historical national accounts statistics.

The second of these assumptions, i.e. the reliability of historical national accounts statistics, may prove difficult to accept in the case of Italy. The existing estimates – ISTAT (1957) and Fua's (1969) revision thereof – date back at least twenty years. Their validity has always been questioned at least on the basis of the authors' parsimony in the disclosure of their sources and methods. Recent work by Fenoaltea on industrial production shows that this distrust is not misplaced. The existing figures underestimate both the level of industrial production in 1911 and the attendant long-term growth rates.[1] Should these upward revisions be confirmed in the case of other industries, our overall view of the time-pattern of Italy's development would be in need of thorough reconsideration. The relevance of this point for the issues addressed by this chapter, and indeed for the entire economic history of modern Italy, can hardly be overstated. Nevertheless, the ranking of Italy with the countries in Table 10.1 is not likely to be altered substantially.

In view of Italy's pronounced economic dualism, any appraisal of her backwardness is likely to be incomplete without some kind of regional breakdown. According to Zamagni (1978), in 1911 the GNP per head of Italy's richer region (the northwest) was slightly lower than that of the whole of France (and therefore much lower than that of the richest comparable French areas). In the same year, per capita income in the south turns out to be only 15 per cent above that of Russia. The gap between north and south is likely to have widened as a result of industrial growth which took place mainly in the former region but it surely existed at the time of unification and much before then. Adopting a strict Gerschenkronian logic, therefore, one could expect a smooth industrialization along French lines in the northwest – where the institutional and cultural winds from across the Alps blew strong – and a state-driven spurt in the south. It is indeed possible to find some traces of these potentially divergent patterns in the first half of the nineteenth century (a market-driven growth of the textile, particularly silk, industry in the northwest, neo-mercantilistic attempts to create industry from above by the Bourbons in the south).

Backwardness, according to Gerschenkron, could not be measured by GNP taken in isolation. Most experts on economic development would agree with this proposition. Indeed, the current literature on economic development offers a number of standard-of-living indicators other than GNP. Among those, we have selected the so-called physical quality of life index (PQLI) devised by Morris (1979). The PQLI recommends itself on two grounds: (a) it is based on data that, when available, are rather accurate for nineteenth-century Europe, (b) it embodies an indicator (literacy) that Gerschenkron considered particularly relevant and two others (infant mortality and life expectancy) that are taken into account by the most recent historical research on standards of living.

The PQLI is an unweighted average of: the literacy rate of the population aged 15 years and older, infant mortality in the first year of life and life expectancy at age one. 'For each indicator the performance of individual countries is placed on the scale of 0 to 100, where 0 represents an explicitly defined "worst" performance and 100 represent an explicit "best" performance' (Morris 1979: 41). The three indicators are equally weighted. Such weighting is no more arbitrary than any other, and tests with different weights show that the *ranking* of individual countries in a large 1970 sample does not change significantly with changing weights.

In adapting the PQLI to nineteenth-century Europe, we made as few changes as possible to the definition of variables and to the parameters used by Morris. Two adjustments, however, were unavoidable. The first concerns the definition of literacy which, in our cases, was measured as the percentage of the population aged 6 or over to which most of our sources referred. The second adjustment relates to the scale (or 0–100 range) employed to index infant mortality and life expectancy. In both cases we had to widen the range in order to avoid negative values.[2] Data for infant mortality were taken from Mitchell (1975); five-year moving averages were preferred, given the large swings in yearly data. Literacy comes from Flora (1983) and from various contemporary Italian sources. When data were not available, literacy was estimated from the percentage of people who signed wedding documents, through regression analysis. In most cases, life expectancy at year one had to be estimated from mortality tables and other demographic material from each individual country. Because of such data limitations, Table 10.2 covers a much more limited range of countries than Table 10.1.

Table 10.2 confirms that, in 1870, Italy was an unmistakably backward country. Backwardness was still very visible in 1910 when Italy lagged more than a generation behind the most advanced European countries in terms of standards of living. At the same time, the data in Table 10.2 allow us to appreciate the considerable progress made by Italy between 1870 and 1900, during a period in which existing historical statistics see practically no increase in per capita incomes. Comparisons with countries less developed than those in Table 10.2 show that

Table 10.2 PQLI: Selected European countries and three main Italian regions, 1870–1910

Year	Country				Italian regions		
	England & Wales	France	Belgium	Italy	North-west	North-east	South & islands
1870	62.9	62.2	na	26.9	40.5	27.1	17.6
1880	70.8	64.4	na	36.9	47.0	41.2	28.4
1890	71.3	67.7	65.5	na	na	na	na
1900	78.9	73.7	75.9	56.7	66.8	62.1	46.0
1910	na	84.0	82.4	62.0	70.5	68.9	49.4

Methods and sources: see text.

infant mortality in Germany and Austria was higher than in Italy throughout the period. Relative to the same countries, however, Italy had a lower percentage of enrolment in primary school for the population aged 5–14 years.

The regional breakdown in Table 10.2 is consistent with income estimates referred to above. By 1910, the northwest was lagging behind the most advanced countries in Europe by about fifteen years, and Italy as a whole lagged by forty. The south was thirty years behind the northwest, despite the rapid progress made after the unification, particularly in life expectancy. These data provide one of the few aggregate indicators of the time-pattern in the welfare *gap* between large Italian regions. Its magnitude and its persistence over time make it difficult to discuss Italy's backwardness meaningfully in aggregate terms. At the beginning of the century, the area of the so-called Milan–Turin–Genoa 'triangle' (the northwestern region in Table 10.2) was larger than Belgium and had a per capita income and, to a lesser extent, a basic standard of living not much lower than the French averages. The south was more similar to Russia than to the northwest in terms of both variables.

INDICES OF INDUSTRIAL PRODUCTION

Gerschenkron's interpretation of Italy's industrialization rests pretty much on his own index of industrial production covering the years 1881–1913. Over the whole of this period the index yields an average annual rate of growth for Italian industrial production of 3.8 per cent (using value-added weights) resulting from a rather good performance during 1881–7 (4.6 per cent per annum), which was followed by a serious crisis that caused virtual stagnation until 1895. Italy had its 'big spurt' in 1896–1908, characterized by a rate of growth of 6.7 per cent. The index shows that during the 'spurt' the production of investment goods grew more rapidly than that of consumers' goods, a pattern consistent with Gerschenkron's expectations derived from the historical experience of other backward European countries.

The construction of Gerschenkron's index in 1955 was certainly a major breakthrough in Italian economic history. Nonetheless its technical pitfalls are quite serious. This is not the place to review them in full: it is enough to point briefly to some of the index's weakest features. Gerschenkron uses twenty elementary series but five of them account for 85 per cent of the index behaviour. Some of them are rather poor proxies for the underlying industries.[3] The index is, therefore, very sensitive to changes in the basic series and in the sample of industries they are supposed to represent.[4] Besides, Gerschenkron derives his weights from a highly questionable source, a survey of 1903 which is a partial and unreliable revision of enquiries undertaken in the 1880s and 1890s (Missaggia 1988). The index is, therefore, based on start-period weights. A reconstruction of Gerschenkron's index using 1911 weights yields substantially higher growth rates for the years 1881–8 (5.6 per cent against 4.6) and 1896–1908 (8.0 per cent against 6.7). This result, incidentally, contradicts the so-called 'Gerschenkron effect' in index numbers. Finally, the index itself is a poor proxy for the omitted industries, which accounted for about one-third of total value-added in 1911. Most of them were slow-growing traditional ones (such as leather works and furniture), their exclusion is, therefore, likely to have raised the rate of growth.

Since 1955 three other indices of industrial production have been estimated: the first by the Italian Statistical Institute (ISTAT),[5] the second – still unpublished – by Carreras (1982) and the third by Fenoaltea (1983).[6]

The present wealth of indices makes interpretation of the overall pattern of industrialization more difficult rather than easier since they yield different results, while none of them is so clearly superior to the others from the point of view of data sources and of method as to recommend itself for acceptance.

According to ISTAT, industrial development was slow and fluctuations limited both in depth and length. Carreras sees an accelerating trend coupled with rather pronounced cyclical swings. Finally, the picture portrayed by Fenoaltea's index of 1983 is similar to Gerschenkron's: slow growth until 1878, rapid development in the 1880s, followed by a serious slump and by a long boom from the mid-1890s onward. Fenoaltea's cyclical swings are, however, much wider then those of Gerschenkron.

None of these patterns seem to fit well with Gerschenkron's interpretation of Italy's industrial development. The most compatible with it is possibly the picture designed by ISTAT which shows a discontinuity with an acceleration of growth rates at the end of the nineteenth-century. But, then, the rate of growth is so slow as to make one wonder whether one might talk of a 'big spurt'. In the index of Carreras, on the other hand, there are no points of discontinuity. Fenoaltea has both the highest rates of growth and the largest cyclical swings: a discontinuity could be found in 1879 rather than in 1896 (a timing much more akin to Romeo's model). This interpretation, however, would conflict with Fenoaltea's denial of the very existence of a big spurt and with his assertion that Italy's industrial growth was cyclical rather than marked by discontinuity (Fenoaltea 1973a, 1988c). His view seems closer to the one put forward by Cafagna (1965: 143) and shared by Bonelli (1978) and Federico and Chesi (1987).

The above-mentioned aggregate indices are actually the sum of three different

Table 10.3 Indices of industrial production, 1861–1913 (annual average rates of growth in real terms)

Period	Gerschenkron	ISTAT	Fenoaltea	Carreras
1861–1913	na	1.95	3.42	2.51
1881–1913	3.78	2.26	4.18	3.19
1896–1908	6.68	5.21	7.87	5.00

Sources: Gerschenkron (1962), ISTAT (1957), Fenoaltea (1983), Carreras (1982).

sectorial patterns. The production of investment goods (engineering, chemicals, iron- and steel-making) shows higher growth rates than that of consumers' goods during both the so-called 'Giolittian era' (1896–1913) and the 1880s. The 1888–92 slump was characterized by a much more rapid decline of the former than of the latter industries. In fact, the whole pattern depends to a certain extent on the huge cyclical swings of the engineering industry (Fenoaltea 1973a; Warglien 1985). Traditional industries such as textile and food-processing industries developed rather slowly with no major cyclical swings. Most 'new' products, such as electric power, rubber and some branches of the chemical industries, started late and showed a high growth afterwards.

THE ROLE OF BANKS IN PROMOTING INDUSTRIAL DEVELOPMENT

At the beginning of the 1890s, Italy experienced a serious banking crisis. It resulted in the failure of one of the six banks of issue (Banca Romana) and the collapse of the two deposit banks (Credito Mobiliare and Banca Generale) which had been established after unification on the model of the French Crédit Mobilier. The void was filled in 1894 and 1895 by two new banks (Banca Commerciale and Credito Italiano), established by German and Swiss capital with German management. Gerschenkron sees the crisis of 1893 almost as a *felix culpa* of the Italian economy – and policymakers, in as much as they were responsible for it – since it brought to an end the existing banking system tailored as it was by the French, and made possible the importation 'of the great economic innovation of German banking in its most developed and mature form' (Gerschenkron 1962: 88). The main feature of such innovation consisted in turning investment banks into real 'department stores' in the field of banking. Their virtue, in a situation of relative backwardness, was to provide – to use Gerschenkronian terminology – efficient substitutes for missing prerequisites of industrialization. In particular, German banks, unlike their French counterparts, are seen as supplying not only long-term credit but also a good deal of entrepreneurship, a factor of production supposedly even more scarce than capital.

Gerschenkron was by no means the first to attribute an important role to the large banks in the development of Italy.[7] Gerschenkron's original contribution to Italian economic history, was to see the role of German banking in a framework in which the industrial development of the country appeared as just one case in the pattern of European industrialization. In the 1950s this was a seminal idea that gave new stimuli to discussion and research. Opinions varied from Cohen's strict Gerschenkronian orthodoxy (Cohen 1967: 382, 1972: 89) to Webster's (1974: 325) and Hertner's (1984) more shaded judgements, and to the decisively negative opinion of Farina (1976, 1980). The latter blames the 'German' banks for having distorted resource allocation in favour of capital-intensive industries and techniques, thus increasing 'dualism' and contributing to the oligopolistic nature of Italian development.

The analysis of quantitative aggregate trends is not of much help in elucidating the role of the mixed banks. An assessment of the time-path of aggregate financial variables carried out along Goldsmith's lines puts Italy's financial intermediation ratio at 0.38 in 1881 and at 0.47 in 1914 (Biscaini and Ciocca 1979: 92–7). Financial deepening did occur but the gap between Italy and the most advanced European countries remained unchanged. During the same period, the share of financial liabilities held by banks grew from 0.19 to 0.29. This positive trend, however, did not exhaust its momentum in 1913. The fact that banks retained an overwhelming importance in financial intermediation at least up to the 1960s is a well-known peculiarity shared by the Italian economy with the Japanese. There is little in these aggregate trends that will confirm or invalidate Gerschenkron's hypothesis.

In fact, Gerschenkron's hypothesis is mainly based on the stimulus provided by the mixed banks to a limited number of 'strategic' firms or industries. Therefore, a proper test of the hypothesis may come from careful archival research on the actual behaviour of the banks. A real breakthrough in this field of research was made by the monumental work by Confalonieri (1974–6, 1982). His conclusions may be summarized as follows: (a) long-term industrial financing came mostly as a result of other banking operations, (b) it resulted from normal scrutiny of clients' demand and from a desire to monopolize the entire range of their banking operations rather than from an autonomous initiative of the banks, (c) the latter, therefore, did not possess much of an *industrial* strategy of their own which was, perhaps, more pronounced in their predecessors of the 'French type', (d) the main novelty of the 'new' banks consisted in underwriting as part of a *banking* strategy directed 'plus à des *affaires* qu'a des *entreprises*' (Confalonieri 1974–6: 469). The early long-term involvement of the banks in the electric power industry is singled out by Confalonieri as an exception in their operations. Moreover, the operations of the French-type banks do not seem to be so different from those of the later German-type banks. The former not only financed the construction of the railways of the 1870s but, what matters more in a Gerschenkronian framework, played a prominent role in the rapid industrial growth of the 1880s.

If reliable, these findings would contradict Gerschenkron's hypothesis. If German-type banks did not provide relevant supply-side stimulus to investment, if they were as a rule not particularly interested in managing industrial enterprises, if they did not hold in their portfolios for long periods of time large quantities of industrial equities, then it is not easy to grant them the role of sole or main 'agents of industrialization'.

A few years ago, Hertner (1984) attempted to redress the balance in favour of 'Gerschenkron's approach which remains a very fertile research hypotheses, even though it requires some revisions and qualifications' (Hertner 1984: 159). His qualifications regard primarily the role of German capital and men in the Banca Commerciale and Credito Italiano which he sees as 'the first example of successful foreign direct investment in Italy in the banking sector'. The early withdrawal of the original German capital was not followed by a repatriation of the banks' top management, which was a crucial factor in maintaining strong links with the international banking world and, thus, assured stability for the two institutions. In general, he sees the two banks as concentrating mostly on the Italian domestic market, thereby giving 'a decisive contribution to the country's industrialization' (Hertner 1984: 155). Ongoing and yet unpublished research carried on at The Historical Archives of Banca Commerciale seems to indicate that, by 1913, the latter had established strong personal links between its own management and that of the industrial firms to which it supplied credit. These results are likely to stimulate new debates and research on the role played by the two German-type banks during the industrial growth of the period 1896–1913.

ECONOMIC POLICIES AND INDUSTRIAL DEVELOPMENT

Inept government policies seem to be, according to Gerschenkron, the single most important cause of the 'disappointingly low' rate of industrial growth during Italy's big spurt (Gerschenkron 1962: 78). The tariff of 1887 'must be viewed as the real pièce de résistance of those policies' (Gerschenkron 1962: 80).

The 1887 tariff marked a real turning point after fifteen years of free trade and ten years of moderate protection to a limited number of industries (Prodi 1965–6; Sereni 1966; Del Vecchio 1978). Italy's tariff policy is criticized by Gerschenkron on three grounds: (a) for subjecting 'the tender plants of industrial growth to the rigors of a protectionist climate in agriculture' (Gerschenkron 1962: 81), (b) for the attention given to cotton textiles, 'an old industry with a moderate rate of modern technological progress and accordingly relatively limited possibilities in a backward country on the European continent' (Gerschenkron 1962: 81), and (c) for neglecting the most promising industries such as chemicals and engineering, the latter being put at a disadvantage also by protecting its main inputs, iron and steel.

This judgement implies the counterfactual hypothesis of a more rational tariff and, therefore, is a much welcome disentanglement from the typical nineteenth-century debate of free trade versus unqualified protection. And it is unfortunate that most Italian economic historians have been unable to follow Gerschenkron along the lines of an assessment of the impact of the tariff on growth in terms of effective protection. Despite the vast literature on the subject, therefore, there is a lack of serious quantitative research on the specific points raised by Gerschenkron. Even the average nominal rate of protection is not precisely known: the only aggregate figure – 18 per cent in 1888 declining to 7.5 per cent in 1913 (Capie 1983) – probably underestimates the actual level.

Federico (1984) has put the average rate of protection for Italian wheat at 52 per cent in 1895. Increasing world prices reduced it thereafter to 33 per cent in 1913. On average, these rates are higher than those computed by Gerschenkron. Looking at the rather fortunate period of free trade, 1915–25, one is inclined to agree with Gerschenkron that 'Italy's agriculture had at its disposal methods of adjustment that were not available to an equal degree north of the Alpine wall'

(Gerschenkron 1962: 81) and that its comparative advantage outside the Po Valley was not in wheat. However, one must pay attention to Italy's social conditions, which Gerschenkron sees as one of the weakening factors in its process of industrialization. The late 1880s and early 1890s, to be sure, witnessed unprecedented social unrest in the countryside that the abolition of the duty on wheat would no doubt have made even more serious.

The cotton industry had already undertaken a process of import substitution under the shield of the 1878 tariff. This process was boosted by the higher duties introduced in 1887. By the end of the century Italy was a net exporter of cotton goods. Fixed capital formation proceeded at such a high rate that by 1907 the sector was burdened by excess capacity and had to resort to *dumping* exports. During the years of the Gerschenkronian spurt, therefore, no 'infant industry' argument could be invoked to justify duties on textile products.

The subsequent development of the Italian manufacturing industry leaves no doubt as to the importance of the chemical and engineering sectors. The demands of the former for adequate protection were met only by the tariff of 1921 (Zamagni 1991). The dynamic effects of the earlier lower duty are difficult to assess given the lack of research in the field. It is likely, however, that chemical production could have benefited from 'infant industry' protection. As for engineering, Toniolo (1977) has shown that its effective protection was negligible, due to the high import duties imposed on its main inputs, iron and steel. At the same time Toniolo has estimated that the most favourable alternative policy (i.e. a subsidy to iron- and steel-making) would have resulted in a 7 per cent increase of value-added by manufacturing in the period 1906–8 (upper bound estimate). The rate of industrial growth during 1896–1908 would have been 7.0 per cent a year against Gerschenkron's 6.7, hardly a dramatic change in Italy's economic history.

Gerschenkron's criticism of the Italian tariff *structure* during the years of rapid industrialization is well taken and its validity has been confirmed by subsequent quantitative research. If the 1887 tariff succeeded in fostering the development of some industries (Zamagni 1984: 14) the price paid by the whole economy in terms of misallocation of resources was probably high. It is difficult, however, to judge how high that price was. And we still 'wonder how much importance one should in general ascribe to tariff policy in the history of European industrializations' (Gerschenkron 1962: 89).

According to Gerschenkron, 'another weakness of the Italian industrialization of 1896–1908 may have derived from the fact that by that time the great period of Italian railroad building was largely a thing of the past' (Gerschenkron 1962: 84). This point was debated with Romeo who held, on the contrary, that the building of railways was a prerequisite for rapid industrialization (Gerschenkron 1968: 98–127).

A general equilibrium model of investment in railways (Fenoaltea 1973b) yields rather discouraging results about the likely magnitude of domestic demand generated by investment in railways, even on the most favourable exchange-rate conditions. Direct estimates (Fenoaltea 1983) show that railway expenditures were a minor component of the demand for engineering goods, which depended to a much larger extent on the building trade, an industry that Gerschenkron did not consider. Moreover, the increasing trade deficit accumulated by the engineering sector during 1896–1908 is clear evidence that its problems consisted of supply rigidities (bottlenecks) rather than inadequate domestic demand. However, the wave of investment in railways which followed nationalization in 1905 took place at a time when, after the 1907 crisis, the rate of growth of domestic demand fell sharply and it therefore provided a timely anticyclical support.

Adding military expenditure to that for railways (Zamagni 1981), a likely guesstimate may be that the state provided about one-third of the total demand for products by the engineering industry during the years 1896–1908. According to recent estimates (Brosio and Marchese 1987) total public expenditure (including that by local authorities) oscillated between 15 and 20 per cent of GNP over the pre-1913 long run. These ratios are higher than those for most other European countries and indicate that, at least in the aggregate, state demand was a relatively more important factor in Italy then elsewhere.

Historians have discussed at length the likely overall effects of fiscal policy on Italian economic development. It has been suggested that deficit spending had a positive macro-economic effect (Barone 1972). Gerschenkron (1962: 82) hinted that state bonds crowded out private investment. Several scholars have stressed the unfavourable redistributive effects (among regions, industries and social classes) of the combination of regressive taxation and high state expenditure on defence and interest on state bonds. At any rate, during 1896–1907, monetary and fiscal policy favoured private investment (Toniolo 1990) so that, all things considered, it is difficult to accept an entirely unfavourable judgement on the role of economic policy during the years of the 'big spurt'.

Finally, Gerschenkron sees in the social situation of the 'Giolittian era' another reason for the weakness of the Italian 'spurt'. The coincidence in time of the 'spurt' with improvements in the workers' standard of living – so the argument runs – shifted resources from investment to consumption. Moreover, 'had the industrial upsurge in Italy taken place one or two decades earlier, in all likelihood it would have been much less disturbed by industrial strife' (Gerschenkron 1962: 86). Three remarks are possible on this subject: (1) While it is true that real wages improved during 1896–1908 (Zamagni 1984), it is likely that product per man in manufacturing grew faster so that the ratio of profits to value-added increased, as did that of gross investment over GNP. (2) The strike figures given by Gerschenkron, according to whom 'between 1901 and 1913 there was only one year when the number of days lost by strikes remained below the million mark' and the number exceeded three million in some years of the period, do not indicate any unbearable loss in production. They include strikes in agriculture and, therefore, should be seen in the context of a labour force totalling about 10 million members, with 2.5 million engaged in industrial production. Even assuming an average of two million days of work lost by strikes in industry alone, the loss in physical output would amount to less than one-third of one percentage point. (3) Contrary to what Gerschenkron thought, 'had the industrial upsurge in Italy taken place a decade earlier' it would have been met by a much larger and widespread working class unrest and discontent. In all likelihood 'Giolitti's conciliatory statemanship' (Geschenkron 1962: 85) was, on balance, a bonus for the economy itself.

THE IDEOLOGICAL STIMULUS

Gerschenkron's opinion on the absence of an ideological stimulus to industrialization is widely shared by Italian scholars. Baglioni (1974) describes a ruling political class coming either from the landed gentry or from the liberal professions. Most entrepreneurs were bound to traditional social and cultural values while, with few exceptions, they shied away from the political arena. The recent business-history literature seems to confirm that most entrepreneurs were bound to the traditional social and cultural values and that their political demands were confined to such issues as tariff protection, subsidies, fiscal policy and, more broadly, to the maintenance of law and order. Some authors (e.g. Hunecke 1982) go as far as saying that most industrialists were reluctant to move their factories from the country to the town for fear of upsetting the existing 'social order'. Generalization is always difficult in these matters. There is, however, a growing literature that seems to indicate that in the 1860s and 1870s Italian entrepreneurs could not prosper without at least the indirect support of local politicians and large landowners. In fact, a number of industrial activities originated directly from the latter. There was, therefore, nothing like a swift emerging of a 'new' entrepreneurial class with an entirely different set of values that enabled it to create and impose its own ideology of industrialization.

Moreover, the Church, which retained a powerful influence on the majority of the population, drastically opposed the new liberal state both for its agnostic stance on religion and, more deeply, for its occupation of the territory of the Papal States. In these circumstances, at least until the death of Pius IX, the Church fought against all attempts at 'modernization' that came from the most far-sighted among the members of the liberal ruling class. With the advent of Leo XIII, the Church took greater interest in social and economic matters, as witnessed by the encyclical *Rerum Novarum* and by the creation of *Opera dei congressi*, an organization that was aimed at spreading the 'social doctrine' of the Church and at promoting engagement by Catholics in such fields as cooperatives and workers' organizations. In principle, the Catholic ideology opposed both capitalism and socialism. In practice, bishops and priests were tolerant of capitalism but resisted rapid changes that would undermine traditional social and moral values. They were, therefore, particularly concerned with keeping their flocks in the countryside. The growth of towns, emigration and large enterprises were seen as major evils.

The Socialist Party, established in 1892, remained in practice hostile to the capitalist system (Satta 1986). The party's propaganda spread among workers the expectation of a new social and economic order and consequently opposition to the actual industrialization process.

There were, therefore, considerable weaknesses in the ideological foundations of Italy's industrialization. Nevertheless, the picture is not as clear-cut as Gerschenkron saw it. The split between the old agrarian ruling classes and the emerging industrial interests was not always very clear. Behind several success stories in industrial entrepreneurship one may detect the financial help of landowners and sometimes the support of local politicians (e.g. Castronovo 1977; Fiocca 1984). Moreover, in the late 1880s and in 1890s the picture began to change from the point of view of the 'ideological stimulus to industrialization' as well. In a most interesting book, Lanaro (1979) has examined the ideology emerging with the rank and file of entrepreneurs, far from the most prestigious academic and cultural circles. A careful examination of pamphlets, speeches and articles in local newspapers had led him to conclude that the protectionist drive was backed by a strong nationalist ideology based on the assumption that, without channelling major resources to industry, Italy could not reach the status of a European power. At the same time, nationalists maintained that given the backwardness of the country only the state had the allocative power needed to promote rapid industrialization. It had, therefore, to be made more efficient by a strong and uncompromising leadership. Nationalists formed an intellectual movement with fuzzy ideological boundaries and multifarious followers rather than a political party.

An industrial ideology was, then, actively present in Italy during the longest period of its pre-war industrial growth. It was based to a large extent on a modified version of German nationalism. It was certainly a minority movement – liberals, Catholics and socialists were contending in the same ideological arena – but, then, Saint Simonism was not the ideology of the French masses either. What matters is that, by the beginning of the twentieth century, a growing number of industrialists and engineers had broken away from traditional values and had developed their own *Weltanschaung* which looked with optimism and hope to the future of Italy as an industrial power. If confidence and moral justification were needed, nationalism was there to provide them.

CONCLUSIONS

As far as Italy is concerned, in the mid-1950s, Gerschenkron's contribution was ahead of its time. A surprisingly deep understanding of the crucial problems in Italian history coupled with sound economic analysis enabled him to produce an elegant interpretation of the industrialization process centred around a limited number of relevant variables.

Backwardness proved to be a much more powerful and operational explanatory variable than others then fashionable such as 'agrarian-industrial concert', 'financial capitalism', 'foreign dependence' and the like. Gerschenkron's index of industrial production has been somewhat improved upon only in recent years. In analysing the likely impact of tariff policy he broke away from the muddling debate on advantages and disadvantages of free trade and set an agenda of research on effective protection that is far from being fulfilled. His assessment of the role of the German banks – possibly the most controversial part of his construction – contains a number of important insights into the working of Italian financial intermediation which are still providing fruitful research hypotheses. There is, therefore, little doubt that Gerschenkron provided a highly seminal contribution to the understanding of the industrialization process in Italy.

Italian historians, with few important exceptions, have been unable to capitalize on this wealth of historical and economic intuitions. It was particularly unfortunate that Gerschenkron's early quantitative seeds did not fall on fertile ground. We still know surprisingly little about a crucial period in the development of one of today's important industrial economies. Some good research has, nonetheless, been done in the field over the past twenty years. In the previous pages we have reviewed the results that seem to be more relevant in discussing Gerschenkron's hypotheses. To sum-up, the following points have emerged. (1) Gerschenkron was not off the mark in his ranking of Italy's backwardness relative to the other major European countries. (2) He was again quite right about the time-path of industrialization, although he underrated the importance of his own quantitative evidence about the industrial development that took place in the 1880s and possibly underestimated the magnitude of the 'spurt' of 1896–1908. (3) On economic policy, Gerschenkron's point about the tariff structure is particularly well-taken and deserves further quantitative analysis. (4) Subsequent research has come to some conclusions that are different from those of Gerschenkron, particularly as far as ideology and banking are concerned. Stress has been placed on the importance of the nationalist movement in providing an ideological climate favourable to industrialization, at least from the beginning of the twentieth century onward. The role of mixed banks as 'agents of industrialization' has been challenged by an analysis of their behaviour that seems to indicate that they were more interested in short-term banking (and profits) than in long-term planning of industrial development. Moreover, it has been argued that the distinction between French and German banks does not stand close scrutiny in the Italian case. However, Italian banking history is developing and new outcomes, more in line with Gerschenkron's hypotheses, may not be ruled out.

In focusing his attention on 1896–1908, Gerschenkron was certainly selecting the most dynamic period in Italian economic history before the 1950s. However, his explanation of the 'spurt' suffered from a neglect of previous industrial growth as well as of some factors that, if taken into account, might contribute to a better understanding of the causes of the rapid growth in the years preceding the First World War.

Quantitative evidence on industrial growth during the 1860s and 1870s is far from satisfactory. According to the existing national accounts estimates, GNP grew in line with population (at the moderate annual rate of 0.7 per cent) leaving per capita income constant. Fenoaltea's (1983) and Carreras' (1982) indices feature a positive but low rate of growth in industrial production per head of population. The overall picture for the 1880s is better established: all the existing indices show that industrial output developed at a respectable pace. There is ample evidence of a wave of private investment, caused by the change in expectations produced by the industrial policy of the 'left', by the resumption of the gold standard in 1882, by substantial government orders to the steel-making and engineering industries, by urban-renewal programmes and by foreign investment (e.g. Toniolo 1990). The banking system played an important role in speeding-up the process of resource allocation to fixed capital formation in industry and building (Confalonieri 1974–6; Sannucci 1989). The lame duck was agriculture: production stagnated and incomes were affected by the fall in prices. During 1896–1908, in contrast, output and productivity grew rapidly in the agricultural sector.

A deep, long depression followed the upswing of the 1880s, characterized by a serious banking crisis. It is surprising that, after drawing so much from Hilferding, Gerschenkron never took into consideration the possibility of a depression transmitted from the financial to the real sector as a result of a combination of large industrial debts, generous lending to risky borrowers, and swift withdrawal of short-term capital (Warglien 1987). This is precisely the story of 1888–1893. In the event, the behaviour of French-type banks contributed to financial instability. But German-type banks were not likely to produce a less volatile financial environment, as witnessed by the inter-war crises in Central Europe. Overall financial conditions were much more stable during 1896–1913. External finance was not as large as it was in the 1880s, there was little foreign short-term capital around, and – last but not least – the embryo of a central bank had been established in 1893. The latter took upon itself the role of lender of last resort, thereby creating a more stable financial environment, as shown during the crisis of 1907 (Bonelli 1978).

Conditions in the world economy must be taken into account when discussing the industrial boom of the so-called 'Giolittian era'. International trade and factor mobility are likely to have affected the behaviour of a relatively small and fairly open economy such as Italy through an export-led growth, particularly of primary goods (Cafagna 1973; Bonelli 1978) and a supply-push by foreign finance (Fenoaltea 1988c). Moreover, emigrant remittances, and to a lesser extent tourism, allowed growth to be free from balance-of-payments constraints.

A thriving agriculture, a stable financial setting, and a favourable international environment are factors likely to have made the industrial upswing of 1896–1913 more rapid and resilient than that of 1879–88. Such factors do not rule out the possibility that German banks played a role of their own as more or less important 'agents of industrialization'. There is indeed much research still to be done on this period but, by now, we know enough to argue that, around 1900, the Italian economy was probably richer and more diversified than Gerschenkron supposed, so that several causes were at work in producing the 'spurt'. This picture is more complex – and therefore intellectually less exciting – than that deriving from Gerschenkron's elegant mono-causal explanation of growth: Clio, as he knew, is often a messy housewife.

ACKNOWLEDGEMENT

The authors are indebted to Giuseppe Gesano and Nicola Rossi for advice, to Stefano Fenoaltea and Richard Sylla for comments, to Pierantonio Dal Lago and Sonia Soncin for research assistance. Financial support from CNR is gratefully acknowledged.

NOTES

1   Fenoaltea's estimates of value-added by mining in 1911 are 46 per cent higher than those of ISTAT (Fenoaltea 1988b: 123); value-added by building and construction exceeds ISTAT's by 82 per cent (Fenoaltea 1988b). Average growth rates (1863–1913) are 2.8 per cent and 3.3 per cent respectively (against ISTAT 0.6 per cent and 1.9 per cent).

2   In fact, the worst European performance (infant mortality of 307 per thousand for Germany in 1870) was 'worse' than the 'worst' one in 1970 for the sample of developing countries used by Morris (Gabon with 229 per thousand).

3   For instance, the production of raw silk is taken to represent silk weaving and a sizeable part of wool production; wheat consumption is taken as a proxy for the entire food-processing industry.

4   For instance, simply by substituting Gerschenkron's estimates of silk production with Fenoaltea's (1988a) estimates of value-added by silk industry (which includes throwing, weaving and dyeing) the rate of growth of the entire textile industry would rise to 3.9 per cent and the overall rate to 4.2 per cent.

5   The index is a by-product of the first reconstruction of Italy's national accounts since 1861. Afterwards it has been incorporated without changes in the Fuà revision (Fuà 1969) and hence in all the international collections of historical statistics (Mitchell 1975).

6   Fenoaltea's index was actually prepared in the mid-1960s and incorporated in his Harvard PhD dissertation. The author is now engaged in a major research aimed at producing a much more reliable estimate of industrial output from 1861 to 1913; partial results have been published in Fenoaltea (1982, 1984, 1985, 1987, 1988a, 1988b).

7   The acrimonious attacks on the Banca Commerciale in 1914–15, for instance, leave no room for doubt that its economic and political power was fully understood at the time by friends and foes alike. Moreover, such contemporary Italian economists as Pantaleoni, Einaudi, Barone, Bresciani-Turroni and Sraffa, if anything overstated the importance of large investment banks.

REFERENCES

Amatori, F. (1980) 'Entrepreneurial typologies in the history of industrial Italy', *Business History Review* 54, 359–86.

Are, G. (1965) *Lo sviluppo industriale italiano nell'età della Destra*, Pisa: Nistri-Lischi.
—— (1974a) *Alle origini dell'Italia industriale*, Naples: Guida.
—— (1974b) *Economia e politica nell'Italia liberale (1890–1915)*, Bologna: Il Mulino.
Baglioni, G. (1974) *L'ideologia della borghesia industriale nello stato liberale*, Torino: Einaudi.
Bairoch, Paul (1976) 'Europe's gross national product: 1800–1975', *Journal of European Economic History*, V, 273–340.
Barone, G. (1972) 'Sviluppo capitalistico e politica finanziaria in Italia', *Studi Storici* a13, 568–99.
Barsby, Steven (1969) 'Economic backwardness and the characteristics of development', *Journal of Economic History*, 449–72.
Biscaini, A.M. and Ciocca, P.L. (1979) 'Le strutture finanziarie: aspetti quantitativi di lungo periodo (1870–1970)', in F. Vicarelli (ed.) *Capitale industriale e capitale finanziario: il caso italiano*, Bologna: Il Mulino.
Bonelli, F. (1968) 'Osservazioni e dati sul finanziamento dell'industria italiana nel secolo XIX', *Annali della Fondazione L. Einaudi* 257–279.
—— (1975) *La cirsi del 1907*, Torino: Fondazione L. Einaudi.
—— (1978) 'Il capitalismo italiano. Linee generali di interpretazione' in *Annali della Storia d'Italia Einaudi*, vol. I, pp. 1126–255, Torino: Einaudi.
Brosio, G. and Marchese, C. (1987) *Il potere di spendere*, Bologna: Il Mulino.
Cafagna, Luciano (1965) 'Intorno alle origini del dualismo economico in Italia', in A. Caracciolo (ed.) *Problemi storici dell'industrializzazione e dello sviluppo*, Urbino: Argalia, pp. 105–50, reissued in L. Cafagna (1989), pp. 187–213.
—— (1973) 'Italy 1830–1914', in *Fontana Economic History of Europe*, vol. IV, reissued in L. Cafagna (1989), pp. 281–319.
—— (1989) *Dualismo e sviluppo nella storia d'Italia*, Padova: Marsilio.
Capacelatro, E.M. and Carlo, A. (1972) *Contro la "questione meridionale"*, Roma: Samonà e Savelli.
Capie, F. (1983) 'Tariff protection and economic performance in the nineteenth century', in J. Black and A.L. Winters (eds) *Policy and Performance in International Trade*, pp. 1–24, London: Macmillan.
Caracciolo, A. (ed.) (1969) *La formazione dell'Italia industriale*, Bari: Laterza.
Carreras, A. (1982) 'La producciò industrial espanyola i italiana des de mitian segle XIX fins a l'actualitat', unpublished dissertation, University of Barcelona.
Castronovo, V. (1977) *Giovanni Agnelli*, Torino: Einaudi.
Cohen, J. (1967) 'Financing industrialization in Italy, 1894–1914: the partial transformation of a late-comer', *Journal of Economic History* 27, 363–82.
—— (1972) 'Italy 1861–1914', in R. Cameron (ed.) *Banking and Economic Development. Some Lessons of History*, New York: Oxford University Press, pp. 58–90.
Confalonieri, A. (1974–6) *Banca e industria in Italia, 1894–1906*, 3 vols, Milan: Banca Commerciale Italiana.
—— (1982) *Banca e industria in Italia dalla crisi del 1907 all'agosto 1914*, 2 vols, Milan: Banca Commerciale Italiana.
Coppa, F.J. (1970) 'The Italian tariff and the conflict between agriculture and industry: the commercial policy of liberal Italy', in *Journal of Economic History* 742–69.
Crafts, N.F.R. (1983) 'Gross national product in Europe 1870–1910, *Explorations in Economic History* XX, 387–401.
D'Angiolini, P. (1972) 'La svolta industriale italiana negli utlimi anni del secolo scorso e le reazioni dei contemporanei', *Nuova Rivista Storica*, 53–121.
De Rosa, L. (1969) 'Difesa militare e sviluppo economico in Italia (1861–1914), in *Rassegna economica*, now in ID (1980), *La rivoluzione industriale in Italia*, Bari: Laterza.

Del Vecchio, Edoardo (1978) *La via italiana al protezionismo*, Rome: Camera dei Deputati.

Ercolani, P. (1969) 'Documentazione statistica di base' in G. Fuà (ed.) *Lo sviluppo economico in Italia*, vol. III, Milan: Franco Angeli, pp. 380–460.

Farina, Francesco (1976) 'Modelli interpretativi e caratteri del capitalismo italiano', *Quaderni Storici*, 32, 487–514.

—— (1980) 'Note sul ruolo della banca mista nello sviluppo italiano', *Societa e Storia*, 19, 919–27.

Federico, G. (1982) 'Per una valutazione critica delle statistiche della produzione agricola italiana dopo l'Unità (1860–1913)', *Società e Storia* 15, 87–130.

—— (1984) 'Commercio dei cereali e dazio sul grano in Italia (1963–1913). Una analisi quantitativa', *Nuova Rivista Storica* LXVIII, 46–108.

Federico, Giovanni and Chesi, Marco (1987) 'Lo sviluppo economico italiano', *Storia della societa italiana, vol. 17 Le strutture e la classi nell'Italia Unita*, Milan: Teti.

Fenoaltea, S. (1969) 'Decollo, ciclo e intervento dello stato', in A. Caracciolo (ed.) *La formazione dell'Italia industriale*, Bari: Laterza.

—— (1973a) 'Riflessioni sull'esperienza industriale italiana dal Risorgimento alla prima Guerra Mondiale', in G. Toniolo (ed.) *Lo sviluppo economico italiano 1861–1940*, Bari: Laterza.

—— (1973b) 'Le ferrovie e lo sviluppo industriale italiano', in G. Toniolo (ed.) *Lo sviluppo economico italiano 1861–1940*, Bari: Laterza.

—— (1982) 'The growth of utilities industries in Italy', *Journal of Economic History* XLII, 601–27.

—— (1983) 'Railways and the development of the Italian economy to 1913', in P. O'Brien, *Railways and the Economic Growth of Western Europe*, London: Macmillan, pp. 49–120.

—— (1984) 'Le costruzioni ferroviarie in Italia', *Rivista di Storia Economica*, n.s. 1, 61–94.

—— (1985) 'Le opere pubbliche in Italia 1861–1913', *Rivista di Storia Economica*, n.s. 2, 335–69.

—— (1987) 'Le costruzioni in Italia 1861–1913', *Rivista di Storia Economica*, n.s. 4, 1–34.

—— (1988a) 'The growth of Italy's silk industry 1861–1913', *Rivista di Storia Economica*, n.s. 3.

—— (1988b) 'International resource flows and construction movements in the Atlantic economy: the Kuznets cycle in Italy 1861–1913', *Journal of Economic History*, XLVIII (3), 605–37.

—— (1988c) 'The extractive industries in Italy 1861–1913: general methods and specific estimates', *Journal of European Economic History*, 17 (1), 117–25.

Fiocca, G. (ed.) (1984) *Borghesi ed imprenditori a Milano*, Bari: Laterza.

Flora, P. (1983) *State, Economy and Society in Western Europe 1815–1975*, London: Macmillan.

Fratianni, M. and Spinelli, F. (1985) 'Currency competition, fiscal and the money supply process in Italy from the unification to World War I', *Journal of European Economic History* XIV, 473–99.

Fuà, G. (ed.) (1969) *Lo sviluppo economico in Italia*, Milan: Franco Angeli.

Gerschenkron, A. (1955) 'Notes on the rate of industrial growth in Italy 1861–1913', *Journal of Economic History* now in Gerschenkron (1984).

—— (1962) *Economic Backwardness in Historical Perspective. A Book of Essays*, Cambridge, Mass.: Belknap Press.

—— (1968) *Continuity in History and Other Essays*, Cambridge, Mass.: Belknap Press.

Hertner, P. (1984) *Il capitale tedesco in Italia dall'unità alla prima guerra mondiale. Banche miste e sviluppo economico italiano*, Bologna: Il Mulino.

Hunecke, V. (1982) *Classe operaia e rivoluzione industriale a Milano 1859–1982*, Bologna: Il Mulino.

Istituto Centrale di Statistica (1957) 'Indagine statistica sullo sviluppo del reddito nazionale dell'Italia dal 1861 al 1959', *Annali di Statistica*, Serie VIII, 9.

Kravis, I.B. *et al.* (1982) *World Product and Income*, Baltimore: Johns Hopkins.

Lanaro, S. (1979) *Nazione e lavoro*, Padova: Marsilio.

Merli, S. (1976) *Proletariato di fabbrica e capitalismo industriale*, Florence: La Nuova Italia.

Ministero Agricoltura, Industria e Commercio (1906) *Riassunto delle condizioni industriali del Regno*, Roma.

Ministero del Tesoro (1988) *Relazione del direttore generale alla Commissione parlamentare di vigilanza. Il debito pubblico in Italia 1861–1987*, Rome: Poligrafico dello Stato.

Missaggia, M.G. (1988) 'Nota sulle statistiche ufficiali per l'industria in Italia: 1885–1903', *Rivista di Storia Economica* 2, 234–54.

Mitchell, B.R. (1983) *European Historical Statistics*, London: Macmillan.

Mitchell, R.C.O. (1975) *European Historical Statistics*, London: Macmillan Press.

Morris D.M. (1979) *Measuring the Conditions of the World's Poor: the Physical Quality of Life*, New York: Pergamon.

Nitti, Francesco S. (1900) *Il bilancio dello Stato dal 1862 al 1896–97*, now in ID (1958) *Scritti sulla questione meridionale*, vol. II, Bari: Laterza.

Nitti Francesco S. (1905) 'La conquista della forza', reissued in F.S. Nitti (1966) *Scritti di economica e finanza*, vol. III.

Pedone, A. (1969) 'Il bilancio dello Stato', in G. Fuà (ed.) *Lo sviluppo economico in Italia*, vol. II, Milan: Franco Angeli, pp. 203–40.

Prodi, Romano (1965–6) 'Il protezionismo nella politica e nell'industria italiana dall'Unificazione al 1887', *nuova rivista storica*, 42–86 and 597–626.

Romano, R. (1977) *Introduzione* in ID, *Borghesia industriale in ascesa: gli imprenditori tessili nella inchiesta industriale del 1870–74*, Milano: F. Angeli.

—— (1980) *I Caprotti. L'avventura economica ed umana di una dinastia industriale della Brianza*, Milan: F. Angeli.

—— (1985) *I Crespi*, Milan: F. Angeli.

Romeo, R. (1958) 'Problemi dello sviluppo capitalistico in Italia dal 1861 al 1887', *Nord e Sud* July–August, reissued in R. Romeo (1961) *Risorgimento e Capitalismo*, Bari: Laterza, pp. 87–120.

—— (1965) *Breve storia della grande industria in Italia 1861–1961*, Bologna: Cappelli.

—— (1974) *Gli scambi degli stati sardi con l'estero nelle voci più importanti della bilancia commerciale*, Torino: Centro di Studi Piemontesi.

Romeo, R. and Gerschenkron, A. (1961) 'Consensi dissensi ipotesi', *Nord e Sud*, November, reissued in A. Caracciolo (1969), pp. 53–81.

Rostow, W. (1963) *The Economics of Take-Off into Sustained Growth*, New York: St Martinus.

Roverato, G. (1987) *Una casa industriale. I Marzotto*, Milan: F. Angeli.

Sannucci, V. (1989) 'The establishment of a central bank in Italy in the 19th century', in M. De Cecco and A. Giovanni (eds) *A European Central Bank?*, Cambridge: Cambridge University Press, pp. 247–81.

Satta, V. (1986) 'I socialisti ed i problemi dello sviluppo economico', in *Clio* XXII, 248–73.

Sereni, E. (1972) *Il capitalismo nelle campagne (1860–1900)*, Torino: Einaudi, (first edition 1947).

—— (1966) *Capitalismo e mercato nazionale*, Rome: Editori Riuniti.

Toniolo, G. (ed.) (1973) *Lo sviluppo economico italiano 1861–1940*, Bari: Laterza.

—— (1977) 'Effective protection and industrial growth: the case of Italian engineering', in *Journal of European Economic History* VI, 659–73.

—— (1990) *An Economic History of Liberal Italy*, London: Routledge.

Warglien, M. (1985) 'Nota sull'invetsimento industriale in macchinari ed altre attrezzature meccaniche Italia 1881–1913', *Rivista di Storia Economica*, n.s. 2, 125–46.

—— (1987) 'Investimenti industriali e instabilità finanziaria in Italia 1878–1913', *Rivista di Storia Economica*, n.s. 3, 384–439.

Webster, R. (1974) 'The political and industrial strategies of a mixed investment bank: Italian industrial financing and the Banca Commerciale Italiana', *VierteGarharchiv fur Sozial und Wirtschaftgeschichte* 61, 320–71.

Zamagni, V. (1978) *Industrializzazione e squilibri regionali*, Bologna: Il Mulino.

—— (1981) *Lo stato italiano e l'economia*, Florence: Le Monnier.

—— (1984) 'Sui salari industriali nell'età giolittiana', *Rivista di Storia Economica*, n.s. I, 183–221.

—— (1988) *Il debito pubblico in Italia dal 1861 al 1987*, Rome: Istituto Poligrafico dello Stato.

—— (1991) *L'industria chimica in Italia* (forthcoming).

Chapter 11

Austria-Hungary

David F. Good

A common way to measure the value of scholarly work is by the volume and quality of research it inspires. By such a standard Alexander Gerschenkron stands out among contemporaries. Only a handful of post-1945 economic historians have stimulated such an outpouring. Much was highly critical, but his approach remains and no alternative has taken its place. Those whose teaching and research benefited from Gerschenkron's seminal ideas are obliged to evaluate 'where we stand' after a quarter century of Gerschenkron-inspired scholarship.[1] What remains of his approach to European industrialization? What are the outlines of a new approach? Answers will be a partial response to the challenge implicit in Gerschenkron's question: 'What more can be expected of any historical hypothesis than to have stimulated research to the point of becoming the stepping stone to a new hypothesis and to new research?' (Gerschenkron 1962: 364).

Any rethinking of the Gerschenkron hypothesis should include Austria-Hungary.[2] Although it played a minor role in most of his work, it took centre stage in his last book and was one of the few cases he studied in detail. Gerschenkron spent his late teens and early adulthood in the intellectual ferment of interwar Vienna, so perhaps it was inevitable that he should look at Austria-Hungary in detail.[3] His intention was, of course, to show how Austria confirms his approach, and although he was not successful in this, the Habsburg case and how he dealt with it offer important guidelines for thinking about European industrialization.

GERSCHENKRON AND THE AUSTRO-HUNGARIAN CASE

How did Gerschenkron fit Austria-Hungary into his framework? We must distinguish between early and later writings.

The early Gerschenkron

In the first statement of his approach in an article in 1952, he referred to Austria-Hungary only casually. His 1962 collection of essays has only eight total page references to the Empire or its sub-units. To support his ideas, Gerschenkron relied mainly on Russia and Italy and to a lesser extent on Germany and France, but even Bulgaria rated a separate chapter.

Despite the limited treatment, Gerschenkron had a clear idea about where the Habsburg Empire fell on the scale of relative backwardness. He viewed the Austrian half as moderately backward – somewhat behind Germany but ahead of Italy – and the Hungarian half as extremely backward – behind Austria and somewhat ahead of Russia (Gerschenkron 1962: 16, 17 and 44). The rankings suggest an earlier, more moderate industrial spurt for Austria and a later, more vigorous spurt for Hungary. He noted, too, that experience *within* the Empire confirmed his idea that the degree of backwardness determines the institutional response during a spurt. Since Austria was moderately backward like Germany, 'banks could successfully devote themselves to the promotion of industrial activities', but in more backward Hungary 'banks proved altogether inadequate, and around the turn of the century the Hungarian government embarked upon vigorous policies of industrialization' (Gerschenkron 1962: 13 and 19–21).

In the late 1960s, two PhD dissertations compensated for Gerschenkron's neglect of Austria-Hungary by testing two of his more important hypotheses. Using quantitative data, Gross (1966: 1–2) declared Austria a 'case study in slow industrialization', demonstrating that 'spurt-like development [was] not the only path' to industrialization. In addition, the consumer goods sector (textiles and foodstuffs) and not the producers' goods sector (iron and machine-building) dominated Austria's industrial structure despite its relative backwardness (Gross 1966: 69–70). Rudolph (1968) challenged Gerschenkron's view that the banks mobilized capital and supplied entrepreneurial skills to overcome Austria's relative backwardness. He found that the big Viennese banks exercised tremendous leverage in the economy, but argued that they were exceedingly cautious, always selecting 'plump-juicy firms with favorable profits, firms with the difficulties and risks of their early years already completed' (Rudolph 1968: 436).

The later Gerschenkron

In 1977 specialists learned with surprise that Gerschenkron himself had been quietly examining the Austrian case while they were using it to test his approach.[4] By his own account (Gerschenkron 1977: ix), the project occupied him on and off for some fifteen years, becoming the basis for two lectures in 1973, and his book in 1977. He had two objectives: first, to piece together and interpret a brief, but important episode in Austrian economic history, and second, to see how the 'facts' of the Austrian case squared with his approach. Here the second theme is more relevant, but a quick review of *An Economic Spurt That Failed* (Gerschenkron 1977) provides a useful introduction.

Gerschenkron's hero is Ernst von Koerber, appointed Prime Minister in 1900 and proponent of an ambitious programme of transportation improvement. The programme called for railroad construction – new lines in Galicia and Dalmatia, plus a direct link between Prague and Trieste – and waterways development – a canal linking the Danube and Oder rivers, and river regulation in Galicia, the Bohemian lands and Upper and Lower Austria. Koerber had twin goals – to stimulate economic recovery and to cool the ethnic conflict that was paralysing political life.[5] Gerschenkron argues that Koerber's plan, passed by parliament in 1901 as the Investment Bill, would have sparked a much-needed 'big spurt' in Austria and promoted the internal cohesion of its provinces. The potential was never realized. The story's anti-hero, the famous economist and then Minister of Finance Eugen Böhm-Bawerk, doomed the spurt to failure, by emasculating the Koerber Plan in calculated, behind-the-scenes manoeuvring.

The bare outline of the Koerber era sets the stage for my main theme: how Gerschenkron uses the episode to fit Austria into his approach. Compared to the 1950s, his view was more sophisticated, but also more ambiguous. He had a much firmer grasp of the archival material on the Koerber era than of the literature of Habsburg economic history. He was aware that specialists found little support for his approach in the Austro-Hungarian case and set out to prove them wrong.

GENERALIZATIONS FROM HABSBURG ECONOMIC HISTORY

Scholars have never been quite sure whether to treat the Gerschenkron hypothesis as a testable theory or as a highly appealing, heuristic framework for interpreting European economic history. Gerschenkron himself seems uncertain. He summarized his views as a set of six propositions that appear quite testable, yet often said that they represented a way of thinking, not a formal model. His empirical analyses of particular cases like the Austrian one are equally ambiguous. In Gerschenkron (1977) he fiercely defends his hypothesis against critics, but makes the Austrian 'facts' fit only after bending his main propositions almost beyond recognition. In the end the evidence for Austria simply does not support a literal reading of his hypothesis. Yet viewing the Habsburg case through Gerschenkron lenses offers insights that otherwise would be lost.

Unit of study

Gerschenkron (1962) uses states, i.e. individual countries, as the units of observation for studying industrialization. In Gerschenkron (1977), he implicitly departs from the states-as-unit approach by focusing on Austria rather than the Empire as a whole. Strictly speaking, pre-First World War Austria and Hungary were not states, but rather sub-units of the larger Habsburg state that granted them autonomy in important areas of policy.[6] But he goes even further when he openly suggests using the region rather than the state to make the 'degree of economic backwardness' operational in cases where 'there were considerable differences in the rate and nature of industrial progress among the various regions of the country involved' (Gershchenkron 1977: 45, but also pp. 46 and 48, footnote 6).

Gerschenkron's shift to a regional approach in the Habsburg case is certainly justified considering the substantial regional disparities. On balance, Austria was more developed than Hungary, but each had its own development gradient (see Figs 11.1 and 11.2). The most advanced regions of Austria (and the Empire) were in the northwest – the Alpine lands (roughly modern Austria) and the Bohemian lands (approximately the western regions of present-day Czechoslovakia). But Austria had its own backward regions. To the east lay the Carpathian lands (now part of Poland and the Soviet Ukraine) and to the south lay the Northern Karst lands and Dalmatia along the Adriatic coast (now part of Yugoslavia).

In Hungary, too, the more developed regions were in the west adjacent to Austria's Alpine and Bohemian lands – Lower Western Hungary (now the heart of modern Hungary) and Upper Western Hungary (roughly the eastern regions of present-day Czechoslovakia). To the east lay more backward regions – Eastern Hungary and Transylvania (now part of Romania). To the south lay Croatia-Slavonia (now part of Yugoslavia).

A regional approach to Habsburg economic development is also consistent with the post-1919 historiography of East–Central European economic history. After the collapse of the Empire, scholars in each successor state began writing their respective national economic histories. For the pre-First World War period, the separate national economic histories amount to regional economic histories of the Habsburg lands making up the post-1919 successor states.

When did growth begin?

In the summary chapter of Gerschenkron (1962), the first of six propositions states: 'The more backward a country's economy, the more likely was its industrialization *to start* discontinuously as a sudden spurt' (1962: 353, my emphasis). In Gerschenkron (1977), he modified his view that industrialization in backward countries *began* with a spurt.[7] Acknowledging that Austria experienced industrialization throughout much of the nineteenth century, he said he never denied 'that some industrialization can take place in advance of the great spurt' (1977: 52). The evidence clearly supports a more stretched-out version of Habsburg economic development.

Much post-1945 research in the field searched for the fundamental discontinuity setting off pre-modern from modern economic life – for historians, the Industrial Revolution; for economists, Rostow's 'take-off' or Gerschenkron's 'great spurt'. Some historians found evidence of industrialization in the Bohemian and Alpine lands early in the nineteenth century (Blum 1948; Purš 1960; Hassinger 1964b). Others acknowledged the industrial stirring before 1848, but believed that sustained industrial growth came only after the mid-century economic reforms had produced a 'revolution from above' (März 1968; Matis 1972; Brusatti 1960). After the late 1960s, 'cliometric' research tried to

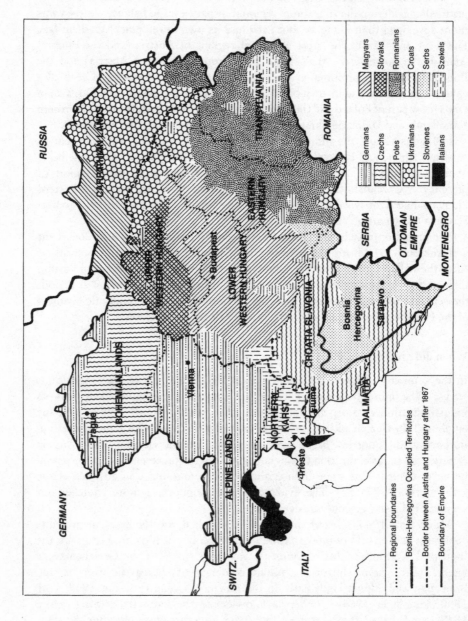

Figure 11.1 The regions and nationalities of the Habsburg Empire, 1890

Legend:

Germans, Czechs, Poles, Ukrainians, Slovenes, Italians

Magyars, Slovaks, Romanians, Croats, Serbs, Szekels

.... Regional boundaries

▓▓▓▓ Bosnia-Hercegovina Occupied Territories

– – – Border between Austria and Hungary after 1867

——— Boundary of Empire

Regions and places: GERMANY, RUSSIA, CARPATHIAN LANDS, TRANSYLVANIA, ROMANIA, EASTERN HUNGARY, Budapest, LOWER WESTERN HUNGARY, SERBIA, OTTOMAN EMPIRE, MONTENEGRO, Bosnia Hercegovina, Sarajevo, BOHEMIAN LANDS, Prague, Vienna, CROATIA-SLAVONIA, DALMATIA, NORTHERN KARST, Fiume, ALPINE LANDS, Trieste, SWITZ., ITALY

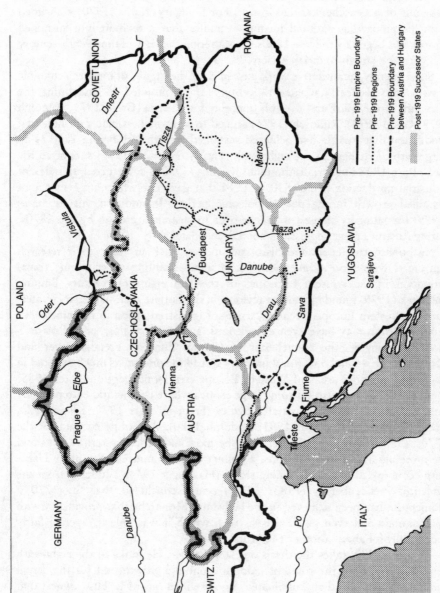

Figure 11.2 The Habsburg Empire and its successor states

resolve the issue with quantitative data. For Austria, the initial efforts of Gross (1966) and Rudolph (1968) focused on the boom from 1867 to 1873 and the growth surge after the turn of the century as potential candidates for a Rostovian 'take-off' or a Gerschenkronian 'spurt'. For Hungary, Katus (1970) concluded from his pioneering national income estimates that a take-off into sustained growth had begun by the late 1880s, thus altering the view of nineteenth-century Hungary as a strictly agrarian society.

Subsequently, quantitative work pushed back the origins of modern economic growth into the early nineteenth century and continued to undermine the relevance of the spurt and take-off concepts for Austria (Gross 1971; Rudolph 1973; Good 1974). Rudolph (1975) argued from formal estimates of industrial production that Austria had achieved sustained growth well before 1850 as an outgrowth of changes in the eighteenth century. Huertas (1977) supported the idea of pre-1848 industrialization and Komlos (1983b) constructed an index of industrial production from 1830 to 1914 that gave overwhelming evidence of sustained growth in the post-Napoleonic period. In addition, his estimates (1989) for Hungary suggest a change-over to sustained growth by the 1870s, during Austria's great depression, not a decade later.

As quantitative economic historians moved back in time, their research converged with more conventional scholarship pointing to economic transformation in the western territories of the late eighteenth-century Empire. Baltzarek (1979) found 'advanced regions' in the Empire that, like their counterparts in Western Europe, became carriers of industrialization in the nineteenth century. Brünn may have even experienced 'a take-off analogous to Rostow's model' making it 'the Manchester of Central Europe' (Freudenberger and Mensch 1975: 44 and 55). Rural industry spread in some areas much as it did in the proto-industrial areas of Western Europe (see Hohenberg and Lees 1985; Mendels 1972), but also on some large estates where aristocratic entrepreneurs directed serf labour in industrial activities (Freudenberger 1975; Klíma 1974, 1985; Komlos 1980; Matis 1981; Rudolph 1980). According to data for the 1770s, the division of labour between the more industrial western regions and the more agrarian eastern regions, a hallmark of the nineteenth-century Habsburg economy, was already taking shape (Hassinger 1964b). Judging from the evidence, Freudenberger (1983: 339) recently concluded that 'by 1770 a momentum had been achieved in the Habsburg Monarchy that provided it with an economic and even political basis with which it was able to operate fairly successfully for about another 140 years'.

Komlos (1989) takes the thesis one step further. He looks to the eighteenth century not just for the roots of modern economic growth, but for the actual economic upswing that culminated in sustained growth. His argues that population pressure in the early part of the century threatened the Empire with a Malthusian crisis. The economic reforms of Maria Theresa and Joseph II ended the age-old Malthusian demographic cycles and initiated an irreversible upswing in the western regions of the Empire.

The debate on the precise timing of growth in the Habsburg Empire will continue. Clearly, however, growth had its origins in a long-term acceleration stretching back into the eighteenth century, not in a short-term spurt sometime in the nineteenth century.

How well did the Habsburg economy perform?

Having conceded (in Gerschenkron 1977) that industrialization could begin without a spurt, Gerschenkron went on to define the spurt's function. 'What I do believe is that the discontinuity of the great spurt provides the basis for a sustained rate of industrial growth and for the reduction of the country's degree of economic backwardness' (Gerschenkron 1977: 52). I interpret him to mean that the spurt was an *acceleration* of industrialization that permitted a slow-growing economy to begin catching-up.

Gerschenkron applied his looser interpretation of the spurt to Austria as follows:

> I cannot consider well-founded the assertion that Austria had been developing just fine and accordingly did not 'need' a great spurt.... It is precisely Austria's failure to have had a great spurt in industrialization, the sluggishness of its growth, the weak cohesion of its provinces and the glaring deficiencies of its communications that make me believe that, in the last years of the nineteenth century, Austria was ready for a spurt of industrialization.... There remains the fact that in the last decades of the past century Austria slid more and more behind Germany ... so that Austria's economic backwardness vis-a-vis Germany was increasing rather than decreasing.
>
> (Gerschenkron 1977: 54)

His view echoes long-standing pessimistic views of the Habsburg Empire. From the early nineteenth century, the Empire was known popularly as 'Europe's China', and, in its final decade, as 'The Sick Man on the Danube' (Hanisch 1978). Its disappearance in 1919 merely reinforced widely-held, negative views. Consistent with its long-term decline as a world power and the growing conflict among its nationalities, many accepted a story of increasing relative economic backwardness and regional economic disintegration.[8]

Gerschenkron believed that the Koerber Plan could have supplied the spurt Austria 'needed'. Even if Austria did 'need' an acceleration of growth at the turn of the century, his interpretation of the Koerber era as 'a spurt that failed' remains puzzling. First, had it been fully implemented, the Koerber Plan would not have been large enough to launch a state-led acceleration in economic development. By adopting such a lofty standard, Gerschenkron automatically built in failure. Second, in 1904 (during Koerber's term in office) the economy recovered strongly from the turn-of-the-century depression in the most vigorous cyclic upswing since the *Gründerzeit* (März 1968; Rudolph 1976; Komlos 1983b). An even faster recovery is hard to imagine. Third, the rail portion of the

Plan was implemented; only the waterways portion fell into limbo. If viewed through the lens of Keynesian economics instead of development economics, the Koerber Plan was perhaps successful. Fiscal stimulus from the truncated Koerber Plan may account for some of the vigour of the post-1904 economic boom.

But did the Empire truly 'need' a spurt around 1900? The answer is not obvious; quantitative economic historians have significantly revised and tempered the overly pessimistic view. They see the economic weakness of the Empire on the eve of the First World War, but stress the economic growth that occurred before.[9] They acknowledge the sharp regional disparities and the growing sectional conflict over resources, but see evidence of economic integration within the Empire (Eddie 1977; 1980, 1989; Good 1981, 1984).

The Habsburg economy was relatively backward in the eighteenth century and, despite economic growth in the nineteenth century, remained so on the eve of the First World War. The issue is whether the gap between the Empire and Western Europe widened or closed in the intervening time.

Sparse data suggest that the relative backwardness of the Empire increased between 1820 and 1870. A regional approach shows how. The western territories of Austria experienced sustained growth about the same time as much of Western Europe (Slokar 1914; Purš 1960; Matis 1969a; Rudolph 1975; Huertas 1977; Komlos 1983b). According to Komlos's data in Table 11.1, industrial output per capita grew at a respectable annual rate of 2.1 per cent from 1830 to 1855.[10] As a follower, Austria relied heavily on Britain and Western Europe for capital and technology (on the role of France, see Cameron 1965). Especially after 1820, the Austrian textile industry began to mechanize and change over to a factory basis. Technical institutes in Prague (1807) and Vienna (1815) spread know-how, and soon Austrians pioneered innovations in both the sugar and brewing industries (Matis 1969b). But by 1870 the western regions had fallen behind as growth slowed in Austria compared to Western European contemporaries from the mid-1850s to the late 1860s. The cause may have been the erratic monetary policy accompanying the Empire's military entanglements between 1848 and 1866 (Huertas 1977).

Economic development spread eastward into the Hungarian lands, but with a delay. The data from Table 11.1 imply rapid, sustained growth in Hungary by the 1870s.[11] In part, the lag was due to the east's isolation from the west, which began to ease only with a surge of railroad development in the late 1850s and 1860s. The main cause was that pre-capitalist land tenure arrangements persisted in the eastern territories. They inhibited economic growth by immobilizing labour, slowing the evolution of a consumer market, and discouraging capital formation and technological change. The eighteenth-century agricultural reforms pushed agriculture onto a capitalist path and the Peasant Emancipation of 1848 abolished remaining feudal vestiges. But both were applied more thoroughly in the west than in Galicia and the Hungarian lands. Obviously, economic growth occurred in the Habsburg Empire without a complete dissolution of pre-capitalist

Table 11.1 Indices of industrial production[a] in Austria-Hungary, 1830–1913 (1913 = 100)

	Austria	Hungary		Austria	Hungary
1830	10.4	11.0	1872	39.3	27.2
1831	10.4	11.5	1873	35.2	24.7
1832	11.0	11.4	1874	34.5	23.7
1833	10.8	11.7	1875	35.4	21.3
1834	10.5	11.7	1876	34.5	21.1
1835	11.5	11.9	1877	35.7	21.7
1836	11.5	12.1	1878	36.5	28.6
1837	12.0	12.3	1879	37.1	26.2
1838	12.6	12.5	1880	35.8	24.9
1839	12.4	12.7	1881	41.5	29.4
1840	13.2	12.9	1882	43.8	38.2
1841	13.5	12.9	1883	47.9	40.3
1842	13.8	13.1	1884	50.5	38.5
1843	13.8	13.2	1885	44.0	38.5
1844	14.5	13.4	1886	45.4	38.5
1845	14.7	14.0	1887	49.0	43.0
1846	16.2	13.2	1888	50.3	41.7
1847	15.3	14.5	1889	52.1	41.6
1848	13.9	11.0	1890	54.5	44.8
1849	15.5	10.6	1891	56.2	52.4
1850	15.9	12.0	1892	56.7	49.2
1851	17.3	13.4	1893	59.4	56.4
1852	18.7	12.6	1894	63.7	58.8
1853	18.1	14.0	1895	65.0	61.8
1854	20.2	14.3	1896	64.3	65.6
1855	20.1	14.9	1897	67.4	61.2
1856	21.2	15.6	1898	72.0	61.8
1857	22.8	17.7	1899	72.5	65.4
1858	23.5	17.4	1900	70.6	61.8
1859	21.5	17.4	1901	72.3	61.0
1860	24.1	18.7	1902	75.1	64.0
1861	25.1	19.1	1903	74.1	69.1
1862	20.9	18.7	1904	75.4	65.1
1863	20.4	18.2	1905	78.7	69.8
1864	19.6	19.0	1906	84.3	76.2
1865	20.5	20.7	1907	95.1	74.4
1866	21.0	19.3	1908	95.9	80.9
1867	26.1	22.2	1909	96.3	87.3
1868	29.0	25.5	1910	93.5	86.4
1869	32.5	21.5	1911	97.9	93.2
1870	33.7	25.4	1912	103.3	98.3
1871	39.7	28.0	1913	100.0	100.0

Source: Komlos (1983b): table E.
[a]Mining, manufacturing and construction except for Austria, 1830–36 and Hungary, 1830–45 – no series on construction.

values and institutions, but the spread eastward depended on their continued decay.[12]

After falling further behind up to 1870, the Empire made up ground in the last pre-First World War decades. Table 11.2 shows that between 1870 and 1910, the Empire grew faster than most Western European economies and began closing the gap with the UK, France, Belgium, and to a lesser extent, Germany.

In the late nineteenth century, railroad expansion fostered interregional flows of financial and human capital, and high levels of interdependence between Austria and Hungary as trading partners.[13] The flow of goods, financial capital and people brought a narrowing of regional differences in commodity prices,

Table 11.2 Real per capita national product in Europe; 1870 and 1910 (in US dollars of 1970)

Country	1870	1910	Annual growth rate 1870–1910
Great Britain	904	1302	0.9
Belgium	738	1110	1.0
*Holland	591	952	1.2
*Switzerland	589	992	1.3
Germany	579	958	1.3
France	567	883	1.1
Denmark	563	1050	1.6
Norway	441	706	1.2
Finland	390	561	0.9
Sweden	351	763	2.0
Austria	450	810	1.5
Hungary	362	616	1.3
Habsburg Empire	413	728	1.4
Russia	252	398	1.3
Italy	467	548	0.4
*Portugal	NA	550	–
*Spain	391	547	0.8
*Greece	312	455	0.9

NA = not available
Sources and methods:
Countries without an *(good national income data): Taken from Crafts (1983: table 1).
Countries with an *(poor national income data): Taken from Crafts (1983: table 5). Crafts estimated a regression equation based on pooled time-series and cross-sectional data for the ten countries with good data using real national product per capita as the dependent variable and letters posted per capita, the share of the age group 15–64 in the total population, coal consumption per capita, and the infant mortality rate as independent variables. Using the equation and values for the independent variables, he estimated real national product per capita for the countries with poor data.
The Habsburg Empire: See Table 3.

interest rates and wages (Good 1977, 1984; Mesch 1984). Perhaps, as many
have argued, the Habsburg Empire made little geographic sense and its ethnic
conflict rendered it politically obsolete (see Good 1984: 96–9 for the arguments).
The data show, however, that the economic union inherent in the mid-century
reforms was becoming a reality.

With economic integration, sustained growth spread eastward into western
Hungary, so after 1870 Hungary as a whole grew almost as fast as Austria.
Relying on capital from abroad, especially Vienna, the Hungarian government
financed infrastructure development and human capital formation (Berend and
Ránki 1974a, b; Komlos 1983b; Eddie 1989). It promoted schooling both as an
instrument of industrialization and as a tool for assimilating non-Magyar
nationalities into Magyar culture, making Hungary's educational revolution 'one
of the most far-reaching of the countries of the European periphery' (Janos 1982:
156).

Productivity grew rapidly in agriculture despite the growing strength of the
large estates (Eddie 1968, 1971). Technological innovations came from abroad
into the iron industry. Hungarian textiles had trouble competing with Austrian
textiles within the Customs Union, but Hungary found its own niche in the flour-
milling industry (Berend and Ránki 1974a, b; Komlos 1983b).

Economic integration promoted sustained growth in the Hungarian regions
around Budapest, but not in Galicia or on the Hungarian periphery (Lampe and
Jackson 1982). As Table 11.3 shows, the most backward regions grew slowly so
the gap between them and the developing regions of the Empire increased at least
until 1900. But they grew fast enough to permit the Habsburg Empire as a whole
to grow more rapidly than most Western European economies from 1870 to 1910.

By 1914 the Empire's position relative to Western Europe was no better and
may have been somewhat worse than a century before, and it had lost out to
Germany for political dominance of Central Europe. But in its final four decades
the Empire began to 'catch-up'.

Politics, society, and Habsburg economic growth

A strength of Gerschenkron's approach is the large role it reserves for non-
economic factors. In the summary of Gerschenkron (1962: 354) is his fifth
proposition: 'The more backward a country's economy, the greater was the part
played by special institutional factors ... [and] ... the more pronounced was the
coerciveness of those factors'.

In Gerschenkron (1977), he modified his view that the degree of backwardness
determined the role of specialized institutional factors in mobilizing capital and
providing entrepreneurial guidance during the spurt. Because he regarded
nineteenth-century Austria as moderately backward, Gerschenkron 'expected the
banks – *qua* investment and promotional banks – to have been of major
significance' (Gerschenkron 1977: 47). The banks were certainly important in
economic life, but they were neither entrepreneurial nor enamoured with

Table 11.3 Real per capita regional product: regions of the Habsburg Empire,
1870 and 1910 (in US dollars of 1970)

Region	1870	1880	1890	1900	1910	Annual growth rate[a] 1870–1910
Alpine lands	517	561	659	930	1089	2.00
Bohemian lands	459	481	551	708	819	1.54
Northern Karst lands	457	487	514	603	789	1.31
Dalmatia	429	455	486	531	650	1.00
Carpathian lands	379	374	427	543	575	1.21
Austria	450	473	539	706	810	1.58
Lower Western Hungary	356	402	468	587	713	1.77
Upper Western Hungary	374	338	433	522	606	1.40
Eastern Hungary	358	330	400	489	566	1.30
Transylvania	378	413	429	483	542	0.88
Croatia-Slavonia	346	405	416	467	542	1.04
Hungary	362	377	434	523	616	1.39
Empire	413	434	495	629	728	1.50

[a] For each region the growth rate is a fitted trend for the five point estimates: 1870, 1880,
1890, 1900, and 1910.
Sources and methodology:
For details see Good (1989). I adapt the method used by Crafts described in Table 2 to
estimate *regional* incomes within the Habsburg Empire. For the same ten countries with
good data, I estimated an equation using Crafts' real national product per capita estimates
as the dependent variable but different independent variables, since most of the variables
used by Crafts were unavailable at a regional level for Austria-Hungary.
    The estimated equation is:

RGNPC = 490.92 + 6.839 LPPC − 0.1256 SQDTHR + 0.1233 RSPC70$
         (11.03)   (13.01)   (−2.03)   (0.605)

$R^2 = 0.843$ $N = 59$ *t* statistics in parentheses
where:
RGNPC = Real national product per capita (US dollars of 1970)
LPPC = Letters posted per capita
SQDTHR = Death rate, squared
RSPC70$ = Real deposits in savings banks (US dollars of 1970)
The coefficients were applied to values for the independent variables for Austria and its
five sub-regions, for Hungary and its five sub-regions, and for the entire Empire to get
estimates of real national-product per capita for 1870 and 1910.
    Data from official government statistics.
Regional definitions (see text for present-day counterparts).

Alpine lands:	Provinces – Lower Austria, Upper Austria, Styria, Salzburg, Carinthia, Tyrol, Vorarlberg.
Bohemian lands:	Provinces – Bohemia, Moravia, Silesia.
Northern Karst:	Provinces – Carniola, Littoral (inc. Trieste).
Dalmatia:	Province – Dalmatia.
Carparthian lands:	Provinces – Galicia, Bukovina.
Lower Western Hungary:	Census units – Danube Right Bank, Danube-Tisza Basin.
Upper Western Hungary:	Census units – Danube Left Bank, Tisza Right Bank.

Eastern Hungary: Census units – Tisza Left Bank, Tisza-Maros Basin.
Transylvania: Census unit – Transylvania.
Croatia-Slavonia: Census unit – Croatia-Slavonia.

industrial finance, especially compared to their counterparts in Germany.[14] Aware of the evidence, he enumerated the 'weighty reasons' that explain bank conservatism. After the 1873 crisis, the 'revulsion in the collective memory', the wave of anti-semitism with banks as victims, and the competition between the government and industry for bank attention, created an unfavourable environment for banks (Gerschenkron 1977: 50). Add to this Austria's structural deficiencies (see also Hertz 1917) – her poor links to the sea, the scarcity and dispersion of natural resources, the power of the aristocracy, and the discriminatory legislation on joint-stock companies – and one sees 'why the German banks, in their so much more favourable environment, could pursue for several decades a policy that was much more innovative and aggressive than the comparatively more intermittent and more timid policies of the Austrian banks' (Gerschenkron 1977: 50–1). Thus, Gerschenkron falls back on the peculiarities of Austria's history and not the degree of her backwardness to explain institutional choice in Austria, i.e. why the state rather than the banks had to guide a great spurt.

Gerschenkron correctly emphasized the major role of politics in the Austrian economy (see Gross 1973). Much eighteenth-century economic history is a history of economic policy, not economic development (Freudenberger 1967; Hoffman 1967; Klíma 1967; Otruba 1967; Tremel 1972; Baltzarek 1981; several contributions in Matis 1981b). Under both Maria Theresa (1740–70) and her son Joseph II (1770–80), policy embodied the mercantilist ideal of using 'government power to achieve economic ends ... and ... economic power to achieve political ends' (de Vries 1976: 236–7). The government tried to encourage trade by regulating rivers, constructing canals, building roads, and abolishing most internal tariffs except for the tariff wall between Hungary and the rest of the Empire (Hassinger 1964a; Sauer 1981; Knittler 1981). It tried to promote industry by subsidizing key export branches, granting privileges for starting factories, and encouraging skilled artisans and mechanics to migrate from abroad (Otruba 1967; Freudenberger 1981; Freudenberger 1983). The agrarian reforms of Maria Theresa improved the peasant's right of occupancy, upgraded his personal and legal position, and encouraged small-scale instead of large-scale farming. Later reforms under Joseph II converted peasant dues and obligations to a money rent and improved the peasant's legal status further (Blum 1948; Rosdolski 1961; Kiraly 1971; Matis 1981a).

How economics and politics interact is also a theme running through work on the nineteenth century (see Gross 1973 for an overview). März (1965, 1968) and Matis (1972) independently developed a Kondratieff-type periodization with major turning points rooted in Austrian political economy.[15] According to the model, growth surged forward after mid-century because the revolutions of 1848 pushed the neo-absolutist state toward dramatic economic reforms in the spirit of liberalism. The peasants received land and freedom from their feudal burdens. The Empire became a full-fledged customs union with the elimination of the tariff wall between Austria and Hungary. The government sold off its railroads to the private sector, promoted more construction with interest guarantees, and created two new joint-stock banks to finance industry.

The crisis of 1873 shattered faith in economic liberalism, gripped the country in a 'depression mentality', and initiated a period of economic stagnation. Chief economic actors, especially the banks, turned cautious and unusually risk-averse. Powerful industrialists and agriculturalists demanded tariffs. Firms formed cartels as protection against unfettered market competition. The bad effects of the depression subsided only in the 1890s. As the banks returned to industrial finance and the state increased its spending, especially on armaments, a new Kondratieff upswing was set in motion.

Some see 1867 as a major turning point in Hungarian economic history. As a partner in the Austro-Hungarian Customs Union, Hungary had no independent tariff or monetary policy. But under the Dual Settlement, the Hungarian government could promote industry directly through tax holidays, subsidies, preferential rail rates, interest guarantees, and support for vocational education (Eckstein 1955).

Cliometric-oriented research offers little statistical support for the *economic* trends implicit in these turning-point hypotheses. According to micro-economic studies, the measured impact of the Peasant Emancipation and the mid-century trade reforms on GNP was small (Huertas 1977; Komlos 1978; see also Rudolph 1983). Economic policy initiatives after 1867 by the semi-autonomous Hungarian government were not large enough to have accelerated industrialization in Hungary (Berend and Ránki 1974a, b; Eddie 1977, 1989; Komlos 1983b). At a macro-economic level, the industrial production data for Austria and Hungary shown in Table 3 give no indication of major trend changes centred on 1848, 1867, 1873 or 1896. Scholars sceptical of cliometric work overestimate both the economic significance of events at the turning points and the extent to which they mark a sharp break with the past.[16]

Austrian economic historians outside North America have roundly attacked the revisionist views. From the outset, some questioned the reliability of the data and the techniques used to construct the underlying estimates (März 1975; Matis 1975; Mosser 1980). But the late Eduard März (1985) unleashed the most stinging attack in one of his last published pieces, a review of work in the field on the occasion of my book (Good 1984). März not only challenged the statistical base, but bitterly criticized the narrowness and 'sterility' of cliometric techniques. He argued that the methodology inherently produces a smoothed-out, continuous version of economic history sanitized of its non-economic environment

Two scholars from outside the field agree in part with März even though they are sympathetic to cliometric approaches. Richard Tilly (1989: 8–9) argues that the revisionist research suffers because 'specifications of the relationship between economic and political change are really quite vague'. (Joel Mokyr (1984: 1098) finds it lacking because 'a systematic analysis of the role of the government in the economic development of the Habsburg Empire is missing'. The criticisms are well-founded. Cliometric research has clarified the strictly economic picture of the Habsburg past and has shown that the economic impact of single policy measures and specific events was probably not large. Yet such research *is* narrowly focused and would benefit from a broader infusion of political economy.

In particular, quantitative economic historians should analyse the formation of policy with as much rigour as the impact of policy. The relevant secondary literature is at hand, since the bulk of historical writing on the Habsburg Empire deals with political and social matters. The problem is that economic historians who draw on the non-economic literature are sceptical of cliometric techniques, while economic historians who know economics and statistics shy away from the literature of social and political history.[17]

Few scholars have tried to synthesize the two literatures, and what exists has limitations.[18] Gerschenkron (1977) is a case in point. For all his flair and erudition in piecing together the story of the Koerber Plan, Gerschenkron explains its demise rather superficially. After masterfully summarizing the political and social milieu of the Koerber era, he places the blame for the Koerber Plan's demise squarely on the shoulders of one person, Böhm-Bawerk. But Böhm-Bawerk, Koerber, and their respective bureaucracies did not operate in a vacuum. The same ethnic conflict and class tensions that the Koerber Plan was to moderate surely explain why, in the end, the Plan was not fully implemented. The reader has to piece together a plausible story.

Two recent works move in the direction of integrating cliometric findings with political economy. Komlos (1989) quantifies change in the eighteenth-century Habsburg economy and draws on Malthus, North (1981) and Boserup (1965, 1981) to build a model of institutional change that explains the patterns. His data show declining stature among peasant military recruits beginning at mid-century. He sees the decline as evidence of a population growth-induced nutritional crisis. The crisis pushed the Crown toward major economic reforms that were to forestall a fiscal disaster and a breakdown of civil order, and to preserve the Crown's power *vis-à-vis* the nobility and the Empire's power *vis-à-vis* neighbouring states. Komlos argues that the reforms reversed the stature decline and initiated modern economic growth by creating a legal environment conducive to capital accumulation and technological change.[19]

Eddie (1989) examines economic policy in the Empire after the Compromise of 1867. He argues that policy in Austria was consistently more *ad hoc* and less purposeful than in Hungary. In Austria, policymakers had to contend with the normal competing classes and interest groups. In addition, they faced provinces with historical traditions of autonomy from central authority and ethnic groups whose national consciousness was rising. Consequently, policy decisions displayed an unusual amount of horse-trading and mutual back-scratching by powerful groups and classes. For example, Wysocki (1975) shows that in regional terms the Austrian federal budget redistributed income from the more developed to the less developed areas. Sometimes conflict became intense, e.g. in the late 1890s when parliamentary obstruction during debates over language rights in the Bohemian lands completely paralysed political life and led to the appointment of Koerber. A major goal of his Plan was to restore order to Austrian political life in one more attempt by the government to 'muddle through'.[20]

By contrast, Hungary's economic policy seems more purposeful and coherent. Hungary's regions had virtually no historic tradition of autonomy under Habsburg rule and its dominant Magyar nationality controlled ethnic minorities with low political consciousness. Yet Janos (1982) shows that class and group conflict shaped policy in Hungary, too. The bureaucracy filled its ranks from the gentry and the traditional, German-speaking urban middle class, two groups hurt by modernization. The bureaucratic élite had a vested interest in Hungary's economic development and single-mindedly pushed programmes in pursuit of the goal. Its main adversary was the landed nobility, which fought the expansion of bureaucratic power and advocated policies to preserve its economic base in large-estate agriculture.

IMPLICATIONS

What lessons can we draw from using the Austro-Hugarian case to rethink the Gerschenkron approach? I believe the exercise has important implications for how we should approach nineteenth-century European industrialization.

The dependent variable

Both Gerschenkron and Rostow focused too narrowly on industrialization. Kuznets's (1966) idea of modern economic growth as the long-term expansion of a diversified productive capacity offers a useful starting point. Modern economic growth consists of sustained increases in output per capita and a fundamental transformation from an agrarian to a non-agrarian (but not necessarily industrial) economic structure. Capacity grows if inputs increase, but long-term growth requires greater input productivity, chiefly through the cumulative impact of new technology and continued adaptations of existing technology. In the long run, productivity change leads to a changing economic structure by fuelling the demand for non-agricultural output as income increases, and by allowing resources to be released from the agricultural sector as demand patterns shift.

States or regions

A comparative approach to European economic history has great value, but the debate on the appropriate unit of study must be resolved. Pollard (1973, 1981) argues for studying European industrialization at the regional level. Regions in different countries often have more in common as economic units than regions within the same state. Much could be learned by comparing industrialization in Alpine Austria and Bavaria or large-estate agriculture in Galicia and Pomerania. Also, some regions in national economies are more closely linked to regions abroad than to regions within.

Yet a host of national economic historians have shown that national boundaries *do* matter. The nation state and industrialization came of age in the nineteenth century. Because it exercised substantial leverage over economic policy, the state could reinforce or offset regional-level forces. A national approach illuminates economic development in the modern period.

In the end, the two levels of analysis are complementary, a point implicit in Gerschenkron's reading of the Austrian case. Cross-national comparisons of regions suffer if they ignore how each regional economy fits into its national economy. The case of Austria-Hungary demonstrates the reverse: that regional analysis is *fundamental* to any study of national economic development. In the early nineteenth century, the Habsburg Empire was a collection of loosely integrated regional and local economies, some more closely linked to economies abroad than to each other. Kuznetsian modern economic growth appeared first in its western regions, i.e. the Bohemian and Alpine lands, not throughout the Empire, so development intensified regional disparities.

The Habsburg pattern was the norm, not the exception among nineteenth-century developing economies. Regional economic disparities were sizeable in larger, geographically diverse economies such as the United States, Germany, Italy and France, but even in small economies such as Belgium they could be discerned. In spatial terms, modern economic growth appeared in concentrated pockets, not evenly spread out, so regional analysis is essential for studying national economic development.

Timing

Like Rostow and historians who interpret the industrial revolution as a rather sudden event, Gerschenkron offers a discontinuous version of modern economic growth. As summarized in Fig. 11.3a he labelled countries as either successful followers (countries that converged on the England after growth spurts whose strength depended on the degree of economic backwardness) or failures (countries that experienced no spurt and fell increasingly behind the leader).

The reality was quite different and certainly more complex, a point Gerschenkron (1977) seemed to acknowledge. As Fig. 11.3b shows, the pattern for nineteenth-century Europe was one of long-term accelerations at different rates, not successful spurts or failures. Some (Germany and Belgium) began to converge on England relatively soon as growth accelerated at a fast pace. Others (the Habsburg Empire) initially fell behind because of slow growth but over time began to converge as the pace gradually quickened. Still others (Spain) grew, but at a snail's pace so that relative backwardness increased. Finally, some countries (Serbia) experienced sharply increased relative backwardness because they did not grow at all.

The behaviour of technological change, the proximate source of modern economic growth, explains why growth was not spurt-like but followed a path of long-term acceleration. Recent work gives little support to Schumpeter's notion that 'gales of creative destruction' produced a clustering of innovations and major discontinuities in economic life. While not denying the importance of key innovations, scholars point to the gradual, piecemeal improvements in new products or production techniques that lend continuity to technological change (Rosenberg 1976, 1982). Of course, well before modern economic growth, periods of intense technological problem-solving and innovative activity led to lengthy upswings in economic activity. But these upswings eventually came to an

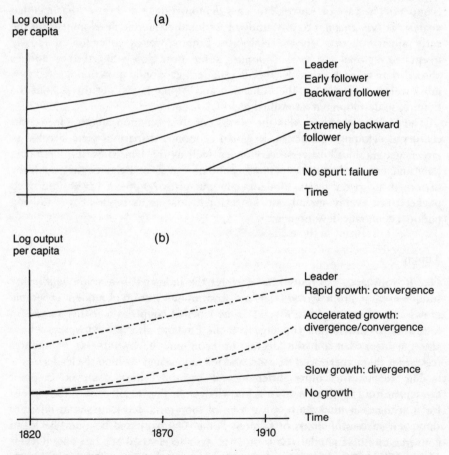

Figure 11.3 (a) Gerschenkron's spurt and convergence patterns (b) Long-term acceleration patterns in Europe

end. Only from the eighteenth century, did technological innovations become so dense and so interrelated that economic growth accelerated irreversibly.

The debate on the timing of growth in the Habsburg Empire continues. But there, as in Western Europe, growth had its origins in a long-term acceleration stretching back into the eighteenth century, not in a short-term spurt sometime in the nineteenth century.

Spatial spread

Gerschenkron recognized that countries and regions develop in contact, not in isolation. Followers benefit as technology is transferred from leaders. Yet transfer does not necessarily involve straight imitation. To have an impact, transferred technology may have to be adapted to fit special circumstances in followers (Rosenberg 1976, 1982). In addition, followers may become technological leaders in specialized niches (Rosenberg 1976; Pollard 1981). Modern technology can spread quickly among and within nations because it has a strong public good component (Baumol 1986). Technological leaders cannot easily stop productivity-raising ideas from diffusing to followers with whom they trade and invest.

But history shows that 'catch-up' is not automatic and that countries 'caught-up' at different rates (Abramovitz 1986). In this sense, Gerschenkron's approach is limited. He wanted to identify patterns of development among successful followers, not explain why latecomers failed to follow, or why they followed at a slow pace.[21] Conditions for realizing potential may not be favourable. For example, poor communications may hinder the diffusion of knowledge. There may be obstacles to the structural changes in output and in the labour force that accompany modern economic growth. More importantly, followers may lack the technical competency to exploit existing technology, i.e. the ability to diagnose and correct problems in the technological system (Rosenberg 1976, 1982).

A society's technical competency depends on its educational system.[22] It also depends on its economic institutions, since innovation is not simply an act of individual genius or a purely technical matter. In particular, economic institutions define property rights in land, labour and capital. A key to economic growth is a property rights structure that rewards individuals for productivity-raising improvements (North 1981; Rosenberg 1982; Libecap 1986).

Habsburg economic history illustrates the spatial dimension of development. Technological transfer was an important key (Freudenberger, unpublished). In the late eighteenth century, mechanics and artisans came with best-practice techniques from all over Western Europe to settle in the Alpine and Bohemian lands. In the early nineteenth century, some industries (textiles), transformed by adapting British technology. After 1870, Hungarian industry depended on a flow of technology and capital from Austria. In addition, niches of technological leadership flourished in industrial sectors tied to agriculture – sugar-processing in Austria and flour-milling in Hungary.

In the eighteenth century legal and natural barriers to trade and resource mobility eased. Growth occurred but for many decades the pace of change was slow and confined largely to the western regions. Already relatively backward, the Habsburg Empire fell further behind the more advanced economies of Western Europe. The Empire's slow growth through much of the nineteenth century reflected the experience of its regional sub-units – the early start in the west and the delayed spread eastward. Gradually, growth accelerated as agriculture became more capitalistic, as the railroad promoted economic integration, and as education produced a more literate labour force. In the half century before its collapse, the Empire began to catch-up.

The political economy of growth

Why do some societies build growth-promoting economic institutions while others do not or do so incompletely? The answer lies in the realm of political economy. The major institutional changes associated with modern economic growth are ultimately hammered out in the political arena. A theory of economic development needs a theory of the state (North 1981; Hayami and Ruttan 1985). Economic historians can draw on standard economic theory to evaluate the impact of government policy. What they lack is an accepted theory of the state that explains why policy takes the form it does (Bates 1981).

We can draw on both society-centred and state-centred views (Staniland 1985). Society-centred views of the state see politics as a function of underlying social and economic forces – class structure according to Marxists or interest group behaviour according to non-Marxists. As classes or interest groups use political means to achieve economic ends they determine the substance of government policy (Bates 1981; Olson 1982). How big and how homogeneous the interest groups are, determines their power. Small, socially homogeneous groups can more easily solve the free rider problem and mobilize for collective action. Their efforts to redistribute income may fuel economic growth if, for example, they advocate a property rights structure that provides incentives for innovation. They will retard growth if they divert income from productivity-raising uses. In addition, they may slow a society's capacity to innovate and reduce factor mobility by delaying adjustment to changing circumstances.

State-centred theories recognize that the state has a life of its own. It can be an autonomous actor and dominate powerful interest groups or classes. Historical sociologists argue that the state is an organization that 'extracts resources from society and deploys them to create and support coercive and administrative organizations' (Evans et al. 1985). Similarly, advocates of the 'new political economy' see the state as an organization with a monopoly of violence that produces public goods in return for revenue (North 1981). Many public goods, e.g. education or transportation, directly affect the economic development. In addition, the state influences the economy indirectly. By specifying, modifying and enforcing 'the underlying rules of the game', i.e. a written or unwritten constitution, it determines property rights in both factor and product markets.

Compared to individual social classes or interest groups, public officials face lower costs of collective action and can impose their will more easily since they have easier access to the means of violence. They enhance their autonomy by using policy to reward friends and punish enemies. The outcome may be growth-inhibiting economic policy. But an autonomous state can be a positive force for economic growth. When institutional innovation does occur, pressure often comes from the top, i.e. from governmental élites. States are in competition within the international political system; in face of stronger neighbours, a state may push new policy measures or even alter the underlying 'rules of the game' to shore up the economic base of its military power.

The interplay between society and state forms a consistent thread through Habsburg history (Good 1989b). Sometimes the state initiated change against the interests of powerful social classes, as in the eighteenth-century reforms of Maria Theresa and Joseph II. At other times, the state responded to social class and interest group pressure from below, as in the post-1848 reforms and the Dual Settlement of 1867. Analysing the interplay would provide raw material for a comprehensive political economy of Habsburg growth – why the Empire grew so slowly and fell behind through the 1860s and how it was able to begin catching-up in its last half century. The story remains to be written.[23]

Gradually, national conflict superseded class conflict as the dominant force in Habsburg political life, a theme running through all discussions of the Empire's final decades. Whether the economy contributed to the Empire's growing internal and external political weakness has been long debated and lies at the heart of Gerschenkron (1977). By modifying the more pessimistic views of observers like Gerschenkron and Jaszi, the revisionist research has, to some extent, rehabilitated the Habsburg economy. But two central questions remain: Would an even faster rate of growth have provided enough military strength for the Empire to have survived the First World War intact? Would an even more rapid spread of economic development within the Empire have reduced national tensions and provided greater internal cohesion?

The answers are not obvious. Had the Empire been victorious rather than defeated in the First World War, it might never have been dismembered. But even a higher per capita income, equal say to that of Germany, might not have been enough to guarantee victory for the Central Powers over the Allies. Also, the ethnic groups that most threatened German ethnic dominance and therefore the Empire's internal stability were not among the poorest – the Croats, Serbs, Ukrainians and Romanians – but among the richest, the Hungarians and the Czechs. The link between politics and economics is complex. Once we unravel the link, we will understand better why the Empire disappeared in 1919 and why after 1750 some European countries grew rapidly, others more slowly, and still others hardly at all.

NOTES

1   The first piece of scholarship I read consciously as a work of economic history was Gerschenkron's *Economic Backwardness in Historical Perspective* (1962).

2   Austria-Hungary and the Habsburg Empire are used interchangeably to refer to the territory controlled by the Habsburg dynasty until it was dismembered at the Paris Peace Conference in 1919. The Dual Settlement of 1867 split the Empire into two relatively autonomous parts with one capital in Vienna and the other in Budapest. Most scholars refer to the former as Austria and the latter as Hungary rather than using their more cumbersome, official names.

3   He graduated *doctor rerum politicarum* from the University of Vienna in 1928. Subsequently, he managed the Vienna branch of a Belgian motorcycle factory from 1928 to 1931 and worked as a research analyst, first with the Austrian Wholesale Cooperative Society from 1931 to 1935 and then with the Austrian Business Cycle Research Institute from 1937 to 1938. He emigrated with his family to the United States in 1938 (Rosovsky 1979: 1010).

4   I learned of his efforts only when Princeton University Press sent me the manuscript for review in autumn 1976.

5   The international depression had come to Austria in 1900 while it was still recovering from the parliamentary obstruction by Czech and German-speaking deputies over the Badeni Ordinances (1897 and 1898) that granted the Czechs concessions in language rights.

6   The position of Austria and Hungary within the Empire was defined in the Dual Settlement of 1867, subject to renewal every ten years. A central bureaucracy in Vienna handled the 'common affairs' of the Empire – military and foreign policy. Since the Empire was a customs and monetary union, separate governments in Vienna and Budapest negotiated and passed *identical* legislation concerning 'dualistic affairs' – setting tariffs, levying consumption taxes, regulating the common currency, and controlling the Austro-Hungarian Bank. The two governments could act independently in most other areas, including transportation, education, agriculture and industry.

7   William Ashworth pointed out the apparent modification in his review of Gerschenkron (1977) in the *Economic History Review* 2nd ser., 31 (1978), p. 172.

8   Gerschenkron echoes Oscar Jaszi's 1929 assessment, typical of the interwar view: 'It is manifest that the principle of free trade was considerably hampered on the territory of the customs union ... There was a tendency toward a diminished interdependency in the last twenty years of [its] existence. ... While the German Empire ... was able to create a powerful and from the standpoint of technique extraordinarily developed industrial system ... Austria-Hungary ... became unsuccessful in the keen industrial competition. ... By 1913, the Austro-Hungarian Monarchy was already a defeated Empire from the economic point of view?' (Jaszi 1961: 191–2, 209–10).

9   For Austria see the growth rate estimates of Gross (1966), Kausel (1979), Komlos (1983), Rudolph (1973, 1975) and Sandgruber (1978). For Hungary see the growth rates estimates of Eddie (1968), Katus (1970) and Komlos (1983b).

10 The estimate is midway between Rudolph's (1975) estimate of 1.7 per cent for the same period and Huertas's (1977) estimate of 3.6 per cent for the period 1841–57.

11 The data show that industrial output per capita grew at 2.7 per cent in Hungary in the period 1865–1913. See also Berend and Ránki (1974a, b), Hanák (1967) and Katus (1970) for more quantitative and qualitative evidence on the same point.

12 For an elaboration see Good (1986) including citations. The slow decay of feudal land tenure arrangements may be another explanation for the increased relative backwardness of Austria by 1870. The eighteenth-century reforms greatly

transformed agriculture in the west, but complete emancipation came only in 1848.

13 Austria took almost 75 per cent of Hungarian exports, chiefly agricultural products, and Hungary took almost 40 per cent of Austrian exports, chiefly manufactured goods (Eddie 1977, 1980). For two key commodity areas the proportions were even higher, which prompted Scott Eddie to speak of the Austro-Hungarian Customs Union as a 'marriage of textiles and wheat' (Eddie 1989). Hungary greatly depended on Vienna for finance in the early stages of growth (Berend and Ránki 1974a, b; Komlos 1983b). Also, Eddie (1989) notes Katus's contention that the non-Magyar areas of Hungary benefited greatly from emigrants' remittances and the indigenous financial institutions that sprang up as a result.

14 Tilly (1986) labels Gerschenkron's approach 'Schumpeterian', in part because of its stress on finance and entrepreneurship. Schumpeter's stress on finance and Gerschenkron's apparent borrowing from Schumpeter are part of a larger phenomenon. Banking and finance play a central role in the theories of two other economists who lived and wrote in Vienna, Eugen Böhm-Bawerk and Rudolf Hilferding. The commonality could be accidental, but most likely reflected the dominance of the big banks in Austrian economic life (Streissler 1981).

15 März draws on Schumpeter (1934) and Matis draws on Hans Rosenberg (1967) to identify three discrete waves in Austrian economic history before the First World War.

16 For example, the reform activity of the 1850s had crucial links with the past. Much of the emancipation had already been carried out in the eighteenth century under the agrarian reforms of Maria Theresa and Joseph II, the tariff wall separating Austria from Hungary was already low by European standards, the railroad expansion followed an earlier building phase in the 1840s, and private banks performed important capital mobilizing functions before 1848. In contrast to his work on the nineteenth century which plays down the impact of economic policy on economic development, Komlos (1989) attributes great economic consequences to the eighteenth-century reforms of Maria Theresa and Joseph II.

17 An exception is the study of unions and wage development in Austria from 1890 to 1914 by Mesch (1984).

18 An early effort was the pioneering work of Nachum Gross (1966, see also 1973) which quantified the Austrian pattern of gradual, slow industrialization and turned to political economy to explain it. According to Gross, the clash between classes favouring industrialization – the industrial bourgeoisie and enlightened bureaucrats – and those opposed – the nobility and the more traditional bureaucrats – was resolved in 1848. After 1848, the bourgeoisie turned conservative so the government was never pushed to pursue a vigorous policy of development. The thesis is plausible, but not supported by the kind of systematic analysis found in his industrial production estimates.

19 Komlos's analysis is thought-provoking but not without some fundamental problems. First, the data on heights are potentially biased and may be unreliable indicators of the standard of living. Second, the standard of living and modern economic growth are related but distinct concepts and measures of them do not necessarily move together or in the same direction. Third, virtually all scholars recognize that the eighteenth-century reforms were favourable to Habsburg economic development. The issue is whether, as Komlos argues, they sparked irreversible growth already in the eighteenth century. The tapering off of the stature decline is not necessarily evidence of irreversible growth.

20 An inadequate but common English translation of *fortwursteln*, the term attributed to Prime Minister Count Taaffe to describe his own policies.

21 Gerschenkron (1962) acknowledged the limited scope of his approach in his 1952

article. He noted that the approach worked for cases 'assuming an adequate endowment of usable resources, and assuming that the great blocks to industrialization had been removed' (Gerschenkron 1962: 8).
22 Easterlin (1981) argues that the unequal distribution of educational attainment explains why the whole world is not developed.
23 Tilly (1989) provides useful suggestions for a possible research agenda – analyses of parliamentary votes, studies of the social origins of government officials, and investigations of social protest actions across space. Tilly's review article shows the value of direct comparisons between the German Empire and the Habsburg Empire on all the issues treated here.

REFERENCES

Abramovitz, Moses (1986) 'Catching up, forging ahead, and falling behind', *Journal of Economic History* 46, 385–406.
Bairoch, Paul (1976) 'Europe's gross national product: 1800–1975', *Journal of European Economic History* 5, 273–340.
Baltzarek, Franz (1979) 'Zu den regionalen Ansätzen der fruhen Industrialisierung in Europa', in Herbert Knittler (ed.) *Wirtschafts-und sozialhistorische Beiträge. Festschrift für Alfred Hoffman zum 75, Geburtstag.* Vienna: Verlag für Geschichte und Politik.
—— (1981) 'Staat und Bürgertum im Zeitalter des Kameralismus und Merkantilismus im Habsburgerreich', in Wilhelm Rausch (ed.) *Die Städte Mitteleuropas im 17. und 18. Jahrhundert*, Linz.
Bates, Robert H. (1981) *Market and States in Tropical Africa: The Political Basis of Agricultural Policies*, Berkeley: University of California Press.
Baumol, William (1986) 'Productivity growth, convergence, and welfare: what the long-run data show', *American Economic Review* 76, 1072–85.
Berend, Iván and Ránki, György (1974a) *Economic Development in East-Central Europe in the 19th and 20th Centuries*, New York: Columbia University Press.
—— (1974b) *Hungary: A Century of Economic Development*, Newton Abbot: David & Charles.
Blum, Jerome (1948) *Noble Landowners and Agriculture in Austria 1815–1848: A Study in the Origins of the Peasant Emancipation of 1848*, Baltimore: Johns Hopkins University Press.
Boserup, Ester (1965) *The Conditions of Agricultural Progress*, Chicago: Aldine Publishing.
—— (1981) *Population and Technical Change: A Study of Long-Term Trends*, Chicago: University of Chicago Press.
Brusatti, Alois (1960) 'Unternehmensfinanzierung und Privatkredit im österreichischen Vormärz', *Mitteilungen des österreichischen Staatsarchivs* 13, 331–79.
—— (ed.) (1973) *Die wirstshaftliche Entwicklung*, in Adam Wandruszka and Peter Urbanitsch (eds.) *Die Habsburgermonarchie 1848–1918*, vol. 1, Vienna: Verlag der österreichischen Akademie der Wissenschaften.
Cameron, Rondo (1965) *France and the Economic Development of Europe, 1800–1914*, Chicago: Rand McNally.
Crafts, N.F.R. (1983) 'Gross national product in Europe 1870–1910: some new estimates', *Explorations in Economic History* 20, 387–401.
de Vries, Jan (1976) *The Economy of Europe in an Age of Crisis, 1600–1750*, New York: Cambridge University Press.
Easterlin, Richard (1981) 'Why isn't the whole world developed?' *Journal of Economic History* 41, 1–17.
Eckstein, Alexander (1955) 'National income and capital formation in Hungary, 1900–

1950', in Paul Horecky (ed.) *International Association for Research on Income and Wealth*, Series 5, London: Bowes & Bowes.

Eddie, Scott (1967) 'The changing pattern of landownership in Hungary 1867–1914', *Economic History Review*, 2nd ser., 20, 293–310.

—— (1968) 'Agricultural production and output per worker in Hungary, 1870–1913', *Journal of Economic History* 28, 197–222.

—— (1971) 'Farmer's response to price in large-estate agriculture: Hungary and Germany, 1870–1913', *Economic History Review*, 2nd ser., 24.

—— (1977) 'The terms and patterns of Hungarian foreign trade, 1882–1913', *Journal of Economic History* 37, 329–58.

—— (1980) 'Austria in the dual monarchy: her trade within and without the customs union', *East Central Europe* 7 (2), 225–47.

—— (1989) 'Economic policy and economic development in Austria-Hungary, 1867–1913', *The Cambridge Economic History of Europe* 8, 814–86.

Evans, Peter B., Rueschemeyer, Dietrich, and Skocpol, Theda (eds) (1985) *Bringing the State Back In*, Cambridge: Cambridge University Press.

Fink, Krisztina (1968) *Die österreichisch-ungarische Monarchie als Wirtschaftsgemeinschaft*, Munich: Rudoklph Trofenik.

Freudenberger, Herman (1967) 'State intervention as an obstacle to economic growth in the Habsburg Monarchy', *Journal of Economic History* 27, 493–509.

—— (1975) 'Progressive Bohemian and Moravian aristocrats', in Stanley B. Winters and Joseph Held (eds) *Intellectual and Social Developments in the Habsburg Empire from Maria Theresa to World War I*, Boulder, Colorado: East European Monographs.

—— (1978) 'Economic progress during the reign of Charles VI', in Jürgen Schneider (ed.) *Wirtschaftskräfte und Wirtschaftswege II: Wirtschaftskräfte der europäischen Expansion*, Nürnberg: Klett-Cotta.

—— (1981) 'Die Proto-Industrialisierung. Zur Funktionalität eines Forschungsansatzes', in Matis, H. (1981b), 355–81.

—— (1983) 'An industrial momentum achieved in the Habsburg Monarchy', *Journal of European Economic History* 12, 339–50.

—— (1986) 'Technology transfer to the Habsburg Empire, 1760–1840', unpublished paper.

Freudenberger, Herman and Mensch, Gerhard (1975) *Von der Provinzstadt zur Industrieregion*, Göttingen: Vandenhoeck & Ruprecht.

Gerschenkron, Alexander (1962) *Economic Backwardness in Historical Perspective*, Cambridge, Mass.: Harvard University Press.

—— (1977) *An Economic Spurt that Failed*, Princeton, NJ: Princeton University Press.

Gold, David A., Lo, Clarence and Wright, Erik O. (1975) 'Recent developments in Marxist theories of the capitalist state', *Monthly Review* 27, 29–43; 36–51.

Good, David (1974) 'Stagnation and "take-off" in Austria, 1873–1913', *Economic History Review*, 2nd ser., 27, 72–87.

—— (1977) 'Financial integration in late nineteenth-century Austria', *Journal of Economic History* 37, 890–910.

—— (1978) 'The great depression and Austrian growth after 1873', *Economic History Review*, 2nd ser., 31, 290–4.

—— (1981) 'Economic integration and regional development in Austria-Hungary, 1867–1913', in Paul Bairoch and Maurice Lévy-Leboyer (eds) *Regional and International Disparities in Economic Development Since the Industrial Revolution*, London: Macmillan.

—— (1984) *The Economic Rise of the Habsburg Empire: 1750–1914*, Berkeley: University of California Press.

—— (1986) 'Uneven development in the nineteenth century: a comparison of the

Habsburg Empire and the United States, *Journal of Economic History* 46, 137–51.

—— (1989a) 'Estimates of regional incomes in the Habsburg Empire, 1870–1910', unpublished paper.

—— (1989b) 'The political economy of regional inequalities in the Habsburg Empire', unpublished paper.

Gross, Nachum (1966) 'Industrialization in Austria in the nineteenth century', unpublished PhD thesis, University of California, Berkeley.

—— (1971) 'Economic growth and the consumption of coal in Austria and Hungary 1831–1913', *Journal of Economic History* 31, 898–916.

—— (1973) 'The industrial revolution in the Habsburg Monarchy, 1750–1914', in Carlo Cipolla (ed.) *The Fontana Economic History of Europe*, vol. 4, pt. 1, London: Collins Fontana Books.

Hanák, Péter (1967) 'Hungary in the Austro-Hungarian Monarchy', *Austrian History Yearbook* 8 (1), 260–302.

—— (1975) 'Economics, society, and sociopolitical thought in Hungary during the age of capitalism', *Austrian History Yearbook* 11, 113–35.

Hanisch, Ernst (1978) *Der kranke Mann an der Donau. Marx und Engels über Osterreich*, Vienna: Europa Verlag.

Hassinger, Herbert (1964a) 'Der Aussenhandel der Habsburgermonarchie in der zweiten Hälfte des 18. Jahrhunderts', in Friedrich Lütge (ed.) *Die wirtschaftliche Situation in Deutschland und Osterreich um die Wende vom 18. zum 19. Jahrhundert*, Stuttgart: Gustav Fischer Verlag.

—— (1964b) 'Der Stand der Manufakturen in den deutschen Erbländern des 18. Jahrhunderts', in Friedrich Lütge (ed.) *Die wirtschaftliche Situation in Deutschland und Osterreich um die Wende vom 18. zum 19. Jahrhundert*, Stuttgart: Gustav Fischer Verlag.

Hayami, Yujiro and Ruttan, Vernon (1985) *Agricultural Development: An International Perspective*. Baltimore and London: Johns Hopkins University Press.

Hertz, Friedrich (1917) *Die Produktionsgrundlagen der österreichischen Industrie vor und nach dem Krieg*, Vienna: Verlag für Fachliteratur.

—— (1929) 'Kapitalbedarf, Kapitalbildung und Volkseinkommen in Oesterreich', *Schriften des Vereins für Sozialpolitik* 174, 41–96.

Hoffman, Alfred (1967) 'Osterreichs Wirtschaft im Zeitalter der Aufklärung', *Osterreich in Geschichte und Literatur* 11, 187–203.

—— (ed.) (1978) *Osterreich-Ungarn als Agrarstaat*, Munich: R. Oldenbourg Verlag.

Hohenberg, Paul and Lees, Lynn (1985) *The Making of Urban Europe 1900–1950*, Cambridge, Mass.: Harvard University Press.

Huertas, Thomas (1977) *Ecoomic Growth and Economic Policy in a Multinational Setting*, New York: Arno Press.

Janos, Andrew C. (1982) *The Politics of Backwardness in Hungary, 1825–1945*, Princeton: Princeton University Press.

Jaszi, Oscar (1961) *The Dissolution of the Habsburg Monarchy*, Chicago: University of Chicago Phoenix Books.

Katus, László (1970) 'Economic growth in Hungary during the age of dualism 1867–1913: a quantitative analysis', in E. Pamlenyi (ed.) *Social and Economic Researches on the History of East-Central Europe*, Budapest: Akadémiai Kiadó.

Kausel, Anton (1979) 'Osterreichs Volkseinkommen 1830 bis 1913', in *Geschichte und Ergebnisse der zentralen amtlichen Statistik in Osterreich 1829–1979*, Vienna: Osterreichisches Statistisches Zentralamt.

Kiraly, Bela (1971) 'The emancipation of the serfs of East Central Europe', *Antemurale* 15, 63–85.

Klíma, Arnost (1965) 'Mercantilism in the Habsburg Monarchy – with special reference to the Bohemian lands', *Historica* 11, 95–119.

―― (1967) 'Die Textilmanufaktur in Bohmen des 18. Jahrhunderts', *Historica* 15, 123–81.

―― (1974) 'The role of rural domestic industry in Bohemia in the 18th century', *Economic History Review*, 2nd ser., 27, 48–56.

―― (1977) Industrial growth and entrepreneurship in the early stages of industrialization in the Czech lands', *Journal of European Economic History* 6, 549–74.

―― (1985) 'Probleme der Proto-Industrie in Böhmen zur Zeit Maria Theresias', in *Osterreich im Europa der Aufklärung. Kontinuität und Zäsur in Europa zur Zeit Maria Theresias und Josephs II*, Vienna: Verlag der österreichischen Akademie der Wissenschaften.

Knittler, Herbert (1981) 'Das Verkehrswesen als Ausgangspunkt einer staatlichen Infrastrukturpolitik', in Matis, H. (1981b), 137–60.

Komlos, John (1978) 'Comment: is the depression in Austria after 1873 a "myth"?' *Economic History Review*, 2nd ser., 31, 287–89.

―― (1980) 'Thoughts on the transition from proto-industrialization to modern industrialization in Bohemia, 1775–1830', *East Central Europe* 7 (2), 198–206.

―― (ed.) (1983a) *Economic Development in the Habsburg Monarchy in the Nineteenth Century*, Boulder, Colorado: East European Monographs.

―― (1983b) *The Habsburg Monarchy as a Customs Union. Economic Development in Austria-Hungary in the Nineteenth Century*, Chicago: University of Chicago Press.

―― (1989) *Stature, Nutrition, and Economic Development in the Eighteenth-Century Habsburg Monarchy: The 'Austrian' Model of the Industrial Revolution*, Princeton: Princeton University Press.

Kravis, Irving *et al.* 'Real GNP per capita for more than one hundred countries', *Economic Journal* 88, 215–42.

Křížek, Jurij (1965) 'Das Finanzkapital in der österreichisch-ungarischen Monarchie', in *Die Frage des Finanzkapitals in der österreichisch-ungarischen Monarchie 1900–1918*, Bucharest: Verlag der Akademie der sozialistischen Republik Rumänien.

Kuznets, Simon (1966) *Modern Economic Growth: Rate, Structure and Spread*, New Haven, Conn.: Yale University Press.

Lampe, John and Jackson, Marvin (1982) *Balkan Economic History 1550–1950: From Imperial Borderlands to Developing Nations*, Bloomington, Indiana: Indiana University Press.

Landes, David (1969) *The Unbound Prometheus*, Cambridge: Cambridge University Press.

Libecap, Gary (1986) 'Property rights in economic history: implications for research', *Explorations in Economic History* 23, 227–52.

März, Eduard (1953) 'Some economic aspects of the nationality conflict in the Habsburg Empire', *Journal of Central European Affairs* 8, 123–35.

―― (1965) 'Zur Genesis der Schumpeterschen Theorie der wirtschaftlichen Entwicklung', in *On Political Economy and Econometrics: Essays in Honour of Oskar Lange*, Warsaw: Pergamon Press/Polish Scientific Publishers.

―― (1968) *Osterreichische Industrie- und Bankpolitik in der Zeit Franz Josephs I*, Vienna: Europa Verlag.

―― (1975) 'Comments', *Austrian History Yearbook* II, 26–32.

―― (1977) 'Einige Besonderheiten in der Entwicklung der österreichischen Volkswirtschaft im 19. Jahrhundert', *Sozialwissenschaftliche Annalen* 1, 87–107.

―― (1985) 'Die wirtschaftliche Entwicklung der Donaumonarchie im 19. Jahrhundert. Gedanken zu einem neuen Buch von David F. Good', *Wirtschaft und Gesellschaft* 11, 367–92.

Matis, Herbert (1969a) 'Der österreichische Unternehmer', in Karl-Heinz Manegold (ed.)

Wissenschaft, Wirtschaft und Technik, Munich: Bruckmann.
—— (1969b) 'Technik und Industrialisierung im österreichischen Vormärz', *Technik-geschichte* 36, 12–37.
—— (1972) *Osterreichs Wirtschaft. Konjunkturelle Dynamik und gesellschaftlicher Wandel im Zeitalter Franz Josephs I*, Berlin: Duncker & Humblot.
—— (1975) 'Comments', *Austrian History Yearbook* 11, 33–6.
—— (1981a) 'Betreibsorganisation, Arbeitsmarkt und Arbeitsverfassung', in Matis, H. (1981b), 41–9.
—— (ed.) (1981b) *Von der Glückseligkeit des Staates. Staat, Wirtschaft und Gesellschaft in Osterreich im Zeitalter des aufgeklärten Absolutismus*, Berlin: Duncker & Humblot.
Mendels, Franklin (1972) 'Proto-industrialization, the first stage of industrialization', *Journal of Economic History* 32, 241–9.
Mesch, Michael (1984) *Arbeiterexistenz in der Spätgründerzeit – Gewerkschaften und Lohnentwicklung in Österreich 1890–1914*, Vienna: Europa Verlag.
Mokyr, Joel (1984) 'And thou, happy Austria? a review essay', *Journal of Economic History* 44, 1094–9.
Mosser, Alois (1976) 'Raumabhängigkeit und Konzentrationsintresse in der industriellen Entwicklung Osterreichs bis 1914', *Bohemia* 17, 136–92.
—— (1980) *Die Industrieaktiengesellschaften in Osterreich 1880–1913*, Vienna: Verlag der österreichischen Akademie der Wissenschaften.
North, Douglass C. (1981) *Structure and Change in Economic History*, New York: W.W. Norton & Co.
Olson, Mancur (1982) *The Rise and Decline of Nations*, New Haven and London: Yale University Press.
Otruba, Gustav (1965) 'Anfänge und Verbreitung der böhmischen Manufakturen bis zum Beginn des 19. Jahrhunderts (1820)', *Bohemia* 6, 230–331.
—— (1967) 'Zur Entstenhung der "Industrie" in Osterreich und zu deren Entwicklung bis Kaiser Joseph II', *Osterreich in Geschichte und Literatur* 11, 225–42.
Pollard, Sidney (1973) 'Industrialization and the European economy', *Economic History Review*, 2nd ser. (26), 636–48.
—— (1981) *Peaceful Conquest: The Industrialization of Europe 1760–1970*, Oxford: Oxford University Press.
Purš, Jaroslav (1960) 'The industrial revolution in the Czech lands', *Historica* 2, 183–212.
Rosdolski, Roman (1961) *Die Grosse Steuer- und Agrarreform Josephs II*, Warsaw: Panstwowe Wydawnictwo Naukowe.
Rosenberg, Hans (1967) *Grosse Depression und Bismarckzeit*, Berlin: Walter de Gruyter.
Rosenberg, Nathan (1960) 'Some institutional aspects of the wealth of nations', *Journal of Political Economy* 68, 557–70.
—— (1976) *Perspectives on Technology*, Cambridge and New York: Cambridge University Press.
—— (1982) *Inside the Black Box: Technology and Economics*, Cambridge and New York: Cambridge University Press.
Rosovsky, Henry (1979) 'Alexander Gerschenkron: a personal and fond recollection', *Journal of Economic History* 39, 1009–13.
Rostow, Walter W. (1965) *The Stages of Economics Growth*, Cambridge: Cambridge University Press.
Rudolph, Richard (1968) 'The role of financial institutions in the industrialization of the Czech crownlands: 1880–1914', unpublished PhD thesis, University of Wisconsin.
—— (1973) 'Austrian industrialization: a case study in leisurely economic growth', in *Sozialismus, Geschichte und Wirtschaft. Festschrift für Eduard März*, Vienna: Europa Verlag.
—— (1975) 'The pattern of Austrian industrial growth from the eighteenth to the early

twentieth century', *Austrian History Yearbook* 11, 3–25.

—— (1976) *Banking and Industrialization in Austria-Hungary*, Cambridge: Cambridge University Press.

—— (1980) 'Social structure and the beginning of Austrian economic growth', *East Central Europe* 7 (2), 207–24.

—— (1983) 'Economic revolution in Austria? the meaning of 1848 in Austrian economic history', in J. Komlos (ed.) *Economic Development in the Habsburg Monarchy in the Nineteenth Century*, Boulder, Colorado: East European Monographs.

Sandgruber, Roman (1978) *Osterreichische Agrarstatistik 1750–1918*, Munich: R. Oldenbourg Verlag.

Sauer, Manfred (1981) 'Aspekte der Handelspolitik des aufgeklärten Absolutismus', in Matis, H. (1981b), 235–65.

Schumpeter, Jospeh (1934) *The Theory of Economic Development*, Cambridge, Mass.: Harvard University Press.

Slokar, Johann (1914) *Geschichte der oesterreichischen Industrie und ihrer Förderung unter Kaiser Franz I*, Vienna: F. Tempsky.

Staniland, Martin (1985) *What is Political Economy: A Study of Social Theory and Underdevelopment*, New Haven and London: Yale University.

Streissler, Erich (1981) 'Schumpeter's Vienna and the role of credit in innovation', unpublished paper, University of Vienna.

Tilly, Richard (1986) 'Alexander Gerschenkron – Modern Historian', unpublished paper.

—— (1989) 'Entwicklung an der Donau: Neuere Beiträge zur Wirtschaftsgeschichte der Habsburger Monarchie', *Geschichte und Gesellschaft* 15 (3), 407–22.

Tremel, Ferdinand (1972) 'Staat Wirtschaft und Recht im österreichischen Merkantilismus', *Osterreich in Geschichte und Literatur* 16, 185–96.

Wysocki, Josef (1975) *Infrastruktur und wachsende Staatsausgaben*, Stuttgart: Gustav Fischer.

Chapter 12

Russia

Olga Crisp

'The relation between any model and specific occurrence in the past, present
or future unfolding of history is problematical.'

(Laue 1975: 8, footnote)

INTRODUCTION

The western student of Russia attempting to assess how the Gerschenkron model
of industrialization stood the test of time in the light of subsequent economic
history literature, faces a difficult task compared with his equivalent in other
European countries. There is a relative paucity of studies in economic history of
Imperial Russia in general, and on industrialization in particular. Those trained
in economics have tended to concentrate on the Soviet Union, whilst historians
with relevant linguistic equipment have devoted most of their attention to
political history, more often than not to the period immediately preceding the
October Revolution, or to the Revolution itself. In so far as economic and social
problems have been studied, they have not been, with a few exceptions, discrete
topics but parts or aspects of a build-up to the Revolution. Where economic
issues are discussed separately, they tend to be approached from an institutional
or socio-political point of view.

The issues which have exercised historians have been the degree of social
differentiation of the peasantry, the extent to which a peasant bourgeoisie or
rural proletariat were emerging; the nature of the working class, its rural
connections and their effects; the failure or otherwise of the commercial and
entrepreneurial classes to act as a force for conservatism and stability; the failure
of Russian educated élites and of progressive political parties to incorporate
property rights as part of their campaign for civil rights; the place of the Russian
state within the system of pre-1914 imperialism; the extent of its independence,
etc. The discussion of these issues involved studying much that is properly the
realm of economic history, but only at the margin and with a specific slant (e.g.
Geyer 1975; Harrison 1977; Rieber 1978; Johnson 1979; Kingston-Mann 1981;
Owen 1981).

Our Soviet colleagues too have been preoccupied with the socio-political rather than the economic aspect of industrialization, but in the process, thanks to their access to archives, they have amassed much valuable factual material. Whether in the areas of agrarian, financial or banking history, early industrialization, and recently prices and markets, much interesting work has been done in the Soviet Union, though inevitably data have been selected and organized within a Marxist–Leninist framework (Kinyapina 1968; Anfimov 1969, 1980; Zaozerskaya 1970; Mironov 1981; Bovykin 1984).

For whatever reason, the Gerschenkron model was not widely discussed. Besides, some of the issues raised by it seemed familiar, and were indeed part of the literature of the build-up to the revolution. Only with regard to the 1870s has a lively debate surfaced questioning the uniformly grim picture of peasant immiseration, which eventually led to a reconsideration of the rate of agricultural growth. However, the macro-economic studies by Falkus (1968), Gregory (1982), Kahan (1978), Barkai (1973) or Metzer (1974) were prompted by the more general interest in the GNP and econometrics sparked off by the studies of W. W. Rostow, S. Kuznets and the literature of development, though indirectly they threw light on the Gerschenkron model.

RUSSIA'S INDUSTRIALIZATION PATTERN AS DEPICTED BY GERSCHENKRON

As is known, the Gerschenkron model of industrialization owes much to his understanding of Russia's economic development. Though his erudition and linguistic talents were exceptional, it would seem, at least on the basis of published work, that he steeped himself most thoroughly in the literature in Russian and pertaining to Russia.

Backward agriculture was Gerschenkron's point of departure. It was backward until 1861 because of serfdom; and it remained backward after 1861 because the serf was so badly emancipated. The Emancipation Edict failed to clear the decks for industrialization. It failed to free the person of the agriculturist, thereby depriving potential entrepreneurs of the stimulus to investment offered by an ample supply of cheap labour. The rural population emerged from the emancipation with inadequate holdings and heavy financial burdens. This limited its purchasing power for products of industry. Finally, the communal system was wasteful of labour and made for low productivity. It encouraged the hoarding of a resource in surplus, i.e. labour, as a means of laying claim to a scarce resource, i.e. land.

As agriculture could not make the contribution to economic growth that it did in more advanced economies, industrialization could only be effected by the state taking on the task of mobilizing the necessary resources and substituting for the inadequacies of the domestic market, entrepreneurship and savings. The state was galvanized into taking on this task because Russia's status as a great power was in jeopardy.

Though the constraints on labour mobility stemming from the provisions of the Emancipation Edict made for an insufficient supply of manpower and skills, capital-intensive industries and large plant and enterprise size substituted for labour and management inadequacies. Whilst agriculture as it operated was not capable of interacting healthily with industry, it could be induced to release some of the essential resources for industrialization by a variety of fiscal measures, though at the cost of falling consumption.

Gerschenkron's model emphasizes discontinuity. It singles out two short spurts of high rates of industrial growth, or two phases of the same spurt: the first in the 1890s with highest rates during 1896–1900 and the second from 1907 to 1913 with highest rates from 1910. During the second spurt or phase, Gerschenkron noted a qualitative change in the pattern. Industry was able to throw away the crutches of government support, banking taking over some of the functions performed by the state. Russia was thus entering a stage of diminished backwardness under which the pattern of industrialization came closer to that specific to Germany, also a latecomer but less backward.

Such a change was possible because during the period of state-led industrialization the economic organism had gathered inner strength, and because of the *volte face* in agrarian policy, as expressed in Stolypin's Reforms 1906–1910 which, by abolishing the commune, made a sound interaction between agriculture and industry possible. 'Though', he wrote 'an agrarian reform was not a *prerequisite* of industrialization in Russia, it may have been – *sit venia verbo* – its *post*requisite' (Gerschenkron 1968: 247).

The above may be a rather simplified rendering of Gerschenkron's model as he applied it to Russia. However, it is not easy to summarize his account, as he was not very specific about the actual policies of the state which he claimed triggered industrialization. Indeed it is often necessary to piece together references to government policies scattered in various reviews by Gerschenkron of books on the Russian economy. He was very detailed in his account of agrarian policies. He was specific in two areas. He had clearly charted the annual rates of industrial growth for the period 1885–1913 (Gerschenkron 1947), and provided an index of per capita output of wheat and rye in fifty provinces of European Russia 1870–1900 (Gerschenkron 1968: 223).

What follows will be an attempt to discuss some of the above aspects of the model in the light of the literature of economic development and industrialization.

RELATIVE BACKWARDNESS

Gerschenkron's judgement as to Russia's level of backwardness relative to other major European countries was undoubtedly correct whatever indicator of backwardness, as listed by him, one applies. Nevertheless, it is desirable to use more rigorous means of ranking Russia relative to other economies but precise recent data on GNP per head for Russia are only those computed by Goldsmith

(1961) and Gregory (1982) for 1913 and for 1861, though for the latter only in a rough order of magnitude.

Some scholars maintain that Russia under Catherine II had an income per head roughly comparable to the leading European countries of the period. E. Tarle, in a famous article in Russian, made this claim basing it on Russia's position as a leading producer and exporter of industrial products, especially iron (Tarle 1909). Gerschenkron rejected this claim, and argued that

> taking into account the structure of Russian industry, its absorptive capacity for raw materials produced (including iron) and its degree of mechanization – as by any other reasonable yardstick – Russia was in the eighteenth century and remained throughout the nineteenth century far and away the most backward among the major European countries.
>
> (Gerschenkron 1968: 435)

Recently Ian Blanchard returned to the issue and concluded that the 'poor, strife-ridden nation of Peter's reign, whose denizens enjoyed a per capita income only two-thirds that of the English and three-quarters that of the French had by 1807 come of age. During the years 1718/22–88 the gap between Russia and the most powerful nations of western Europe had rapidly closed until the average Russian was only 15 per cent poorer than his French counterpart and less than 5 per cent worse off than the average Englishman'. When, as a result of the decline in French incomes during the period of French revolutionary wars, Britain assumed economic leadership in Western Europe, in 1807 the average British citizen was barely richer than his Russian counterpart. 'The two nations – Britain and Russia – stood at the very top of the European national-income league table' (Blanchard 1989: 282).

Whatever the case might have been, by 1861 the gap separating Russia from other major European countries was again wide in per capita incomes. By 1913, though in the aggregate Russia compared favourably with several countries (almost equalling the UK, and only falling behind Germany) in Europe, in per capita terms between 1861 and 1913 the gap widened markedly with most countries; though relative to Italy the gap on this evidence seemed to have somewhat narrowed. Goldsmith (1961) puts Russia on a level with Italy (Gregory 1982).

The most recent estimates of per capita national product by N. Crafts confirm Russia's position at the bottom of the league table of European countries at three dates: 1870, 1890 and 1910 (Crafts 1983).

On the basis of another criterion commonly used to assess the ranking of economies, that of infant mortality, Russia's dismal position is confirmed both in absolute and relative terms (Gatrell 1986: table 2.2). The criterion of literacy points to a similar situation. Unfortunately data for the Russian Empire are available only for 1897, and though the evidence strongly supports very important progress in this respect, the rates of literacy, especially female literacy, also increased in other European countries, so that the ranking is unlikely to be much more favourable than it was around 1900 as portrayed by Cipolla (1969: 126–8; Gatrell 1986: 34).

Nevertheless there were important changes in levels of literacy as a result of the educational reforms of the 1860s, but also as a product of industrialization. This was reflected in higher literacy rates among industrial workers, especially males, and in the two capital cities, Moscow and St Petersburg, which were also among the largest industrial centres. The Baltic Region, today's Latvia and Estonia, had levels of literacy in 1897 on a level with Austria and Belgium in 1900 (Guroff and Starr 1971; Crisp 1978).

Whatever criterion of backwardness one applies, account has to be taken of important regional disparities. However, the data are not such as to allow for comparison in this respect with other countries. Certainly if Italy had its south, the Russian Empire had its eastern periphery. It also had something akin to the Milan–Turin–Genoa triangle in the provinces of Moscow and St Petersburg. These two provinces accounted for nearly one-third of all the incomes of over 1000 roubles in the whole Empire in 1910 (Ministry of Finance 1906–10).

AGRARIAN POLICIES 1861–1906

Gerschenkron's negative assessment of the Emancipation Edict of 1861 and of the subsequent agrarian policies of the Russian government up to 1906 closely resembled conventional wisdom on the subject and was acceptable to most students of Russia. His association of a stagnant agriculture with a specific pattern of industrialization was novel, but the subtlety of his interpretation was often missed. Instead there was a tendency in the literature to identify the industrialization policies of the 1880s and 1890s with the notorious Stalinist forced-draft industrialization of the 1930s. Thus the relationship between the agrarian and industrial sectors under the Gerschenkron models applied to Russia was described as 'the resource raid perpetrated upon one sector [agriculture] for the benefit of the other [industry]' (Trebilcock 1981: 219). 'Emancipation', in this view, 'should be recharacterized as the institutional source of non-feudal serfdom, harnessing the new peasantry to the requirements of an autocracy prepared to *coerce* the desired measure of development from its populace.' Reference was made to 'grain levies' suggestive of compulsory deliveries to the state under the Soviets.

Not everyone, however, accepted the importance which Gerschenkron attached to the provisions of the Emancipation Edict and of policies associated with them. The Edict – they maintained – was above all a political act motivated by contrition, revulsion or humiliation felt by enlightened members of the Imperial Family, of the bureaucracy and the educated classes who, having internalized Western ethical and cultural values, had found continuing 'slavery' no longer supportable (Field 1976).

Though there were members of the land-owning classes who shared these sentiments, and though the nobility at large acquiesced in the decision of the

Emperor, in order to be acceptable the settlement had to be in the nature of compromise.

For these reasons, the emancipation statute was unlikely to contain an ideal set of provisions designed to smooth the road to economic modernization, even if this had been in the minds of the legislators (which was not the case). Nevertheless, an analysis of the provisions suggests that, contrary to Gerschenkron's view, the statute contained many potentially positive features whether approached from the angle of purchasing power, agricultural productivity, or labour supply to industry (Crisp 1976: 17–21).

Even Gerschenkron's basic assumption about the retention of the communal system – it is argued – needs qualifying. 'What is true of serfdom', Gerschenkron wrote, 'is *mutatis mutandis* true of the commune' (Gerschenkron 1968: 436) N. A. Militun, the man most responsible for the form which the legislation of 1861 took, is quoted:

> the lawgiver does not impose on the rural class any one form of property preferably to others: it may be individual or communal according to the custom prevailing in each region, and it will be left to the purchasers' own pleasure whether they will transform the lands acquired by the communes into private or individual property.

It did not work out that way. Far from letting the commune live or die as the natural inclination of the peasants dictated, the government shored it up by legislative devices of all kinds, especially during the 1880s and 1890s (Schapiro 1986: 58). However, though at the time of the promulgation of the statute, communal land tenure accounted for about four-fifths of all peasant households in European Russia, the 1861 statute contained a number of clauses which gave much scope for choice in favour of private property. That this choice was rarely made indicates the peasants' 'natural inclination'.

Nevertheless, during the 1860s and 1870s the prevalent official view tended to be in favour of private property. The two ministries most involved, Interior and Finance, worked in tandem during this period to facilitate a transfer to household property where the Edict allowed for it, and to limit the restrictive effects of communal retention. Even in the 1880s, when the clauses allowing for privatization were largely rescinded, the foundation of the Peasant Land Bank by N. K. Bunge in 1882 to advance credit for land purchase, increased the area of land over which the peasant could have choice untrammelled by collective decisions and collective responsibility for taxes (Crisp 1989: 41–2). By substituting indirect for direct taxes, Bunge made much of the interference by governmental and village authorities redundant. Collective responsibility for taxation finally went in 1903, but right up to 1917 peasants tended to apply the principle of mutual guarantee, by choice, in a variety of contractual transactions, an indication that they found it a useful arrangement in the specific conditions of Russian rural life (Crisp 1989: 55).

The above would suggest that government policy was far from monolithic, and that the agrarian policies *per se* could not have had the uncompromisingly negative influence on the development of agriculture or the conditions of the rural population that Gerschenkron's analysis implied. Moreover, as market forces grew in strength in consequence of the monetization of the rural economy, the expansion of the railway network and the growing integration with the European economy, these forces rather than individual acts of government became decisive for agricultural development.

There is no evidence that communal land tenure *per se* impeded growth of agricultural productivity. Peasants, whilst valuing highly the security of tenure provided by joint ownership, were nevertheless keenly involved in the land market as buyers. There is no evidence that purchased land was cultivated significantly better than land held in the commune, largely because communal arrangements were far from rigid. Improvements on both were slow, but they occurred wherever there was opportunity and know-how (Crisp 1989: 62–3; Pallot 1983).

As regards the constraints imposed upon peasant mobility by the communal system institutionalized by the 1861 Edict, the evidence seems to suggest a great deal of mobility. Millions migrated to Asiatic Russia, millions more left the village for seasonal employment, many worked full time in cities and factories. For the majority, however, the pull of factories was not strong enough to persuade peasants who valued the security provided by land to move. The indices of real wages for St Petersburg, which indicate that real wages in industry rose by an insignificant percentage between 1853–60 and 1910–13, show that the urban sector was provided with all the unskilled labour it required at a roughly constant wage. There was no overall labour bottleneck and the legal arrangements of the 1861 Edict were redundant or, at most, neutral in this respect. Gerschenkron identified the commune with serfdom. However, serfdom, as it operated in Russia in the nineteenth century, was far from being the drag on the national economy commonly assumed (Crisp 1978: 362–70, 408–13).

AGRICULTURAL OUTPUT AND CONSUMPTION LEVELS

'In the last quarter of the nineteenth century', wrote Gerschenkron, 'Russian agriculture, taken as a whole, made a valiant effort to keep the per capita output constant. But it failed' (Gerschenkron 1968: 223). His index of per capita output of wheat and rye in fifty provinces of European Russia, 1879–1900, seemed to confirm this failure. The index suggests a fall in output per head during the 1880s and 1890s, a fall which in association with the increased share of exports in total output under the pressure of government policies was a clear indication of pressure on consumption levels, especially of the rural population. The latter, burdened with high taxation, an essential part of government policy of mobilizing resources for industrialization, high land prices and deteriorating terms of trade, was marketing cereals at the expense of their own consumption (Gerschenkron 1968: 224–9).

Recent research suggests that Gerschenkron had underestimated agricultural growth, was wrong about the rate of retention of food production in the country at large and in rural areas in particular, and consequently overestimated the pressure on consumption levels of the population. The study of the statistics of grain production 1860–1900 by the Soviet specialist, Nifontov (1974), the work on Russia's national income, 1885–1913 by Paul Gregory, and the most recent monograph by Heinz-Dietrich Löwe (1987) on the conditions of the peasants in Russia 1880–1905, indicate that contrary to the Gerschenkron model, Russian agriculture as measured by growth rates of cereals and potatoes output and consumption levels of the population, did not decline but in fact rose.

Nifontov's data, which embrace the two post-emancipation decades as well as the 1880s and 1890s most closely associated with the industrial spurt, point to sustained growth of food grains and potatoes from the 1860s to 1900 if annual averages over ten-year periods are considered, smoothing out fluctuations from year to year. Similarly, net output (i.e. net of seed) per head of the total population and per head of the rural population grew strongly relative to the 1860s, especially during the 1870s and 1890s (Nifontov 1974: 198, 266, 269, 284, 303).

Wheatcroft (1980: ch. 4) calculated that during the whole period 1850–1900, three-quarters of the increase in output in European Russia was on account of higher yields, only one-quarter was due to area expansion. In the Empire at large about 90 per cent of output growth between 1883 and 1895 was on account of higher yields; after 1895 about 60 per cent of the increased output was on account of area expansion.

Gerschenkron was right that exports represented an increased share of the gross harvest except during the 1890s, when the percentage share slightly declined (13.7 per cent as against 14.3 per cent in the 1880s) (Nifontov 1974: 143, 214, 307–10). However, the internal market accounted for 60 per cent of the marketed grain, and was throughout decisive for the growth of commercial agriculture, not only because it was one-and-a-half times larger than the export trade, but also because it was more stable whilst exports fluctuated from year to year depending on external circumstances (Nifontov 1974: 303). It also comprised a larger assortment of produce though, with prevalence of rye and oats. It is a not well-known fact that Witte, far from forcing exports, was anxious to prevent mass sales in falling markets and attempted to influence the military authorities to make reserve purchases internally to forestall the cheapening of exports (Kitanina 1978: 170ff).

In the 1880s there was a significant shift in the ownership and utilization of land in production and marketings in favour of family farms. However, the bulk of food grain grown on allotment land held on communal tenure was used for subsistence or on the farm. The bulk of the produce from land purchased from the estates and about one-fifth of that grown on land rented from estates was marketed (Nifontov 1974: 303). This confirms Gregory's finding in Chapter 4 about the rationality of peasant behaviour, and refutes the view that the purchases of land were made at prices which exceeded the income from the land, because 'survival' purchases were involved.

Gregory's study of Russia's national income, 1885–1913, calculated on the basis of final expenditure, provides the most powerful refutation of Gerschenkron's thesis. Its calculations suggest that the volume of retained cereal crops rose both in absolute terms and as a proportion of net output between 1885–9 and 1897–1901. Rural consumption increased at the same rate as the net national product, although retail sales in urban and rural areas grew faster still. During the period 1897–1901 to 1909–13, the growth of retained grain exceeded the growth rate of both total retail trade and the net national product. This, Gregory suggests, implied availability of extra grain in part for personal consumption, and in part for feeding livestock and workstock, thereby raising their quality, with potential impact on productivity (Gregory 1980: 135–64).

As regards average household consumption, Gregory believes that there was no decline in absolute terms during the whole period under investigation, 1885–1913. There was no substantial difference between the growth of rural and urban consumption taking the period as a whole. A tentative comparative study suggested to him that the rural–urban differential in Russia did not depart markedly from that in more affluent societies (Gregory 1976: table II). The finding which seemed most to run counter to conventional wisdom, was that concerning the growth of the grain retention rate per head of the rural population. However, both the Nifontov data for the period up to 1900 and Löwe's interpretation give strong support to Gregory's finding.

Moreover, there is much confirming evidence from the growth of rural savings, land purchases, diets, regional peasant budgets, and, paradoxically, from the treasury success in collecting revenue from indirect taxes, to indicate that the rural sector at large disposed of purchasing power which, far from declining, was actually growing.

Löwe maintains that Russian agriculture, measured by growth rates of output and yields of cereals and potatoes, compared favourably with German agriculture (Löwe 1987: 43). Concentrating on peasant farming, he draws attention to a neglected aspect of Russian small-scale family farming: its ability to produce and market, usually at local markets, a variety of crops and products based on more intensive land and labour utilization, thereby contributing by small individual sales to the value of output, levels of consumption, and variety of diets. He finds the calorific content of diets in Russia and Germany more or less comparable. He underlines the flexibility, and responsiveness to market demand, and points to the fallacy of conventional wisdom with its concentration on the size of allotments. He stresses the dynamism of smaller units (Löwe 1987: 117–47).

FISCAL PRESSURES

The element of fiscal pressure is of double significance in the Gerschenkron model of Russian industrialization. First, it was an integral part of his thesis that in the absence of ability or willingness to invest, it was the task of the state to channel 'through the means of taxation much larger portions of national income on investment than otherwise would have been made available'.

Second, he maintained that fiscal pressure on agriculture during the 1880s and 1890s, and especially on the peasantry, though it made Russian industrialization possible, also tended to inhibit the development of a healthy interaction between agriculture and industry, which Paul Mantoux emphasizes as an essential element in the industrial revolution in England (Gerschenkron 1968: 246). Hence the slump at the turn of the century, evidence of the exhaustion of the tax-paying capacity of the population and the agrarian disturbances of 1902 culminating in the Revolution of 1905, indicated that the limit of endurance had been reached (Gerschenkron 1968: 230).

Recent literature paints less dark a picture of fiscal pressures and their effects during the 1880s and 1890s. It is said that direct fiscal pressure was more acute in the 1860s and 1870s. The redemption operation was long drawn out; only in 1881 did redemption become obligatory. During the period of transition, some peasants were still paying rents or performing labour services; others were already under pressure to pay redemption payments, arrears of which started to mount almost from the start. The Poll Tax was raised several times by the Finance Minister Reutern as it became clear that collective responsibility for taxes and charges ostensibly assured by preserving the commune, was a very ineffectual instrument of fiscal exaction. Government resources were under enormous pressure in coping with the financial legacy of the Crimean War, the financing of the emancipation, founding banks, building railways, etc. (Kahan 1978: 266; Crisp 1989: 46).

In the 1880s direct taxes were reduced to one-third of their 1862 level (Trebilcock 1981: 226; Löwe 1987: 374). The totality of direct tax payments per head of the rural population in the 1890s represented less than 5 per cent of computed per capita expenditure of the rural population (based on Simonova 1969: 168). Redemption payments, not strictly speaking a tax, accounted according to Gerschenkron for only 6 per cent of treasury receipts from taxation (Gerschenkron 1968: 226). The arrears in payment, it is maintained, were an index of unwillingness not of inability to pay, because the peasants believed that the land was theirs in the first place. In any case there were so many write-offs, and reschedulings that peasants believed that sooner or later payments would be cancelled, as they eventually were (Simonova 1969: 158–95). From 1886, indirect taxation became the main source of exchequer revenue which, as Gerschenkron pointed out, continued to mount throughout the 1890s. It certainly proved a very efficient, flexible, easily collectable tax, looked at from the viewpoint of the treasury.

True, it was a regressive tax and it fell on several articles of mass consumption, but it is not easy to say how much of this tax was paid by the rural population. Arcadius Kahan quotes calculations by Vainshtein showing how heavily indirect taxes fell upon the peasants and agricultural producers, thus supporting Gerschenkron's thesis in this respect (Kahan 1978: 276, footnote 21; Gatrell 1986: 201). Simms, however, argued that one cannot have it both ways. If the treasury coffers were filled with receipts from indirect taxation, then peasants must have consumed the articles or used the services thus taxed (Crisp 1976: 27–8; Simms 1977; Wilbur 1983). Others maintained that not peasants, but city dwellers and industrial workers were the main consumers. Peasants had a variety of substitutes and consumed a much smaller proportion of the articles taxed than their sheer numbers would suggest. If indirect taxes were paid by city dwellers and industry, then financing of industrialization was not only at the expense of agriculture and rural dwellers. If this was the case, then the alleged fiscal pressure could not have been all that great, and the consequent impoverishment of the village was less than Gerschenkron thought.

Moreover, a closer study of Russian taxation policy suggests that Russian industry bore a rather high share of overall taxation at the very time when the state was ostensibly involved in all-out industrialization allegedly at the expense of agriculture.[1]

On the whole, the issue of fiscal pressure allied to that of consumption levels puts quite a different complexion on the relationship between industry and agriculture. Löwe (1987: 374–7) suggests that there was in Russia, as elsewhere, an interaction between agriculture and industry, the one stimulating the other, rather than one growing at the expense of the other.

THE ROLE OF THE STATE

The role of the state was central to the Gerschenkron model of industrialization under extreme backwardness. As this aspect is discussed elsewhere in this study only a few general points will be made here. Gerschenkron did not consider that under extreme backwardness the 'state' itself might not be capable of acting. For backwardness might mean lack of a central authority capable of asserting its power for the mobilization of resources internally, and of commanding enough confidence and stability to seek and obtain the missing resources externally. In this sense the Russian state was not any 'state' but one which certainly until 1905, and because of the country's great power status subsequently too, until 1917, had the capacity referred to. Moreover, it was a state most careful and proud of its reputation for creditworthiness, and there was a general recognition of this in investing circles abroad. Finally, the state was always highly visible, and throughout Russian history was expected to lead.

Gerschenkron used interchangeably the term 'state' and the more narrow entity 'government' which he considered separately from society, as a kind of autonomous institution. He wrote that it did not matter if society at large did not share the business ethos as long as the government was committed to industrialization. This raises the question whether and how much the government was committed, and forces us to narrow still further the definition of 'state' in this respect, to the views and activities of the Ministry of Finance. During the vital

period between the emancipation and the 1905 Revolution, the finance ministry
was dominated by four men. M. Kh. Reutern, N. Kh. Bunge, I. A. Vyshnegradsky
and S. Yu. Witte, all ministers of the highest calibre. Of the four, Reutern and
Witte were self-professed industrializers, and during the whole period the
ministry was associated with 'new' rather than 'old' Russia: with the world of
bankers, Russian and foreign, railway tycoons, factory owners, Jewish entrepreneurs and middlemen, mining specialists and engineers. By universal consent
the ministry consisted of a number of exceptionally intelligent, conscientious,
and highly skilled professionals. Especially under Witte, they formed a cohesive,
highly motivated and progressive group who under his 'revered authority' were
involved in the earnest task of financial management of the country (Lieven
1989: 192–6). However, though under Witte the activities of the financial
department reached into practically every area of Russia's economic life, so
that his ministry could be described as a 'state within a state', with its own agents
in major capitals, there is still no certainty of how truly representative it was of
the thinking and policies of the government at large. Was there ever such a thing
as a consciously designed and collectively agreed policy of industrialization?
There was throughout a consensus that the highest priority be accorded to
maintaining great power status externally and stability and order internally. The
two sets of priorities were, however, in conflict. Under conditions of modern
warfare, industrialization was a *sine qua non*, but it was also likely to be
destabilizing. Hence ambivalence, indecision and dichotomy. Representatives of
business interests as a pressure group, notwithstanding the encouragement of the
finance ministry, carried relatively little weight and did not articulate their views
clearly. Within the government the voice which sounded loudest was for preserving 'old' Russia, whilst the élites tended to share the views of the government
majority either out of concern for stability, for welfare considerations or for a
romantic belief in the uniqueness of rural Russia.[2]

Nevertheless, there was already an inner dynamism of forces put into motion,
however half-heartedly, or of measures taken with a view to protecting the
currency, or the funds, or of raising state revenue, which had *effects* of an
economic nature, entailing an industrializing role for the government. Soviet
historians had this in mind when maintaining that though the Tsarist government was not comfortable with developing capitalism, 'objectively' they
promoted it (Crisp 1976: 24–5; 1978: 334–5).

Von Laue's book graphically depicts the struggle Witte had to wage against
critics inside and outside the government. Indeed the gloomy picture conjured up
for us about the conditions in Russia in consequence of Witte's policies of
industrialization, is largely based upon this criticism. The various memoranda
produced by Witte and quoted by scholars as setting out his strategy of
industrialization, were more often than not defensive pleas to the Emperor with
the aim of forestalling possible changes in policy under the pressure of Witte's
critics. Under the Russian system of government the Emperor was the ultimate
arbiter, and he belonged to 'old' Russia, though as foreign bankers and

governments acknowledged, he could be relied upon to meet the country's financial obligations (Laue 1954, 1963).

With regard to specific issues raised by Gregory, it is clear that a close analysis of quantitative data so far yields a more modest role for government during the Gerschenkron spurts. However, if some things cannot be quantified, it does not necessarily mean that they were not important.

If one looks at Russia's industrialization not as confined to Gerschenkronian spurts but as a continuous process starting in the eighteenth century, then Russia's industrialization pattern emerges as one of interaction between autonomous, i.e. market driven, and 'induced', that is state initiated or assisted, development. This appears to have been the case over time and at any given time. It is immaterial whether the state undertook the role of industrializer consciously, as under Peter the Great, or whether the industrializing role was the effect of policies designed to overcome balance of payments constraints, to increase treasury revenue as was the case with Kankrin's 1822 tariff, or a mixture of both under very different domestic and international circumstances from 1877 through the 1880s and 1890s (Crisp 1976: 12–17; 1978: 413).

OTHER ASPECTS OF THE MODEL

In the context of the Russian government's concern for the country's great power status, the development of heavy industry was undoubtedly a priority issue. However, in an age when coal and steel played such a decisive role in the international economy, and given that the resources were available in relative abundance and could be made accessible by the railway, it was only 'natural' to develop them, especially as consumer goods industries could take care of themselves. Moreover an attempt to build railways by importing the hardware, as during the 1860s and 1870s, led to a balance of trade crisis. Consequently, the alleged emphasis on producers' goods in the industrialization pattern of latecomers in the Gerschenkron model may be a coincidence where Russia is concerned.

Furthermore, government bias notwithstanding, the share of producers' goods industries whether measured in terms of employment or value of output, was easily outstripped by consumer goods industries, especially fibres and food-processing. Consumer goods industries, especially textiles, grew steadily right across the emancipation divide (but for the effect of the American Civil War which cut off raw cotton supplies), through the 1893–1900 period with its heavy industry bias, and were practically unaffected by the slump that followed. It would seem, therefore, that Russia's pattern of industrialization was not all that different from earlier industrializing economies, where industrialization affected first of all consumer goods industries (Goldsmith 1961: 460; Gregory 1972; Crisp 1976: 36–44; 1978: 351–5).

Two elements of substitution inherent in the model, that of capital to make up for labour inadequacy, and the large size of business units to economize on management are also subject to some criticism. Crisp has shown that most industries and most plants combined modern technology with primitive manual processes. There was no shortage of unskilled labour, and conditions undoubtedly improved as regards skilled labour with rising literacy and more formal schooling (McKay 1970: 242–67; Crisp 1978: 387–94).

As regards the size of units, the literature suggests that size, if measured by numbers employed, was most often due to low productivity and to the need to provide for workers a variety of services not directly connected with the main activity. Of course Russia was inadequately provided with managerial and technical talent, and had to import it at considerable cost together with capital. Though the situation was undoubtedly improving, the large numbers of foreign personnel still employed in Russian enterprises by 1913 was in part testimony to the fact that 'ignorance' was still a factor in Russia's relative backwardness, but it also indicates that the growing supply of managerial and technical talent was being overtaken by the growth in demand as the economy developed. One could also question Gerschenkron's proposition regarding size as a means of spreading management. In the cotton industry units tended to be very large, and yet this was Russia's oldest modern industry, whose management is known to have become by the 1870s well educated and professional, and mainly ethnic Russian (Rimlinger 1961; Crisp 1978: 396–99; Portal 1963).

In so far as size of businesses is measured by nominal capital issued, it would appear that changes in the taxation of profits encouraged companies to enlarge their capital. Moreover, by using this criterion of size, one leaves out a very large segment of enterprise which did not take corporate form. In any case, even though official statistics seriously under-recorded small units, the distribution of Russian business units by size does not suggest a special position for Russia in this respect. Nearly 70 per cent of all firms extant in Russia in 1903 had a workforce of under 50. More than two-thirds of these small units were created during the decades of the 1880s and 1890s, a period commonly associated with the formation of large joint-stock companies (Carstensen 1978).

CONTINUITY VERSUS CHANGE THROUGH SPURTS

Gerschenkron (1968: 207) believed that 'the more backward a country, the more likely it is that the early stages of industrialization will be characterized by a sudden violent spurt in investment and output'. The abolition of serfdom and the upsurge of industrial growth were separated by nearly a quarter of a century during which, in his view, there was a very moderate rate of industrial growth. Gregory (1982: 70) seems to concur, whilst Goldsmith's (1961: 464) own computations seem to contradict his generalization to this effect. His breakdown of the period 1860–1913 into sub-periods 1860–83 (or 1887) and 1883–1913, suggests that growth rates in the earlier sub-period did match those in the later one, in other words no 'sudden violent spurt'.

As indicated in the section dealing with the role of the state, Russia's industrialization pattern seems to have been one of continuity. In his Cambridge lectures Gerschenkron (1970a: lecture 3) emphasized that Peter the Great's industrialization effort had undoubtedly yielded high annual growth rates but, he believed, it could not be successfully sustained because of the introduction of industrial serfdom. Arcadius Kahan, on the contrary, stressed continuity in economic development in post-Petrine eighteenth-century Russia, not on account of state activity about which he was less than enthusiastic, but because of the importance of market forces, the efforts and needs of the Russian population, and of the commercial relations with Europe, which made for continuity in economic activity (Kahan 1965). Jennifer Newman (1985) and Ian Blanchard (1989) have similarly stressed the interaction between economic development in Russia and the industrial revolution in Britain in the later eighteenth and early nineteenth century.

For the first half of the nineteenth century Yatsunsky (1959), Rozhkova (1959), Ryndzyunsky (1966), Strumilin (1926), and in the West Blackwell (1968) and Portal (1963) have done detailed research on various aspects of industrial development. Some of this development was in the nature of 'proto-industrializ-ation'. Though the phenomenon of proto-industrialization became an important topic of research in the West in the 1970s, Russian historians have been discussing the phenomenon without thus naming it, for over a century. For those who wished to preserve 'old' Russia, the spread and resilience of rural industries was evidence of the possibility of avoiding capitalist industrialization. However, the literature suggests that these industries were part of an ongoing process of industrialization, which also involved growth of factory industry in continuous interaction in a variety of patterns with rural industry. Blackwell described industrial development in the first half of the nineteenth century as 'preparatory', implicitly therefore as an integral part of the later development. In an otherwise favourable review of the book, Gerschenkron (1970b) rejected Blackwell's interpretation and stressed elements of discontinuity as characterizing Russia's later development (Crisp 1976: 17). According to Crisp industrial development in the 1840s was more than preparatory, it marked the beginning of industrializ-ation based on modern technology. The authors of a recent article stress that Russia seemed to have been the greatest beneficiary of the repeal of the British ban on machinery exports (Farnie and Yokenava 1988).

The rate of growth of gross output of a selected series of industries for the period 1845–63, adjusted for price changes, was estimated as between 3.5 and 4 per cent. This was much lower than the average rate of growth in the next fifty years, it nevertheless represented respectable growth in a period which tended to be described as one of stagnation because of serfdom and the ostensible inertia of the government of Nicholas I, or rather his finance minister, Count G. F. Kankrin (Strumilin 1926: 250; Pintner 1967). On balance, it seems that continuity rather than discontinuity characterized Russia's industrialization process.

SUMMARY AND TENTATIVE CONCLUSION

It would appear from the above account that Gerschenkron's interpretation of the pattern of Russia's industrialization has not fared well at the hands of recent historians. It is fair to say, however, that recent literature is not very extensive, and is overwhelmingly revisionist.

The revision of the behaviour of agriculture, and of the consumption levels of the population have removed one of the most important planks of the model as it relates to Russia. However, the revisionists may not have the last word as some scepticism, if muted, of Gregory's revisionist views has been expressed by at least two scholars.[3]

The second important plank, the role of the state, is shaken but not entirely demolished. Here the number of protagonists is larger, and the arguments more varied. The arguments hinge on the extent to which the 'state' can be defined, its contribution measured, and to what extent its role is specific to backwardness or is historically conditioned by the country's past and its political system. However, if one ignores the big spurt as the strategic element in the industrialization pattern of backward countries, it is undoubtedly right to emphasize the significance of the 1890s because this period was characterized by intensified involvement of the government through the agency of Witte's ministry in the economy, in particular through the vast programme of railway construction, supported by a high import tariff, offering substantial markets to the fast-growing heavy industry. It was also a period of highest agricultural growth so far, which does not fit neatly into the pattern.

In 1972, in summing up my account of government policies, I wrote

> the ... policies of the state bear out Gerschenkron's thesis on the role of the state in conditions of backwardness, but not without some qualifications. [Government] policies proved by and large successful because by the 1890s there was already in Russia a fair sized market, a firm monetary system and financial institutions which had gradually evolved during the preceding decades, a skeleton of transport and educational facilities, and most importantly a pattern of commercial and financial relations abroad backed by the prestige of the Russian state and its excellent record as a debtor.
>
> (Crisp 1976: 33)

I would still stand by this view, which I think suggests that government successes of the late 1890s were possible because they were built upon prior achievements. Were I to write it today, I would stress the interconnection of these developments with respectable rates of agricultural growth and would put more emphasis on the strategic role of the railways.

The work on the impact of the railway on Russia yields contradictory results. Metzer (1974) concluded that its impact on growth rates was not very significant. White (1975) and Lyashchenko (1912) on the other hand demonstrated its importance for agriculture and marketings. However, I believe that the railway was of strategic importance in the Russian economy and it is to be hoped that scholars will turn their attention to it in the not too distant future. It certainly was more significant than the abolition of serfdom. The latter was of immense political importance in that it opened the way to modernization in the sphere of law, education, municipal and local government and military reform, which ultimately benefited the economy too. But in the short term, from the point of view of industrialization, the abolition of serfdom was almost an irrelevance. If one must have landmarks or watersheds then the date of the foundation of the Principal Railway Company in 1857 with a programme, which was more or less in place by 1875, of connecting food-producing regions with markets inside Russia, and with ports, is as good as any, and undoubtedly of more significance for the growth of agricultural output in the late 1860s and 1870s.

Löwe's hypothesis that agricultural growth and high grain prices of the 1860s stimulated the industrial boom of the 1870s due to increased demand for consumer goods, especially textiles, and that the boom of the 1890s accompanied as it was by higher than ever rates of agricultural growth was equally evidence of an interaction between two sovereign sectors, rather than one growing at the expense of the other, seems to make sense at least in so far as consumer goods industries were concerned (Löwe 1987: 374).

If it does, then another scenario suggests itself. Gerschenkron's concentration on the period from the mid-1880s, which may be a reflection of more reliable data based on N. D. Kondrat'ev's index rather than of the path of industrial growth as it really occurred, blots out the industrial boom of the 1870s. Goldsmith who based his computations on the whole period from 1860 reveals that the average growth rate of industry during the period 1860–83 or 1860–87 was equal, or even slightly exceeded that of the period 1885–1913. Furthermore when he breaks down the period 1860–1913 into four sub-sections of twelve years each, one finds that the average rate derived from various indices for the period 1874–87, whilst obviously lower than during the period 1888–1900 (6.7–7.6) was within the range of 5.4–6.6 per cent. Goldsmith used these data for the purpose of testing his computations not in order to demonstrate a different growth path, but is clear that scholars will need to look more closely at the first two decades after 1860 and not just dismiss them as a period of slow growth (Goldsmith 1961: 464).

Moreover, one will have to look again at the thesis which associates industrialization with fiscal pressure. The nominal level of taxation was high during the period 1862–85, though treasury revenue from taxes was well below it. No one has suggested that during this period the government was mobilizing resources for industrialization. It is extraordinary, therefore, that on the very eve of accelerated government activity on the industrialization front a tax reform in 1885–6 should drastically cut taxes. As is known, indirect taxes eventually filled treasury coffers much more efficiently than direct taxes ever did, but the rise in treasury revenue also meant effective demand. Consequently, one may question the applicability of the Gerschenkron thesis about fiscal pressure to Russia's industrialization during the vital period 1885–1900.

To sum up it would appear that Gerschenkron's model of industrialization, in so far as it relates to Russia, was more in the nature of brilliant intuitive insight of which the most valuable aspect was the concept of substitution, even though it does not quite fit the Russian case. However, it is through such intuitive insights that the frontiers of knowledge are extended.

NOTES

1   For example, in 1897 direct taxes on industry and commerce accounted for 46 per cent of the total, another 15.6 per cent came from taxes on money capital, a share as high as in the affluent, industrially developed United Kingdom. By then indirect taxes had become the mainstay of the Russian budget, but in this respect too Russia did not depart significantly from the experience of other countries (see Brokhauz and Effron).
2   In spite of the respect the ministry commanded, only 19 of 215 members of the highest governing authority, the State Council, were former members of the ministry (Crisp 1976: 24–5; Rieber 1977, 1978; Lieven 1989: 192–6).
3   See Feinstein (1985) and Trebilcock (1987).

REFERENCES

Anfimov, A.M. (1969) *Krupnoye pomeshchich'ye khozyaystvo Europeyskoy Rossii ...*, Moscow: Nauka.
—— (1980) *Krestyanskoye khozyaystvo Europeyskoy Rossii, 1881–1904*, Moscow: Nauka.
Barkai, H. (1973) 'The macro-economics of Tsarist Russia in the industrialization era: monetary developments, the balance of payments and the gold standard', *Journal of Economic History* 33, 339–71.
Blackwell, W.L. (1968) *The Beginnings of Russian Industrialization*, Princeton, NJ: Princeton University Press.
Blanchard, Ian (1989) *Russia's age of Silver; Precious-metal Production and Economic Growth in the Eighteenth Century*, London: Routledge.
Bovykin, V.I. (1984) *Formirovaniye finansovogo kapitala v Rossii*, Moscow: Akademiya Nauk, Institut Istorii.
Brokhauz, F.A. and Effron, I.A. (eds) (nd) 'Rossiya', *Entsiklopedichesky Slavar*, 198ff.
Carstensen, F.V. (1978) 'Numbers and reality: a critique of foreign investment estimates in tsarist Russia', in Lévy-Leboyer, M. (ed.) *La Position Internationale de la France*, Paris.
Cipolla, C.M. (1969) *Literacy and Development in the West*, Harmondsworth: Penguin.
Crafts, N.F.R. (1983) 'Gross national product in Europe 1870–1910: some new estimates', *Explorations in Economic History* 20, 387–401.
Crisp, O. (1976) *Studies in the Russian Economy*, London: Macmillan.
—— (1978) 'Labour and industrialization in Russia', in P. Mathias and M.M. Postan (eds) *Cambridge Economic History of Europe*, vol. VII, part 2, Cambridge: Cambridge University Press, 308–415.
—— (1989) 'Peasant land tenure and civil rights implications before 1906', in O. Crisp

and L. Edmondson (eds) *Civil Rights in Imperial Russia*, Oxford: Oxford University Press.

Falkus, M.E. (1968) 'Russia's national income, 1913: a revaluation', *Economica* 35 (137), 52–73.

Farnie, D.A. and Yokenava, S. (1988) 'The emergence of the large firm in the cotton spinning industries in the world, 1883–1938', *Textile Industry* 19 (2), 185.

Feinstein, Charles (1985) 'Review of Gregory's book', *Economic History Review* XXXVIIi (2).

Field, D. (1976) *The End of Serfdom: Nobility and Bureaucracy in Russia, 1855–1861*, Cambridge, Mass.: Harvard University Press.

Gatrell, P. (1986) *The Tsarist Economy 1850–1917*, London: B.T. Batsford.

Gerschenkron, A. (1947) 'The rate of growth of industrial production in Russia since 1885', *Journal of Economic History* VII-S, 144–74.

—— (1962) *Economic Backwardness in Historical Perspective*, Cambridge, Mass.: Harvard University Press.

—— (1963) 'The early phases of industrialization in Russia: afterthoughts and counterthoughts', in W.W. Rostow (ed.) *The Economics of Take-off into Sustained Growth*, New York: Cambridge University Press.

—— (1967) 'Problems and patterns of Russian economic development', in C.E. Black (ed.) *The Transformation of Russian Society, Aspects of Social Change since 1861*, Cambridge, Mass.: Harvard University Press, pp. 42–71.

—— (1968) *Continuity in History and Other Essays*, Cambridge, Mass.: Harvard University Press.

—— (1970a) *Europe in the Russian Mirror, Four Lectures in Economic History*, New York: Cambridge University Press.

—— (1970b) 'Review of Blackwell's book', *Soviet Studies* XXI (April), 507–15.

Geyer, D. (ed.) (1975) *Wirtschaft und Gesellschaft im norrevolutionaren Russland*, Köln: Kiepenheur und Witsch.

Goldsmith, R.W. (1961) 'The economic growth of tsarist Russia 1860–1913', *Economic Development and Cultural Change* 9 (II), 441–75.

Gregory, P.R. (1972) 'Economic growth and structural change in Tsarist Russia: a case of modern economic growth', *Soviet Studies* 3, 418–49.

—— (1976) 'Russian national income in 1913', *Quarterly Journal of Economics* (August), 445–59.

—— (1980) 'Grain marketings and peasant consumption in Russia, 1885–1913', *Journal of European Economic History* 17, 135–64.

—— (1982) *Russian National Income, 1885–1913*, New York: Cambridge University Press.

Guroff, G. and Starr, S.F. (1971) 'A note on urban literacy in Russia 1890–1914', *Jahrbücher für Geschichte Osteuropas*, n.s., XIX (4), December, 526–31.

Harrison, M. (1977) 'Resource allocation and agrarian class formation: the problems of social mobility among Russian peasant households, 1880–1930', *Journal of Peasant Studies* 4, 127–61.

Johnson, R.E. (1979) *Peasant and Proletarian: The Working Class of Moscow in the Late Nineteenth Century*, New Brunswick, NJ: Rutgers University Press.

Kahan, A. (1965) 'Continuity in economic activity and policy during the post Petrine period in Russia', *Journal of Economic History* 25 (1), 61–85.

—— (1978) 'Capital formation during the period of early industrialization in Russia, 1890–1913', in P. Mathias and M.M. Postan (eds) *Cambridge Economic History of Europe*, vol. VII, part 2, Cambridge: Cambridge University Press.

Kingston-Mann, E. (1981) 'Marxism and Russian rural development: problems of evidence, experience and culture', *American Historical Review* 86, 731–52.

Kinyapina, N.S. (1968) Politika russkogo samoderzhaviya v oblasti promyshlemnosti (20-50-ye gody XIX v.), Moscow: Moscow University.

Kitanina, T.M. (1978) *Khlebnaya torgoviya Rossii v 1875–1914*, Leningrad: Akademiya Nauk, Institut Istorii.

Laue, F.C. (1975) 'The role of governments in economic growth in early modern times', *Journal of Economic History*, 35, 8–17.

Laue, T.H. von (1954) 'A secret memorandum of Sergey Witte on the industrialization of Imperial Russia', *Journal of Modern History* 26, 60–75.

—— (1963) *Sergei Witte and the Industrialization of Russia*, New York: Columbia University Press.

Lieven, Dominic (1989) *Russia's Rulers under the Old Regime*, New Haven, Conn.: Yale University Press.

Löwe, Heinz-Dietrich (1987) *Die Lage der Bauern in Russland 1880–1905*, St Catharinen: Scripta Mercaturae Verlage.

Lyashchenko, P.I. (1912) *Khlebnaya torgovlya na vnutrennikh rynkakh Evropeiskoy Rossii*, St Petersburg.

McKay, J.P. (1970) *Pioneers for Profit: Foreign Entrepreneurship and Russian Industrialization, 1885–1913*, Chicago: University of Chicago Press.

Metzer, J. (1974) 'Railroad development and market integration: the case of Tsarist Russia', *Journal of Economic History* 34, 529–50.

—— (1976) 'Railroads in Russia. Direct gains and implications', *Explorations in Economic History* 13, 85–111.

Ministry of Finance (1906–10) *Documents Relating to the Project of a State Income Tax. I*, The result of an approximate calculation of the national revenue in Russia from various sources and according to size of income, St. Petersburg.

Mironov, B.N. (1981) *Vnutrenny rynok Rossii vo vtoroy polovine XVIII-pervoy polovine XIX v.*, Leningrad: Akodemiya Nauk, Institut Istorii.

Newman, J. (1985) 'Russian foreign trade 1680–1780: the British contribution', unpublished PhD thesis, University of Edinburgh.

Nifontov, A.S. (1974) *Zernovoye proizvostvo Rossii vo vtoroy polovine XIX veka po materyalam ehegodnoy statistiki urozhaev Evropeyskoy Rossii*, Moscow: Akademiya Nauk, Institut Istorii.

Owen, T.C. (1981) *Capitalism and Politics in Russia: A Social History of Moscow Merchants 1855–1905*, Cambridge: Cambridge University Press.

Pallot, J. (1983) 'The development of peasant land holding from emancipation to the revolution' and 'Agrarian modernization on peasant farms in the era of capitalism', in J.H. Bates and R.A. French (eds) *Studies in Russian Historical Geography*, London: Academic Press, vol. I pp. 83–108, vol. II, pp. 423–49.

Pintner, W.M. (1967) *Russian Economic Policy under Nicholas I*, New York: Cornell University Press.

Portal, R. (1963) 'Industriels Moscovites: Le Secteur Cotonier (1861–1914)', *Cahier du Monde Russe et Sovietique* IV, 5–46.

Rieber, A.J. (1977) 'The Moscow entrepreneurial group', *Jahrbücher für Geschichte Ost-Europas*, Neue Folge 43, 174–99.

—— (1978) *Merchants and Entrepreneurs in Imperial Russia*, University of North Carolina Press.

Rimlinger, G. (1961) 'The expansion of the labour market in capitalist Russia: 1861–1917', *Journal of Economic History* XXI, 208–15.

Rozhkova, M.K. (1959) *Ocherki economicheskoi istorii Rossii*, Moscow, Akademiya Nauk, Institut Istorii.

Ryndzyunsky, P.G. (1966) *Krest'yanskaye e promyshlennost' v Rossii*, Moscow: Nauka.

Schapiro, L. (1986) 'The pre-revolutionary intelligentsia and the legal order', in E.

Dahrendorf and H. Willetts (eds) *Russian Studies*, London: Collins Harvill.

Simonova, M.S. (1969) 'Otmena Krugovoy Poruki', *Istoricheskiye Zapiski* 83, 159–95.

Simms, J.Y. (1977) 'The crisis in Russian agriculture at the end of the nineteenth century: a different view', *Slavic Review* 36, 377–98.

Strumilin, S.G. (1926) *Ocherki Sovetskoy Ekonomiki*, Moscow-Leningrad: Izdatelstvo Ekonomichesky Literatury.

Tarle, E. (1918) 'Bylali Ekaterinskaya Rossiya ekonomicheski otslaloy stranoy', *Zapadi Rossiya*, Petrograd.

Trebilcock, C. (1981) *The Industrialization of the Continental Powers, 1780–1914*, London: Longman.

—— (1987) 'Review of Gatrell's book', *Business History* XXXIX (3).

Wheatcroft, S. (1980) 'Grain production and utilisation in Russia and the USSR before collectivisation', unpublished PhD thesis, Department of Commerce, Birmingham.

White, C.M. (1975) 'The impact of Russian railway construction on the market for grain in the 1860s and 1870s', in L. Symons and C.M. White (eds) *Russian Transport*, London, G. Bell & Sons.

Wilbur, Z. (1983) 'Was Russian peasant agriculture really that impoverished?', *Journal of Economic History* 43, 137–44.

Yatsunsky, V.K. (1959) 'Krupnaya promyshlennost Rossii v 1796–1860 gg', in M.K. Rozhkova (ed.) *Ocherki promyshlennosti Rossii pervoy poloviny XIX veka*, Moscow: Akademiya Nauk, Institut Istorii.

Zaozerskaya, E.I. (1970) *U istokov krupnogo proizvodstva v russkoy promyshlemnosti: k voprosu o genezise kapitalizma v Rossii*, Moscow: Akademiya Nauk, Intitut Istorii.

Index